ROMAN CENTURY

Photo Alinari

GIUSEPPE GARIBALDI

ROMAN CENTURY

A Portrait of Rome
as the Capital of Italy,
1870–1970

GLORNEY BOLTON

NEW YORK   THE VIKING PRESS

TO

CECIL PARKER GLORNEY

CONTENTS

LIST OF ILLUSTRATIONS

PREFACE

ON NOVEMBER 11th, 1969, a few Italian monarchists entered the Pantheon in Rome and discreetly observed the centenary of the birth of Victor Emmanuel III, their King for forty-six years. He was scarcely four weeks old when Pope Pius IX opened the First Vatican Council: eight months old when Pius proclaimed the new dogma of infallibility; ten months old when Italian troops breached a Roman wall and caused the old Pope-King to be called 'the prisoner of the Vatican'; and thirteen months old when news that the Tiber had overflowed its banks brought his grandfather, Victor Emmanuel II, hurrying southwards from Florence. On the last day of 1870, and at four o'clock in the morning, the grandfather set foot in Rome for the first time as its King. Before fireworks proclaimed the dawn of a new year, he was already on his way back to Florence.

The grandfather had no love for Rome. He dreaded the day when he must return, proclaim the city as his capital, and henceforward live in the sombre Quirinal Palace. If he had his way, Turin would never have ceased to be the capital of his Kingdom. As a northerner, he had lived among people who seldom travelled far south. Cavour, his greatest statesman, never saw Rome. Neither did Manzoni. When northern ideas of Rome were not romantic, they were usually censorious. Manzoni's son-in-law, Massimo d'Azeglio, was about the only former Minister who once lived in Rome. He thought it madness to make such a 'sewer' the Italian capital.

Apart from the railway built by defeated Pius, Rome had lost almost nothing of the loveliness known to Keats, Shelley, Stendhal and Walter Scott. More than half the capacious area within the Aurelian walls was devoted to villas, parks and gardens; farmsteads, vineyards and olive groves; bridle paths and shaded lanes. The Piedmontese, as Pius and his supporters called the newcomers, cared for none of these things. The city was the Pope's no longer, and strangers were intent on making it the worthy capital of Europe's new Great Power. Yet Rome was still smaller than Naples or Milan. Not until Mussolini's day did it become Italy's largest city, with a population above a million.

Mussolini, another man from the north, resolved to make Rome the still worthier capital of a still Greater Power. Five years after his violent death, there came a pilgrim horde for the Holy Year of 1950; but there also came a hectic building boom. Critics have called it the second sack of Rome. Unless this second sack is halted in good time, old Rome will be lost, just as old Milan is lost.

On one side of the Capitoline Hill stands the Tarpeian rock, from which the Romans hurled their traitors. The rock takes its name from Tarpeia, a legendary maiden who agreed to open a gate to the Sabines if they would give her the golden bracelet which each warrior wore on his left arm. The Sabines kept their promise. They cast their bracelets at Tarpeia, but they also cast their heavy shields. The weight killed her.

Italians are often no more grateful to their century-old capital than were the Sabines to Tarpeia. The contrast between the dream of the united country ruled from Rome and its prosaic reality has been too striking. In the Middle Ages, Florence led the way in the arts of communal self-government, but the long years of theocracy in Rome have left their mark. Today other Italian cities are shocked by the vastness of Rome's debts.

Cavour, Mazzini and Garibaldi were all enslaved by their vision of the Eternal City. So was Mussolini. So, throughout the past century, have been millions of Italians and foreigners. How should Rome be judged—by its buildings, old and new, or by its people? Byron, never much of a sightseer, embraced Venice like a lover because it teemed with youth and life. Ruskin, more solitary, cared chiefly for its buildings. Seeing their neglect and decay, he decided that Venice was already doomed.

Modern Rome has become a mushroom city. Yet, as hideous suburbs spread towards the Alban and Sabine Hills and monotonously border the Tyrrhenian Sea, it is well to remember that their dwellers are all old in their origin. Saracen, Phoenician, Etruscan or Greek: they have come, as in ancient times, to Rome in search of work or fortune. Spiritually their influx has not impoverished the city of the Popes.

Once a man from Turin lived in the Quirinal Palace as the first King of Italy. Now another man from Turin lives there as the fifth President of the Italian Republic. Rome changes less than appearances suggest. The Kings have gone; the Popes remain. So does the city's fascination.

The letters quoted in this book are from Matilda Lucas, William James, George Gissing, Oscar Wilde, H. G. Wells, Sigmund Freud, Rainer Maria Rilke, James Joyce, D. H. Lawrence, George Santayana and Hilaire Belloc. Their writers knew that there were depths in the Italian character which they could not fathom. If George Santayana came nearest to an understanding, his blood was Latin. It is all part of the fascination that Rome and the Romans will never be fully known.

Among English-speaking people in Rome there seem to be no agreed rules about the places to be named in English and those in Italian. If mine are illogical, they represent a present-day, though transitory, usage.

ITALY in 1815 after the Congress of Vienna

ROME
- Tivoli
- Vatican City
- Fiumicino
- Frascati
- Rocca di Papa
- Ostia
- Castelgandolfo
- Nemi
- Velletri
- Anzio

0   10   20 miles

I KINGDOM OF SARDINIA (including Savoy, Piedmont & the Island of Sardinia)
II LOMBARDY–VENETIA (then a province of the Empire of Austria)
III DUCHY OF PARMA
IV DUCHY OF MODENA
V DUCHY OF MASSA
VI DUCHY OF LUCCA
VII GRAND DUCHY OF TUSCANY
VIII PONTIFICAL STATE
IX KINGDOM OF THE TWO SICILIES

SWITZERLAND

EMPIRE OF AUSTRIA

KINGDOM OF FRANCE

- Aosta
- L. Maggiore
- Stresa
- Trento
- Rovereto
- Vittorio Veneto
- Aquileia
- Bergamo
- Salo
- Treviso
- Monza
- Garda
- Padua
- VENICE
- MILAN
- Brescia
- Verona
- TURIN
- Mantua
- Parma
- Modena
- BOLOGNA
- Genoa
- Imola
- Ravenna
- Forli
- Rimini
- Predappio
- Rep. of San Marino
- Viareggio
- Lucca
- Prato
- Fiesole
- Ancona
- Pisa
- FLORENCE
- Loreto
- Perugia
- Assisi
- Foligno
- Spoleto
- Bolsena
- Viterbo
- Pescara
- Civitacastellana
- Civitavecchia
- ROME
- Frascati
- Anagni
- Ostia
- Carpineto
- Sora
- Anzio
- Sermoneta
- Monte Cassino
- Teano
- Capua
- Benevento
- Tarracina
- Gaeta
- Caserta
- Pozzuoli
- NAPLES
- Bari
- Capri
- Vesuvius
- Pompeii
- Salerno
- Brindisi
- Maddalena
- Caprera

OTTOMAN EMPIRE

ADRIATIC SEA

CORSICA (French)

CAGLIARI

TYRRHENIAN SEA

- Messina
- PALERMO
- Reggio Calabria

MEDITERRANEAN SEA

TUNISIA (OTTOMAN EMPIRE)

- Tunis

0   50   100   150 miles

ROMAN CENTURY

CHAPTER ONE

TALE OF TWO CITIES

'*FACCIA gialla, fang' o' miracolo!*' 'Yellow face, get on with the miracle!'

The cry often came from women huddled within Naples Cathedral on the morning of September 19th, feast day of St. Januarius, who was patron of the city. It was heard again in 1870 while a multitude stood waiting for the blood of the patron to liquefy. The miracle was a token that a dead Bishop of Benevento, victim of Diocletian's persecution, still blessed Naples and the neighbourhood. In other years, his intervention enabled grapes, oranges and lemons to grow more abundantly in the Campagna; checked a scourge of cholera; rescued fishermen about to drown in the Bay; calmed even the wrath of Vesuvius.

A Bishop who blesses can also curse, and fear gripped the supplicants whenever the patron of their city was slow to liquefy his blood. They knew too well the cruelty of storm, pestilence, earthquake and boiling lava. On the feast day, the setting sun must not crimson distant Capri until Januarius has liquefied the blood which he shed long centuries ago.

In sober fact, he performs his miracle three times a year: on the feast day, September 19th; on the first Saturday in May, when a phial of the cherished blood is exposed in the Franciscan church of Santa Chiara; and, on December 16th, in the Cathedral. The summer miracle commemorates the day when he was thrown to the lions kept in nearby Pozzuoli and emerged from their den unscathed; but the winter miracle is a latecomer and marks an eruption of Vesuvius which, in 1631, devastated the countryside for miles around. Januarius intervened in time to make Vesuvius spare the actual city, and in gratitude the people erected a monument to him just outside the Cathedral. They also turned the anniversary into a new opportunity for the performance of his miracle. Yet Januarius did not always comply with their wishes. Some of the oldest citizens inside the Cathedral on this feast day of 1870 could have recalled a fateful morning when—on the first Saturday of May, 1799—he cheated at Santa Chiara.

The French were then the military masters of Naples as well as Rome, and Pope Pius VI was their prisoner. As King Ferdinand had fled from his palace and gone to Palermo, the French set up their own Partheno-pean Republic. This angered the people, and especially the unnumbered swarms of cut-throats, thieves and vagabonds to whom the Spaniards, when they first overlorded Naples, gave the enduring name of the *lazzaroni*. Though steeped in ignorance and superstition, the *lazzaroni* loved kingship and their religion. They were monarchists, not republicans. They hated the foreigners from godless Paris all the more for being regicides. They became conspiratorial, enlisted in bands of the 'Holy Faith', and showed a courage which the French themselves were soon driven to admire.

To the outward eye, life in Naples went on very much as before, though flags and uniforms were changed. The poor walked barefoot and unhurrying through the streets. Donkey-carts and painted wagons with high wheels drawn by a team of white bullocks scraped past each other in steep and narrow alleys which the womenfolk festooned each morning with their washing. Everywhere echoed raucous voices, the clatter of hooves and the cracking of whips. Now and again careless laughter accentuated the plight of the galley-slaves—as prisoners were always called—who shambled through the streets in chains or carried enormous burdens on their shoulders. Most galley-slaves wore yellow tunics, but the shirt of a killer was scarlet. The laughter was deceptive. No one was free, least of all the French. Death might come to them stealthily in a city honeycombed with obscure passages, broken stairways and unlit courtyards.

The *lazzaroni* placed their trust in Januarius. On the first Saturday in May, they thronged the church of Santa Chiara. For once—and for once only—they wanted him to withhold the miracle. By his deliberate abstention, he would bring a curse, and not a blessing; but the cursed would be the French. As each quarter-hour passed without a miracle, the shouting inside Santa Chiara became more uproarious, and excitement was soon spreading throughout the city. When word reached the French commander, General Championnet, he recognized the danger and promptly sent an officer to Santa Chiara with a secret order. The officer forced his way to the altar rail, where he whispered a few words to the priest who held the phial in his hands. Almost at once, the blood began to liquefy.

Soon the message given to the priest became known to others. It had told him that unless he caused the blood to liquefy within ten minutes, he would be put against a wall and shot. A sceptic might have blamed the priest for cowardice or commended him for prudence, but nothing assuaged the fury of the *lazzaroni*. They were believers who knew that a miracle is always a saint's work. Januarius alone was the offender.

As soon as the French quitted Naples, the Parthenopean Republic fell like a house built with a pack of cards, and the people showed their joy by punishing Januarius. They dragged his statue through the streets and hurled it into the sea. St. Anthony took his place as patron of the city. He was a lover of animals, and a chaplet of flowers hung from the neck of each horse, donkey and bullock seen in the streets of Naples on his feast day, January 17th. It was his misfortune, however, to be an African, and few Neapolitan legends could be woven around him. He was also quite ineffectual when again lava began to flow towards the city. The *lazzaroni* brought his statue right to the path down which the lava was pouring, but the flow continued until it reached the Maddelena bridge.

At the spot where the lava was halted stood another, and hitherto neglected, statue of Januarius. Here was an unmistakable sign that, once again, the martyred Bishop of Benevento intervened to spare the city. Whereupon the *lazzaroni* forgave him for his sins, even as he had now forgiven them for theirs.

A city so close to Vesuvius could not bear to live without a true patron; for, as Edward Gibbon observed, its inhabitants 'seem to dwell in the confines of paradise and hell-fire'. In a later century, a second English historian saw that this capital of a southern kingdom was like no other place. 'As soon as you enter Naples,' wrote Thomas Babington Macaulay in 1838, 'you notice a striking contrast. It is the difference between Sunday and Monday.' Without a worker of miracles, the people had no protection from Vesuvius or from earthquakes. So they brought religion down to earth and earthiness into religion. This shocked a sensitive young don from Oxford. 'Religion,' John Henry Newman complained, 'is turned into a mere occasion of worldly gaiety —as in the history of the Israelites—and the sooner we are out of so bad a place the better.'

If Newman had stayed in Naples a little longer, his scorn might have given place to pity. The elements were, indeed, fearful and seemingly capricious; but so was the tyranny under which the people were compelled to live. Once it was possible to speak of Naples as an enlightened city. Keen speculative thinkers, from Thomas Aquinas to Giambattista Vico, had taught or written within its walls. No Inquisitor ever succeeded in setting up his office in Naples. Yet the people were kept deliberately in ignorance.

As the eighteenth century drew nearer its close, a small, but increasing, number of aristocrats, merchants and lawyers became ashamed of the cultural gulf between them and the people. They read the literature of Paris, and in the first flush of the Revolution they realized that their own King was a Bourbon and that his consort, Maria Carolina, was an older sister of Marie Antoinette, Queen of France. In Naples, as in Paris, monarchy and the Church might be swept away. All men might be equal, fraternal and free. 'Man is born free', but the chain which fettered the Jacobins of Naples was their isolation from the people. They believed that a Republican army would liberate the multitude. Instead, the populace refused to be released from its own chains. In the eyes alike of the King, the Queen, the shopkeepers and the *lazzaroni*, whoever embraced the new ideas from France was a traitor.

Fabrizio Ruffo, both a Neapolitan nobleman and a Cardinal, knew how the people felt. He had not wanted the King to leave Naples, but he followed him to Palermo, where he pleaded that a Prince of the Church should be allowed to win back the throne. The Cardinal appealed to the sense of justice which, he was certain, all men at heart possessed, whether they were bandits roaming through the valleys or *lazzaroni* picking the pockets of strangers. He invited them all to fight for the Holy Faith and to call themselves the *sanfedisti*. The rabble brought the King and Queen back to Naples.

The appeal to the sense of justice had not been in vain. It was strong, even if narrow-visioned, in the Cardinal himself. Now was the time, he believed, to introduce a few basic reforms and to ensure social harmony. He reckoned without the royal couple. The King called the populace 'an ugly beast', and he feared it. Under his wife's domination, he also persecuted the men of wealth or intellectual influence. One caustic observer wrote that he had 'executed the whole of his Academy.' Even if these words were exaggerated, death on the gallows or brutal imprisonment on the desolate convict island of Favignana awaited many who failed to escape from the Kingdom.

In younger years, the Queen used to discuss ideas of good government with her brother, the Emperor Joseph II, and her first reaction to the French Revolution was one of approval. The pace of reform needed to be hurried; but when her sister was condemned and put to death, her old respect for men with ideas became hatred. Only a thorough-going purge of the elevated classes could restore stability in the Kingdom of the Two Sicilies. The dynasty and the people, the Queen told Madame de Staël, were no longer capable of trusting each other.

The social pyramid which used to rise, however haphazardly, from the people at its base to the King at its apex was now disrupted. Between King and people stood only the machines of tyranny and police invigilation. Whether they returned to Versailles near Paris or to Caserta near Naples, the Bourbons learned nothing and forgot nothing.

As individuals, they had redeeming features. Even Maria Carolina's grandson—Ferdinand II, called by his subjects *Re Lazzarone*, and by foreigners King Bomba—was not quite the monster whom Englishmen of the day imagined him to be. He hated to sign a death warrant; he behaved bravely whenever cholera was rampant in the city; he kept the taxes low; and his railway between Naples and Portici was the first to be built in Italy. If he named each engine after a favourite saint, so did Pope Pius IX when he, in turn, became a railway builder. The King's railway, moreover, ran between Vesuvius and the Bay. It was earthquake country.

For his wife, Ferdinand chose Maria Cristina, youngest daughter of Victor Emmanuel I, King of Sardinia. She was born on the pleasant hill-top in Cagliari, where royal palace and Cathedral adjoin each other, and a new world opened to her when, at the age of thirteen, she spent four months in Rome during the Holy Year of 1825. Whenever she made a separate pilgrimage on foot to each of the major basilicas, she was heavily veiled and carried a coronet in her hand. A handsome youth of eighteen from Nice may have seen her in the street; for a thirty-ton boat in which Giuseppe Garibaldi had sailed before the mast docked at Fiumicino. Then, laden with wine, the boat was drawn by oxen up the Tiber to Rome, where Garibaldi and his father stayed for a month. Thereafter, the son knew what his life's work ought to be. 'Rome to me was Italy. Rome to me was the one and only symbol of Italian unity.'

Maria Cristina had other dreams. Rome showed that it was her vocation to be a nun. She was overwhelmed with grief on hearing that she must marry the King of the Two Sicilies. For a long time not even her father could persuade her to believe that a dedicated princess may find her true vocation by living in the world as a queen.

Ferdinand liked boorish pranks and barrack-room language, but he soon became ashamed to act foolishly in the presence of a wife who gently begged him not to use those 'soldier words', and who rebuked a groom when she saw him on horseback ahead of her carriage and clearing the way through a crowd of *lazzaroni* with his riding whip. The Neapolitans loved their 'holy queen', and they mourned when, not yet 24, she died after giving birth to a sickly boy: Francis, heir to the throne.

The widower married again, and under the influence of a bigoted Austrian consort, Maria Teresa, his religiosity became more pronounced. He approved the way in which his confessor, Monsignor Cocle, placed under lock and key all the immodest statuary found during excavations in Pompeii or Herculaneum. The first question which he put to every caller at the Palace was: 'Have you been to church today?'

His nickname of King Bomba was not altogether deserved. It came to him after September 8th, 1848, when General Carlo Filangieri—in the opinion of a British admiral on the spot—shelled Messina for eight hours longer than was necessary. The King was nowhere near the stricken city. Yet the fact that Messina was shelled showed how troubled was the condition of his dual Kingdom. The revolutionary trend of events throughout Europe in 1848 compelled him to grant his people a constitution. None the less, he detested the liberals because each reform which they proposed seemed to be contrived to undermine his personal authority as King. His ideas were absolutist. As soon as possible, he forgot even the existence of a constitution.

Before the year ended, Pope Pius IX fled from Rome and took shelter in the naval fortress of Gaeta. Later he went to live in Portici at the far end of King Bomba's first railway. The Neapolitans had seen him as he drove through the country lanes or blessed them from a balcony of the King's Palace. Now—on this feast day of St. Januarius, 1870—many may have prayed for the Holy Father, whom they loved far more than their sovereign from the hard-faced north, King Victor Emmanuel II. Though news travelled none too quickly from Rome to Naples, they realized that the Pope's city must soon be attacked by the King's soldiers. It would have been a token of calamity if, at this hour, their saint and patron withheld a liquefaction.

'*Faccia gialla, fang' o' miracolo!*' 'Yellow face, get on with the miracle!'

While the people inside Naples Cathedral were waiting for St. Januarius to liquefy his blood, Pope Pius drove from the Vatican Palace to the summit of the Lateran Hill, where he entered a building which contains the *Scala Santa*. They are the 'Holy Stairs' which, according to tradition, belonged to the hall in which Pontius Pilate sat in judgment. When the Emperor Titus destroyed Jerusalem, he carried away the ornaments of the Temple: the seven-branched candelabra, the ark which enclosed the Tables of the Law, and the silver trumpets which were sounded in a jubilee year. He brought back to Rome many hundreds of Jewish prisoners, whose descendants still live by the banks of the Tiber. More than two centuries later, Helen—mother of the Emperor Constantine—brought back from Jerusalem the Holy Stairs which Jesus of Nazareth had climbed after his scourging and condemnation to death.

So pilgrims have believed as they humbly ascend the stairs on their knees. One of them—in 1510—was Martin Luther, a German priest and formidable theologian. He was approaching the topmost step when he reflected that his action could neither save his soul nor the souls of others. In later centuries the sceptical spirit became more dominant, and an American visitor was surprised when a priest forbade him to walk up the stairs. At that time three young French soldiers were racing each other to the top on their knees. No one tried to stop them. The French kept order in Rome. To offend them was dangerous.

Now a new soldiery was at the gates. Pius, when looking from the Vatican, had seen Monte Mario 'white with the tents of the Piedmontese waiting, like vultures, to descend'. Rome was a besieged city and doomed to fall. The last Pope-King, as he climbed the Holy Stairs on his knees, was suffering and deeply contrite. The faults which brought the Eternal City to this plight were many, and not a few were his own.

When the penitential climb was over, Pius left the building to speak words of encouragement to the zouaves who were defending St. John's Gateway. He gazed for a moment at the view which visitors to Rome sometimes acclaimed as the finest and most spacious to be seen within the Aurelian walls: the homely avenue of mulberry trees which linked the Cathedral of St. John's Lateran with the smaller basilica of the Holy Cross; the long skeletal arches of the Claudian aqueduct; the white and almost unbending line of the new Appian Way as it stretched to Albano; the villa of Castelgandolfo; the vineyards around Frascati; the olive groves below Tivoli and, beyond the Sabine Hills, the higher peaks of the Apennines which are snow-capped in the winter. The entire region, smiling in autumnal splendour, was once the Pope's; but now only the Aurelian walls, just sixteen centuries old, stood between the Piedmontese and the papal zouaves.

The walls were themselves a reproach. In the Imperial days, Rome would not have needed their protection. A symbol of its former freedom is the equestrian and contemporary statue of Marcus Aurelius which, in Michelangelo's time, was moved from the Lateran Hill to the Capitoline Hill. The horse has no bridle and its rider no guiding reins: wherever, by the pressure of a knee, the philosopher-Emperor directs his horse, it strides over Roman soil. The Empire had been a world, but the Aurelian walls showed that Rome was an open city no longer. Even as a defence, they were a failure; for the barbarians, instead of scaling them, cut the aqueducts. The French had breached the walls in 1849. The Piedmontese would breach them on the morrow.

This Pius no longer doubted. Cardinal Giacomo Antonelli, his powerful Secretary of State, had told him that further resistance was useless. It was better, he said, to admit the Piedmontese into the city and to let them find the zouaves standing to attention with each man's firearms laid at his own feet; but Pius had a better understanding of his soldiers' pride, and he wished to spare them this humiliation. Let them defend the walls until they were breached. Then capitulation must follow.

Fighting within the city he would not permit. Too many men—French, Germans, Poles, Belgians, Swiss and Irish—had died in defence of his Temporal Power. Each fought for a supranational and, it seemed, a spiritual cause; but as soon as a big war started between France and Prussia, volunteers from those two countries were impatient to get back to their homeland. Pius never spoke a word of blame. Patriotism counted even in Rome. This deepened the tragedy of its siege, for the majority of zouaves were as Italian as the Piedmontese; and as Italian as Pius. The conflict was not racial. It arose from a clash of principles. Pope's men or Emperor's men, Guelphs or Ghibellines: the struggle raged in Dante's day. It was raging still.

CHAPTER TWO

GUELPH AND GHIBELLINE

PIUS, AS he surveyed the Roman countryside from the Lateran Hill, happened to be standing almost immediately below a famous mosaic. For more than a century this mosaic had been exposed to the open air, but originally it adorned the *triclinium*—the vast banquet hall of the Lateran Palace—which Pope Leo III had built soon after he had crowned Charlemagne as the Holy Roman Emperor on Christmas Day, 800. Dante may have seen it when he wandered entranced round the Lateran Hill during the first Holy Year of 1300. It illustrated a doctrine which, as a Ghibelline, he did not accept.

Within an arch, the mosaic shows Christ surrounded by the Apostles. With one hand He blesses, and with the other He holds a book in which is written: *Pax vobis*—'Peace be with you!' To the left of the arch, Christ is shown again, and this time He is seated. On one side kneels Pope Sylvester; on the other side kneels Constantine, the first Christian Emperor. Christ gives to Sylvester the keys of heaven and hell, and to Constantine a banner surmounted by a cross.

To the right of the arch, there is another figure; but he is Peter, and not Christ. On one side of Peter kneels Pope Leo III, and on the other side kneels Charlemagne. While clinging to the keys, Peter gives the pallium of an archbishop to Leo and the banner of a Christian army to Charlemagne.

Over the centuries the Church exalted the authority vested in the Pope through Peter. In the words of Thomas Aquinas, the Pope is 'the Sovereign Priest, Peter's successor, the Vicar of Christ, to whom all the Kings of the Christian people owe submission, as to Our Lord Jesus Christ Himself'. Dante, when he watched a papal procession on the Lateran Hill, might have heard the heralds preceding Pope Boniface VIII and shouting:

'Behold two swords; behold the successor of Peter; behold the Vicar of Christ.'

Within the Lateran church—the Pope's Cathedral as Bishop of Rome—another cry was raised:

'The Pope is King; temporal and spiritual Sovereign; above all, whoever they may be; and he holds the place of God.'

Dante believed that this teaching was faulty, and in the Latin prose of his *De Monarchia* he strove to correct it. The Lateran mosaic was right when it showed Christ giving the keys of heaven and hell to Pope Sylvester and a banner to Constantine. It was even right when it showed Peter conferring a pallium on Pope Sylvester, but it erred sadly in making Charlemagne the recipient of a banner from Peter. For the Guelph all power, ecclesiastical and civil, came from Christ through Peter. For the Ghibelline, on the contrary, the Emperor's civil power came directly from Christ, and not through Peter at all. Accordingly, Dante amended the teaching of Aquinas. In *De Monarchia*, he wrote of 'the Sovereign Pontiff, vicar of Our Lord Jesus and Peter's successor, to whom we owe what is the due not of Christ, but of Peter'.

For Italians, more often than not, the Emperor had been a shadowy figure seldom seen south of the Alps, and the word '*Imperator*' is hard to find anywhere in the writings of Aquinas. Whatever hopes Dante once placed in the actions of the Emperor Henry VII were dashed when his hero died—probably poisoned—near Siena. Yet he clung tenaciously to the idea that universal peace would prevail when harmonious partnership was established between Pope and Emperor: one, the head of the universal Church; the other, head of the universal Empire; and each supreme in his own sphere. 'Let Caesar,' he wrote, 'show for Peter the reverence which a first-born shows for his father,' but Caesar's authority was no less divine than Peter's.

This idea, wherever it took root, gravely weakened the Pope's claim to Temporal Power, and *De Monarchia* found no favour in Rome. Within eight years of Dante's death, Pope John XXII condemned the book to the flames; in 1554, Pope Julius II—a militant defender of his Temporal Power—put it on the Index; and for a while Italian Protestants eagerly disseminated copies.

For just over a thousand years there had been a Holy Roman Emperor. Although this grandiloquent title did not survive the Napoleonic wars, Dante's idea of universal rule as the harbinger of universal peace continued to fascinate Italian minds. Rome was majestic and universal long before it became the seat of a Papacy. Napoleon I, more Italian than French, named his son the King of Rome.

Yet, when his wars were over, Rome remained almost unchanged. Once the world's largest city, it was now barely half the size of Naples. Three-fifths of the area within the Aurelian walls were rustic. Handsome villas crowned the Celian Hill, and the northern crag of the Palatine Hill was a Cardinal's hanging garden. Vienna dominated Milan and Venice; Kings ruled in Naples and Turin; a Grand Duke in Tuscany and a Grand Duchess in Parma; Dukes in Modena and Lucca; and the

Pope in Rome. This patchworked sovereignty was a grievance not only for the Italian who had begun to dream of national unity, but also for a number of Catholic thinkers outside Italy. Why, they asked, should the Pope be an Italian princeling content to exchange his nuncios with the ambassadors of other and larger courts? His authority was spiritual. Better than any concordats or alliances between throne and altar would be a full acknowledgment that, as guide of the Christian conscience, the Pope was infallible.

So argued Félicité Lamennais, a brilliant Breton priest. At one time the ultra-conservative Catholics in France regarded him as their spokesman, but they were soon disillusioned. For one thing, he cared almost nothing for governments. Their concern for religion was always hypocritical. Napoleon I expressed their attitude when he said:

'There is only one way of securing morality, and that is to re-establish religion. Society cannot exist without inequality of possessions, and inequality of possessions cannot subsist without religion. When a man is dying of hunger alongside another who is bloated, it is impossible for him to accept this contrast unless there is an authority which says to him: "God wills it to be so. There must be the poor and the rich in the world, but afterwards and during eternity things will be shared out differently." '

Back on his ancestral throne, Louis XVIII paid, as he was bound, a copious lip-service to the altar and to the Gallican liberties won in an earlier century for the Church in France, but those closest to him knew that he admired Voltaire. To the end of his days he remained a sceptic. Far more sincere was his successor and brother, Charles X, who, after a period of dissolute living, showed such devotion to the altar that, according to the gossips, he was a Jesuit in disguise and had been secretly consecrated a Bishop. None the less, the men around him who pulled the actual strings of power feared sincerity in others. It was a blemish in Lamennais. No apologist was more widely read in Paris. Yet at the very time that the ultra-conservatives looked to him to defend a tottering throne, Lamennais preferred to show how often the French Government flouted the will of Rome and how often the Gallican liberties stood in the way of the Church's spiritual freedom.

As Lamennais knew, no return to the days before the Revolution of 1789 was possible, and no amount of posturing as a Christian State would enable the Government of France to assist the Church in its task of regenerating society. The mask was ripped away when, in 1830, the devout King Charles abdicated and Louis-Philippe, the 'citizen-King', took his place on the throne. This mild July Revolution may have involved few changes in the Constitutional Charter, but the article which declared the Catholic religion to be the religion of the State was suppressed. Henceforward, as Lamennais noted, the State was 'atheistic'.

It was better so. The Church needed to be separated completely from the State. The centre of its unity on earth was Rome. The spiritual authority of the Pope transcended all barriers of State. Only through his active leadership as the Vicar of Christ could a revitalized Church achieve the regeneration of society. For this reason, all Catholics must acknowledge the Pope's infallibility.

In temporal matters, it was true, the Pope had no authority over Kings or Governments. It followed, therefore, that if the Catholic could not put his trust in Kings or princes, he must put it in the people. Louis-Philippe was not, like Charles X, the King of France. He was 'King of the French'. Pope Pius VIII, whose reign lasted no more than twenty months, had hastened to address him as the 'Most Christian King of the French'. The change in the regal title was, none the less, far more significant than its authors or the Pope had realized.

Sheer intellectual honesty drove Lamennais out of the conservative camp and into the liberal. His response to the July Revolution of 1830 was to launch a daily newspaper called *L'Avenir*. For its motto, he chose '*Dieu et la Liberté*': 'God and Liberty'. The journal was Catholic because, while arguing that the Church must be separated from the State, it called for steadfast loyalty to the Pope as Vicar of Christ and for wholehearted acceptance of his infallibility. It was also liberal because it demanded full religious liberty, full liberty of education, liberty of the press, liberty of association, and universal suffrage. Finally, as a check against any revival of tyrannical rule, it demanded a decentralization of the Government. For the first time, Paris was faced with a new phenomenon: the Catholic liberal.

Though a new phenomenon in Paris, the Catholic liberal was not entirely so elsewhere. The Belgians, for instance, had no old régime of their own to which they longed to return. After Napoleon's defeat, the Congress of Vienna joined their country to Holland and created a new Kingdom under William of Nassau. He was a Protestant who treated the Belgians as though they were inferior to the Dutch. So doing, he brought the Belgian Catholics and liberals close together, and their alliance forced the pace for a separate Belgian Kingdom. Their first sovereign—Queen Victoria's uncle, Leopold of Saxe-Coburg —was not the King of Belgium, but the King of the Belgians; he led a people.

The Catholic liberal was not even a new phenomenon in distant Warsaw. From old St. Petersburg, there issued one Imperial edict after another to humiliate the people of a once independent country and to infringe the freedom of their Catholic worship. Lamennais, in fact, started his daily journal in a revolutionary year. In Belgium and in Poland, Catholics were the revolutionaries.

Another country, too, showed that it might soon become a hotbed of Catholic liberalism. A young French aristocrat, Charles de Mont-alembert, was distressed by what he saw during a holiday in Ireland. Catholic emancipation, which a Parliament in London had recently granted, was emancipation solely for the well-to-do: it was not emancipation for the Irish people. The established Church in Ireland was still the Church of a Protestant ascendancy, and in countless ways it kept the Catholics impoverished. The one benefit which they possessed was the complete separation of their Church from an alien State. They were scorned and kept in economic bondage, but spiritually they were free.

Montalembert was in Ireland when a friend sent him the prospectus of *L'Avenir*. It was just the document which he needed. At last, he wrote, 'a splendid destiny now opens for Catholicism. Disengaged for ever from its alliance with political power, it is going to recover its force, its liberty and its primal energy. . . . If *L'Avenir* wants me, I give up everything for it.' Another close collaborator was Jean-Baptiste de Lacordaire, who began his career as an eloquent pleader at the Paris bar and later, as Father Dominique, crowded Notre-Dame whenever he occupied its pulpit. Peerless in his style, he shared to the full his friends' vision of a Church which should be as liberal and as democratic as it is Catholic.

Discerning men understood that Lamennais was building a bridge between the Catholic and the liberal, but it was a bridge which almost no conservative layman wanted to cross. Nor did the average liberal; for he was too apathetic, or else too militantly anti-clerical. The battle for popular assent would have been long, and at no time did the circulation of the newspaper rise above two thousand. The actual readership was much larger, for the purses of young priests and teachers were slender, and many copies passed from hand to hand; but when the Bishops forbade their clergy to read its pages and dismissed offending teachers from their posts, they struck a deadly blow.

Accordingly, *L'Avenir* lasted only for thirteen months. In its final issue, the triumvirate—Lamennais, Lacordaire and Montalembert —explained why they had suspended publication. It was not because they lacked funds, but because they were appealing to Rome. They must find out for themselves whether or not the Pope approved their enterprise. They declared that they must leave the battlefield and, like the soldiers of Israel, go 'to consult the Lord in Shiloh'. If the Pope approved, they would resume the publication of *L'Avenir*. If not, they would submit.

The three Catholic liberals left Paris convinced that they would come back armed with the Pope's blessing. The Pope was Gregory XVI, who had just succeeded the short-reigning Pius VIII. As a young and austere Camaldine monk, he had written a book called 'The Triumph of the Holy See', in which he argued that the Pope's infallibility must be acknowledged and his Temporal Power supported. It seemed certain, therefore, that he would appreciate the emphasis which *L'Avenir* had placed on his infallibility and on his capacity, as Vicar of Christ, to rejuvenate the Church. He would confound the journal's ecclesiastical foes in France. *L'Avenir* would circulate once more and renew its demand for the separation of the Church from the State. No priest, teacher or seminarist could ever again suffer punishment for buying a copy and discussing its ideas.

Lamennais and his friends were pinning their hopes on a phantom. If his book, published as far back as 1799, gave Gregory a reputation for foresight, this was scarcely justified. His mind was as plain as his features. It was priestly and monkish, but it was not prophetic. It had nothing in common with the questing minds of the three young Frenchmen, and Gregory did not intend to receive them without taking careful advice beforehand.

For one thing, on hearing of the appeal to Rome, the French Government told its Ambassador to warn the Pope that, in spite of their personal loyalty to him, the three men held views injurious to the Church and State in France. For another, *L'Avenir* had roused the suspicions of Prince Metternich in Vienna. He was almost the only statesman of his day to understand, however imperfectly, that Europe is unitary. For this reason, the sovereigns must league together and support each other's interests.

The one sovereign whom Metternich refused to recognize and whom he dreaded was the people. Yet Demos was the sovereign hailed by Lamennais, a Catholic priest. In turn, therefore, the Austrian Ambassador in Rome was ordered to give a warning. The Pope must be protected against an anarchist in ultramontane clothing.

Lamennais had been in Rome before, but now his eyes were more fully opened to a prevalence of social injustice. Time and again *L'Avenir* had denounced the inhumanity of rule in France, Poland and Ireland. Could it be less inhuman in the Pontifical State? Was not the Temporal Power a crippling fetter on the Pope's spiritual rule over the Church?

The three Frenchmen had not gone far into the Pontifical State when they saw on every side the tokens of misery, penury and neglect. 'We came across a troop of poor wretches,' Lamennais wrote, 'who were led by the papal police and chained together two by two. By their looks several betrayed suffering rather than crime. They all pressed round us, stretched out their hands and in a pathetic way asked for a *bajocco* or two. Under our eyes were descendants of the world's masters.'

Within Rome, Lamennais might often have passed a prison with its cells occupied by political offenders and its walls dampened by the flooding Tiber. More than once, too, he might have seen a group of hooded men walking before a cart in which a wretch sat backwards with his hands tied behind his back and a thick belt clasped round his neck. To a man about to lose his life it was hardly a consolation that the death warrant required the signature of a Cardinal or that the revolutionary French, when they first entered Rome, taught authority to displace the gallows with the guillotine. Soon Lamennais was writing:

'I need air and movement and faith and love and everything that one vainly seeks amid these ancient ruins, over which, like filthy reptiles, the vilest human passions creep. The Pope is pious and means well; but he knows nothing about the world or about the state of the Church and the state of society. Motionless in the thick darkness by which he is surrounded, he weeps and prays. Another twenty years of this kind of thing, and Catholicism would be dead. God will save it through his people.'

With his two companions, Lamennais waited in Rome for more than two months before Gregory received them. He spoke with them for a quarter of an hour and then looked for a small silver replica of Michelangelo's 'Moses', which he wanted to show them. He gave them gilt medals of Pope Gregory I, blessed their rosaries and 'dismissed us graciously, without having uttered a single word that had the least bearing on our mission or on the fortunes of the Church'.

Gregory took a long time before pronouncing judgment, and he expressed it in *Mirari vos*, the first Encyclical Letter to be written since his election. Without actually mentioning *L'Avenir* by name, he forthrightly condemned its political teaching. It was wrong, he declared, to suppose that the Church needed regeneration, that liberty of conscience should be guaranteed to all, or—a grievous fault—that it was possible for Catholics and non-Catholics to unite for the advancement of political liberty; and he quoted with approval the dictum of an eighteenth-century predecessor, Clement XIII, that the only way to deal with erroneous books was to burn them. In particular, it was wrong to attack 'Our dearest sons in Jesus Christ, the princes'; for their authority was given to them for the defence of the Church. This meant that Gregory also condemned the revolt of Catholic Poland against the Tsar, even though her Russian ruler belonged to a Church in schism.

The appeal to Rome was lost. *L'Avenir* could never be published again, and in a letter to a friend Montalembert underlined some of the scornful words which Gregory had used. The Pope, he wrote, 'calls liberty of conscience *sheer madness*, liberty of the press *abominable*, science *impudent*, and proclaims the necessity of the union between Church and State. This act . . . compels us to lay down our arms.' Lamennais resolved to serve liberty and the cause of Polish nationhood with his prayers, since 'God forbids me by the voice of his Vicar on earth to serve them with my pen'.

Montalembert and Lacordaire remained loyal sons of the Church. Yet, so far from laying down his arms, Montalembert continued to argue that true democracy and Christianity were inseparable. The more one is a democrat, 'the more it is necessary to be a Christian, because the fervent and practical cult of God made man is the indispensable counterweight of that perplexed tendency of democracy to establish the cult of man believing himself God'. Lamennais alone was too radical in his thinking to retain any loyalty to Rome. He left the priesthood and the Church, and he died, in 1854, unreconciled.

Gregory, while condemning Catholic liberalism, had taken care not to condemn the idea of papal infallibility, and this idea took root in the minds of men who seldom, if ever, acknowledged their debt to Lamennais. The apostate went on writing, and his last work, published after his death, was a prose translation of Dante's *Divina Commedia*. Like Henry Francis Cary—an Anglican clergyman who rendered the *Divina Commedia* into English verse—Lamennais wanted his age to recognize the grandeur and the genius of the Roman Church's most illustrious layman. Guelph no longer, he paid tribute to a Ghibelline.

While Lamennais waited in Rome for his audience with Gregory, another priest and man of letters was writing a book, which for many years he dared not publish. He gave it the challenging title of *Della Cinque Piaghe della Santa Chiesa*: 'Five Wounds of the Church'. Antonio Rosmini, who was its author, came from Rovereto, close to the northern shore of Lake Garda, and he knew from harsh experience how deeply many of his neighbours resented Austrian rule. Yet political freedom was not enough. The people needed spiritual freedom even more. The Church could not give them this full freedom until five inflicted wounds had been healed.

First of the five wounds, Rosmini wrote, was the division between the clergy and the people in their worship. Its cause was the use of Latin. The language of the Church had long ceased to be the language of the people, who were thus left in darkness. They 'should be actors in the liturgy as well as hearers, while in fact they are mostly present at Mass like the columns and statues of the building. Only the Catholic clergy can bring a remedy to this wound.'

The second wound was the imperfect education of the clergy. The seminaries established after the Council of Trent represented a distinct improvement, but too much of their teaching was still left to the lower and often less educated clergy. In consequence, their students became men of memory rather than men of thought.

The third and fourth wounds were inflicted on the Church through the defective methods of appointing Bishops. In the Venetian Republic, the Bishoprics went to the cadets of famous or wealthy families: the more territory they possessed, the less accessible they became to the lower clergy and to the people. Yet, in the first Christian ages, Bishops were elected *per clerum et populum*: 'by the judgment of the clergy and the people'. Nothing was more wounding to the Church than the concordats which the Holy See signed with sovereigns for regulating appointments to Bishoprics. Only in the United States were Catholic Bishops genuinely free.

Finally, there was the wound inflicted by the Church's wealth. No one save the Pope could cure this slavery of ecclesiastical riches. In a modern State, Rosmini pleaded, the Church should not be over-privileged in the possession or use of property. Moreover, it should pay its share of a country's taxation. Any failure to do so imposes an unfair burden on the other citizens.

Rosmini kept actively in touch with other thoughtful priests and laymen. He used his personal influence to prevent the Holy See from putting an earlier book by Lamennais—*Des Progrès de la Révolution*—on the Index. He saw that the sway of many dialects was a barrier to full Italian unity. A single dialect should be the literary medium for the whole of Italy, and his plea that this medium should be Tuscan—the language of Dante—persuaded Alessandro Manzoni virtually to re-write his novel, *I Promessi Sposi*: 'The Betrothed'.

Two other close friends of Rosmini exerted a marked influence on the struggle for national unity. One was Niccolo Tomasseo, who worked with Daniele Manin in a valiant effort to throw the Austrians out of Venice. He was sent to prison for defending the freedom of the press and was then compelled to live as an exile in Corfu, where he wrote two books. In one, he advocated the abolition of the death sentence; and in the other, he argued that the Church's influence for good would be far greater if only the Pope were deprived of his Temporal Power.

The second friend was Vicenzo Gioberti. Orphan reared in a cloister, court chaplain in Turin, exile in Paris and Brussels, and eventually Prime Minister of Piedmont, Gioberti played with ideas quite as boldly as did Lamennais and Rosmini; but he believed that Italy should attain her unity without violence and, therefore, in gradual stages. The first stage he announced in a book—*Il Primato Morale e Civile degli Italiani*: 'The Moral and Spiritual Primacy of the Italians' —which he published in 1843, when he was an exile and Italy still the political patchwork imposed by the Congress of Vienna.

The separate Italian States, Gioberti declared, should federate under the presidency of the Pope. 'I see religion placed at the summit of all things human. I see princes and people vying in reverence and love for the human Pontiff, recognizing and adoring him not only as successor of Peter, Vicar of Christ, head of the universal Church, but as doge and standard bearer of the Italian confederation, fatherly arbitrator and pacifier of Europe, heir to Latin greatness, and amplifier of it by natural and pacific modes.'

Gioberti would have been a great man, 'if only he had common sense'. So said Camille Cavour, Prime Minister of Piedmont and a principal architect of Italian unity. He was expressing the attitude of a practical statesman to a man of ideas. Yet he himself shamelessly exploited ideas and idealistic action; for without them Italy would never have become a nation. From Montalembert, for example, he borrowed and made memorable the phrase 'a free Church in a free State'. The men of ideas included Giuseppe Mazzini and many other anti-clericals, but they also included priests, each of whom was anxious about the part which a Pope should play in the Italy of the morrow.

Should the Pope be the President of an Italian Federation? Or, stripped of all Temporal Power, should he be hailed throughout the Catholic world as infallible? There was an obvious conflict of ideas. Who was right: Gioberti or Lamennais?

In the end, both Gioberti and Lamennais forsook their original ideas about the Pope, and both died alienated from the Church; but what they had written continued to influence a renascent Italy. Their readers—some of them humble parish priests—knew how much depended on the emergence of a Pope able to speak the language of a new age and to make the Church contemporary.

Gregory was not that Pope. The few who knew him well liked him. Rosmini, who had often consulted him in younger years, claimed that the office of Pontiff in no way spoilt his gentleness and courtesy; he was 'still the same man'. An American visitor complained that his appearance was untidy, 'his nose, hands and breast being completely covered with snuff', but he was 'mild and unassuming in manner, easy and pleasant'. None the less, he was a recluse and unadventurous. 'I am too old to reform the State,' he admitted, 'and the world will get along somehow.' He called a railway a *chemin d'enfer*—'a road to hell'—and allowed none to be built in the Pontifical State.

Although Rosmini spoke well of Gregory, he was himself a sufferer. Tomasseo wrote as an exile in Corfu, and Gioberti wrote as an exile in Brussels; but Rosmini worked on Italian soil. He knew that, as long as Gregory was the Pope, he could not publish 'The Five Wounds of the Church'. Even if he passed his manuscript from one discreet friend to another, more than fifteen years had to go by before he gave it to a printer. No doubt, many other men put pen to paper, well knowing that what they wrote could never be published. Though Rosmini did not mention it, a grave wound of the Church was censorship. 'Ignorant people,' a papal official once explained, 'are easier to govern.' None the less, the simile of a shepherd and his flock had long since lost its charm. Man is not born to be sheep-like, and the prophets could not be silenced for ever.

If Gregory neglected the world, he seems in turn to have been neglected; for Massimo d'Azeglio—painter, novelist, guitarist, military commander, and Cavour's immediate predecessor as Prime Minister of Piedmont—recorded a story of his death in 1846. 'A poor gardener who loved the Pope knew that he was on the point of death. The man took it into his mind to see him once again: he finds the private staircase open and arrives at an ante-room; knocks; no one; he goes through and finds himself in the Pope's bedroom; but he is lying as though he had been trying to raise himself in a fit of choking, lying curled up on his side, with his head dangling over the side of the bed.

'The poor gardener rushes to help him and lift him back on the bed as best he can: he calls to him, feels his pulse and finds him cold: he goes down on his knees weeping and recites a *de profundis* for the dead Pope. Just then one of the household enters, perhaps just back from hiding things: he is taken by surprise, shouts and threatens the man lest he should tell tales, and chases him out. But the gardener talked.'

On the afternoon of June 14th, 1846, fifty Cardinals entered the church of St. Sylvester on Monte Cavallo, listened to a Latin sermon and then walked in solemn procession up to the Quirinal Palace, where all was made ready for their Conclave. Two days later they elected Cardinal Giovanni Mastai-Ferretti as Pope, and he took the name of

Pius. It was then well past midnight, and no cannon was fired until the morning of June 17th. Cardinal Mastai had not been well known to the Romans, and for a time the people who gathered in the square showed little enthusiasm. Yet, when he stepped on to the balcony of the Quirinal Palace to give his first papal blessing, many were astonished by his elegance, pleasant looks, aristocratic bearing and melodious voice. Though he was 54, not a single grey hair could be seen.

Here, at last, was a new Pope for a new age. The struggle between Guelph and Ghibelline, however, is not new. Some wanted a Pope to preside over Italy, and others wanted a Pope who would be deprived of all Temporal Power. What would Pius IX be: the first Pope-President, or the last Pope-King?

No one remembered a Pope who was similar in temperament or upbringing to Giovanni Mastai. He was 23 when Napoleon's victors restored the Pontifical State to Pope Pius VII on the distinct under-standing that it would be well governed. As he liked soldiering, Giovanni Mastai wanted to become an officer in the Papal Guard. He was rejected because he had periodic fits of epilepsy. All hopes of marriage, family life and a military career vanished. Pius VII, however, had an affection for him, recognized his simple piety, persuaded him to wear the tonsure and then, ignoring a mother's passionate plea that he should stay in Rome, sent him to Chile as a secretary to the Apostolic Vicar.

The voyage was long and perilous, and a two years' sojourn in Santiago gave him a distinctly different political horizon. He returned to Rome still very young and responsive to ideas of freedom. Always neatly dressed, he spent only a little money on himself, although he was expansively generous in his help for others. In Rome he felt at a disadvantage because he was not scholarly and may have lacked a thorough theological training. Uncertain of himself, he needed to rely on others; and as the years brought him advancement in the Church, it became increasingly important that his advisers should be large-visioned men.

For five years he was Archbishop of Spoleto, and for fourteen he was Bishop of Imola. This was the important Bishopric held by Pius VII, then Cardinal Luigi Chiaramonti, before his election as Pope. In 1797, Chiaramonti had said that there was no necessary conflict between the principles of the Gospels and those of a good republican. A man could be both a good Catholic and a good republican. First in Spoleto and then in Imola, Giovanni Mastai heard enough to know that papal rule was corrupt and Austrian rule intolerable.

One evening two fugitives—Prince Louis Napoleon and his mother,

Queen Hortense—arrived at his palace and asked for aid. To ensure their safe arrival in Piedmont, the Bishop sent them away in his own carriage which, since it bore his episcopal arms on its two doors, no police officer would have dared to stop. On one occasion, he was adoring the Holy Sacrament in Imola Cathedral when the police chased a man right into the building and killed him. On another, he heard screams beyond the Cathedral's open door, rushed into the square and arrived to comfort the dying victim of an angry mob.

He had been a Cardinal for about six years when news reached him that Gregory was dead. From a friend he borrowed six hundred crowns for his journey to Rome. As it would be long and often tedious, the wife of Giuseppe Pasolini, a liberal-minded friend, gave him three books to read. One was Gioberti's 'Moral and Spiritual Primacy of the Italians'. Its strong appeal turned the Cardinal's journey into a pleasure, and he decided that he would not go back to Imola until he had made the new Pope promise to read it.

Instead, and very unwillingly, he became himself the new Pope. Among the first to feel the wind of change were the political prisoners. Two years beforehand, for example, Felice Orsini was lodged for a political offence in a secret dungeon immediately below the *conforteria*: the room in which men condemned to death received the last sacrament. He saw a blood-stained guillotine carried past the window, and he was himself condemned to the galleys for life. This meant that one day he would be fastened by a yard-long chain to a dungeon wall in Civita-vecchia; for as each galley-slave died, another took his place at the wall.

Orsini was still kept waiting in the fortress of Civita Castellana when he and his fellow-sufferers were told that the new Pope had granted an amnesty to political prisoners. Each signed a paper 'never in any manner to abuse this act of sovereign mercy'. Most of them signed it willingly, and nearly one thousand men were set free. Reforms soon followed. Pius allowed a greater freedom for the press. He established a Consulta for the Pontifical State and a municipal council for the city of Rome. For the first time, laymen had an effective share in ruling the State, and one of the Ministers was Giuseppe Pasolini.

Leo XII, the successor of Pius VII, had forbidden the Jews either to buy land or to leave the ghetto after dark. He had also revived an insulting regulation which periodically required them to listen to a Catholic sermon in the church of Sant' Angelo in Pescheria. Pius lost almost no time in having the regulation abolished. He tore down the walls of the ghetto and permitted the Jews of Rome to live wherever they chose to go.

In this changed climate, Rosmini was at last able to publish his

'Five Wounds of the Church'. Whether or not Pius read it carefully, he kept a copy on his writing desk, and he let it be known that he intended to make the author a Cardinal. Through an old friend, he sent a message to Lamennais. 'I have an overture to make to you,' wrote Father Ventura. 'It is on behalf of the angel whom heaven has sent us, from Pius IX whom I saw this morning. He has charged me to tell you that he blesses you and is waiting to embrace you.'

Like many others, Garibaldi believed that the new papal reign marked 'the dawn of an era of Italian liberty'. 'We were prepared for everything except a liberal Pope,' Metternich admitted to the Sardinian Minister in Vienna. 'Now that we have one, there is no telling where it will end.'

Yet the end was already near. If Lamennais and his two compatriots once pursued a phantom Pope, so did the men who believed that Pius could become the President of Italy. 'Good God, bless Italy!' These were the vibrant words which Pius uttered on February 10th, 1848. Five weeks later, Metternich was in flight from Vienna, and the Italian rulers—those of Naples, Tuscany, Modena and Parma—were ready jointly to free Italy from the Austrian. Pius alone held back. As a prince, it would have been his privilege to collaborate with his fellow-princes of Italy; but he was more than a prince. He was Pontiff. 'I am more Italian than you are,' he told the Ambassadors of his fellow-princes, 'but you refuse to make the distinction in me between the Italian and the Pontiff.'

Pius called the Cardinals together, and in an Allocution he explained why he was not at war with Austria. 'We, though unworthy, represent on earth Him who is the author of peace and the lover of concord, and, according to the order of our supreme Apostolate, We seek and embrace all races, peoples and nations, with an equal devotion of paternal love.'

With these words, Pius both destroyed the dream of a papal presidency over Italy and pronounced the eventual doom of the Temporal Power. At the same time, he proclaimed, and was able to preserve, the international character of the Papacy. An act, judged by many contemporary critics to be weak, happened to be the strongest and most enduring of his reign.

Ten months later, Pius was an exile in Gaeta.

CHAPTER THREE

FATHER OF HIS PEOPLE

ON DECEMBER 4th, 1848—feast day of St. Barbara, patroness of artillerymen—Pope Pius IX sent a letter from Gaeta to tell Queen Victoria in England of the 'utterly unheard-of violence which, provoked by a nefarious conspiracy of abandoned and most turbulent men,' made it necessary 'to depart for a time from our Holy City and from the whole state of our pontifical dominions'. His letter, when it reached Windsor Castle, raised a problem: how should the sovereign lady who was head of the established Church of England and Ireland address the Pope?

The Foreign Office took nearly a month before finding the right answer and drafting a suitable reply. To judge from the records preserved in the State Paper Office, only one English sovereign since the days of Henry VIII's break with Rome had ever sent a letter to the Pope. This was George IV, an uncle whom Queen Victoria thought not at all desirable. It was true that Queen Mary I, faithful daughter of an offending Tudor monarch, signed a number of letters to be despatched as soon as her expected child was born. They included one for Pope Paul IV; but, as the birth did not occur, none of the prepared letters left England. The precedent to follow was clearly set by George IV. As Prince Regent, he wrote letters to Pius VII which began 'Most Eminent Sir' and styled him 'Your Holiness'. When he became King, he continued to address his letters to Rome in the same way.

'Most Eminent Sir,' wrote Queen Victoria in her reply to Pius IX, 'Your Holiness has given so many proofs of being animated by a sincere desire to improve the condition of the people whom, under Divine Providence, you have been chosen to govern, and the clemency of your heart and the rectitude of your intentions are so well known and so truly appreciated, that I cannot but hope that the trials which you have experienced in consequence of popular emotion will speedily come to an end, and will be succeeded by a cordial good understanding between Your Holiness and the Roman people.'

No sooner was her letter sent to Gaeta than the Queen received one from Prince Louis Napoleon, telling her that he had been elected President of the new French Republic. As the nephew of a once mighty Emperor, he was not shy in addressing a monarch. His letter began '*Très chère et grande Amie*', and it ended '*Votre ami, Louis Napoléon Bonaparte*'. Just two months later, a letter arrived from Turin. The writer addressed Queen Victoria as '*Ma très chère Soeur*', signed himself '*votre très cher Frère, Victor Emmanuel*', and announced his accession to the throne of Sardinia.

Pius IX, Louis Napoleon, Victor Emmanuel: none of them could have foreseen how, in the next two decades, their paths would cross and re-cross; and none of the three letters which reached her in such quick succession could have pleased the English Queen. Behind each letter was the story of a loss of nerve. To most of the European monarchs in 1848 and 1849, the future seemed dark and menacing; but, as Queen Victoria told her uncle—Leopold, King of the Belgians—'I never was calmer and quieter and less nervous. *Great* events make me quiet and calm, and little trifles fidget me and irritate my nerves.' She believed that if King Louis-Philippe had stayed in Paris, there would have been no need for him to abdicate. He was the architect of his own misfortunes. Pope Pius betrayed a similar weakness. He announced that he would never leave Rome. Then, the Queen complained, he left his Holy City the very next day.

Weakness, too, had brought Victor Emmanuel to his throne at the age of 29. Charles Albert, his father, had grown up as an exile in Napoleon's France, and he was sixteen before he set foot in Piedmont. His temperament, however, was so completely Piedmontese that he might have lived all his life in Turin, 'half-barrack and half-cloister', where the censorship of books and plays was the severest in Italy, and where the favourite motto of the War Ministry was 'Books make a soldier unlearn his trade'. He was a pious man taught to believe that no life was nobler than a priest's or a soldier's, and he imposed on his own three sons a religious upbringing and spartan discipline not dissimilar to his own.

Though merciless to men who shared Mazzini's ideas of political freedom, he longed to see the last armed Austrian soldier driven off Italian soil, but he was nearly always uncertain how and when to act. Courteous critics called him Hamlet; others called him King Wobble. Then came the revolutionary surge of events in 1848. If these events compelled Charles Albert in Turin, as they compelled Ferdinand in Naples, to grant a Constitution, or Consulta, they also provided an unmistakable opportunity for declaring war on Austria. When the citizens of Milan rose against the Austrian Governor of Lombardy-Venetia—the 82-year-old Marshal Radetsky—Charles Albert was driven to go to their aid.

For a time, fortune favoured the arms of Piedmont. Her soldiers were brave, but the generalship was poor. At Novara they were beaten, and the shame of defeat was too much for the King of Sardinia. Charles Albert abdicated and went into a final exile in Oporto. Victor Emmanuel, his elder son and successor, had two notable assets: a good name as a fighting soldier, and a determination never to submit to a demand from Austria to revoke the Consulta. The soldier-King must keep the word which his father pledged to the people. For this reason, his Prime Minister, Massimo d'Azeglio, called him *Re Galantuomo*: 'the upright King'.

Legend and reality, however, often part company. Little was kingly in the appearance or manner of the new monarch. As a child less than two years old, he was staying with his maternal grandmother, Grand Duchess of Tuscany, at the villa of Poggio Imperiale. The bed caught fire, and although the nurse rescued him, the story persisted that he had died and that another child of about the same age was found to take his place as heir to the throne of Sardinia. Victor Emmanuel was ill-shaped and ugly, selfish and vain. Though he seemed to treat all men alike and to ignore distinctions of rank, he had an inordinate pride in his House of Savoy, and he never forgot that it was the oldest ruling house in Europe. Thus he drew a firm line between its members and other people, whether they bore many titles or none. 'I can refuse a gentleman neither a title nor a cigar,' he once admitted. The royal pedestal was high, but the floor beneath it was even. His mother tried hard to make him a good Catholic, and he admired the saintly spirit of his Austrian wife, Maria Adelaide; but he was himself more superstitious than genuinely religious. His enemies said that he feared the devil more than he feared God.

Because he was shy and painfully aware of his physical uncouthness, the King tried to avoid all ceremonies where he could not be seen in full military uniform and on horseback. If he was made to attend a banquet, he never opened his napkin nor ate a morsel of food. Glowering at his guests, he waited until his ordeal—and theirs—was over. What he wanted was life in the open air, a day's shooting, and a simple midday meal cooked like a peasant's and eaten in a mountainside camp.

Victor Emmanuel was obsessively attracted to women, and he preferred them to be common. Soon after he came to the throne, his glance fell on Rosa Vercellona, the sixteen-year-old daughter of a regimental bandmaster, and he wasted no time in setting up a second establishment. Even in Stupinigi, where he went with the Queen and the royal offspring for the summer months, Rosa—later known to all the gossipers as Rosina—was lodged in a small house at the further end of the park.

A hypocrite would have taken more care to conceal his numerous infidelities alike from his wife and from his mistress, but Victor Emmanuel had the rather unkingly habit of saying just what he thought and hiding almost nothing. If at times he dissimulated, it was done clumsily. He preferred to be frank. This capacity for truthfulness makes his letters still as refreshing to read as those of Queen Victoria. Every oblique deed or falsehood—and there were many—seemed to be attributable to his Ministers or advisers. He could not help remarking that Rosina's children were more beautiful than the Queen's, and then came the inevitable boast that the mixture of royal and common blood was good. The Queen bore him five children and Rosina bore him three. One day the Queen found Rosina's eldest child playing in the park. She kissed him tenderly and did not hide her tears. A few weeks later she died in childbirth.

Within a fortnight of her death, the King also lost his mother and his brother, the Duke of Genoa. The court was not merely in mourning; it was virtually in complete abeyance. The citizens of Turin adored the Duke of Genoa, but they had no love for his sharp-tongued Saxon widow. According to the gossipers of the day, she was determined to marry her bereaved brother-in-law and become the Queen of Sardinia. When she knew that she would be rebuffed, she ostentatiously married an obscure Lieutenant Rapallo. Victor Emmanuel was furious and meant to send her back to Dresden in disgrace. Later he relented and allowed her to live in a villa by Lake Maggiore with her two children, but all three were forbidden to stay in any city in his Kingdom. The husband was made a marquess and became a chamberlain to his own wife.

Victor Emmanuel was untravelled, narrowly educated and courtless: a crowned provincial. This troubled Cavour at a time when he wanted some international support for his Italian aims. He joined England and France in a blundering war against Russia because he believed that this would give him or his successor the right to take part in an eventual peace conference. The Kingdom of Sardinia must figure more impressively on the European chess-board. For the sake of their country's prestige, therefore, fifteen thousand Piedmontese troops were sent as cannon-fodder to the Crimea. 'Theirs not to reason why'; but one result of Piedmont's alliance with England was an invitation to Victor Emmanuel to stay with Queen Victoria and the Prince Consort in Windsor Castle. Cavour went with him and hoped earnestly that his own sovereign would not be too ill-behaved.

On the contrary, the Queen liked him. One fundamentally truthful person faced another. Though extremely startling at first, wrote the

Queen to her uncle Leopold in Laeken, he is 'so frank, open, just, straightforward, liberal and tolerant, with much sound good sense'. 'He is shy in society, which makes him still more brusque, and he does not know (never having been out of his own country or even in Society) what to say to the number of people who are presented to him, and which is, I know from experience, a most odious thing.' The Queen was particularly pleased to invest him with the Order of the Garter. 'He is more like a knight or King of the Middle Ages than anyone one knows nowadays.'

None the less, there was another side to the story. Victor Emmanuel hated to wear any ceremonial dress likely to emphasize his distorted figure, and he also hated even to be touched by a man. The day before his investiture in St. George's Chapel, the court tailor arrived to take the measurements for his robes. The King sternly forbade him to approach too near. In dismay, the tailor walked slowly round him several times and judged the correct measurements with his naked eye.

Though the hour which Victor Emmanuel chose for his departure from Windsor Castle was four o'clock in the morning, England must have pleased him; for in the following autumn he proposed marriage to Queen Victoria's first cousin, Princess Mary of Cambridge. The Queen stipulated that the princess must decide for herself whether to accept or to decline the offer. It was declined on the plea that the young lady did not intend to change her religion and that, as the Protestant Queen of Sardinia, she would put herself in a false position. Instead of becoming a Queen, she married an impecunious Duke of Teck, who constantly complained that he was only a Serene Highness, while his wife took precedence over him as a Royal Highness.

Five princely children were left in Piedmont without a mother and with a father who saw them only when it pleased him to do so. The two girls—Clotilde and Maria Pia—grew up in a remote wing of the palace in Turin. The three boys—Humbert, Amadeus and Odo—were sent to Montcalieri, two miles outside Turin. The boyhood of Humbert and Amadeus had to be as spartan as was the boyhood of their father and grandfather. Before five o'clock each morning they were out of bed. They rode each day, but never beyond a prescribed distance. Except on Sundays, when they visited their sisters, they were not allowed to enter Turin. The severe discipline could not be applied to Odo, the youngest and ablest of the three boys, because he was crippled and destined to be short-lived. His brothers loved him, and they were watching over him when an urgent summons brought the King to the sick-room. On hearing that Odo had only a few more hours of life, Victor Emmanuel left again. He was driven away not by heartlessness, but by a superstitious dread of death.

Rejected by an English princess, Victor Emmanuel soon abandoned the search for a royal consort. Yet Turin could not be left for ever without a court. Apart from his two sons, the King's nearest male kinsman was the Prince of Carignano, a distinguished admiral. He was excellent as presiding over a council in the King's absence, but he loved Turin's most popular actress quite as much as his sovereign loved Rosina Vercellona. Only a royal lady could be the guiding spirit of the court in Turin. The King wisely forgot his quarrel with the Duchess of Genoa. He ended her exile on a bank of Lake Maggiore, and she went back to Turin with the Marquess Rapallo, her second husband, in attendance.

Victor Emmanuel grew fond of her again, and Henry d'Ideville, a young attaché at the French Embassy, recorded the story of the King's unexpected call on the Duchess. The two were talking together when there was a quiet knock on the door. The Duchess went on talking as though nothing had happened.

'There's a knock,' said the King. 'Why don't you answer?'

'Why bother? It can only be Rapallo. He doesn't know that Your Majesty is with me.'

'But why such severity, dear sister?' And, in the same breath, the King added: 'Come in!'

The chamberlain opened the door, advanced to the centre of the room, bowed low and was told by the Duchess to bring the King a glass of water. As soon as the Marquess Rapallo had retired, the King asked why a husband should be treated in this way.

'You are cruel, Duchess, and I don't understand.'

The Duchess went on talking as though there had been no break in the conversation.

Nor was it only with his former sister-in-law that Victor Emmanuel renewed friendship. He did not fail to notice that her daughter, Margaret, was an intelligent and well-bred child. If he could not find a royal consort for himself, he thought it probable that he had found one for Humbert, his heir.

Queen Victoria was not alone in liking Victor Emmanuel. Deep in his heart, Pope Pius also liked him, even though a clash of principles made one the foe of full Italian unity, and the other a monarch eventually excommunicated by his Church. Between them was a bond of soldierly simplicity. In other circumstances, they might have fought bravely side by side; but one was an epileptic denied admission to the Papal Guard, and the other a sovereign destined to rule over the Italian people from the Quirinal Hill. Cardinal Antonelli was reading aloud an account of the King's successful fighting against the Austrians at Palestro, when Pius suddenly exclaimed:

'*Vittorio, Vittorio, figlio mio!*'

On seeing a look of horror on the face of his Secretary of State, the Pope added:

'And why not? After all, we are Italian.'

Pius knew that most of the King's failings stemmed from moral weakness. Victor Emmanuel meant well and was endowed with physical courage, but he was unable to pursue a line of his own. Cavour, ten years his senior and a master of statecraft, treated him as though he were unintelligent and a boor. In the clumsiest fashion, the great Minister tried to end the scandal of his sovereign's intimate life with Rosina. Pius had more charitable advice to give to the wild widower. Rather than put away his mistress, let him marry her!

If weakness in the King often distressed Pius, he was not always blameless himself. Queen Victoria may have judged him too harshly for his flight to Gaeta the day after he had said that he would never leave Rome. The circumstances were terrifying. His Prime Minister, Pellegrino Rossi, had been hacked to death as he was about to enter the Chancellery, while Bishop Palma, as he gazed innocently from a window of the Quirinal Palace, was shot dead by a sniper perched on the campanile of Borromini's beautiful little church of St. Charles of the Four Fountains. In this time of danger, only two of the Cardinals stood by the Pope. One was Giacomo Antonelli, whose physical bravery Pius never forgot.

Antonelli was the grandson of a peasant who lived near Terracina and had endeared himself to the blind Cardinal Alessandro Albani, builder of a spacious Roman villa and one of Europe's greatest patrons of the arts. Through the Cardinal's influence, the peasant secured a fine education for his grandson, who entered the papal service and soon showed that he had a remarkable financial acumen. Though he rose to be a Cardinal and the Secretary of State, Giacomo Antonelli never became a priest. He was content to remain in minor orders and, in consequence, he did not say Mass. Like many others born of the Italian peasantry, he was charming in his manner, adroit, cunning and wholeheartedly devoted to the material interests of his own family. He would have been handsome if it were not for a protruding jaw which, according to Ferdinand Gregorovius, the Prussian historian of medieval Rome, was 'thousands of years old and belonged to the creatures of the mud who devoured, devoured, devoured'. Aristocrat and peasant get on well together in Italy, but in allowing himself to be identified so completely with Antonelli's views and methods, Pius took the path which led all the more speedily to his destruction as a temporal prince.

There was one good priest who might have stopped him from taking this path. Antonio Rosmini followed Pius to Gaeta and begged him to reflect seriously on the future. Let him not rescind the Constitution granted to his people. Otherwise his reign would be cut sharply into two parts: the one liberal, and the other reactionary. Let him not even stay in Gaeta, which was territory belonging to the Kingdom of the Two Sicilies. If Rome was too dangerous for a speedy return, let him go to Bologna. Then he would be back on the soil of his own State and among his own people.

At first, Rosmini seemed to be influencing Pius, and there was a report that the Pope might go to Loreto; but the good priest from Rovereto was no match for Antonelli. If he were to re-write his book, Rosmini might have changed the title to 'The Six Wounds of the Church'. The sixth wound was the power of Cardinals who were not priests. Rosmini served the Church, but Antonelli served the Pontifical State. The servant of the Church and the servant of the State lived on spiritually different planes. There came a day when the police—and they were King Bomba's—served an expulsion order on Rosmini. He refused to leave Gaeta until he had seen the Pope. Antonelli did his best to prevent the audience. The priest whom Pius once intended to make a Cardinal found that his 'Five Wounds of the Church' and other writings were put under the scrutiny of the Holy Office. Foes did not shrink from accusing him of heresy.

If Pius and Victor Emmanuel secretly liked each other, they barely concealed their disdain for Louis Napoleon Bonaparte. In spite of a martial name, the French ruler lacked the simpler soldierly qualities which Pope and King appreciated. Fundamentally, as Bismarck once admitted, he was a good-natured man, but he could not resist practising his own gifts of guile and dissimulation. He was a born conspirator.

In earlier years he knew the Italian scene well and showed sympathy with Mazzini's ideas and methods. He remembered how the former Archbishop Mastai had helped him and his mother to reach Piedmont in safety, and he was eager to show gratitude. He was elected the first President of a new French Republic, and almost at once he committed himself to the task of destroying a new Roman Republic led by Mazzini and Garibaldi.

'We must act,' Mazzini said, 'like men who have the enemy at the gates, and at the same time like men who work for eternity.' At first, the enemy was Ferdinand of the Two Sicilies, who, delighted to be the Pope's host and protector, hurried to make war. In his own mind, he was also working for eternity, and he brevetted St. Ignatius Loyola as one of his Marshals.

Eventually it was the French who occupied Rome. This they did in the name of public order, which, in point of fact, the new republicans had kept remarkably well. No doubt, thousands of Romans were sorry when the Pope went away. Yet their anger was unbounded when the French broke into the city and compelled them to surrender. The French restored 'order', and General Oudinet sent his chief of staff to Gaeta to lay the keys of Rome at the Pope's feet. Whether the year was 1799 or 1849, and whether the conquered citizens were Neapolitans or Romans, the invader from France trod on Italian dreams.

The cause of republicanism had been betrayed, but Louis Napoleon was an imperialist in republican clothing. Later on—at the cost of 27,000 arrests and 215 deaths in Paris alone—he made himself a dictator and then restored the Empire. Yet, when Felice Orsini was condemned for an attempt to assassinate him and the Empress Eugénie outside the Opera House in Paris, he tried—perhaps half-heartedly—to save the Italian from the guillotine. On his authority alone were published the two letters which Orsini wrote to him in his death-cell.

'Remember that so long as Italy is not independent,' the first letter stated, 'the peace of Europe and of Your Majesty is but an empty dream. May Your Majesty not reject the words of a patriot on the steps of the scaffold! Set my country free, and the blessings of twenty-five million people will follow you everywhere and for ever.' Orsini plotted to kill the Emperor Napoleon III because he was the enemy of Italian freedom. Then, in the last hours of his life, he begged the Emperor to become Italy's liberator. What induced Napoleon III to publish the two letters? Good nature and admiration for courage, or a passion for conspiracy? Even the generous words of a doomed man could be made to serve an ambiguous purpose.

Napoleon was willing to free the northern half of Italy from Austrian domination, but at a double price. From Cavour the statesman, he demanded Savoy and Nice: one, the homeland of the Royal House; and the other, the native city of Garibaldi. From Victor Emmanuel the father, he asked for the hand of Princess Clotilde for Prince Jerome Bonaparte. For himself he had chosen Eugénie de Montijo, a Spaniard outside the royal circle, but for his cousin—a middle-aged beater of mistresses and known throughout Paris as 'Plon-Plon'—he selected a girl demurely sheltered in Turin.

'What's the bastard up to now?', Victor Emmanuel exclaimed on one occasion. 'He's a *parvenu* of a monarch, an upstart amongst us. He forgets what he is and what I am—the head of the first and oldest house to reign in Europe.' Savoyard pride was hurt. Clotilde was the King's first child, and Pope Gregory XVI had been her godfather. The English princess to whom Victor Emmanuel offered marriage was given full freedom to accept or reject a reigning monarch. The same freedom must now be accorded to his daughter who, as he told the Emperor, was 'a member of a house which had carried its head high for 850 years and followed the path of honour without reproach'. The letter did not offend Napoleon. Good naturedly, he said that he liked it; and Clotilde married Plon-Plon as dutifully as another princess of Savoy had married King Bomba.

Garibaldi never forgave Cavour for sacrificing Nice, and France's new acquisitions roused such fears in England that, within a few months, about 130,000 civilians joined the Volunteers. None the less, the formalities of popular consent were observed; for it had been agreed that there should be a plebiscite in Savoy and Nice and that, if its verdict was favourable, the result would be endorsed by the Parliament in Turin.

Although the number of people who possessed the vote was limited, the majority of them showed that they wanted cession to France. This was good enough for Napoleon, and he waited with ill-tempered impatience for Cavour to go through the motions of gaining the approval of his Parliament. The mood in Turin was sullen, and Victor Emmanuel wept when he bade farewell to the officers and men of the Savoyard Brigade. Though prepared to serve a new sovereign, they asked that their Brigade should not be disbanded. The Emperor refused the request. As individual soldiers, they were scattered among his other regiments.

Yet he kept part of his pact with Cavour, for he had joined Piedmont in a war on Austria. Together with Victor Emmanuel, he rode triumphantly through the streets of Milan. After bitter fighting and severe losses, the French took Solferino and the Piedmontese took San Martino. A promise to free northern Italy 'from the Alps to the Adriatic' seemed likely to be fulfilled when, without any warning to his ally, Napoleon called for an armistice and made peace with Austria. Vienna continued to hold sway over the Venetian provinces and Mantua. The City of the Lagoon, the once emancipating University of Padua, the birthplace of Virgil: all were still diadems of an alien Austrian crown. No ally—least of all, Napoleon III—was to be trusted. If the Italians wanted full freedom, they must win it by themselves alone.

This view was not confined to the King, the Ministers and professional soldiers. It was the burning faith of Garibaldi and his followers. The struggle for unity suddenly changed its direction when—on April 4th, 1860—Garibaldi set sail from Genoa for Sicily with his thousand volunteers. Hitherto the struggle for unity had meant liberation from the Austrians and from the petty courts dominated by Vienna. Now an independent Kingdom, in which Austrian influence was indirect, came under the hammer of Italian patriotism.

Pius stayed in Portici until the midsummer of 1850. For all the papal devotion, King Bomba would never have allowed him to interfere in the affairs of his own Kingdom. None the less, it was fortunate that Pius had already left by the time William Ewart Gladstone arrived in Naples for a winter holiday. James Lacaita, legal adviser to the English Legation in Naples, persuaded the statesman to attend the trial of Carlo Piero, a former liberal Minister who, against impossible odds, had tried to work the short-lived constitution. Gladstone heard him sentenced to twenty-four years' imprisonment in chains. This so shocked him that he insisted on visiting the victim in his cell. He soon discovered that there were about 24,000 other political prisoners languishing as galley-slaves under filthy conditions.

Tales could still be told of savage sentences and inhuman treatment in other Italian prisons. The amnesty which Pius had granted was confined to political prisoners. Galley-slaves who were not political prisoners still rotted in captivity. The punishment of wickedness and vice was inexorable, though the offence which brought a man to the galleys might be trivial, the evidence marshalled against him biased, and the trial too summary.

Nor was Gladstone concerned with the sufferings of thieves or cheats or moral corruptors. What troubled him was the fact that in Naples—capital of a Kingdom and Italy's largest city—men were punished for their political views and actions in exactly the same way as were the criminals. He knew no peace of mind until he had written an open letter to Lord Aberdeen condemning 'the wholesale persecution of virtue . . . the awful profanation of public religion . . . the perfect prostitution of the judicial office . . . the savage and cowardly system of moral as well as physical torture . . . the negation of God erected into a system of government.'

The words were scathing and written in anger, and a friend who was born an Italian feared that Gladstone had damaged his case against King Bomba by excessive vehemence. As a young lawyer in Modena, Anthony Panizzi had plotted secretly against its reigning Duke. When this was discovered, he escaped and made his way to Liverpool, where for a while he lived precariously as a teacher of Italian. None the less, the Duke of Modena had him hanged in effigy and then sent him a bill for 225 francs and 25 cents to cover the cost of his execution and the fee for the hangman.

Later Panizzi became the famous Librarian of the British Museum. In this position, he cultivated the friendship of influential people partly because he liked good dinner parties, but chiefly because he was an active champion of Italian unity. The good will of present and former Cabinet Ministers was very important. So was the accuracy of their information. Panizzi decided, therefore, to go to Naples and to see things for himself.

He was well aware of the danger. As soon as he set foot in the city, the secret police might send word to the King or lay false evidence against him. To forestall them, he promptly sought, and obtained, an audience. On the way to the palace, he stepped for a moment into a church because he already knew the first question which the King would ask him: 'Have you been to church?'

The King was cheerful, and their parting gay. 'Farewell, terrible Panizzi!' Terrible, indeed: on his return to London he confirmed every word which Gladstone had written.

Though born in Palermo, Ferdinand regarded Sicily as the plague-spot of his Kingdom. The Sicilian differs from the Neapolitan as the Irishman differs from the Englishman. He holds himself aloof from the 'Continent', a bare five miles away from Messina. In 1837—the year in which Queen Victoria ascended her English throne—Ferdinand abolished the Ministry of Sicilian Affairs in Naples. The old principle of separate rights gave place to a new one of 'common possession'. Against the wishes of the Sicilians, the Kingdom became unitary. Palermo's jealousy of Naples was ignored.

Here was a political blunder which Ferdinand might have mitigated by spending a part of each year in Sicily, so that curses turned occasionally to cheers. After all, General Filangieri was lustily cheered when he visited Messina a few years after he had bombarded it. Gladstone may have heard this view while he was wintering in Naples; for when, eighteen years later, he became England's Prime Minister for the first time, he gave his sovereign the unheeded advice that she should go to Ireland as often as she went to Scotland and that the Prince of Wales, heir to the throne, should live in Dublin as her Viceroy.

As the ruling dynasty in England, the Hanoverians were only two decades older than the Bourbons in Naples. There had been time enough for the Bourbons to become indigenous and Neapolitan, but Ferdinand dared not accept political change. Fear was his unfailing companion. 'I am ready to believe that the King of Naples is naturally mild and kindly,' wrote Charles de Tocqueville, 'but he is afraid, and the worst of all tyrannies is the tyranny of cowards.'

In the summer of 1859, King Bomba died a few days before the once

powerful Prince Metternich, and papal Rome showed its grief by
heavily draping the basilica of Santa Maria Maggiore for a Requiem
Mass. Before the year was out, the political map south of the Alps
made nonsense of Metternich's old assertion that Italy was only 'a
geographical expression'. Lombardy, Parma, Lucca and Tuscany were
all freed from Austrian tutelage. Their princes, puppets of Vienna,
ruled no more. Apart from the Venetian provinces and the tiny
Republic of San Marino, Italy's rulers were reduced to three: the King
of Sardinia in the north, the King of the Two Sicilies in the south, and
the Pope in his Pontifical State. Each was born and bred an Italian.

Not everyone who had wanted to expel the Austrian agreed that
the whole of Italy should be united under one sovereign. Massimo
d'Azeglio, for one, struggled hard to free his fellow-Italians from the
foreign yoke; but he had little sympathy with the idea of full Italian
unity, and he saw no reason why an independent Kingdom of the
Two Sicilies should disappear. Early in the New Year, in fact, Victor
Emmanuel sent an envoy to Naples to assure the new King—Francis II,
a kinsman—that he had no designs on his Kingdom. 'There could be
no greater security for Italian independence than a good understanding
between the two largest Italian States.'

The future, therefore, did not look too bleak for Francis. He was
only 23 and far from impressive in his appearance. Older people,
however, acclaimed him as the only child of a saintly mother, on whom
Pius bestowed the rare title of Venerable. Memories of her sanctity
were revived on the seventeenth anniversary of her death; for then the
coffin was opened at Santa Chiara in the presence of the Cardinal
Archbishop, the Nuncio, three surgeons and three ladies of the court
who had seen the Queen die. The body was not corrupted. Instead of
the gangrene detected at the time of her death, there was now a fragrant
odour.

Religion and earthiness dance together in Naples, and Francis had
also the mundane advantage that the people adored their new Queen
—Maria Sofia of Bavaria, the last princess to be married by proxy—
because she was high-spirited and beautiful. In Munich, she was said
to be quite as lovely as an older sister, Elizabeth, the ill-starred Empress
of Austria. With youth, courage and time on their side, the royal
couple might have changed the court at Caserta as Queen Victoria had
changed the court at Windsor.

Time alone was denied them. Revolution started not in Naples, but
in Palermo. In answer to an appeal from Francesco Crispi, a fiery
Sicilian, Garibaldi and his thousand volunteers sailed from Genoa to
Trapani. Within four months he made himself dictator of Sicily, crossed

the strait of Messina and was heading for Naples in advance of his
volunteers. On September 7th, 1860, he completed the last part of the
journey on King Bomba's first railway, and then drove through the
streets of Naples amid tumultuous cheering. No soldier dared to fire
from the ramparts of the Castel Nuovo.

Garibaldi had been a republican in Rome. Now he was a monarchist
and had won more than half a Kingdom, from Naples southwards,
for Piedmont. The Neapolitans were not yet capable of feeling any
affection for a King in remote Turin; but they loved Garibaldi, the
bearded hero who looked gentle and Christ-like, who was himself a
'poor man's king', and whose descent on Naples had been a miracle.
Many brought him their infants to baptize, and great was the joy when
it became known that he would enter the Cathedral on the feast day
of St. Januarius and await the liquefaction of blood. His behaviour in
the Cathedral was exemplary. So was the saint's; the blood soon
liquefied.

Like a man born to be a benevolent dictator, Garibaldi imposed his
own legislation on Naples. He decreed the immediate opening of twelve
homes for parentless children found on the streets; the replacement of
the national lottery by a savings bank; a reduction in the price of salt;
a halt to the enclosure of common lands; and better treatment for cab
horses. Religion was to be free and, as a first token of its freedom,
Garibaldi allotted land for the building of an English Protestant Church.

As soon as reports of these activities reached Turin, Cavour decided
that there was no time to lose. He had wanted to stop Garibaldi and his
thousand volunteers from leaving Genoa, but the success and speed of
their expedition turned the scales. Assurances given to King Francis
were now completely forgotten, and Victor Emmanuel hurried his
troops southwards by invading the papal territory of Umbria and the
Marches. 'The King,' wrote Cavour, 'must not receive the Crown of
Italy from Garibaldi. It would wobble too much on his head.' Luigi
Farini, who had never before set foot in Naples, was sent to administer
the city. In particular, he was to reject Garibaldi's reforms. 'Take a
whip,' Cavour told him, 'and sweep them all into the sea. Without
mercy sweep away all the muck left in that stable.'

The King was more gracious, for he insisted that Garibaldi should
be at his side when he drove through Naples for the first time. On
November 7th, the dictator waited on the railway line at Caserta to
salute his sovereign. The King got into the train, and Garibaldi set off
post-haste in a carriage. Both reached the railway station in Naples at
almost the same time. None the less, both arrived too soon and were
compelled to wait for the Mayor and the city council. A loyal address

was read, and then none of the royal carriages could be found. Out of love for King Francis, perhaps, the coachmen had driven them elsewhere. There was torrential rainfall, and Victor Emmanuel made no attempt to hide his impatience and annoyance.

Eventually, one royal carriage drew up. Victor Emmanuel and Garibaldi climbed into it, and they were followed by General Solaroli in a public cab. The procession went to the Cathedral, and in the negligible distance between the street and the main entrance, the rain drenched alike the King and the dictator.

Dictator no more; for on the same day the King wrote a letter to tell him that, while in Naples, 'I shall govern both militarily and civilly. When I go away, the Government will assume that form and character which is the necessary consequence of the fundamental laws of my monarchy. You will understand, therefore, that I cannot confer on you powers which would be constitutionally divided.'

Garibaldi's work in Naples was done, and he embarked on one more journey to Caprera, his lonely island home off the northeasterly tip of Sardinia; but he did not leave the harbour in Naples without telling Carlo Persano, the Piedmontese admiral, what he thought of Cavour and their King. 'They use men,' he said, 'just as they use oranges. They suck the juice out to the last drop and throw the peel away in the corner!'

Nor was Garibaldi the only sufferer. Victor Emmanuel's letter applied to all former subjects of a Bourbon king. A plebiscite may have shown that the majority of eligible voters favoured incorporation into the Kingdom of Sardinia, but it was taken before most of them had realized that 'the fundamental laws of my monarchy' were all laws introduced in Piedmont to meet Piedmontese needs. Many of these needs differed from those of Naples, and still more from those of Palermo, which by land lies a full thousand miles to the south of Turin.

For a few weeks, Francis held the strong fortress promontory of Gaeta, which a French fleet prevented Admiral Persano from bombarding. He lodged with the Queen in two dismal rooms which were badly furnished and without carpets. The Queen was gracious to the defenders, but rather too coquettish, and she wore a Calabrian cap to show that she was still living in the Kingdom of the Two Sicilies. Napoleon III, however, was concerned for Rome, not for a lost Kingdom. He was a Bonaparte and cared nothing for a Bourbon. Piedmontese had swept through Umbria and the Marches; but once he was assured that they would not attack Rome, he agreed to withdraw his fleet from Gaeta. The Bourbons were doomed.

Gaeta lies less than ninety miles to the south of Rome, and news that it had fallen brought a jubilant crowd into the Corso, Rome's main thoroughfare. Every balcony seemed to be filled with spectators, and some places were illuminated. Yet the excitement subsided almost as quickly as it had begun. Freedom for Naples and Gaeta was not freedom for Rome. Under the protection of French bayonets, the theocrats ruled once more, and Antonelli filled the prisons with political offenders.

The last Bourbon King of the Two Sicilies and his consort were allowed to sail from Gaeta to Terracina, where a detachment of zouaves waited to escort them on the straight road through the Pontine marshes to Rome. A papal delegation greeted them at St. John's Gateway, and Antonelli received them at the entrance to the Quirinal Palace, which was placed at their disposal. A few hours later, the Pope left the Vatican to pay a ceremonious call. At first, it was thought that the King and Queen would leave Rome for Munich, but the days became weeks, and Pius grew anxious about the expense of lodging his guests in the Quirinal Palace, which, since his return from Portici, he had never again occupied.

Eventually, Francis realized that, as lawful King of the Two Sicilies, the smaller and far more beautiful Farnese Palace was his own property. Ever since his great-grandfather, Ferdinand I, had removed its treasures and sent them to Naples, the Palace remained uninhabited and neglected. Stout doors had to be built for privacy and glass to be introduced as a protection against draughts. Most of the rooms were left bare.

'Rome is a magnificent theatre with bad actors.' So Metternich once declared, and Rome can seldom have witnessed more indifferent actors than the Bourbons from Naples. Ferdinand Gregorovius watched them when—on Palm Sunday, 1861—they attended the celebration in St. Peter's. 'Francis had a very bored and misanthropic air. His pose was unforced, neither military nor princely; he looks older than his years. Queen Sofia pale and suffering. The Duke of Trapani ugly and insignificant, like all the other princes.' Nor did Gregorovius spare the King's stepmother, the overbearing Queen Maria Teresa: she 'is more like a workman's wife than a queen. The whole royal family seemed to me at St. Peter's like dead leaves swept together by the wind.'

CHAPTER FOUR

FROM THE PO TO THE ARNO

O N FEBRUARY 18th, 1861—five days after the fall of Gaeta—
many new Senators and Deputies entered the Parliament in
Turin for the first time. Most of them came from Tuscany,
Emilia, the Marches, Umbria and the broken Kingdom of the Two
Sicilies. Voting in the recent plebiscites was restricted, as in Savoy and
and Nice, to privileged persons. Roughly they amounted to one person
out of every forty-four; but they formed the political élite of the day.
All Italy—save Venetia and Latium, of which Rome was the centre—
had her representation in the new Parliament. A law was passed and
contained only one article: 'King Victor Emmanuel assumes for himself
and his successors the title of King of Italy.' The monarch himself
chose to be 'King of Italy by the grace of God and the will of the
nation'.

As Europe possessed a King of the Belgians and an Emperor of the
French, a more appropriate title might have been King of the Italians.
The King of Sardinia, however, wished to be the King of Italy.
Though Italy's first King, he was still called Victor Emmanuel II. If
the title was new, the dynasty was old. The original homeland might
be forfeited to a *parvenu* Emperor born of Corsican stock, but the
glamour of Savoyard lineage must remain uncontaminated. The new
Kingdom of Italy, moaned its critics, was Piedmont 'writ large'.

They expressed only a half-truth. A new Kingdom of Italy without
Rome was misshapen. So it was without the Venetian provinces, and
Venice was almost as large as Rome. Five weeks after Garibaldi's entry
into Naples, Cavour had told the old Piedmontese Parliament that
Rome must become 'the noble capital of a rejuvenated Italy'. For
most of his listeners, Rome was then a legendary and far-off city, a
new Jerusalem, which they were unlikely ever to visit. Except among
the clergy, his words did not rankle unduly in Turin. The new Italian
Parliament, however, contained spokesmen for Bologna, Umbria and
the Marches, and they knew from personal experience what theocratic
rule was like. They longed to see it ended in Rome, and the first
Parliamentary session was not brought to a close without a vote 'that
Rome, the capital acclaimed by national opinion, be joined to Italy'.

Cavour faced problems far more urgent than the future of Rome.

The speed with which Garibaldi advanced on Naples had taken him by surprise. No plans existed for amalgamating the northern and southern Kingdoms, and no railway linked them together. 'To harmonize north and south,' Cavour admitted, 'is harder than fighting Austria or struggling with Rome.' Speed must answer speed, and one of the statesman's earliest decisions was to build a railway from Bologna to Rimini and the Adriatic port of Ancona. As soon as possible, his railways must reach those which had been built or started in the south by King Bomba. Nor would the spectre of fighting against Austria be finally laid until the Venetian provinces were freed from her rule. Without them, the independence of the new Kingdom would be constantly threatened. For its protection, therefore, Venice was more important than Rome.

'The Roman question,' Cavour told Parliament, 'cannot be solved by the sword; only moral forces can overcome moral obstacles.' The best weapon of moral forces is persuasion. The French must be persuaded to retire from Rome, and the Pope must be persuaded to believe that if he renounced his Temporal Power and accepted definite guarantees of full freedom in the exercise of his ministry, the Church might become spiritually renewed.

There seemed to be no hope of persuading Pius to make such a surrender, even though expert theologians admitted that his Temporal Power was not based on a dogma; but he was now 68, and many reports indicated that he might not live much longer. He was still prone to epilepsy. Antonelli once told the Duc de Gramont, French Ambassador in Rome, that the Pope could not be held responsible for all he said when an attack of this nervous disease was approaching. The symptoms were shown in his eyes and hands. Whenever the Cardinal noticed them, he avoided many subjects during an audience.

When Pius died, Cardinals from other European countries would enter Italy well briefed on the attitude of their particular Government to the Roman question. However secret a Conclave may be, the Cardinals could not meet together without heart-searching discussions on the Italian threat to the Pontifical State. For this reason, Cavour was concerned less with Pius than with his unknown successor. The cruel future was hidden from him. In this first year of a new Kingdom, the angel of death spared Pius and took away Cavour, who was only 50. According to the medical practice of the day, his doctors bled him time and again. The excessive bleeding helped to kill him.

Though Father Giacomo da Poirino, a parish priest, knew that Cavour had been excommunicated, he heard his confession and gave him extreme unction. Later he saw a cousin entering the bedroom to kiss the hand of her dead kinsman. 'Do not weep,' said the priest. 'No one knew better than he did how to forgive and to offer help.' None the less, the priest was punished by the Holy Office for what he had done.

As King of Italy, Victor Emmanuel became the owner of more palaces than any other sovereign in Europe. Few were statelier than Caserta or more richly endowed with paintings than the Pitti Palace in Florence. The King cared almost nothing for them. It was hard to drag him away from a hunting box in Piedmont. With the utmost difficulty, he was persuaded to show himself to a large number of new subjects by travelling down Cavour's railway line from Bologna to Ancona as soon as it was ready for traffic.

Bologna, where he stayed the night, received him coldly. At each station on the line, he put his head out of the window of his compartment and, for a brief moment, acknowledged the cheers of a people who were gaily attired in the traditional costumes of their own locality. Henry d'Ideville, who was travelling in the royal train, wondered what was causing the greater excitement among the people: a curt nod from their King, or their first sight of a railway engine.

At midday, the train reached Rimini, where a banquet had been prepared inside the station. Victor Emmanuel left his railway coach and condescended to attend the feast. Within six minutes, however, he decided that the train must leave at once for Ancona. Other passengers were amazed, and shamelessly many seized food from the tables to eat on their renewed journey. Lackeys in magnificent red and gold livery hurried to the train with bottles of sparkling wine tucked under their arms. Thus the people who had been waiting in the stations between Rimini and Ancona found three things to divert them: a railway engine, a brusque King, and at least four uproariously drunken lackeys.

Late in the afternoon, the train reached Ancona. In the incomplete station there was a tent, in which the Mayor and other dignitaries of the city waited to present the King with an address. Instead of entering the tent, the King went straight to a carriage outside the station. In the evening he was more gracious, for he sat through a banquet and stayed for as long as ten minutes at the theatre.

On the following morning a deputation from all the notables of the province arrived at their meeting-place only to be told that the King was already on his way back to Turin. He wanted to be among his own people again. Each of his two separate families spoke the Piedmontese dialect, and even Princess Margaret, his future daughter-in-law, never lost her Piedmontese accent. The King of Italy was still a provincial.

So, for that matter, were nearly all his subjects, old and new. If the citizens of Turin once accepted calmly Cavour's statement that Rome must eventually become Italy's capital, their reaction was very different when, within four years, they heard that the King would transfer his capital from Turin to Florence. The decision was made not by the King, but by his Prime Minister, Marco Minghetti, after a secret correspondence with Napoleon III.

Like Cavour before him, Minghetti realized that the new Kingdom would not have enough freedom of action until Venice and its provinces were snatched from Austria. The Emperor of the French seemed still to be the strongest monarch in Europe, and his troops occupied Rome. If he regretted this occupation, he was too much of a schemer to abandon it without some thought of compensation for himself and for France. There was more than a hint that he wanted Sardinia. The blow to Savoyard pride would have been too heavy. Despite the loss of Savoy and Nice, Victor Emmanuel had not deliberately forfeited the old Kingdom of Sardinia for a new Kingdom of Italy. The architects of this embracive new Kingdom paid, like Pius in Rome, a heavy price for French support, but they did not intend it to be enclosed in the west by France. Italy was not her satellite.

For all his scheming and dictatorial authority, the Emperor dared not offend the ultra-conservative Catholics in Paris. Nor would the Empress Eugénie let him forget that Pius was the godfather of their only child, the Prince Imperial. He was bound to support the Temporal Power. In an effort to escape from his dilemma, he expressed the hope that the Pope would himself reach an agreement with the Piedmontese. 'My goodness!' Pius exclaimed. 'I can do that whenever I wish, and without the help of foreigners. When all is said and done, we are Italian.'

He spoke the disconcerting truth. The Temporal Power was not based on a dogma. It derived from an old political fragmentation of the Italian peninsula, and now the Pontifical State was no more advantageous to the Church than had been the pre-Napoleonic status enjoyed by the Prince-Bishops of Mainz, Cologne and Trier. Even a Roman Congregation, when examining the theological arguments, decided that the Pope might renounce his Temporal Power if the interests of the Church required its surrender. The quarrel persisted because Pius had no wish to reach a settlement with the Italians alone.

In consequence, Napoleon III and Victor Emmanuel's Ministers drew up their own makeshift convention whereby the Italians promised not to invade any more papal territory and the French undertook gradually to withdraw their troops, while allowing the Pope enough time in which to strengthen his military defences. No Minister in Paris or

Turin believed that this convention would be permanently binding. In the end—perhaps, in the twentieth century—Rome would enter the Kingdom. By then, Cavour's assurance that Rome would be its capital and the vote taken by the first Italian Government might have little meaning. Behind the King's back, Minghetti agreed with Napoleon III that Florence should forthwith become Italy's capital city.

The King was furious and tried to prevent the change. All his own affections, he protested, were centred on Piedmont. Why, when his people had sacrificed Savoy and Nice, should they be asked to make a sacrifice that was even harsher? Minghetti came from Bologna, and not from Turin. 'It doesn't matter to others,' the King complained, 'but my heart is broken.' He told his Prime Minister that he was voicing the true feeling of Turin, and he was right. People of all classes denounced the demotion of their comely city. Throughout two September nights there was rioting in the streets.

Massimo d'Azeglio thought that the transfer was a mistake. So, in his opinion, was the idea that Rome—'a sewer'—should be the final capital. Manzoni, his father-in-law, thought otherwise. Though it was mid-winter and he was approaching 80, Manzoni left Milan for Turin to vote as a Senator in favour of the transfer. He knew that he would displease Pius; 'but, close as I am to death, how should I dare to present myself to God if I hesitated to render this service to the Church?' True Italian unity demanded its unifying language and, once Rosmini had converted him to the literary use of Tuscan, Manzoni longed to hear Dante's language exalted from one end of the Italian peninsula to the other. The court would go to Florence, and Tuscan would be its language. Gone were the days when the King of Sardinia often communicated with Cavour in French.

Going, too, were the days when Elizabeth Barrett Browning wrote that Florence was 'cheap, tranquil, cheerful, beautiful, within the limits of civilization, yet out of the crush of it'. The Pitti Palace became the chief official residence of the King of Italy, who—on May 14th, 1865—observed the sixth centenary of Dante's birth in Florence by unveiling a statue of the poet in the Piazza della Santa Croce. Victor Emmanuel made no claim to culture. His gifts, as he told a friend, were limited to a practical knowledge of men, common sense and courage. The ceremony, however, enabled him to appeal for a fuller national unity. Only a few who heard him may have realized the weight of his own personal sacrifice. In January, when he had held his last State ball in Turin, a crowd jeered at his guests as, magnificently apparelled, they drove through the streets to the royal palace. All his sympathies were with the angry citizens.

Even his appeal for more national unity might have proved less effective if Dante himself had not come to his rescue. Less than a fortnight after the sexcentennial celebrations, workmen repairing a wall in the cloisters of the Franciscan church in Ravenna unearthed the casket which contained Dante's bones. More than three centuries beforehand, the Florentines had gained papal permission to bring the bones from Ravenna, where Dante died, and place them in their own Franciscan church of Santa Croce. Michelangelo was eager to carve a splendid tomb. The Franciscans of Ravenna, determined that the bones should never be taken away, hid them within the cloisters.

Whatever Italy may have meant to Dante, he can hardly have envisaged Italian nationhood, for he fixed his hopes of universal peace on an Emperor who came from north of the Alps, and who should be the temporal ruler of all Christendom. None the less, his bones were prized from their hiding place at a time when Italy needed a national poet. Dead Dante filled the part even more effectively than did Giosue Carducci, a young and patriotic professor from the University of Bologna.

'Cursed be he that moves my bones'[1] is the inscription on William Shakespeare's tomb in Stratford-on-Avon. His plays sometimes suggest that he once travelled into Italy and knew what a sailor's life at sea was like. If he voyaged through the Adriatic and entered the wine taverns of Ravenna, then much nearer to the coast than they are now, older men could have told him how the Franciscans had hidden the bones of a poet to prevent anyone from carrying them off to distant Florence.

Florence was no longer claiming them. They belonged to the Middle Ages, and the Piedmontese wanted their new capital to bear a closer resemblance to Paris, where Georges Haussmann was cutting spacious *boulevards* through a labyrinth of medieval streets. Massive buildings began to rise just in that part of Florence in which Dante was born. Hotels were needed for Senators and Deputies. Government officials required dwelling houses as well as offices. A building boom brought newcomers from the countryside in search of work. The city grew larger, and not a few staunch supporters of the Pope's Temporal Power began secretly to wish that the despoilers would one day leave the banks of the Arno for those of the Tiber.

For no matter what agreements the Italian Ministers might have reached with the Emperor of the French, the Roman question could

---

[1] Good frend, for Iesus sake forbeare
To dig the dust encloased heare:
Bleste be yᵉ man yᵗ spares these stones,
And curst be he yᵗ moves my bones.

not remain unanswered. 'Rome or death!' Garibaldi once shouted. Like Mazzini, he rivalled Pius in his assumption that Rome, the Eternal City, was more precious than any other. His followers were hero-worshippers who detested the more prosaic levels of practical states-manship. For them a new Kingdom of Italy without Rome was robbed of more than half its poetry and meaning.

Early in his reign Pius declared: 'A great gift from heaven is this: one of many gifts which He has bestowed on Italy; that a bare three millions of our subjects possess two hundred million brothers of every nation and every tongue.' He penned these words when many had begun to share Gioberti's dream of a Pope-President of Italy; but now the Pope's subjects were reduced from 'a bare three millions' to little more than seven hundred thousand. Diminished and isolated within a new Kingdom, the Pontifical State looked shabby, spiritless and sepulchral. The loss of the Temporal Power would not make Italy less Catholic. Her people would still belong to a community of 'two hundred million brothers of every nation and every tongue.'

Political isolation, moreover, made Rome a danger to the Kingdom. Within its walls lived many ducalists from Tuscany, Parma, Modena and Lucca. The city became a club for absentee landlords and disgruntled ex-officers, while hundreds of Romans had to escape from the Pontifical State to avoid imprisonment by the orders of Cardinal Antonelli. Even more menacing was the court which the last King of the Two Sicilies held in the Farnese Palace. If most of its rooms were left unfurnished, Francis needed his money for winning back a throne. At the turn of the century, Cardinal Ruffo encouraged rascals to enlist in his *sanfedisti* and to drive the French out of Naples. Now, from the city in which almost all the curial Cardinals were living, Francis plotted with a different generation of Neapolitan rascals. South of Terracina, bandits were again at war with the enemies of a Bourbon King.

If King Bomba had blundered in imposing unitary rule over the Two Sicilies, Cavour and his immediate successors created another legacy of resentment and distrust by clamping, like a straitjacket, Piedmont's Constitution on a southern people. Their young men, mostly unable to read or write, were snatched from the fields, orange groves and vineyards to be conscripts of an army led by northern generals with exacting and almost Prussian ideas of military discipline. Neapolitan officers had a more liberal tradition. They understood the dialects of their men and hated to see them punished for disobeying orders which were hard to grasp; but without military discipline and constant vigilance, the Piedmontese army could not have held its own against the Austrians and the French.

Northerners believed that the indolent and sun-kissed south needed muscle. Accordingly, they applied their laws, their penalties and their methods in a realm which hitherto almost none of them had seen. Few men from the north, even among its leaders, travelled to the south. Neither Cavour among statesmen nor Manzoni among men of letters ever visited Rome, let alone Naples or Palermo. Victor Emmanuel himself had been a stranger. The Piedmontese imagined that the south was rich and that its wealth would be made manifest, once the evil of Bourbon misrule was overcome.

Massimo d'Azeglio knew better. As a young painter, he had lived in Rome or on the Alban Hills. He was also familiar with Naples, where an older brother—Prospero, an eminent Jesuit—worked for about three years. 'At Naples,' Massimo wrote, 'we overthrew a sovereign in order to set up a government based on universal suffrage. And yet we still need today sixty battalions of soldiers to hold the people down, or even more, since they are not enough, whereas in the other provinces of Italy nothing of the sort is necessary. One must, therefore, conclude that there was some mistake about the plebiscite. We must ask the Neapolitans once again whether they want the Piedmontese or no.'

Napoleon III knew that the French maintenance of order in Rome was a sham if it allowed the city to be a nerve-centre of Bourbon plots and intrigues against the new masters of southern Italy. He, therefore, told his Ambassador in Rome to ask for the expulsion of King Francis and his exiled court. The Pope refused. A predecessor—Pius VII, in whose honour he had himself taken the name of Pius—was proud to receive the kinsfolk of fallen monarchs. For a time, the mother of Napoleon I and a sister of Louis XVI were both living in the same Roman street. It was the prerogative of the Popes always to shelter the unfortunate princes of other nations: 'of this,' commented the ninth Pius, 'the Bonapartes are a striking example'.

The Ambassador then went to the Farnese Palace and offered to restore to Francis a substantial part of his former fortune if he would agree to leave Rome. For once, the King showed true dignity. 'Sir,' he replied, 'I have heard that in all ages great and good men have ended their days in obscurity and poverty, and it can be no source of dread to me if I am numbered among them.'

In the long run, the solution to the Roman problem rested not with a foreigner, but with the Italians. Their choice was between force and consent. The more thoughtful wanted the way of consent to be taken. Their family ties were strong. Within their intimate circle of brothers and cousins, priest and anti-clerical met and argued with each other. The bond of blood they seldom, if ever, ignored. When Victor Emmanuel was King of Sardinia and Massimo d'Azeglio his Prime Minister, they shamelessly discussed their conquests with women and their desire to be rid of more than one unbending Bishop. Yet the King was constantly influenced by his pious mother, and he feared the lash of papal rebukes. Nothing seemed to mar the affection which the Prime Minister and his Jesuit brother showed for each other. Even when he was in office, Cavour lived and entertained in the house of his older brother, Gustavo, a close and religious friend of Rosmini; and Antonelli sometimes found it effective to remind the statesman that his paternal grandmother belonged to the same family as Francis de Sales, patron of Catholic writers, whom Pius was later to declare a Doctor of the Church.

The deeper springs of the Italian Risorgimento were spiritual. In many ways the movement was less anti-clerical than anti-temporal. With a natural gift for reaching compromises, priest and anti-clerical often discussed within the family how the Roman problem should be solved. The right solution might involve defeat for papal policy, but not humiliation for the Pontiff.

Encircling the neighbourhood of St. Peter's and the Vatican Palace are the Leonine walls which, in the middle of the ninth century, Pope Leo IV built in a belated effort to keep out the Saracens. From time to time, it was suggested that the Pope should be sovereign of this Leonine city and possess a strip of territory to the sea. Rome itself would become an integral part of the Kingdom of Italy and send its own Deputies to the Parliament in Florence. It would become the capital of honour, to which the King and his successors, each in their turn, travelled in state for their crowning by the Pope in St. Peter's. Florence would remain the royal city and the seat of the Italian Government; but Rome would still be the city where, as its Bishop, the Pope went wherever he chose to go.

On these terms, Victor Emmanuel need have troubled Pius IX no more than Charlemagne troubled Leo III. South of the Alps, Dante's dream of harmony between spiritual and civil authority would have been brought nearer fulfilment. Pius would have kept the pallium, while Victor Emmanuel acquired the Christian banner. In Italy, as in the United States, there could have been a free Church within a free State.

Pius misread the signs of the times because he lacked a long vision. He had been the first future Pope ever to cross the Atlantic and to live in a republic of the New World. Throughout the rest of his life, he admired the Americans for the absolute freedom of religion which they accorded to their Catholic fellow-citizens. He never whole-heartedly condemned the principles which were said to justify the

French Revolution of 1789: 'There was yet some good in them; equality before the law, for instance.' He failed, however, to realize that the French Revolution and the Italian Risorgimento were both logical consequences of the American War of Independence. It was impossible to speak of a free world when Rome was fettered and lived under a clerical theocracy. Amid tumultuous difficulties, Pius VII had been able to look beyond the tribulations of his Napoleonic era, but Pius IX saw in the assaults on the Pontifical State a continuous action of sacrilege and impiety.

In 1864—the year in which the decision to make Florence the Italian capital was taken—Pius issued the Encyclical Letter *Quanta cura*, in which he condemned the principles of freedom of opinion, freedom of the press, the absolute sovereignty of the people, and the juridical supremacy of the State over the Church. By itself, the Encyclical Letter might have provoked little popular excitement. Pius, however, agreed that all the errors mentioned in his previous encyclicals, apostolic letters and allocutions should be assembled in a Syllabus of Errors and published as an annex to *Quanta cura*.

These errors, each stated as a proposition, numbered eighty. Propositions 77 to 80 related to the errors of modern liberalism. The final one condemned the belief that the Roman Pontiff 'can and should reconcile himself with progress, with liberalism and with recent civilization'. Papal defeatism could hardly have been more explicit. Those who believed that it was possible to be both a good Catholic and a good democrat received a blow sharper than the one which Gregory XVI had inflicted on the followers of Lamennais.

Sharper, but not more deadly; for Pius published his Syllabus within a decade which was to give the thinking world Charles Darwin's 'Origin of Species', Ernest Renan's 'Life of Christ' and Karl Marx's 'Capital'. If the errors of this decade abounded, its unceasing quest for truth deserved a just tribute; and Georges Darboy, Archbishop of Paris, made a dignified protest. 'You have distinguished and condemned the principal errors of our epoch,' he told Pius. 'Turn your eyes now towards what it may hold that is honourable and good and sustain it in its generous efforts.'

Whether he was Gregory or Pius, a Pope walked in darkness whenever he failed to understand, or else ignored, the spirit of his own age. Mazzini had a completely different message. 'Space and time are ours,' he wrote. 'We can quicken or retard it. We cannot stop it.'

CHAPTER FIVE

THE LAST POPE-KING

L IGHT FELL at last on the precarious papal path when Pius declared that he was calling all the Bishops to Rome for a new Council of the Church. The last Council, held almost exactly three centuries beforehand in Trent, had given the Catholic answer to a contemporary Protestant challenge. Ruling princes had been invited to participate in the deliberations in Trent; but Pius was at war with civil ideas of authority, and he decided that no ruling prince, except himself, should have any say in the Vatican Council. He asked representatives of the non-Roman communities to enter the Council, but all refused.

The refusal of the Orthodox Churches—in spite of Rome's recognition that their orders and sacraments were valid—was already foreshadowed by the answer given to Pius when, in 1848, he wrote an Encyclical Letter to the Christians of the East. 'In the Eastern Churches,' its Patriarchs told him, 'neither the Patriarchs nor the Councils have ever been able to introduce anything new, as the depository of the faith is with us the body of the whole Church; that is to say, the people itself.' The ruler of the Eastern Church was Demos. The Vatican Council—the twentieth Ecumenical Council of the universal Church —would be restricted, therefore, to Bishops in communion with Rome.

Mazzini had no faith in the Vatican Council. 'Science,' he wrote to the Bishops, 'goes forward, regardless of your doctrines, caring nothing for your denunciations and your Councils, tearing up, with every new discovery, a page of the book that you call infallible.' Very different, however, was the attitude of David Urquhart, a Scottish Catholic who exerted no little influence in England's Foreign Office. He saw that this Roman Council had a supra-national character and might achieve tasks hitherto not attempted in a nineteenth-century world. For one thing, it could bring this world back to a respect for fundamental human rights. The Pope, who had never allowed military conscription in his own State, might call a halt to its alarming increase in most other countries of post-Napoleonic Europe. In addition, Urquhart urged him to establish an 'academy' which would be independent of the Vatican Council and yet brief the Bishops on all technical aspects of international law. Through the sponsorship of the Pope and the

Bishops, this academy might open a new path towards universal civil rule and universal peace.

Though Urquhart sent his memorandum to Rome, it was quietly ignored by those members of the Curia who were preparing the preliminary documents for the Vatican Council. They knew what the theologians closest to the Pope wanted the Council to give him. In 1854, he had promulgated the dogma of the Immaculate Conception of the Virgin. Now his more intimate advisers sought a dogmatic assertion from the Bishops that, when the Pope spoke *ex cathedra*, he was infallible.

The idea of his infallibility as the Vicar of Christ was neither new nor illogical. It was not even new when, at the close of the previous century, the future Gregory XVI wrote his book in its defence. Lamennais had given it prominence because he distrusted the power of the civil princes. At that time, he believed that an infallible Pope was needed as a buttress for Catholic democracy. Thus he invested the idea with a political significance and made it dangerous. The mere mention of papal infallibility roused suspicion in foreign courts and chancelleries, whether they were Protestant or Catholic.

Apart from a few striking exceptions, the Bishops who did not favour a dogma of papal infallibility expressed dissent not because it might have been theologically an error, but because it was 'inopportune'. Pius himself had gone far to make it inopportune; for what political harm could not be done by an infallible Pope who claimed to have two hundred million religious followers and who explicitly refused 'to reconcile himself with progress, with liberalism and with recent civilization'? The promulgation of the dogma would be more opportune, perhaps, when the question of the Pope's Temporal Power was finally solved and when a Pope free from all political ambitions or preoccupations sat on Peter's throne: a Pope who had not a single armed soldier under his final command.

Amid great ceremony Pius opened his Vatican Council in the right-hand transept of St. Peter's on December 8th, 1869, feast day of the Immaculate Conception. About seven hundred fully robed Bishops were present. Two hundred were Italian; one hundred and twenty were English-speaking; and the rest came mainly from France, Spain and other Catholic countries in Europe. Rome had never before witnessed so large a gathering of Cardinals, Patriarchs, Archbishops and Bishops; and although rain was pelting with an almost tropical intensity, the people crowded into the basilica.

Some estimated their number to be not less than eighty thousand. 'Only from a distance,' wrote Gregorovius, 'was I able to see the interior of the Council's open hall, where shone the rows of red seats, the medallions of the Popes and the decorated tribune. I saw nothing of the procession; not even a Bishop's mitre. The heat was unbearable; clouds of vapour were issuing from drenched clothing and from the dripping umbrellas which transformed the marble floor into a muddy pool.'

No one in Rome under the age of twenty-five recalled a time when Giovanni Mastai was not yet Pope. Almost all the Bishops at the Council received their consecration during his reign, and what he wanted done carried a special weight with them. No doubt many Bishops went to Rome with open minds. They would listen to the arguments and vote as their consciences dictated, but it would be hard to vote against the known wishes of the Pope, and especially for those Bishops who were to stay in Rome at his expense.

The crucial document on infallibility would be presented by the Commission of Faith. To this Commission Henry Edward Manning, Archbishop of Westminster, was elected. He owed this triumph not to his fellow-Bishops in England and Wales, but to the Italians. Cardinal Antonelli, who was not even a priest, could take no open part in the Council. Manning's was now the master-mind which Pius needed.

Born of rich parents and Gladstone's rival as an eloquent debater at the Oxford Union, Manning sought a political career. His father's bankruptcy compelled him to change his plans. He took orders in the Church of England, married his rector's daughter and became Arch-deacon of Chichester. When his wife died, he was inconsolable and composed many of his weekly sermons while sitting beside her grave. For a long time, his friendship with Gladstone was unbroken. Both were deeply religious, and Gladstone would have been a clergyman himself if he had disregarded his father's wishes. Each, in fact, became what the other had wanted to be. Manning as England's Prime Minister and Gladstone as Archbishop of Canterbury might still have achieved an enduring fame. At the opening of the Vatican Council, England's Prime Minister was Gladstone. Manning could not help envying the power which his former friend exerted at home and abroad.

Gladstone loved Italy, spoke her language well and often quoted Dante in a parliamentary debate. The Colosseum in Rome was the place in which he chose to offer marriage to Catherine Gwynne. He hated the injustices of King Bomba in Naples all the more because he believed that, at his best, the Italian represented the highest type of a Christian gentleman. At one time, he alarmed Robert Peel, then the Prime Minister, by offering to leave his Cabinet and become the

English Minister in Rome. In this lesser office, he thought, he might help to convince the Vatican that his own Church of England was genuinely Catholic in its traditions; it maintained the standards upheld by the universal Church in the first four centuries of its life and was substantially free from all subsequent deviations.

As head of the Church of England, Queen Victoria appointed its Bishops and Deans on the recommendation of her Prime Minister. Gladstone regarded this duty as the highest privilege of his own office, and he took immense care over each appointment. While the Vatican Council was in session, the Deanery of St. Paul's fell vacant. Gladstone insisted that the new Dean should be Richard Church, a quiet country clergyman who had been a close friend of John Henry Newman in his famous pre-Roman days at Oxford, and whose invalid son lived long enough to publish the first English translation of Dante's *De Monarchia*.

Hitherto St. Paul's had been more a museum than a place of genuine Christian worship. Its services were dreary, and at all other times no member of the public could enter the Cathedral without paying a twopenny fee. The poor were virtually excluded. Dean Church had an intimate knowledge of St. Peter's and many other famous churches in Italy. He knew that a country's greatest Cathedral should belong to the people. In his own words, he began to make St. Paul's 'the parish church of England'. In fact, he did more, for he helped to give St. Paul's a closer spiritual resemblance to St. Peter's. The Catholic from the Continent, as he wandered into the Cathedral during a service, could hardly fail to notice its reverence and dignity.

At this time, when Catholic and Anglican needed to acquire a better understanding of each other's worship, Gladstone was troubled by reports which Lord Acton was sending him from Rome. Manning was hurrying a process which must set Roman and Anglican further apart. Papal infallibility, Gladstone was eventually to write, made the Papacy 'an Asian monarchy; nothing but one giddy height of despotism and one dead level of religious subservience'. As in his old denunciation of King Bomba, he weakened his case by exaggerated language. More relevant was the critical attitude of Newman. Like Manning, he was the son of a banker who failed in his business; but even if the family affluence had continued, it seems certain that he would have remained steadfast in his vocation. He was a poet and thinker endowed with the historical imagination. The idea of the Pope's infallibility presented no difficulty for him; but, unlike Manning, he could not forget his own Anglican past. He knew that his old Oxford friends and countless others thought constantly of Rome. Time and patience were needed.

'To understand Scripture and history,' he wrote, 'was to become Catholic, and children of the Reformation would find their way home.'

Convinced that in time Roman and Anglican would be reconciled, Newman distrusted the speed with which Manning's 'aggressive and insolent faction' was forcing the issue. The proposed promulgation of the dogma of papal infallibility was clearly 'inopportune'. 'You are going too fast at Rome,' wrote Newman to a friend. 'We do not move at railroad pace even in the 19th. century. We must be patient and that for two reasons, first in order to get at the truth, and next in order to carry others with us. The Church moves as a whole; it is not a mere philosophy, it is a communion.'

Manning hustled because he did not know how to wait on time. The historical imagination was denied him, and he had no notion of the harm which he might be doing. He realized that about 150 Bishops regarded the promulgation of the dogma as inopportune, and he took various steps to reduce their number and to curb their influence. The task was relatively easy because the Bishops, when they first assembled in Rome, were mostly unacquainted with each other. Private meetings of more than twenty Bishops were actually forbidden during the Council. Archbishop Darboy of Paris, a leading inopportunist, complained to his Emperor about their lack of freedom. He even suggested that the Government should come to the rescue of the minority.

If any Government left the Bishops an absolute freedom of choice, it was the Italian. Not a single Bishop with a diocese in the Kingdom of Italy was forbidden to go to Rome for the Council. Visitors to Florence found the ministerial circles indifferent to what was happening in St. Peter's or the Vatican; it was a squabble in the sacristy.

For one thing, the Italian Government had too much to do. By joining Prussia in her war against Austria in 1866, Italy had at last gained the Venetian provinces; but each war in which Victor Emmanuel and his troops took part was costly. Taxes increased, and the burden was felt in former States which, like the old Kingdom of the Two Sicilies, had hitherto been lightly taxed. 'It is shameful how they tax us,' a Neapolitan woman cried. 'Yet they can't even allow Victor a new pair of trousers.'

When Prince Humbert at last obeyed his father's order to marry his first cousin, Princess Margaret of Savoy, it was decided that their first child should be born in Naples and, if a boy, bear the title of the Prince of Naples. On November 11th, 1869, cannons were fired from Neapolitan forts and thus compensated for a lack of the sound of church bells. A prince was born. One name given to him at his baptism was Januarius. If he lived long enough, he would eventually come to the Italian throne as King Victor Emmanuel III.

The hopes of the Bourbons, however, were not yet completely frustrated. In command of the zouaves which accompanied King Francis and Queen Maria Sofia from Terracina to Rome was a handsome Belgian, Count Armand de Lavayss, with whom the Queen soon fell in love. Rome bored her, and eventually she went back to Bavaria. The court in Munich announced that, after her tragic experiences in Gaeta, the Queen of Naples had retired to the Ursuline convent in Augsburg, where her physician was given a special dispensation to visit her. Within its walls she gave birth to a daughter of the Belgian count. The child was at once taken away from her mother, and the Wittelsbachs carefully guarded their secret.

Without his beautiful wife, King Francis and the Bourbon cause were at a grave disadvantage, and the Queen startled her own family by announcing that she would go back to Rome on one condition: she must tell her husband the whole truth. Francis heard and forgave, and while the cannons in Naples fired their salute in honour of a future King of Italy, the Farnese Palace was busily preparing for the birth of another royal child, for whom the bells of the Neapolitan churches would ring, though the cannons might be silent.

The Empress of Austria went to Rome to be near her sister, and the visit coincided with the opening of the Vatican Council. Though she was supposed to be travelling *incognita*, Elizabeth insisted on taking her place in the tribune reserved for crowned heads. The surge of people outside St. Peter's was so vast and confused by the rainstorm that it delayed her entry for at least a quarter of an hour, and the Swiss Guard had to open a way for her. 'One looked out over an ocean of mitres,' she wrote to the Emperor Francis Joseph, 'but one visit was more than enough.' She paid a state visit to Pius and 'all the crawling about on one's knees struck me as very comical'.

The whole household in the Farnese Palace was waiting on its knees when Pius returned the call. None the less, the Empress was doing her best to make the birth of an heir to Francis a glamorous occasion; but the child, born on Christmas Eve, was a girl and died within three months. Not long afterwards, Francis and Sofia Maria left Rome, never to return. When Gregorovius again saw Francis, he was walking alone through the streets of Munich: 'forgotten by Naples, by the world, and probably by his own people'.

Certainly, he was soon forgotten by Rome, where hostesses were entertaining Cardinals and Bishops from foreign countries and hoping that Franz von Liszt, the Hungarian composer and pianist who had taken minor orders, would end his temporary retirement to the Villa d'Este in Tivoli and attend their salon. Hitherto time had moved slowly in the Eternal City. In the previous summer, Henry Wadsworth Longfellow paid his second visit after a lapse of forty years. He wrote to tell a friend that 'Rome is quite unchanged since you and I were here forty years ago. I said so to Cardinal Antonelli the other day, and he answered, taking a pinch of snuff: "Yes, thank God." '

A few months later Henry James arrived in Rome. He left his luggage in the Hotel Inghilterra and at once set off for a five hours' walk through the city. 'At last—for the first time—I live'; so he told his brother William. By this time the American community in Rome had passed its century. The first American artist to live in the city was Benjamin West, who arrived in 1760. Johann Winckelmann, the greatest antiquarian of his day, introduced him, though a Quaker, to the blind Cardinal Albani, who had befriended Antonelli's humbly born grandfather. The Cardinal touched West's face and asked: 'Is he black or white?'

Thereafter came a steady and increasing succession of artists and writers from the United States. Ralph Waldo Emerson, when in Rome in 1833, was delighted to find fifteen people from Boston alone. Most artists and writers were young, poor and glad to know that life in Rome could be cheap: 'with care,' a Frenchman told Raphael Steele, 'fifty dollars a year will enable you to appear like a *Milord*'.

Their chief meeting place was the Caffè Greco, then three dark and untidy rooms, in the Via Condotti. Opposite the Caffè Greco was the Trattoria Lepri, where, in 1857, Herman Melville 'dined at 19 cents'. He might well have dined for the same amount of money twelve or thirteen years later. The Trattoria Lepri provided separate eating rooms for the Germans, the French, the Americans and the English; for, although the Italians called all the Americans as well as the English *inglesi*, they knew that the American regarded the English-man as aloof and cold. He misunderstood the torment of shyness.

As a rule, the Americans and the English took lodgings somewhere near the Spanish Steps, where Italians of striking appearance and of almost every age waited to be hired by the hour or by the day as an artist's model. Whenever a new picture was on view, the Roman spectator could at once tell who had been the model, whether he was St. John, Satan, or the Eternal Father. After looking at a painting of 'Christ at the Well', Nathaniel Hawthorne went with Franklin Pierce, a former President of the United States, in search of the model, only to find that the bearded young man with a gentle and blameless face had left the city and become a soldier.

Henry James could see the Rome once known to Hawthorne. The Caffé Greco, like the Via Condotti itself, might have become tidier and more fashionable, but Biblical and half-starved models were still lounging on the Spanish Steps. Yet something was missing, and Henry James wished he had known Rome when Hawthorne and William Wentmore Story, an unusually successful sculptor, first went to live within its walls. He thought, perhaps, that there had been more freedom. 'Rome,' Hawthorne declared, 'is not like one of our New England villages where we need the permission of each individual neighbor for every act that we do, every word that we utter, and for every friend that we make or keep. In these particulars the papal despotism allows us freer breath than our native air.' He was right, however, in thinking that the Pope's Government wanted the people to enjoy the fine arts because they turned their minds away from politics. In every authoritarian State, the police watched the class called thinkers, especially if they were foreigners. No thoughtful person in papal Rome was really free.

If few men were more discerning than Henry James as an interpreter of the social scene, he was already twenty-six when he took his first long walk through Rome. At that time two children—Violet Paget and John Singer Sargent—saw the living Rome with fresh and radiant eyes. The girl, aged twelve, was staying with her English parents just opposite the Palace of the Propaganda Fide. On arriving in Rome, they gave perfunctory glances at St. Peter's, the Colosseum and the tomb of John Keats, and then they settled into a smaller world bounded by the Pincian Gardens, the Villa Borghese 'and the evening stroll down the deserted Corso'.

The boy—living at the top of the Spanish Steps, not far away—was more fortunate. His father had made enough money as a surgeon in Philadelphia to retire at the age of thirty-four and to fulfil his wife's dearest wish by living in Europe; and Emily Sargent knew how to make excursions in Rome and beyond exciting for her son and his friend. Together, from the high Pincian terrace, the boy and girl hurled pebbles and acorns at the pigs kept outside the Flaminian Gate. Sometimes in their wanderings they saw Pope Pius, 'a white sash around his portly middle, distributing benedictions with two extended fingers among the bay hedges and mossy fountains of the Villa Borghese'. Guided by Emily Sargent, they learned in their impressionable childhood how to look at the true Rome in its sweetness and rankness, its grandeur and poverty: a splendid backcloth for 'beggars and loafers, inconceivable squalor and lousiness'.

They were a happy pair of children: the American boy, a future portrait painter, 'in his pepper-and-salt Eton jacket, bounding his way among the models and mendicants down the Spanish Steps'; and the English girl, later to write under the name of Vernon Lee, looking from the window at the Palace of the Propaganda Fide and 'watching the Cinderella coaches, with emblazoned hammercloth and hanging gold-braided footmen and the various Eminences—was that the villain Antonelli?—alighting, draped in scarlet mantles and followed by scarlet ill-furled umbrellas of state.'

The two children had no regrets for a past which they did not know. Rome was alive and in a constant state of change; for even if time seemed to move slowly, it was never stationary; and Rome could not be completely isolated from a changing world. Pius himself looked forward to the day when the Vatican Council would vote in favour of the dogma of papal infallibility. People who saw him in the street noted that he looked more than ever serene. 'Once, before I was Pope,' he was reported to have said, 'I believed in infallibility. Now I feel infallible.'

A year beforehand, almost every town and village in the Pontifical State had sent him a present to mark the jubilee of his ordination. Faithful subjects, it seemed clear, greatly outnumbered the discontented. Already plans were being made to celebrate, in the summer of 1871, the twenty-fifth anniversary of his Pontificate. By then he would have reigned as Bishop of Rome even longer than Peter.

Nor was Pius alone in anticipating change. Hundreds of political prisoners and active exiles resented the condition to which theocratic rule in Rome had brought them. There were also some powerful landowners whom Antonelli dared not touch. One was Prince Michelangelo Caetani, Duke of Sermoneta, whose acres stretched right across the Pontine marshes from near Velletri almost to Terracina, and who was a collateral descendant of the imperious Pope Boniface VIII. He had been one of the Pope's Ministers before the flight to Gaeta, and while Pius turned his back on a liberal past, the Duke remained loyal to his own political principles.

For all his wealth, Michelangelo Caetani was a man of simple tastes, and although generous to others, he became quite eccentric in his reluctance to spend money on himself. When cataracts were falling over his eyes, he refused the services of an eminent surgeon and entrusted himself to a local doctor, who bungled the operation and permanently blinded him. He was a fine Dantean scholar and, in spite of his affliction, he gave lectures which left his listeners with the firm impression that Dante was a poet who sang for the whole of Italy. Only a few outstanding European men of letters stayed in Rome without a welcome at the Caetani Palace. Already there was a white as well as a black aristocracy in Rome.

Other signs of restlessness within the papal city abounded. Bishops from Northern Europe were surprised to see the word 'Verdi' written on many walls. It looked like the tribute of a musical people to the composer who had not yet produced his popular 'Aïda'. In actual fact, 'Verdi' stood for *'Emanuele, Re d'Italia'*. As Bishops passed behind the Braschi Palace, which Pope Pius VI built for his family, they might also have seen more than one lampoon fastened to an ancient and unlovely statue of Pasquino. These lampoons, or pasquinades, revealed the views of Romans who had no free press of their own. During the Vatican Council one widely quoted lampoon read:

> *Quando Eva morse, e morder fece il pomo,*
> *Gesu per salvar l'uom, si fece uomo;*
> *Ma il Vicario di Crist, il Nono Pio,*
> *Per render chiavo l'uom, si vuol far Dio.*[1]

Pius, however, was now far more concerned with the ultimate fate of the proposed definition of his infallibility than with the sentiments of his subjects. When a vote was taken in the Council Hall on July 13th, eighty-eight Bishops expressed their dissent, while another sixty-two gave only a modified approval. For a moment, Pius hesitated. The final vote was due to be taken on July 18th and Antoine Dupanloup, Bishop of Orleans, wrote a very private letter to show how Pius might yet evade the clutches of Manning's group. Immediately after the Council had voted on the text, the Pope might express two things. First, he could thank the Council Fathers for giving so large a vote in favour of his prerogatives as the Pontiff. Secondly, he could declare that, after long prayer, he thought it prudent to delay his confirmation of the Council's vote and to wait for a time more propitious and for a greater calmness of the spirit.

The proposal, however, was not accepted, and when they realized that the cause of the 'inopportunists' was lost, fifty-five Bishops—among them, Dupanloup and Darboy—left Rome. There was thus a substantial reduction in the number of mitred Bishops to be seen when, on July 18th, the final voting brought a vast crowd once more into St. Peter's.

This time there was a violent thunderstorm: perhaps, the worst which any Roman could remember. The darkness thickened, and when

[1] 'When Eve bit the apple and caused it to be eaten, Jesus made Himself man in order to save him; but the Vicar of Christ, Pius the Ninth, wants to make himself God in order to render man a slave.'

the result of the voting was presented to the Pope, a large lighted taper had to be placed at his side. Thunder incessantly reverberated through the huge basilica; it shattered a window almost over the Pontifical throne; and even those members of the congregation who stood nearest to the Council Hall could not follow what was happening. Yet, as soon as they heard the Bishops clapping their hands, they knew that the definition had at last been promulgated. They waved handkerchiefs as they shouted 'Viva il Papa Infallibile! Viva il trionfo dei Cattolici!' The shouting which they had begun was spread throughout the building and stopped only by a solemn recital of the Te Deum and the Benedictus, when—as Thomas Mozley, Newman's brother-in-law, wrote in his dispatch to the 'Times' newspaper in London—'the entire crowd fell on their knees as I have never seen a crowd do before in St. Peter's, and the Pope blessed them in those clear sweet tones distinguishable in a thousand'.

The definition was now a dogma which 'divinely revealed that the Roman Pontiff, when he speaks ex cathedra, that is,—when in the exercise of his office as pastor and teacher of all Christians, he defines by virtue of his supreme apostolic authority doctrine concerning faith or morals to be held by the Universal Church,— is by the Divine assistance promised to him in the person of St. Peter possessed of that Infallibility wherewith the Divine Redeemer willed that His Church should be endowed in defining doctrine concerning faith or morals; and that, therefore, such definitions of the Roman Pontiff are unalterable of themselves and not by reason of the consent of the Church'.

Out of 535 Bishops in the Council Hall, all save two— the Bishop of Little Rock in Arkansas and the Bishop of Caiazzo, near Caserta— voted in favour of the definition. Before the Pope left the Council Hall, and in full view of his episcopal brethren, the Bishop of Little Rock stepped forward and made his submission. So did the Bishop of Caiazzo. He seemed to have voted non placet by mistake. None the less, the liberals in his diocese concluded that his adverse vote was deliberate, and they gave him a rousing reception on his return.

Time now began to move swiftly, even in Rome; a little more than twenty-four hours after the final voting in St. Peter's, France declared war on Prussia. Many Infallibilists and Inopportunists alike were eager to get home and not a few must have hoped that the Pope would immediately suspend the work of the Council. Then, when the war was over, he might recall them to Rome to discuss their future relations with him, and they could speak more freely of their own need for curial reform. The machinery of the Curia was antiquated, creaky and yet secretive. Many Bishops suffered from the lack of sympathy and understanding in the Vatican. The new dogma made it more than ever important that their relations with the Pope should be simple and direct.

Nor were all the Italian Bishops living outside the Pontifical State unmindful of the freedom with which the Government in Florence allowed them to go to Rome. The King, when he addressed his Parliament, actually said that he was hoping to hear a conciliatory word from the Bishops at their assembly. So far, that word had not been uttered. Yet, as all the chief actors of the Roman drama knew, the problem of the Temporal Power was not insoluble. The alternative courses of action were still those of force and consent. Armed spiritually with a new dogma of infallibility, the Pope needed his Temporal Power less than before. The expense and burden of ruling a State— geographically, only a province within the Italian peninsula—could be lifted from him. In St. Peter's he could crown a King whose Government stayed in Florence. He could even meet him at a gateway of the city and escort him in state to St. Peter's for his crowning. The mind alone created barriers. Among seven hundred Council Fathers, there must have been not a few who, whether back in their own diocese or still in Rome, wanted to repair the damage done by the Syllabus of Errors and somehow to reconcile the Pope 'with progress, with liberalism and with modern civilization'.

They pinned their hopes on a short war, and it took time to realize how deep was the gash which the Emperor Napoleon III, military patron of the Pontifical State, inflicted on Europe when he quarrelled with Bismarck ostensibly over a successor to the Spanish throne. In nearly every mess, French officers drank to the day when they could meet each other again in Berlin. By the valour of their arms, they would regain the left bank of the Rhine, which the first Napoleon had won for France, and which his victors took away. The new war was swift, but instead of victory for France, it brought defeat.

Though mortally sick, Napoleon III held supreme command for a whole month. He withdrew his garrison from Rome, appealed to Victor Emmanuel for help and sent his cousin, Jerome Napoleon, to Florence to plead personally with the King, his father-in-law. The Emperor wanted not less than seventy thousand Italian troops. Victor Emmanuel remembered the day when he and the Emperor entered Milan together, and he was eager to be at the Emperor's side again. He gloried in war. All his sympathies were now with Garibaldi, whom Italian ships were watching, lest he should leave his humble house at Caprera to fight for France or, worse still, to set up an independent republic in his native Nice.

The King, however, could not act against his Ministers. The image of a constitutional monarch had become too firm. Led by Quintino Sella, the Ministers were determined to keep the new Kingdom out of a suicidal war.

'I understand,' said the King, 'that making war requires courage.'

'Yes,' Sella replied, 'but resisting Your Majesty requires more courage than making war.'

The remark caused the King to lose his temper.

'One sees very clearly that you descend from clothiers.'

'That is true, Sire, but clothiers have always honoured their signature. This time Your Majesty would be signing a bill without being sure of your ability to pay.'

Victor Emmanuel was compelled to yield. The battle of Sedan made the Emperor a prisoner. The Empress fled to England. Besieged Paris was ruled by republicans who had no intention of ever sending French troops back to Rome. Would another power try to take the place of France in the Pontifical State? Would the Pope-King use the new dogma of infallibility solely as a spiritual weapon? What harm might not be done if he used it for political ends? Or would Catholic Europe leave Rome to its fate as it had once left Constantinople?

By comparison with the fall of Constantinople, the loss of the Temporal Power would be almost a parochial affair. In 1453, the Turks took the largest city in Christendom and turned the great Cathedral of St. Sophia into a mosque. In 1870, the struggle for a city and its province would be waged between fellow-Catholics and fellow-Italians. Not a single church within its walls need suffer damage, though convents might feel the lash of anti-clerical legislation. The French withdrawal from Rome was not gradual, but precipitate; and it created a problem of security for a new Kingdom now living under the menacing shadow of a major European war. The Italian Government met the unexpected challenge by sending troops into the Pontifical State under the command of General Raffaele Cadorna.

If the image of a constitutional ruler remained firm, the original image of the King who kept his word was tarnished by the Ministers. So Victor Emmanuel believed, for they had twice broken his word for him: they refused aid to the Emperor of the French, and they repudiated the September Convention which bound the Italians to refrain from invading the Pontifical State. Under these conditions the *Re Galantuomo* had no wish whatever to set foot in Rome. To dream of riding in triumph into Berlin with the French Emperor at his side was one thing. To lead his troops towards the city of the Pope was quite another. He stayed in Tuscany, well knowing that his troops would reach the walls of Rome.

Thus—on the feast day of St. Januarius and within two months of his spectacular theological triumph in St. Peter's—Pius made his penitential climb up the *Scala Santa* on the Lateran hill. After he had spoken to the zouaves guarding St. John's gateway, he got into his carriage and told the coachman to drive very slowly back to the Vatican. He knew that he would never again be seen in the streets of Rome. The Pope-King was giving his subjects a final blessing.

Pius had kept the taxes low, walked freely in his city, and visited the prisons and asylums. Knowing that good soldiers are born and not made, he had spared young men the torments of military conscription. Soon, in Rome as in Naples, new taskmasters would raise the taxes, impose rigid northern laws and drag unwilling Romans to their barracks. The spirit of the age was on the side of the Piedmontese, as their foes still called them; and this spirit Pius condemned.

At heart he knew that his fellow-Italians were a Catholic people and that their King, though a sinner, hated to wound him. His long reign began gloriously, and he had paid a cruel price for his just refusal as Pontiff to make war on Austria. Often, perhaps, he reflected on the advice which Rosmini gave him in Gaeta; for by a prompt return to the Pontifical State and by upholding the Constitution which he had granted, his reign would not have been divided into two parts: the one liberal and the other reactionary. Had he continued to be a constitutional ruler and eventually renounced his Temporal Power at the request of his own people, Italian unity might have been achieved with far less bloodshed. At least, there would not have been the shame of the military occupation of Rome by a foreigner.

Pius had sent greetings to the troubled Lamennais and rejoiced when Rosmini was at last rescued from the heresy-hunters. Nor did he forget Montalembert's steadfast loyalty to the Church even after Gregory XVI's condemnation of Catholic Democracy. Montalembert upheld the Temporal Power, but, when near to death, he protested against the way in which the Bishops were being hustled into accepting the definition of the Pope's infallibility. After his death it was arranged that Dupanloup should deliver the oration at a Requiem Mass in the church of the Ara Coeli on the Capitoline Hill. Under Jesuit pressure, Pius gave orders that the funeral service should not be held. Next day, however, he went himself to the lesser-known church of Santa Maria della Traspontina and asked that a Mass should be at once prepared for 'a certain Sir Charles'.

'Let me not be attached to the things of this world.' That was his constant prayer, and amid all the pomps of the Vatican Pius lived simply. Garibaldi, Mazzini and himself, he once observed good-naturedly, seemed to be the only men who had got nothing out of the Risorgimento. Fundamentally, his sympathies were with the prophets. What he lacked was their strength. He had to lean on others.

There was time, even now, to go beyond the walls and invite the King's troops to enter unmolested into the papal city; but this vision of the truth, even if fitfully granted to Pius, was denied to almost all his court. He was driving back not to a home, but to a prison. Henceforward thousands would call him 'the prisoner of the Vatican'. In actual fact, he was already a prisoner; for a long emphasis on the Temporal Power had made Rome ghetto-minded. If he had wanted to parley with the King's troops, the court and his own officers might have dragged him back.

In Gaeta, less than ninety miles away, the inhabitants were talking of another prisoner. Many remembered when Pius and some of his Cardinals lived in their midst. Still more recalled the days when the last King of the Two Sicilies and his Queen shared the privations of a beleaguered garrison. Pope or Cardinal, King or Queen: they were nothing in comparison with a patriot who, throughout the greater part of his life, had been almost penniless and was now confined to a fortress. As the process of uniting Italy reached its climax, the King's Ministers did not want to be embarrassed by the presence of Garibaldi or Mazzini. Their day was over. Garibaldi had obligingly left for a baffled France, but Mazzini was found in Palermo. It was necessary, therefore, to arrest him and to take him in custody to Gaeta.

He was a philosopher and knew how to endure privation. The prison library provided him with Tasso's *Gerusalemme* as well as bad translations of Shakespeare and Byron. This did not matter; for in the late September of 1870, he was consoled by the beauty of the sky at night. The stars 'shine with a lustre one sees only in Italy. I love them like sisters, and link them to the future in a thousand ways. If I could choose, I should like to live in absolute solitude, working at my historical book or at some other, just from a feeling of duty and only wishing to see—for a moment, now and then—someone I did not know, some poor woman that I could help, some working man I could advise, the doves of Zurich, and nothing else.'

Mazzini seemed not to know what pride and affection he had roused among unseen neighbours living within reach of his prison walls. The stories told about him were legion. As an exile in London, he led a crusade against the white-slave traffic of poor Italian country lads whose contracts which promised high pay and good living were not valid in England, and who were often beaten and half-starved. He opened a school for them, and friends like Joseph Toynbee taught them without accepting any fee.

In the days of the short-lived Roman Republic, when he was one of the triumvirate, he walked through the Quirinal Palace until he found a room small enough in which to live. Once, when the crowd fetched confessional boxes out of the churches to make barricades, he begged that they should be taken back. From these confessionals, he explained, had come words of comfort to their mothers. His one act of severity was to fine the Canons of St. Peter's because they had refused to conduct the customary Easter services.

Although the people in Gaeta knew why Mazzini was famous, they were mostly too unlettered to read his books and articles. He was prophet as well as patriot; and, like Garibaldi, he hated the contrast between the glorious dream of Italian unity and the unfurling shabby reality. Once there was Rome of the Caesars, then Rome of the Popes. There ought now to have been Rome of the people. Instead, there was about to be Rome of a King surrounded by generals and commercial magnates. Such a monarchy, the prisoner believed, could not last. One day a republic must succeed it. Even united Italy was too small for Rome. Her place must eventually be taken by united Europe: 'that great European federation, whose task is to unite in one association all the political families of the old world, destroy the partitions that dynastic rivalries have made and consolidate and respect nationalities'.

Dante wrote of the universal Emperor, but Mazzini wrote as though the universal Emperor and the universal people were one. The Church and the State would both attain a more universal status. 'We will march from the Church of the past to the Church of the future, from the dead Church to the living, the Church of freemen and equals. There is room for such a Church betwixt the Vatican and the Capitol.' On the other hand, nothing is Caesar's, 'except in so far as it conforms with the divine law. Caesar—in other words, the civil power—is only the mandatory, the executor, when its own efforts and the times allow it, of God's design.' In the end, the good Guelph and the good Ghibelline are one.

Revolutionary and anti-clerical, Mazzini never realized that at heart he was still a Catholic who had much in common with Francis of Assisi. Thus the people loved him; and because the harsh noise made in unlocking a prison gate might have jarred on Mazzini's nerves, the jailer in Gaeta took as long as three minutes each time he opened the door of his cell.

CHAPTER SIX

VATICAN AND QUIRINAL

ON THE morning of September 20th, 1870, the Pope said Mass at an hour later than usual, so that members of the Diplomatic Corps might attend. He was talking with them quietly in his private library when a Monsignore announced that the Aurelian walls had been breached near Porta Pia. At once he gave orders for the white flag to be hoisted above the Castel Sant'Angelo and for General Kanzler to capitulate. From that moment, all Rome outside the Leonine walls passed to the King of Italy by right of conquest.

Within the Leonine walls were zouaves still ready to die for their Pope-King. Next day they paraded in St. Peter's Square and presented arms to the shout of *'Viva Pio Nono Pontefice Re'*: 'Long live Pius the Ninth, Pope-King.' Pius came to the window and, with the sweet voice which old age had scarcely impaired, he blessed them. Soon afterwards, Cardinal Antonelli was compelled to ask that Italian troops should forthwith enter the Leonine city for the sake of maintaining order. The King's soldiers waited in vain for a glimpse of the Pope. He never again blessed the people in the Square.

Though Victor Emmanuel had opposed the assault on Rome, he rejoiced in the news of victory, and he made amends for past rudeness by sending his powerful Minister of War a photograph of himself inscribed: *'All'amico Quintino Sella, Vittorio Emanuele—Roma libera 1870.'* Giovanni Lanza, the Prime Minister, acted quickly by choosing October 2nd—less than a fortnight after the Pope's loss of his Temporal Power—as the date for a plebiscite throughout the fallen Pontifical State.

Though the right to vote was restricted, not even Pius doubted that the result would be favourable to the King. A few patricians closed the outer gates of their palaces or villas and protested that they would never re-open them until the rule of the Pope-King was restored. Prince Torlonia, whose banking interests made him fabulously wealthy, changed the livery of his servants, so that it should no longer bear the royal colours. None the less, many courtiers were feeling the wind of change. Only two years had passed since Pius refused Antonelli's request that the patricians should be forbidden to subscribe to a handsome wedding present for Prince Humbert and Princess Margaret.

The King's Ministers were, in fact, so certain of the result that, on the day before the plebiscite, they decided that the Quirinal Palace should be his official Roman residence.

Pius declined to live in this summer palace again after his return from Portici; but, like Gregory XVI, he had been elected Pope in its stately chapel. Lanza would have preferred to leave the Quirinal Palace untouched and he was distressed to hear that no suitable alternative could be found. Rome abounds in palaces; but if the city was to become the permanent capital of the Kingdom, it needed a royal palace which compared not too meanly with the Pitti Palace in Florence or the vast Royal Palace in Caserta. No private palace could be commandeered, and although Cardinal Antonelli produced receipts to show that the average annual fund for the upkeep of the Quirinal Palace came from the Pope's private purse and not from the State revenues, the northerners brushed his argument aside. Antonelli refused to hand over the keys.

Here was the first direct challenge to the Italian Government's authority in Rome. There could be only one result. Officers burst open the main gate. All the Swiss Guards found inside the Quirinal Palace were sent back under escort to the Vatican.

Tempers were frayed, and Pius—so calm and dignified on the day of the capitulation—used harsh language in a bull which announced his suspension of the Vatican Council. 'Suddenly,' the bull stated, 'the sacrilegious invasion of this beloved city, our seat, and the other provinces of our temporal dominion has reduced us to such a condition that, through God's will and inscrutable judgments, we find ourselves completely under enemy dominion and power.' Yet, if Pius was really 'under enemy dominion and power', at least his foes allowed him full freedom to declare it.

After the plebiscite, the blind Duke of Sermoneta led a delegation to Florence and, at a solemn ceremony in the Pitti Palace, he announced the figures to the King. Altogether 133,681 voters favoured incorporation into his Italian Kingdom, while only 1,507 of the Pope's former subjects voted against it. In no more than two small places—Marano and Roiate—did the 'noes' outnumber the 'ayes'. Rome was now the King's both by right of conquest and by the will of its people.

To the outward eye, the changes within the city were at first few, but striking. Like the French soldiers, the papal zouaves were no longer to be seen. Their place was taken by bersaglieri, crack Italian riflemen who walked at a quick pace and wore hats with their plumes streaming downwards on one side. More newspaper stalls were erected at street corners, and the journals for sale were no longer restricted to the *Voce della Verità* or the *Osservatore Romano*, which Marcantonio

Pacelli had founded ten years beforehand. There were now copies of the *Nazione* of Florence and other Italian newspapers from beyond Rome. Sometimes there were also belated copies of the 'Morning Post' and the 'Times' from Protestant England. The fall of papal Rome spelt far more freedom for speech and freedom for the press.

Yet fear was not entirely overcome. Many clergy still hesitated to walk alone through the streets, and if a Cardinal went out-of-doors, his coach bore the draperies of mourning. A Roman was either a Pope's man or a King's man, a Guelph or a Ghibelline; but when Gregorovius paid his first call on the Duke of Sermoneta after the capitulation, he found him entertaining Cardinal Silvestri. Guelph and Ghibelline had to learn how to live in a society which refused to be static. Only the wide-minded could point the way to conciliation.

Their task became harder when Pius pronounced the major sentence of excommunication on the King and all others held to be responsible for the loss of his Temporal Power. Victor Emmanuel felt the wound both as a man of honour and because he was superstitious. The Ministers, by forcing him to break his word, had brought the *Re Galantuomo* to the verge of damnation, and he asked to see a copy of the act which marked his father's abdication. He hated more than ever the thought of setting foot in Rome, and an Archbishop reminded him that the Capitoline Hill—where, it seemed likely, the Italian Parliament would have its future seat—embraced the fearsome Tarpeian rock, from which the malefactors of other years were often hurled.

Lanza and the other Ministers knew their King. His fears and scruples were an additional reason for swiftness of action. The Senator of Rome gave place to a *Sindaco*, or Mayor, and local government in Rome and the former papal provinces followed the example adopted elsewhere in the Kingdom. Then came elections to the provincial and municipal councils as well as to the Parliament in Florence.

The parliamentary elections caused less excitement than the plebiscite, for the Pope's ex-subjects were not yet fully in touch with the issues which dominated political life on the banks of the Arno. Many, too, were troubled by the major excommunication, and enough happened to show the strength of clerical feeling. Terracina, for example, paid Cardinal Antonelli the tribute of electing his brother, Gregorio, to be a provincial councillor. As he had no intention of sitting with the King's supporters, he promptly resigned.

As Christmas drew near, the Romans became more aware of the Pope's physical alienation. On December 8th—feast day of the Immaculate Conception and the first anniversary of the opening of the Vatican Council—many patricians and other citizens illuminated their palaces or houses as a sign that they were faithful to the Pope; but Christmas was made deliberately grey. There was no Pope to be seen outside the Vatican: and no King of Italy within the walls of Rome.

Yet tribulation was soon to bring the citizens closer together; for, early on the morning of December 28th, the Tiber overflowed its banks. Water, gushing down the Corso and through the tortuous alleyways of Trastevere and the Campo Marzio, submerged the ground floors of almost all the buildings between the Spanish Steps and the foot of the Janiculum Hill. In the old ghetto, where most of the Jews continued to live, the damage and the suffering were terrible. Towards nightfall, when the wind was gentler and the water becalmed, the city resembled Venice as members of a new National Guard rowed boats with a lantern at the bow or the stern and carried out their rescue work, not heeding whether the victims were Jews or Christians, monarchists or papalists. More than one priest declared that the flood was sent from God as a punishment; but Pius—the Bishop of Rome isolated from his own people by a voluntary incarceration—rebuked a Monsignore whom he heard speaking in this way.

Victor Emmanuel's reaction to the news of Rome's worst flood since 1805 was soldierly and prompt. The victims were his new subjects. On December 30th, while the city was still flooded, the Marquess Spinola called on Cardinal Antonelli as the bearer of an urgent personal letter from the Pitti Palace: the King was already on his way to Rome.

The royal train brought him to Termini station at four on the morning of New Year's Eve, and torchbearers escorted his carriage through the empty streets to the Quirinal Palace. At dawn the news of his arrival was spreading through the city, and there were large and boisterous crowds when, a few hours later, Victor Emmanuel drove to the Capitoline Hill. As Mayor of Rome, Prince Francesco Pallavicini began to arrange a ceremonious welcome, but time was against him. Shortly after five o'clock in the evening, the royal train was taking the King back to Florence. The visit was private. A duty had been done: brusquely, but well.

Awake or asleep, Victor Emmanuel was still in his train while fireworks in countless Italian villages and towns heralded the demise of 1870 and the advent of 1871: the year in which he was to make a solemn return to Rome and to take possession of his last and permanent capital. 'Here we are in Rome,' he would say on that occasion, 'and here we remain.'

Three weeks later Prince Humbert drove with his consort and the fourteen-month-old Prince of Naples through decorated streets to the Quirinal Palace. Princess Margaret, first lady of the land, was wholeheartedly a Catholic, and it must have been with mixed feelings that she became the hostess in a palace cluttered with papal associations. No priest was now permitted to say Mass in the Quirinal chapel. On her first Sunday in Rome, therefore, the princess accompanied her husband to the basilica of Santa Maria Maggiore, where obliging Canons placed elaborate faldstools before them.

The Canons knew that their own position had become invidious. An ancient tradition made the sovereign of Spain a Canon of Santa Maria Maggiore, just as the sovereign of France was a Canon of St. John's Lateran and, before the Reformation, the sovereign of England was a Canon of St. Paul's-beyond-the-Walls. The war raging in France had begun because Napoleon III and Bismarck quarrelled over a successor to the Spanish throne; but the candidate finally chosen was not a Hohenzollern. He was, in fact, none other than Victor Emmanuel's second son, Prince Amadeus.

Thus, in the basilica of Santa Maria Maggiore, a Savoyard had a canon's stall within the sanctuary. Kingship and priesthood are nearly allied; and when Pius was asked how the children from Catholic schools ought to greet Princess Margaret on seeing her in the street, he replied: 'As a princess. Is she not a member of the Royal House of Savoy?'

This deep and instinctive tie between monarchy and the Church—the tie which helped to make Pius and Victor Emmanuel sympathetic to each other, even though destiny had brought them into conflict—caused profound sorrow for Mazzini; for he never doubted that one day the monarchy would betray the people. Soon after the result of the plebiscite was known, the Government had allowed him to leave Gaeta. He spent one restless night in Rome and then took the train to Livorno. His aim was to reach Genoa, where he might see his mother's grave.

'The only thing really touching to me,' Mazzini wrote, 'was in the churchyard—it was late—and the place was quite empty, but a keeper had, it seems, recognized me, and coming out of the gate, some poor people, a priest among them, were drawn up in a line, bowing and almost touching the earth. Not a smile, no attempt at absurd applause, they felt my sadness, and contrived to show that they were sharing it.'

Though death has often failed to silence a prophet, contemporary Rome treated the living Mazzini as a man of the past and his republicanism as a lost cause. Whoever ruled in Rome—Pius or Victor Emmanuel—he was a King, and not a republican. Monarchists and papalists alike were shocked when Paris fell into the hands of revolutionary Communards, who seized Archbishop Darboy as a hostage and later shot him.

Although Darboy hated the hustling methods which Manning adopted at the Vatican Council and was determined to leave Rome before the Bishops took their fateful vote on the definition of papal infallibility, he managed to get a message out of besieged Paris to let Pius know that he condemned the loss of his Temporal Power. He also accepted the new dogma. Hitherto, he explained, he opposed the definition only because he believed it to be inopportune. When Manning passed through France on his next visit to Rome, he went to the fortress at La Roquette and knelt in prayer on the spot where his valiant ecclesiastical foe met a brutal death.

Darboy was the third Archbishop of Paris to be shot within a century. The times seemed to be diabolical, and pious French Catholics believed that their country's defeat in war was a moral judgment. Their priests spoke of the need for penitential suffering. As an act of contrition, the National Assembly agreed to build the basilica of Sacré Coeur on the summit of Montmartre, and Pius showed his approval by contributing fifty thousand francs towards its cost. Few were the Frenchmen who, like Ernest Renan, knew how to view military defeat with detachment; for if the French possessed the better arms, the Prussians had the abler plans of campaign. In war, Renan observed, one side is the victor, and the other side is the loser. Defeat, as in a game of chess, is a consequence of inferior skill or miscalculation; it is not a spiritual degradation.

While France was licking her wounds, the Parliament in Florence endorsed a skilfully drawn Law of Guarantees which, many hoped, would pave the way to a final reconciliation between the Italian State and the Holy See. This Law conferred sovereign honours on the Pope; granted him an annual subsidy; guaranteed the full freedom of his spiritual ministry; and assured the immunity of the Vatican, the Lateran and the Villa of Castelgandolfo from the jurisdiction of the Italian State. Pius, however, would have nothing to do with the Law of Guarantees; for it put him 'under hostile domination' and made him appear before the whole Catholic world as a mere Italian subject. The Temporal Power, he still insisted, was essential to the independence of his ministry.

On Easter Day, the chief festival of the Church, Pius entered the Paoline Chapel, but not a crowded St. Peter's. For the first time since his return from Portici, he did not go to the outer balcony of the basilica to give his Easter blessing *urbi et orbi*: 'to the city and the world'. On June 16th, he reached the twenty-fifth anniversary of his election. The King sent a general to the Vatican to convey his personal greetings, but the emissary was not received. In fact, almost all the former preparations for commemorating the longest Pontificate since St. Peter's were in disarray; and when, for the first time since the fall of Mazzini's brief Roman Republic, the Waldensians held a service within the city walls, their preacher declared that St. Peter had never entered Rome.

To the Pope's burden of griefs was soon added the seizure of eight large convents which the Government needed for housing some of its Ministries. All were in the centre of Rome, and all were rich in their links with its history. San Silvestro in Capite, chosen for the Ministry of the Interior and later for the central Post Office, was the convent to which Vittoria Colonna, Michelangelo's friend, retired in her widowhood. The Minerva, selected for the Ministry of Agriculture, was the convent in which Galileo faced his trial for heresy.

Not all the buildings which the Government seized were religious foundations. The Madama Palace, once the Roman house of the Medicis from Florence, became the Senate. A palace designed by Gianlorenzo Bernini and known as Montecitorio was the future Chamber of Deputies, while the Braschi Palace, which a long-suffering Pius VI had built as a town house for his brother's family, was at first favoured for the Ministry of Agriculture. A new and bureaucratic Rome could not be built in a day, and edifices suitable for its needs were not always easy to find; but, in seizing the convents, the northerners trampled alike on Roman piety and Roman pride. Within the Vatican and among the Jesuits were heard voices urging Pius to leave Italy.

Where should he go? Some said to Malta; but he could not forget that England had played a decisive part in enabling Garibaldi's thousand volunteers to cross the Strait of Messina unmolested. Others said to Corsica; but he knew how the Romans had resented the presence of French soldiers in their city, and when they eventually departed, he had himself expressed the hope that they would not return. The one country of which he always spoke well was the United States, where Catholic citizens were given a full freedom for their worship. His journey as a young priest across the southern Atlantic had been far from fruitless. Sometimes when he spoke at ease with an American, he came near to uttering the phrase which Cavour borrowed from Montalembert: 'a free Church within a free State'. Perhaps he forgot that if the Catholic Church in the United States has an unfettered freedom, it is also unprivileged. There was, however, a much more important question to be answered: not where, but why should the Pope go?

For all his personal failings, Pius did not lack the capacity for self-criticism. Queen Victoria's verdict that King Louis-Philippe should never have left Paris made sound sense. Pius should never have left Rome for Gaeta. His flight could not be explained, except as a momentary loss of nerve. He had then been in Rome for not much more than two years; but now two full decades had passed since his return from Portici and, at the age of 78, he preferred to stay where he was. For a time France—humiliated by defeat and resenting Italy's failure to go to her aid—was the only country likely to attempt a restoration of his Temporal Power. The others all agreed that their Ambassador in Florence should follow the King to Rome. When Louis Thiers, hitherto a champion of the Temporal Power, gave similar instructions to the Duc de Choiseul, Pius knew that his wish to stay in Rome was justified. If he had left Rome, his successors might never have found it again; and almost certainly not without the risk of involving Europe in another war.

The times were not markedly happier for Victor Emmanuel than they were for Pius. On July 2nd, which was a Sunday, the King arrived shortly after twelve in the morning for his official entry into Rome. The citizens were already bedecking their streets and raising the standard of each Italian city along the Corso when he sent a telegram to Prince Francesco Pallavicini forbidding all signs of festivity. None the less, the streets were crowded with onlookers, and even the prisoner of the Vatican could not fail to hear the cannons as they fired salutes from the ramparts of the Castel Sant'Angelo, where at his own command, less than ten months beforehand, the white flag had been hoisted.

Women standing on the balconies of their apartments threw flowers at the carriage in which the King was sitting 'with an air rigid, gloomy and ugly'. As Gregorovius wrote in his diary, all was 'without pomp, vivacity, grandeur and majesty; and that was very prudent. This day signs the end of the millenary rule of the Popes over Rome.'

A Minister who came from Turin urged the King to cross the river to Trastevere because its working-class inhabitants had prepared a great ovation. 'No!' said the King firmly. Then, speaking in the Piedmontese dialect which few, if any, of his other listeners were likely to understand, he added: '*Il Papa li a doi pass a sentirà. I l'hai già faire abastansa a coul pover veii!*' 'The Pope is only two steps away and he would feel hurt. I have done enough already to that poor old man!'

The King cared nothing for the Quirinal Palace, and he would have found his first Roman winter intolerable if he had not spent most of it in the Villa Ludovisi, which the Duke of Sora rented to him. Here lived Rosina Vercellina, now his morganatic wife and the Countess of Mirafiori.

This secluded and stately villa was an architectural gem in a city which had changed little since the end of the seventeenth century. As in Napoleon's day, three-fifths of the area within the Aurelian walls were still adorned with the villas, gardens and parkland of Cardinals and lay princes. There was a remarkable similarity in the plans of Rome published by Giovanni Battista Nolli in 1748 and by John Murray in 1869. In the intervening period, scarcely a single new villa had been added or a park reduced in size. Each was built by a magnate who wished to give style to his wealth and whose descendant gladly received visitors of culture and taste.

Even a request to see a property well beyond Rome was seldom refused; and when an Englishman asked whether he might look at Sermoneta Castle, which stands on a hill above the Pontine marshes, the Duke wrote: 'Certainly, pray go by all means. I only regret that I cannot offer you luncheon, but our cook at Sermoneta died at the end of the sixteenth century.'

No one enjoyed his walks through the gardens and parks of the villas more thoroughly than did Stendhal, who made Italy virtually his own country. He went often to the Villa Negroni to converse with friends amid its thirty fountains and to the neighbouring Villa Strozzi to sit at midday beneath its sheltering trees. His favourite haunt was, however, the Villa Ludovisi. To most English visitors its garden, which covered seventy-five acres, appeared to be rather too French and formal, but Stendhal insisted that they made those of the Tuileries and Versailles look like 'a feeble imitation'.

The interior of the villa pleased him with its abundance of frescoes by Guercino, and he thought it unfair to blame the Duke of Sora for not wanting to receive thirty to forty English visitors each day. 'If I had the luck to possess this charming place,' he wrote in 1828, 'I should be blamed still more severely. Never, while I was there, would anyone set foot in it. In my absence, there would be an admission fee of two piasters for the benefit of poor artists.'

Even in the first half of 1871, a Duke of Sora was admitting visitors who had first applied to his banker. Then came Rosina, and the gates were firmly shut against the Roman world. Almost everyone was excluded, save the King and their surviving two children, Vittoria and Emanuele Alberto, now both full-grown and handsome. Society, black or white, had nothing to do with the Countess of Mirafiori, and she had nothing to do with society. Many who once sauntered in the gardens took revenge by talking maliciously of her ignorance and vulgarity. 'She beats her husband'—wrote Matilda Lucas, an English Quaker—'and sometimes shuts him out for a day or two.' Whether

the gossip was true or false, the Countess had already kept the affection
of a fickle lover for well over twenty years, and both adored their
children. The King was ready enough to be a constitutional monarch
and, within reason, to do what his Ministers wanted from him; but
his private life was his own.

Even if he had been gracious in his manner and married to someone
of royal blood, he could not have reconciled a divided society in his
own lifetime. The flood which brought him hurriedly to Rome on a
New Year's Eve was itself an omen of change. His capital city could
not be left to the menace of periodic inundations. The Italian Government knew that it must fulfil a task which the Popes had left undone,
and the building of stout embankment walls would involve the
disappearance of many attractive landmarks from the edge of the
Tiber. In addition, Rome had to get ready for an invasion of newcomers: Ambassadors, Ministers, Senators and Deputies from Florence
—to say nothing of the humbler civil servants, whom some estimated
to exceed forty thousand. Embassies, hotels and houses were urgently
needed.

Under Savoyard rule, Turin acquired a fine architectural tradition,
and the city on the Po was made magnificent through the buildings of
Ascanio Vitozzi, Carlo di Castellamonte and Guarini Guarini, a priest
who—like his English contemporary, Christopher Wren—travelled as
far as Paris in his search for new architectural designs and ideas. With
this tradition in full play, the Piedmontese might have earned the
enduring gratitude of future generations. Three things impeded them:
the lack of preparation, the pressure of time, and the decline of their
own tradition.

If Pius and the Italians had agreed to make Rome the 'capital of
honour' to which the King went for his crowning, there need have
been no seizure of palaces or convents within the Aurelian walls and
no building of many new Embassies, hotels and houses. Florence alone
would have been marked down for architectural spoliation. Even
when Rome had fallen, there might have been an agreement to build
an administrative centre for the Italian Kingdom outside the Aurelian
walls. Within the walls, the older city of medieval, Renaissance and
baroque builders could have remained unharmed, while a new
Savoyard city arose outside them. Bergamo in Lombardy provides
the Italian prototype of a dual city. Upper Bergamo, perched on a
hill, contains the Cathedral and many palaces, while lower Bergamo
is modern and built on a plain. Yet they form a single municipality.

Savoyard Turin had the right patronage, the right architects and
town-planners, and the right spaciousness of time and place. Savoyard

Rome lacked, in particular, the right spaciousness of time. The political unity of Italy had been a hectic, and not a gradual, achievement. Naples fell unexpectedly because the Bourbon army was too inefficient to check Garibaldi's lightning advance, and the northerners rushed to the task of administering a southern Kingdom about which they knew almost nothing. A quarrel over the next King of Spain led suddenly to a war between France and Prussia, and when French troops withdrew from the Pontifical State, they left a vacuum. Europe's loveliest city was soon at the mercy of northerners who had lost their own tradition as town-builders.

They built their new Rome in a hurry; they also built it cheaply and without refinement. First in their minds was the thought that its conquest had made Italy one of the European powers. Henceforward their country must play a part in power politics. Italy needed, therefore, a first-class army and a first-class navy. The King regarded himself as a warrior, and Prince Humbert was cast in the stiff mould of a professional soldier. The military tradition of Piedmont, when imposed on the whole Kingdom, was both a blessing and a curse: a blessing because the two services were finely disciplined and free from corruption; and a curse because the Italian genius is exploratory and individualistic. The new Kingdom had something better to offer Europe than playing a part in power politics that was beyond its strength. Papal Rome had, at least, an international significance, and Savoyard Rome should never have become exclusively nationalistic.

None the less, the swift defeat inflicted on France gave a new and terrible dimension to modern warfare, and much of the audacity and courage of the Risorgimento began suddenly to look old-fashioned. Garibaldi, it seemed, was bound to be the last of the great *condottieri*. The heroic age was over, and the years of prosaic nation-building lay ahead. For one thing, the King had been constantly engaged in war, and wars are costly. Count Giovanni Lanza, the Prime Minister, believed with Gladstone that a generation which waged war must be the one to pay for it. He also believed that no country prospers until it achieves a parity between income and expenditure. The taxes were increased.

Lanza lived in a Spartan way himself, and he expected the Italian people to follow his example. Many were too ignorant to understand. On poor agricultural workers fell eventually a double scourge: a grist-tax which helped to pay for the army and the navy; and military conscription which took their sons away from the fields and vineyards. These afflicted peasants formed the majority of Victor Emmanuel's subjects.

Before 1876, most of the Ministers came from the north, and on the whole the men in Parliament shared their economic views. Many of them took their meals for two lire a day at Valiani's restaurant in Termini station. Free railway passes were their only financial gain. Power had not yet enriched anyone in the Italian Kingdom.

Ministers and Deputies were all the children of an optimistic era. Like Cavour, they believed in the wealth-making power of railways. The opening of the Mont Cenis tunnel between Italy and France added more lustre to the eventful year of 1871. Later, when a railway reached Bari and was then extended to Brindisi, the English who ruled in India were provided with an overland route through Italy which greatly reduced their journeys to and from the homeland. Together the Calais-Brindisi land route and the Brindisi-Bombay sea route in Italian ships offered the shortest time-distance between England and India until the century of commercial flying.

The railways also lowered the costs of transport, but it was with a tragic lateness that the Government discovered the enormous extent of the damage caused in the south through wanton deforestation. Whole river courses were changed or lost. The more the Ministers studied the actual conditions in the south, the more they realized how stark were its poverty and ignorance. A priest's blessing, it was widely believed, did more good than a hundred manurings.

One brutal example of poverty was the plight of the *caruso* who worked in the sulphur mines of Sicily. The *caruso* was a boy, often no more than eight or nine years old, who went down the shaft to carry sulphur out of a mine. He bore his heavy load through hot and tortuous passages which reeked with sulphur fumes. Although he worked completely naked, he had always to struggle with his load for some distance in the open air, no matter how low the actual temperature might be. A miner paid the *caruso* or his parent a sum ranging from fifty to three hundred lire, and the child continued to work for him until the money was paid back. The wage was so trifling that the child was virtually condemned to a long period of servitude. Army Medical Boards had to reject more than forty per cent of the Sicilian recruits who came from the sulphur-mining districts.

Before long the Government began to see the spectre of southern poverty hovering on its own Roman doorstep. News of a building boom brought whole families from distant Puglia or Calabria to Rome. The father sought work as a navvy and the mother as a domestic slut, while the children—miserably clad and hungry—wandered about the streets until nightfall, when they dropped to sleep on the outer steps of a church or else in the colonnades of a palace where the princely owner was too pitying to deny them a roof. The supply of unskilled labour exceeded the demand. In an effort to cope with a social evil, the Municipality of Rome asked for a loan from the Government in order to start the work of building embankments for the Tiber. The loan was granted, but the Municipality had no settled plan of action. Like the Popes before them, it considered one ingenious scheme after another; but it always procrastinated. Then Garibaldi made his first entry into Savoyard Rome and demanded to know why nothing had been done to prevent a future flooding.

His days as a fighting soldier were over. He had fought for France in her last war, and a grateful National Assembly in Paris waited to welcome him as a fellow-member. He cared nothing for parliamentary life—in Italy or in France. He was a knight-errant ready to sponsor one particular cause after another. People had laughed at him when he urged the building of a bridge across the Strait of Messina to link Sicily with the Italian mainland. They were less disposed to laugh at him now, even though he protested that a deviation of the Tiber would make it possible to give Rome a seaport of its own.

Deliberately, he made his presence felt in Rome. 'Lately,' Pius observed, 'we were two here. Now we are three.'

Victor Emmanuel, who had always liked his tiresomely independent subject, gave Garibaldi a warm welcome; but, as a constitutional monarch, he was bound to refuse a request. Garibaldi wanted the King to grant the annulment of his marriage to Giuseppina Raimondi, so that he might marry Francesca Armosino, by whom he had two living children. The annulment, so he believed, would enable her children to become legitimate. 'If I could legitimize your bastards,' the King explained, 'I would first legitimize my own.'

Garibaldi spent eighteen months in Rome trying to raise the money with which to build a seaport. Though this project came to nothing, he shamed the Roman authorities into building the embankments for the Tiber. The long and costly work was almost completed when, in 1900, another flood arose. But for the embankments there might then have been a devastation even more ruthless than the one which Rome experienced in the closing days of 1870. Thus Garibaldi earned the gratitude of another generation and another century.

To the generation now ruling in Rome, he was a man of the romantic past and belonged to an age when everything was simpler. He saw no reason why life should ever cease to be simple, and he went back to his single-floored house on the island of Caprera, content with the few things which he possessed and loving the wide horizon and loneliness of his surroundings. The Court of Appeal found a way to obtain his divorce from Giuseppina Raimondi: the marriage contract had been made under Austrian law, which permitted divorce for non-consummation. Once, and once only, Garibaldi owed something to Austria. Henceforward all he wanted was a quiet evening, a dignified death and a simple burial.

On the next island of Maddalena lived Captain Roberts, an old Englishman who had helped Byron to burn Shelley's body when, in 1822, it was washed ashore at Viareggio. 'Tell me the exact story of your poet's fire-burial,' Garibaldi asked. 'Only the priests oppose it. It hurts their trade.' He told Francesca, now his lawful wife, that a pyre of acacia, myrtle and linden should be made in his garden when he was dead. He wished to be dressed in a red shirt and to have his face turned to the sun. His ashes were to go into a pot: 'any old pot will do'. No one outside the household must know of his death and 'fire-burial' until the following morning.

Garibaldi lived until 1882, and his death was not kept secret for a single hour. Authority forbade the burning. Although burial in the garden was permitted, the grave stood empty until many representative men from Rome and the Kingdom were present. Uniformed or top-hatted, they clambered out of boats and ascended a winding and rocky bridle-path to the house. Most of them were anti-clerical, but Italy had been spared the shock of a pagan incineration. Respectability triumphed over poetry.

CHAPTER SEVEN

BEHIND THE CURTAIN

SOME TIME before the cannons of Castel Sant'Angelo fired their
salute to the King of Italy, Joseph Severn paid a casual visit to the
basilica of St. John's Lateran. A full half-century had gone by since
two young Englishmen—one a painter, and the other an ailing poet
—entered Rome through St. John's gateway. There were no friends
to greet them, but a Scottish doctor took pity on the poet and found
rooms in a lodging house at the foot of the Spanish Steps. John Keats
knew that he must soon die. It was the penalty for having nursed a
consumptive brother, and he had set off for Italy 'with the sensation
of a soldier marching up to a battery'. Rome was almost the last city
in the Mediterranean world to which a man in his wretched condition
should have been taken.

Joseph Severn was not a great artist, and his own name might have
been 'writ in water' but for the steadily accumulating fame of a dead
and long neglected friend. He lived in Rome for many years and,
though a Protestant, he was once commissioned to paint an altar-piece
for the basilica of St. Paul's-beyond-the-Walls, which Gregory XVI
had rebuilt after a disastrous fire. As the acknowledged friend of Keats,
he went back to London in late middle age and lived a rather Bohemian
life in Pimlico. The years had made him Rome's prisoner. He became
impatient to return and, in 1860, Gladstone's personal influence enabled
him to be appointed the English consul.

Thereby Severn acquired a higher social status, just as Henri-Marie
Beyle, who wrote under the name of Stendhal, acquired it when King
Louis-Philippe made him the French consul in Civitavecchia. He had
long outgrown the boisterous company to be found in the Caffè Greco,
but this was also true of other artists whom he had known when he
was young and who were still in Rome to welcome him back.

Chief among them was John Gibson, an attractive and quiet-
mannered sculptor who had been the pupil first of Antonio Canova
and then of Albert Thorwaldsen, a Dane. He hated all forms of ostenta-
tion and wanted a simple funeral; but when he died, in 1866, the French
were still in military occupation, and they remembered that he had
been decorated with the Legion of Honour. Accordingly, they sent a
platoon to the Protestant Cemetery. After the body had been lowered,

each soldier in turn fired into the grave. 'Look at that!' cried a startled Italian onlooker. 'He is dead, and they are killing him again.'

Another artist in Rome was Richard Rothwell, an Anglo-Irishman and formerly the favourite pupil of the fashionable portrait-painter, Thomas Lawrence. In his youth he had been remarkably handsome, and he set out for Italy well furnished with letters of introduction from Queen Victoria's mother, the Duchess of Kent. The palaces of all the dynasties then reigning in Italy might have been open to him, but he offended the Duchess by presenting none of her letters. Without patronage he was lost. Yet, like Severn, he was Rome's prisoner, and he went back to a city where the models waiting on the Spanish Steps to be hired were lovelier and more natural than the royal ladies whom he might once have painted in Parma, Modena and Lucca.

Within a year of his own return to Rome, Severn was given the additional office of consul for the new Kingdom of Italy; for Turin and Rome were both agreed that it should be held by a non-Italian. The dual consulate made a fine listening-post; but Severn was a painter, and not a diarist. Otherwise he might have cast some light for posterity on Thomas Dessoulavy, who died in 1869, and who, according to the inscription on his tombstone in the Protestant Cemetery, 'during 53 years painted the classic scenes of Rome with truth and beauty and never ceased to be an Englishman'.

At the time when Severn was making his way to St. John's Lateran, only a few of the social customs in Rome were changed. From its outer steps, he could still gaze at a countryside unaltered since the day of his first arrival with John Keats. He could still hear a similar clattering of horses' hooves. As fifty years beforehand, carriage-folk were constantly arguing about the type of coachman whom they ought to employ: *un giovanotto elegante o un 'uomo di presenza?* An elegant youth or an older man of good appearance?

The young Roman coachman with a comely figure and an innate sense of dress caused many young hearts to lose a beat, but he drove too fast. Like his charioteer ancestor, he believed that it was a pedestrian's duty to slink close to a wall whenever he ventured down a narrow street without a pavement. Horses, as they shied at strange sights or noises, were often soon out of control. The wages of an *uomo di presenza* cost a little more than those of a *giovanotto elegante*, but the breakages of limb or carriage-wheel were less likely to be frequent.

Inside the basilica—and by no means for the first time—Severn looked at the full-length portrait which Thomas Lawrence had painted of his own English sovereign, King George IV. There was more than one reason why Rome should show honour to this unconventional

Hanoverian Protestant. He was not merely the first sovereign in England to send a personal letter to a Pope; he had also paid a delicate tribute to his distant Stuart kinsmen who were buried in St. Peter's. Last among them was Henry Stuart, known in Rome as Cardinal York and to his more ardent English and Scottish supporters as King Henry IX. For many years he was Archpriest of St. Peter's and Bishop of Frascati. He died—the last of the direct Stuart line—in 1807 and bequeathed his claim to the English throne to King Charles Emmanuel IV of Savoy.

By this time, Charles Emmanuel had abdicated in favour of his brother, Victor Emmanuel I, and was living in Rome as a Jesuit. If the claim to the English throne was eventually transmitted to Victor Emmanuel II, neither he nor Queen Victoria seemed to know anything about it, still less to allow any ruffling to spoil a State visit to Windsor. Nor did it impair the regard which George IV showed for the exiled Stuarts. At his own expense, he commissioned Canova to carve a graceful memorial to them in St. Peter's.

Lawrence also painted a full-length portrait of Pius VII. The exchange of courtesies between Catholic and Protestant rulers was admirable; and the Protestant painter of an altar-piece in one arch-basilica could scarcely complain if a Protestant's portrait of a Protestant King was found in another; more especially since it was in George IV's reign that the Catholics of Great Britain and Ireland obtained their political emancipation.

Severn, however, was no longer the young painter who left Regency England for Rome. In late middle age he had gone back to Victorian London, where the only English monarch since Charles I who had any sense of taste—however eccentric it may have been—was now numbered among the Queen's 'wicked uncles'. Great was his distress when, entering St. John's Lateran in the early summer of 1871, he saw that a whole row of peasants from the countryside were reverently kneeling in front of the royal portrait. They believed that they were looking at the image of a saint.

Monsignori listened with respect to the protest of a painter-consul. Lawrence's portrait of an English King was withdrawn from the Lateran church and did not regain any prominence until, more than half a century later, Pius XI built a separate picture gallery in his new Vatican City State. The days of Severn's consulate, however, soon drew to a close. He belonged to a leisurely age. Rome may have been slow to change outwardly during the first year of Savoyard rule, but the tempo quickened. Younger and more active consuls were needed.

Each Embassy brought its permanent staff, and few who had worked in Turin welcomed the move first to Florence and then to Rome. Ambassadors talked as though they had reached Italy's final capital, but they were seldom in a hurry to rent an unfurnished residence or to bring the Embassy furniture from Florence. Savoyard rule might have lasted no longer in Rome than Mazzini's. It was a fortunate day for King Francis when the French Government rented his partially furnished Farnese Palace and used it as the Embassy. At last a republican France brought benefits to a Bourbon.

Meanwhile the Governments which had Embassies in Rome before the loss of the Temporal Power retained their diplomatic relationship with the Holy See. In a time of uncertainty, this was a double insurance. The Kings of Italy and Spain were father and son, and for a while the historic Spanish Embassy, from which the Piazza di Spagna takes its name, was used by both of Spain's Ambassadors: one half for the Ambassador to the Holy See, and the other for the Ambassador to the Kingdom of Italy. Few observers seriously believed that an Ambassador never met his opposite number or that there were no ties of personal friendship or blood between the black and the white patricians; but the façade of two *corps diplomatiques*, two societies and two men entitled to sovereign honours, was zealously observed. The world had to know that there was a family quarrel.

A Cardinal loved his three nephews. Each in turn was called to the colours. Before donning military uniform, each called on his uncle. The Cardinal charged each one never to cross his threshold again until the military uniform was laid aside.

As a prisoner, Pius refused to go to his people, but they came to him. Each Sunday afternoon the people of a parish went in turn with their priest to the Sala Regia, where, as their Bishop, Pius humbly expounded the Gospel of the day. He could be rude to a Government and use harsh epithets, but he was never rude to the people. There were times when he looked on Victor Emmanuel more as a fellow-prisoner than as a King invested with power. The Ministers he did not deign to know, but Victor Emmanuel was the head of a family which had produced a galaxy of saints, Bishops, priests and warriors. One day, perhaps, each would need the help of the other.

It so happened that Rome's Cardinal Vicar was troubled by a complaint from the head of a small seminary in a crowded part of the city. Close to the seminary was a house tenanted by young women of easy virtue, and they were distracting the students. The Cardinal Vicar asked the Pope what ought to be done. After an impressive silence, Pius said that he had found the answer. The Cardinal Vicar could go away in peace. As soon as he was alone, Pius sent for the Marquess

Crispolto Crispolti, who was the lieutenant of the Noble Guard on duty for that day.

'Crispolti, we have a very delicate task to entrust to you.'

'I await your orders, Holiness!'

'We must send you abroad on a confidential mission.'

'I go where Your Holiness commands.'

'Very well then! Go and change straight away into civilian dress and come back here.'

As Crispolti later told his friends, he expected at least to be sent to Washington or to Constantinople.

On his return, the Pope said with more than a touch of irony. 'You must place this letter in the hands of the person to whom it is addressed. Look and see to whom it is going.'

Crispolti read: 'To King Victor Emmanuel, at the Quirinal.' Though astounded, he did what he was told to do. At the Quirinal Palace, he said: 'I am the Marquess Crispolti, lieutenant of His Holiness's Noble Guard, and I have a letter to deliver personally to His Majesty the King.'

Crispolti was at once led to the room of the adjutant on duty.

'His Majesty is at present resting,' the adjutant said. 'Please give me the letter.'

'No sir! Like you, I am a soldier, and I know my duty. I can deliver the letter only in person to His Majesty.'

'Then, please wait!'

When the King awoke, he showed his annoyance that anyone sent to him by the Pope should have been kept waiting, and he received Crispolti warmly. He read the letter and begged the bearer to tell the Pope that his request would be met within twenty-four hours. Soon he called his Ministers together and read the letter to them.

After describing the plight of the young seminarists, the Pope continued in his letter:

'I am more than ever convinced that Rome cannot be the seat of the Vicar of Christ and of Belial. May Your Majesty take action within the limits of your powers and in agreement with your Ministers . . . Full of paternal affection, I pray to God for Your Majesty, I pray to Him for Italy, I pray to Him for the Catholic Church.'

The King, as he read the letter aloud, stressed and repeated the reference to Belial. Hitherto he alone had been Belial in the papal vocabulary. The Ministers noted with approval that Pius expected the King to act strictly in agreement with them. 'As Your Majesty will see,' one of them said, 'the Pope has indeed become constitutional.'

At this point Lanza, now Minister of the Interior, observed that the

King exceeded his own powers when he gave an oral promise to the lieutenant of the Noble Guard. Not even the head of the Government could turn tenants out of a house which they had rented if, so doing, he broke the law. There were no legal means of forcing the young women to leave the house.

Which should the King break: the law, or his promise to the Pope? Victor Emmanuel solved the problem by paying the women to go away within twenty-four hours; and he paid handsomely out of his own pocket.

It was not long before the Cardinal Vicar admitted to the Pope that the young women were back in the house under a new lease. 'If,' the Cardinal Vicar began, 'Your Holiness should wish to return to the system which worked so well last time . . . '

'Poor son,' the Pope replied. 'No, I don't want him to spend any more money.'

As the prisoner of the Vatican, Pius was unable to see the physical changes of his former capital. Visitors judged them to be good or bad according to their temperaments. It was fortunate that, when Henry James went back to Rome in 1872-73, his older brother, William, eventually joined him. Henry had already lost his heart to the city, but William—the philosopher who ought to have been a novelist— was seeing it for the first time. His sympathies were with Emerson's daughter, Ellen, who 'actually grew afraid at last that she might be going to think Rome a greater place than Concord'.

Like many other visitors to Rome, Henry James received his first warning of a fundamental change when he saw a newspaper stand in which journals other than the *Osservatore Romano* and the *Voce della Verità* were on sale. It meant the loss of an old connection with 'the extraordinary leisure of thought and stillness of mind to which the place admitted you'. New people, moreover, were now strolling along the narrow Corso. Although Henry James enjoyed the spectacle of many finely attired Italian dandies, 'these goodly throngs of them scarce offered compensation for the absent Monsignori, treading the streets in their purple stockings and followed by the solemn servants who returned on their behalf the bows of the meaner sort; for the mourning gear of the Cardinals' coaches that formerly glittered with scarlet and swung with the weight of the footmen clinging behind; for the certainty that you'll not, by the best of traveller's luck, meet the Pope sitting deep in the shadow of his great chariot with uplifted fingers like some inaccessible idol in his shrine. You may meet the King indeed, who is as ugly, as imposingly ugly, as some idols, though not so inaccessible.'

Like Pius and Joseph Severn, Henry James enjoyed looking at the unspoilt view from the top of the Lateran Hill. During his former visit, he had 'wasted much time in sitting on the steps of the church and watching certain white-cowled friars who were sure to be passing there for the delight of my eyes. There are fewer friars now, and there are a great many of the King's recruits, who inhabit the ex-conventual barracks adjoining Santa Croce and are led forward to practise their goose-step on the sunny turf . . . Here too the poor old Cardinals, who are no longer to be seen on the Pincio, descend from their mourning coaches and relax their venerable knees. These members alone still testify to the traditional splendour of the Princes of the Church; for as they advance, the lifted black petticoat reveals a flash of scarlet stockings and makes you groan at the victory of civilization over colour.'

The Cardinals chose to exercise their limbs between the Lateran church and the smaller basilica of Santa Croce for no better reason than the attraction which the Pincio gardens now had for the Royal family and other newcomers to Rome. 'Yesterday,' Henry James wrote, 'Prince Humbert's little *primogenito* was on the Pincio in an open landau with his governess. He's a sturdy blond little man and the image of the King. They had stopped to listen to the music, and the crowd was planted about the carriage-wheels, staring and criticising under the child's snub little nose. It appeared bold cynical curiosity, without the slightest manifestation of "loyalty", and it gave me a singular sense of the vulgarization of Rome under the new régime. When the Pope drove abroad it was a solemn spectacle; even if you neither kneeled nor uncovered you were irresistibly impressed. But the Pope never stopped to listen to opera tunes, and he had no little popelings under the charge of superior nurse-maids, whom you might take liberties with.

'The family at the Quirinal make something of a merit, I believe, of their modest and inexpensive way of life. The merit is great; yet, representationally, what a change for the worst from an order which proclaimed stateliness a part of its essence!'

Before Henry James made his return visit to Rome, the newcomers had stripped the foliage from the Baths of Caracalla, where Shelley once loved to roam, to meditate and to read; they uprooted from the Colosseum 'the high-growing wild flowers', on which an Englishman had written a learned book; they tidied up the Roman Forum; they provided a live wolf with a grotto on the edge of the Capitoline Hill; and they had, indeed, begun to build a new European capital. Yet the young American writer was free to pace the shady country lane 'which connects St. John's Lateran with Santa Maria Maggiore'. He rode at ease through the cork-woods of Monte Mario, which reminded him of New Hampshire, or else over the pleasant meadows which led from the Villa Doria-Pamphili to the basilica of St. Paul's-beyond-the-Walls. From most of the gateways, half an hour's progress through winding lanes brought him to open country. He particularly liked a canter and a gallop to Veii, citadel of the Etruscans, who, if only they had defeated the Romans in a crucial battle, might have altered the course of human history; 'over acres of daisied turf, a long, long gallop is certainly a supersubtle joy'.

Sometimes the newcomers rescued old buildings from their neglect or misuse under the old papal rulers. Henry James was grieved to discover that mud and stones made the road to the Villa Madama on a slope of Monte Mario almost impassable, while the Villa itself was turned into 'the shabbiest farm house'. 'Margaret Farnese was the lady of the house, but where she trailed her cloth of gold, the chickens now scamper between your legs over rotten straw.' Nor was Henry James altogether pleased to find beggars and peasants lounging on the great steps which lead to the church of the Ara Coeli: 'this huge black staircase, moulding away in disuse, the weeds thick in its crevices and climbing to the rudely solemn façade of the church'.

He wrote too soon. In a subsequent year, the Italian Government restored the Villa Madama to its former dignity and elegance, so that it might be used for the entertainment of State visitors. Before long, the steps of the Ara Coeli were weeded and repaired, while the loafers were turned away. Attitudes were changing, even in the Vicariate of Rome. Don Roberto, wrote Matilda Lucas, 'has mortally offended the artists because he has refused to hear confession from any girl who sits as a model; the artists are very offended because the girls are afraid to sit to them'.

In the end, the newcomers treated the artist models in the same way as they treated the loafers on the steps of the Ara Coeli, and they were forbidden to wait on the Spanish Steps to be hired. St. Johns, Satans and Eternal Fathers went out of fashion; and when the Sicilian sculptor, Mario Rutelli, was commissioned to carve the water-nymphs for Rome's largest modern fountain, close to the church of Santa Maria degli Angeli, he went to Anticoli, a mountain-village beyond Tivoli, for his models. New Rome was spiritually at war with the old.

William James saw more clearly than his brother, Henry, that the conflict was good. He respected art more as an activity than as an artifice. 'The ancients,' he argued, 'did things by doing the business of their own day, not by gaping at their grandfathers' tombs—and the

normal man of today will do likewise.' He loved Rome's 'geological
stratification of history' all the more because he was seeing its continuous and often painful changes with his own eyes. Rome was becoming
as volcanic as Naples.

The first assault on Rome's garland of villas was the destruction
of the Villa Negroni, soon to be followed by that of the neighbouring
Villa Strozzi. The trees were felled, the gardens and their fountains
dismantled, and the whole area between Termini station and Santa
Maria Maggiore webbed with commonplace streets, a few hotels and
many tall apartment houses. Later, when the Countess of Mirafiori
ceased to be its tenant, the Duke of Sora once more admitted to the
Villa Ludovisi those visitors who had first applied to his banker; but
within a short period of time the villa and its spacious garden slid into
the clutches of the speculative builder. The Roman region beloved by
Stendhal disappeared.

While William and Henry James sparred with each other about the
merits of Victor Emmanuel's new capital city, Augustus Hare voiced
the grievances of the titled and well-to-do English visitors to Rome.
One and all, he believed, regarded the newcomers from the north as
philistines and spoliators. 'The absence of Pope, Cardinals and monks;
the shutting up of the convents; the loss of the ceremonies; the misery
caused by the terrible taxes and conscription; the voluntary exile of
the Borgheses and many other noble families; the total destruction of
the glorious Villa Negroni and so much else of interest and beauty;
the ugly new streets in imitation of Paris and New York, all grate
against one's former Roman associations. And to set against this, there
is so very little—a gayer Pincio, a live wolf on the Capitol, a mere
scrap of excavation in the Forum, and all is said.'

A decade later the spoliation was more intense. Almost the whole
of the Esquiline Hill was limbed with streets, mean or pretentious, and
through their centre ran the new Via Nazionale intended to deprive
the Corso of its status as Rome's chief thoroughfare. The Castel
Sant'Angelo was no longer the bastion which once sharply divided the
city from the countryside, and no window of the Vatican now enabled
the Pope to see the meadows which hitherto sloped gently from its
walls to the rustic banks of the tawny-coloured Tiber; for they were
covered by a maze of housetops. 'Twelve years of Sardinian rule,'
moaned Hare, 'have done more for the destruction of Rome, with its
beauty and interest, than the invasions of the Goths and Vandals. The
whole aspect of the city is changed, and the picturesqueness of old days
must now be sought in such obscure corners as have escaped the hand
of the spoiler.'

Other writers made similar complaints. George Gissing, for example, saw Rome for the first time only in 1888; and that was the year when the Celian—the most graceful of the city's seven hills—was robbed of the Villa Campana and the Villa Casali, so that enough space might be found for a new military hospital. All the district round the Castel Sant'Angelo, Gissing wrote, 'is now being built upon, and great ugly barrack-like houses are rising thick. Indeed modern Rome is extremely ugly'. Five years later, John Addington Symonds declared that the Rome which he had loved in 1863 was lost. 'But I cannot deplore change when change means prosperity. Does it so here? The Ludovisi Villa has become a nest of bourgeois habitations . . . I see little of real wealth about. The faces of the shops in the vast new quarters are poor, like stores set up by squatters in some Californian mining stations.'

The newcomers from the north were not only the spoilers of old Rome. They arrived in a hurry; they had given no previous thought to town-planning; and they were pressed for time. The King and his heir believed in military strength, no matter how much it might cost, while the Ministers struggled to secure a balanced budget. Almost all the new buildings arose within the Aurelian walls. They included barracks and banks as well as Embassies, consulates and Government buildings; and houses were needed for a population which grew from about 244,000 in 1871 to about 300,000 ten years later. The value of the land within the walls increased sharply, so that owners of villas began to sell portions of their parkland or gardens. Then, seeing that the harmonious pattern of architecture and landscape was lost, they were soon tempted to sacrifice the actual villa.

If the newcomers were blamed for putting temptation in the way of Roman landowners, their victims offered little resistance. A handsome bank balance meant more than outward style. Where their forebears built for show, the Romans were now building or selling for profit. The difference of aim was fundamental.

Nor was speculation in land an entirely new feature of Roman life; for when land was needed for building the Via Nazionale and other streets on the Esquiline Hill, one of the chief vendors was Monsignor François-Xavier de Merode, the Belgian brother-in-law of Montalembert and the Pope's former Minister of War. He had been an almost fanatical supporter of the Temporal Power; but, unlike Antonelli, he wanted Pius to leave Rome after his capitulation. Whether the Pope went or stayed, de Merode was willing enough to sell his land at a high price. Business, after all, could be done with the newcomers. Every property-owner in Rome, ecclesiastical or lay, craved for stability.

Augustus Hare expressed the views and prejudices of a conservative coterie of well-connected English ladies who, whether residents or visitors, liked ivy-clad ruins, balconies draped with foliage and glimpses of picturesque, if sunless, alleys. Rome was a romantic city in which to sketch or to saunter, but the northerners were flaying it with their tidier ways and bustle. Yet, in the very year when William and Henry James sparred with each other over the virtue or vulgarization of the new Rome, the English residents were planning to build their own Anglican church within the Aurelian walls. So were the American Episcopalians.

Each community chose for its separate church the same English architect, G. E. Street. The Americans built their church of St. Paul's-within-the-Walls on the new Via Nazionale, which was, at least, an appropriate site. The English, on the other hand, deliberately built their church on the old Via Babuino, which leads from the Piazza di Spagna to the Piazza del Popolo. For more than a century, the Piazza di Spagna had been their Roman ghetto, and if the new church marred the architectural charm of the Via Babuino, it was well within walking distance. As faithful Protestants in a Catholic country, they had not forgotten that horses, like oxen and asses, must do no work on the Sabbath day.

Though Americans employed the same architect as the English and commissioned Edward Burne-Jones to paint the frescoes in the apse, no one in Rome seems to have thought it strange that the Americans and the English should worship in separate Protestant churches. The alienation was a legacy of the American War of Independence. Before 1776, all the American 'Plantations' as well as all the stations of the East India Company were under the spiritual jurisdiction of the Bishop of London, who ruled them indifferently from Fulham Palace on a bank of the Thames. Hitherto no Protestant Bishop had ever set foot in North America. George Berkeley, the philosopher from Ireland, lived for a while in Rhode Island, but he was then a Dean, and not yet Bishop of Cloyne. Thus the day of independence left the American Episcopalians without any Bishops of their own. They were aggrieved by Canterbury. On the advice of Martin Routh—the President of Magdalen College, Oxford, who died in his hundredth year—they elected their own Bishops and then sent them to Scotland, and not to England, for their consecration.

The Church of England was rooted in national, and almost insular, pride. Yet its Prayer Book followed the flag and was used by every captain of an English ship whenever he conducted a Sunday morning service or presided over a burial at sea. When the English church in the Via Babuino was completed, Augustus Hare and his friends would follow the familiar prayers for 'our sovereign lady Queen Victoria', for 'Albert Edward Prince of Wales', and for 'the High Court of Parliament'. They were the prayers heard in Bombay Cathedral, where the side aisles were occupied by men and women whose blood was mixed with Indian, or whose parents, though both English, had failed through poverty to give them an education outside India. They belonged to the Church of India's governors. In a hostile and caste-ridden country, it was their hall-mark of social superiority.

In the previous decade, Charles Longley, Archbishop of Canterbury, made a bold attempt to transcend the national spirit by inviting all the Bishops who were in Anglican orders to journey to London for the first Lambeth Conference. The experiment was not an unqualified success. William Thomson, Archbishop of York, refused to attend, and Dean Arthur Stanley forbade the Bishops to hold a special service in Westminster Abbey. Full reconciliation between the English-speaking people lay far in the future. If the first Lambeth Conference was recent history, so also was the Alabama dispute; and some old American and English residents in Rome vaguely remembered the time when their two countries were again at war with each other. Unlike worshippers in the English church in the Via Babuino, no American would enter his church in the Via Nazionale to pray for the granddaughter or other descendants of King George III. The separate churches showed that, like the Romans, the Anglo-Americans had their own family quarrel.

Separateness, in fact, has never been completely absent from Roman worship. Pilgrims from the different countries have always travelled together, and they like to hear Mass together when they reach Rome. In 728, King Ina founded the church of Santo Spirito, not far from St. Peter's, for the benefit of his fellow-pilgrims from Saxony. In 775, King Offa of the East Saxons founded another church which, when rebuilt in the twelfth century, was dedicated to Thomas Beckett, the martyred Archbishop of Canterbury.

To this day, every nation in Europe has its own church in Rome, and so has every Italian region. Lombards, when they live or stay in Rome, go to San Carlo in Corso; Tuscans to San Giovanni dei Fiorentini; and Neapolitans to Santo Spirito dei Napolitani. To this day, too, English Catholics go to San Silvestro in Capite, and American Catholics to Santa Susanna. Even as Catholics, English and Americans keep apart. So also do the English and the Irish. If Rome is one of the world's most cosmopolitan cities, it gives a fair play to individual nationhood.

CHAPTER EIGHT

RENDERING UNTO CAESAR

THE CONFLICT between Church and State was bound to be long and acrimonious. Men who sought reconciliation and harmony feared that they were outnumbered by men who, on both sides, hugged petty triumphs over their adversary. Prelates were often more papal than the Pope, and statesmen more royalist than the King. Those who once governed the Pontifical State in the Pope's name were conditioned to theocratic rule. They did not care to know how much they should now render unto Caesar. The freedom which the Church demanded, so Marco Minghetti told the Chamber of Deputies in 1873, 'is not freedom, as we understand it; that is to say, common right. On the contrary, it is privilege; independence from the laws of the State; and exclusive control over education, charity and civil acts. This is not freedom, but monopoly.'

Catholics, ran a Vatican decree, were to be 'neither electors nor elected'. They were free to take part in municipal elections, but no man was to enter the Chamber of Deputies as a faithful Catholic or with the votes of other faithful Catholics. In a country of about twenty-four million inhabitants, little more than half a million were accorded the right to vote. None the less, the enfranchised few represented the nation's élite, and almost all of them were Catholics by baptism and upbringing.

If the Savoyards were usurpers in Rome, they were not usurpers in Sardinia or Piedmont; and only the Austrians might have regarded them as usurpers in Lombardy or Venetia. Charles Albert's Constitution was never revoked by his son. Victor Emmanuel was a constitutional ruler; and in those parts of Italy where the Pope had hitherto acknowledged his sovereignty, the Vatican decree was an interference with the civil rights of the people.

The decree, in fact, defeated its own purpose. If every Catholic in Italy had obeyed the Pope, the elections would have been a farce and Parliament a mockery. The political élite soon learned how to be Catholic with the Pope and liberal with the State. Parliament worked all the more effectively because there was no clerical caucus within the Chamber of Deputies to obstruct liberal legislation. The sense of freedom and maturity grew stronger in Rome, while the memory of interminable visits to police office or sacristy were vanishing.

Yet if prelates forgot what they should render unto Caesar, statesmen had often vague notions of what they should render unto God. The first few years of parliamentary life in Rome were marred by legislative measures which need never have been introduced. In Protestant England, for example, no clergyman received the accolade of knighthood from his sovereign because it was judged to be unseemly that anyone should require a 'clerk in holy orders' to wield the sword. It was not long, however, before the Parliament in Rome agreed that priests and seminarists should be made liable for military service. In the next century, the Church might be ruled by a Pope who had once served in the ranks of the Italian army.

Bitterness was largely the product of fear. Pius spoke as though the loss of his Temporal Power was not permanent. One day an ally would come to his rescue; but the most powerful man in Europe was now Bismarck, Chancellor in the new and victorious German Empire. His Lutheran background made him react sharply against the 'retrograde' dogma of papal infallibility. In the belief that Pius was as much a fallen sovereign as his own former prisoner, Napoleon III, he mocked at the triple tiara, which symbolized the power to loosen and to bind in hell, on earth and in heaven. Let the Pope have his power over heaven and hell, said Bismarck, 'but the earth is mine'.

Angered by retaliatory words from Pius, the German Chancellor reflected that it was no longer possible to punish the offender by sending a naval ship to threaten his old port of Civitavecchia with bombardment. Stripped of all territory, Pius was free to hurl denunciations at the Italians and at the rulers of foreign countries. The papal quill, when wisely used, was stronger than the sword.

Sometimes, when Pius quarrelled with a Government, the blow fell indirectly on an individual. One victim was Ferdinand Gregorovius who, like Bismarck, came from East Prussia. He had spent many years collecting the material for his elaborate and imaginative 'History of Rome in the Middle Ages'. Almost all the Roman libraries, including the vast one in the Vatican, were accessible to him. Through the Duke of Sermoneta, he met Cardinal de Luca, Secretary for the Congregation of the Holy Office. The Cardinal knew German and had read the first volume or two of the 'History'. Later, when the early volumes were translated into Italian and published in Venice, they attracted the attention of the Jesuits and were severely criticized in their influential journal, *Civiltà Cattolica*.

Few readers of this 'History', which became a best-seller with the
Italians nearly a century later, can have doubted that it was written
by a non-Catholic: a man of letters who loved Rome and was yet
unable to feel completely at home within its Church. He could have
remained a sympathetic outsider, but the spirit of partnership warred
against him. At the end of March 1870, when the definition of papal
infallibility was becoming the dominant issue with the Bishops in St.
Peter's, he was refused certain manuscripts in the Vatican Library. He
saw the malicious smile of Father Bollich, a Jesuit, and he knew that
his hour had come. Yet he was not greatly troubled, for his massive
work was now almost finished.

Four years later Gregorovius heard that the 'History' had been put
on the Index. The particular decree was published in the *Osservatore
Romano* and it bore the signature of Cardinal de Luca. According to
an ancient custom, copies of a decree which put a book on the Index
were affixed to the entrances of St. Peter's, St. John's Lateran, Santa
Maria Maggiore, the Chancellery and the Curia Innocenziana. The loss
of the Temporal Power made it impossible to affix copies of the decree
to the entrances of the Chancellery and the Curia Innocenziana, but
Gregorovius hurried to the three basilicas.

Unknown friends, he found, had torn down the notices in St. Peter's
and Santa Maria Maggiore. The one in St. John's Lateran, however,
was put beyond their reach, and Gregorovius showed it proudly to
his brother, an army officer, when he arrived in Rome a week later.
'If the priests had prohibited my book after the publication of the
first volume, the work would not exist today because they would have
closed all the libraries to me . . . Only now have they shot the arrow,
not so much against me as against Prussia, where Bismarck, like a new
Diocletian, persecutes Christianity, as the priests insist, and perhaps also
against the municipality of Rome, which subsidizes the printing of my
'History' in Venice. My work is completed and circulates throughout
the world: the Pope now makes propaganda out of it.'

Father Bollich, the Jesuit with a malicious smile, was not an Italian,
and it is strange how many unkind gestures recorded in the closing
years of Pius's reign were made by foreigners who saw the surfaces
of action, but not its hidden springs. Augustus Hare and his English
ladies, Protestant though they were, bemoaned the seizure of the
convents. They did not notice how often the inmates were given alternative and, perhaps, more convenient accommodation. Benedictines,
Dominicans and Franciscans still walked through the Corso in their
traditional garb, and some of the sandal-wearers were men of world
renown. The mean new streets failed to rob the ordinary Roman of

his gentleness and courtesy. If orders were harsh, a way was sought to make their execution smooth.

Cardinal de Luca read the first volume of the 'History of Rome in the Middle Ages' long before Gregorovius found himself excluded from the Vatican Library. The offender was popular neither with the Jesuits nor with German professors jealous of the prestige gained by a writer who had no University chair. The Secretary to the Holy Office could have acted much sooner. To his credit he let time slide away, and the historian was enabled to finish a life's work. Though Gregorovius joked about the Index, he pondered sadly on the libraries which he must never again enter and on their scholarly readers or staff whose friendly glances and words he had valued. Once he belonged to a Roman commonwealth. Now he was officially an alien. On another level, however, he was not an alien at all; for the municipality enrolled him as a Roman citizen.

No matter how proudly Victor Emmanuel swaggered through the salons of the unlikeable Quirinal Palace, he was obsessed with the feeling that Rome did not yet belong to him. He shared it with another: the priestly ruler who, Sunday after Sunday, received the people of a Roman parish; the prisoner who, when he went to the top of the Vatican garden, saw all Rome at his feet.

To please his Ministers, Victor Emmanuel paid State visits to the Emperor Wilhelm I in Berlin and to the Emperor Francis Joseph in Vienna. He did not hesitate to tell the German Emperor that, if allowed his own way, he would have fought for France in the recent war. Rome should have witnessed the return State visits of these two Emperors—the one a Protestant, and the other a Catholic. Victor Emmanuel, however, shared their reluctance to offend the Pope. Accordingly, he went to Milan to receive the German Emperor, and to Venice to receive the Austrian Emperor. As long as he reigned in Rome, no other crowned head entered the palace which was once the Pope's.

Though Italians were masters in the arts of compromise and good personal relations, they seldom realized how often their invective and sharpness of statement startled or stung the foreigner. Nicholas Wiseman lived for many years in Rome as Rector of the English College. An early meeting with Newman, then still an Anglican, encouraged him to believe that the English people were slowly turning towards the Catholic Church. He waited patiently and Gladstone, when he called at the college on the feast day of Thomas Beckett, was delighted to find that its Rector was not a proselytizer. Yet, when Pius made him a Cardinal and the first Archbishop of Westminster in 1850, Wiseman issued the famous letter 'out of the Flaminian Gate' which infuriated the English and convinced them that they were soon to be the victims of a papal 'aggression'.

At present, the letter declared, 'and until such time as the Holy See shall think fit otherwise to provide, we govern, and shall continue to govern, the Counties of Middlesex, Hertford and Essex as Ordinary thereof, and those of Surrey, Sussex, Kent, Berkshire and Hampshire with the islands annexed, as administrator with ordinary jurisdiction'. Even if Wiseman did not actually draft the letter which bore his name, only the long years spent in Rome or in Monte Porzio on the Alban Hills could excuse the bombastic and Italianate style. It made Queen Victoria ask: 'Am I the Queen of England, or am I not?'

In vain Gladstone spoke against a bill which forbade Wiseman and his fellow-Bishops to use English territorial titles. He knew that Wiseman might have used gentler language. Yet, nearly a quarter-century later, he was himself hurling denunciations at Rome, and he called his pamphlet 'The Vatican Decrees in their Bearing on Civil Allegiance'. If he sold 150,000 copies in a few weeks and made about £2,000, he owed not a little of his luck to Pius, who declared that he was 'a viper attacking the bark of St. Peter'. Gladstone was an Anglo-Catholic and by no means anxious to rekindle the fires of Protestant indignation; but, even if distressed by reports from Lord Acton on the support which Pius gave to Manning's manoeuvres at the Vatican Council, he forgot that after the storm there came calm, and even forgiveness. Three years went by before Pius made any new Cardinals, and his list was fair and objective. Not until 1875 did he make Manning a Cardinal. Outside Italy Pius was never the foe of true civil allegiance.

Words envenom. The Catholic Bishops in England defied the law against the use of their territorial titles. It became a dead letter and was at last repealed; but the young men who read Gladstone's pamphlet had been children when parents and nursemaids alike still talked about the papal 'aggression'. The Church of Rome was the 'scarlet woman', and some were unable to escape from their early indoctrination. This explains, but does not excuse, the conduct of an unnamed Englishman employed at the Embassy. During an audience, wrote Matilda Lucas, he 'crossed his legs, folded his arms and kept his seat, staring rudely at him. The Pope was furious and raised his stick. The Cardinals, fearing an undignified outburst of temper, pushed him out of the room. Sir Augustus Paget sacked him.'

There was an unfortunate sequel. 'The other day,' Matilda Lucas continued, 'a perfectly inoffensive woman went to an audience with her family, and when the Pope heard what nation they were, he made a gesture of disgust and contempt, and passed on without even looking at them. The English lady was so much shocked that she nearly fainted. Father Smith, who called here the other day, said that there were strict orders to admit no English to the Vatican.'

Pius bore burdens far heavier than the rudeness of an English stranger. For years he had been unfaltering in his loyalty to the Cardinal who stood by him while the mob was assailing the Quirinal Palace. In the end, he knew that his once powerful Secretary of State was avaricious and worldly. In 1876, when he heard that Antonelli was dying, he sent word bidding him to make a good death. Then came one shock after another. Antonelli's fortune was enormous, and his three brothers were its inheritors. Soon the Countess Lambertini claimed that she was Antonelli's daughter, and she started a legal process in Rome to obtain a share of the fortune. The viper which had attacked 'the bark of St. Peter' was not Gladstone, but a peasant's grandson; a spiritual child of the Renaissance; a lover of jewels and fair women born in the wrong century.

Pius lived simply because he loved the things which money cannot buy: music, the open air, the play of wit and the friendliness of the poor. He delighted in the singing of Father Giovanni del Papa, a humble Capuchin who lived at the Ara Coeli, the convent on the Capitoline. 'Music,' said the Capuchin, 'is the prelude to Paradise.' He came from Lucca and, when a young man, he fell from a cart and broke a leg so badly that the chance of saving it was slender. Whereupon he vowed that if his leg was spared, he would become a friar.

This did not exempt him from army service, and his two years in the artillery were spent chiefly in tracking down brigands. Then a brother volunteered to take his place in the ranks, and the friar went back to the convent. He preached to the 'galley-slaves' and heard confessions. Later, preaching and the confessional were abandoned: 'the shouting of the one and the whispering of the other are equally injurious to his voice'. Father Giovanni often used to sing in the salons of the black aristocracy, but his love for the Pope prevented him from accepting the King's invitation to sing in the Quirinal Palace.

After Pius had stopped him from going out in society, he sang in the homes of personal friends. One evening a little girl told Pius that Father Giovanni had arrived at the apartment of an officer and his wife who lived inside the Vatican. A few minutes later, a servant appeared at the door with a bottle of Bordeaux wine and a pineapple. He also brought a message in which Pius told Father Giovanni that he must take some refreshment before going out into the night air.

Rome in the night air had an ashen splendour. Stars shone in a smokeless sky. Fountains cascaded in deserted streets. Water dripped from balconies and window-sills laden with flowers. Cats prowled as stealthily as panthers. Voices were stilled or lost their harshness. Blemishes were revealed only by daylight; for some old streets and houses which Hare's friends called picturesque were even meaner in their original construction than the new ones rising near the Castel Sant'Angelo or on the site of the Villa Negroni. Yet the elements had reshaped and coloured them. They hummed with life, present or departed.

If a returning visitor found that a new building marred his once favourite view, time was the healer and might soften the crudeness of an ugly contour: 'nature, while she worketh, sleepeth as a dream'. By day or by night, the Roman light was the gentlest in the Mediterranean world, and most newcomers were enchanted by what they saw. They looked on Rome as a city still invaded by the countryside.

In the summer of 1877, Oscar Wilde entered it for the first time. He was barely 22, but he read Greek with ease, and his eyes had recently feasted on the ancient glories of Athens and Mycenae. The Acropolis might have dimmed the grandeur of the Forum, or Agamemnon's open-natured Kingdom of olive groves surpassed the charm of Latium, but Wilde loved Rome as he rode with a Miss Fletcher through unspoilt lanes and beyond the Aurelian walls. Perhaps, since he had an inborn dislike of walking, he went on horseback along a well-shaded road to the Protestant Cemetery, where Keats—the Greek who knew no Greek—was buried. 'Someway standing by his grave I felt that he too was a martyr, and worthy to lie in the City of Martyrs. I thought of him as a Priest of Beauty slain before his time, a lovely Sebastian killed by the arrows of a lying and unjust tongue.'

Pius had ruled over the Church for thirty-one years. He outlived Gregory's Cardinals, and those who would elect his successor owed to him their elevation to the Sacred College. Rome talked incessantly about the likely successor and how he might change the attitude of the Holy See to the House of Savoy and the Kingdom of Italy. All men and women live under sentence of death, but few endure the knowledge that a chattering world awaits the day when the sentence is carried out. The loneliness of the victim deepens; he reads men's thoughts. Pius—so unmistakably an Italian—turned to an English Cardinal for friendship. Did he know that Manning would never accept election? Or was the friendship based on a shared secret?

Manning was a widower. To this day a visitor to Chichester Cathedral may see the memorial which, as Archdeacon of Chichester, he erected to his wife. Many years later, when he was Archbishop of

Westminster, a friend told him that his wife's grave was in disrepair. 'It is best so,' he replied. 'Let it be. Time effaces everything.' He had loved; he grieved; and there was work to do. Thereafter he hid his sorrow.

He did not forget. To Bishop Herbert Vaughan, later to succeed him as Archbishop of Westminster, he left a message to be delivered at his death. 'For years you have been a son to me, Herbert: I know not to whom else to leave this—I leave it to you. Into this book my dearest wife wrote her prayers and meditations. Not a day has passed, since her death, on which I have not prayed and meditated from this book. All the good I may have done, all the good I may have been, I owe to her. Take precious care of it.'

How much of his private sorrow did Manning indicate to Pius? And what could Pius have told him in return? Augustus Hare put in writing a story which he heard from Edward Craven Hawtrey, Provost of Eton. Though manifestly wrong in some of its details—and Hare was always an embroiderer—the story may have the substance of truth.

According to the Provost of Eton, there was a Madame de Salis who spent many unhappy years in Rome and then, in her widowhood, returned to Ireland, where her father, William Foster, was the Protestant Bishop of Kilmore. Even in Ireland, she still saw the room in which she had suffered. The remedy, it seemed, was to take her back to this room; but she refused to return to Rome unless her unmarried sister went with her. The family agreed on condition that she never allow her sister to marry a foreigner.

In Rome, however, the sister met young Count Mastai, an officer of the Noble Guard, and now it was her turn to become the invalid. She loved him so much that Madame de Salis had to choose between 'breaking her word and saving her sister's life'.

'When the day came,' Hare's account continues, 'all the friends of Madame de Salis collected in the Church of San Luigi dei Francesi, where the marriage was to take place. According to the custom of brides in Rome, Miss Foster, accompanied by Madame de Salis, came first to the altar and waited for the bridegroom. He never came—he never came at all—he never, never, never was heard of again.'

By his own version of the Provost's story, Hare showed that people certainly heard of Count Giovanni Mastai-Ferretti again. He wrote that the young man set off for the West Indies. Letters were intercepted, and the would-be bridegroom was induced to believe that the Protestant Bishop's daughter no longer cared for him. He was then persuaded to take orders. In the process of time, he became Pope, 'and Miss Foster lived to know of it'.

To become an officer in the Noble Guard was Mastai's early ambition, and the refusal to enrol him must have been a shattering blow. Could a man afflicted with epilepsy dare to embark on matrimony? Or was there a ruthless dual and conflicting conspiracy: a Protestant Bishop determined not to have another foreigner—and a Catholic— for a son-in-law, and a family well esteemed by the Roman aristocracy no less determined to oppose a 'mixed' marriage? Mixed marriages, if they existed at all in the Rome ruled by Pius VII, would have been extremely rare. Miss Foster, it is true, might have already become a Catholic; but why was the church of San Luigi dei Francesi—the church of the French community in Rome—chosen for the marriage of an Anglo-Irish convert?

Yet, even if the Provost's story is dismissed as a fable, it was by no means improbable that a handsome, attractive and well-born subject of the Pope-King fell in love with a girl from a good family in Ireland. There was some discerning reason why Pius VII, whose gentleness influenced even Napoleon I, wanted a frustrated young man to accept orders and then, against the pleadings of his mother, sent him to distant Chile. If Pius once craved for the love of a woman, he was akin to Manning—and akin to countless Bishops and priests who, against their natures, chose the celibate's life for God's greater glory. In old age, when liberated from the promptings of the flesh, Pius and Manning might have spoken dispassionately of the married state. At least, they knew that many dedicated priests found the sacrifice hard to make and to endure.

Peter the prisoner lived on one side of the Tiber. On the other side lived Caesar. Peter ruled the Church. His spiritual authority was absolute. He alone decided who should be made a Cardinal, and when he spoke *ex cathedra*, he was infallible. Caesar was not an absolute ruler. He spoke and acted through his Ministers, and they were dependent on the support of Parliament. The years revealed many short-comings in the Constitution granted by Charles Albert, but the principle of limited monarchy gathered strength. It allowed ample room for development and for a widening of the franchise. In the end, the limited monarchy might be broad-based on the active consent of the Italian people.

Victor Emmanuel displayed his natural common sense when, in 1876, Minghetti and his Cabinet colleagues achieved their goal of a balanced budget and were soon afterwards defeated in the Chamber of Deputies. The leader of the triumphant Opposition was Agostino Depretis, an old supporter of Garibaldi. One of his chief lieutenants was Francesco Crispi, the Sicilian whose entreaties made Garibaldi embark on his fateful expedition. For the sake of Italian unity, Crispi abandoned his former republicanism. 'The monarchy unites us,' he said. 'The republic would divide us.' Many members of the Opposition were probably still republican at heart. Their hostility to the Church might be too wounding. Very much, therefore, depended on how the King would act.

Minghetti and his colleagues, nearly all men from the north, were the avowed heirs of Camille Cavour. They were well-to-do, understood finance and paid a willing tribute to the English parliamentary system. They believed themselves to be liberals, but they became increasingly conservative because they had been in office too long. They had no sure touch with the south, where the average wealth of an individual was only half the average wealth of an individual in the north; where illiteracy was rampant; and where a tax was levied on a peasant's donkey, but not on his landlord's saddle horse. The Right had been Gladstonian in its determination to balance the budget and achieve a parity between revenue and expenditure, but the Left was no less Gladstonian in its desire to make primary education available to every Italian child and to widen the franchise.

The King knew what he must do. As he never cared for the wealthy and the privileged, he let them grumble. The Constitution allowed him enough power to exert his influence; he trusted the new men, and they did not abuse his trust. Depretis won a widespread respect, all the more because he did not hesitate to make politics look prosaic. 'When I see an international question on the horizon,' he once declared, 'I open my umbrella and wait until it has passed.' He continued to live simply, and those who wished to see him at home had to climb more than a hundred steps to his apartment.

Though a northerner, Depretis brought Crispi and other southerners into the Government. They soon showed that, like him, they were practical men. The distinctions between Right and Left became blurred. In later years, when the southern element increased, scandals became numerous, and northerners complained that the south had looser standards of political integrity. They forgot the frank confession of Cavour, their political hero. 'If we did for ourselves what we are doing for Italy,' he told Massimo d'Azeglio, 'we should be great knaves.'

Almost all the low-lying districts of Latium were infested with malaria. This, as the King well knew, provided a sound argument against the choice of Rome for Italy's capital. In the first week of 1878, he fell a victim himself to malaria, though he was not yet 58. On the morning of January 9th, he wanted to go into the fresh air, and he tried in vain to get himself dressed. His condition rapidly worsened. Ministers came and went. The Pope made constant enquiries and lifted the major sentence of excommunication. About midday, the oldest of the three doctors told the King that his last hour was approaching. 'Ah, well then!' he said calmly. 'Here we are!'

A priest heard his confession, and he prepared himself for the Viaticum. When he was no longer capable of speech, he looked in turn at the two half-brothers who were kneeling at each side of the bed. One was Prince Humbert. The other was Count Emmanuel Albert Mirafiori, Rosina's son.

At about half-past two, the King died. The news was at once brought to the Pope, who gave orders for a Mass to be sung in St. John's Lateran. 'He will need a good bath,' Pius said, 'but Heaven is merciful.'

A daughter—Maria Pia, Queen of Portugal—hurried to Rome for the funeral. As she did not want to sleep under the roof of a palace which had been seized from the Pope, she stayed at the Portuguese Embassy. Emmanuel Albert Mirafiori went back to the palace to bid farewell to the father who loved him. 'You may see your father,' the new King was reported to have said. 'But, remember, this is the last time that you cross the threshold.'

Romans in their thousands went to the Quirinal Palace to pay homage to Victor Emmanuel, who was dressed in full uniform with boots, gloves and the cloak of the Grand Master of the Order of the Annunziata: the highest Savoyard order, which was instituted as far back as 1362. The body was displayed at so steep an incline that it seemed to be almost upright. 'It did not look human,' Matilda Lucas complained: 'more like a mastiff or bulldog.'

'The King is dead. The Pope is well.' So wrote Giuseppe Sacchetti in his newspaper. Prince Altieri did not attempt to cancel a ball in his villa, and although all Rome appeared to be watching the long funeral procession to the Pantheon, a conspicuous feature was the absence of the clergy.

Meanwhile the court was offended because Queen Victoria—now the 'grandmother of Europe'—was represented only by the Earl of Roden, a young and unmarried lord-in-waiting. Gladstone had been succeeded as Prime Minister by Benjamin Disraeli, whose father was racially an Italian Jew. Through the centuries, the interregnum between the death of a Pope and election of his successor was always a period of acute anxiety for the Jews living in the Roman ghetto: would the new Pope be a persecutor like John XXII, who had the Talmud publicly burned, or an active protector like Martin V? Less than half a century had passed since Leo XII still compelled the Jews to listen to a Catholic homily in the church of Sant'Angelo in Pescheria. If Pius had died before 1870, who could have been sure that his successor would not re-impose this humiliation? For the Jewish community in Rome the end of theocratic rule had long become a moral necessity.

Quite apart from her Prime Minister's ancestral links with Italy, there was a special reason why Queen Victoria ought to have been more ostentatiously represented at the funeral of Italy's first King. Victor Emmanuel may have been a good and fearless soldier, but his main distinction had been the firm refusal to allow the Constitution of his country to be revoked. Thus the nature of his rule contrasted sharply with the pretentious sabre-rattling of Louis Napoleon, the conspirator who managed to wear an Emperor's mantle for eighteen years. So long as Victor Emmanuel's successors remained strictly constitutional in their actions, Savoy might be still the oldest reigning House in Europe. Or was Mazzini right? Should Demos alone be King?

Ten days after his father's death, Humbert drove in state to the Montecitorio Palace, where he swore to uphold the Constitution. Already he had made an important concession to his Ministers. As King of Sardinia, he would have been Humbert IV, but Crispi insisted that the King of Italy must be called Humbert I. None the less, the motto of his House was still 'Avanti, Savoia!' His consort was also a Savoyard; and in his speech in the Montecitorio Palace, he paid tribute to Queen Margaret, 'who had educated their dearly loved son according to the glorious example of his illustrious grandfather'. Were those examples primarily constitutional or military?

Without military lustre in the past, the House of Savoy could not have endured, and the love of military glory coursed through the King's blood. Humbert had his father's physical courage without the bombast. He shared the disappointment that the Ministers forbade his father to aid the French in their war against the Prussians. Yet, when the war was over, he turned his sympathies against the French. They had been beaten by their own bad generalship.

The Italians and the Germans had struggled almost simultaneously for their national unity. A plebiscite followed each conquest made by Victor Emmanuel's troops or by Garibaldi's volunteers. In outward form, Humbert's Kingdom was based on the people's consent. German unity, like the Italian, should have become a liberation; but, in the hour of victory, Bismarck decided to annex Alsace and Lorraine. There was no question of holding a plebiscite in the two provinces, for the Chancellor was indifferent to the feelings of their inhabitants. Might was right. The liberals who were once the vanguard of the German struggle for unity became contemptuously ignored.

If liberal Germany was now an adventurer, what temptations might not befall the new Italian Kingdom which stretched southwards from the Alps to Marsala, where the coastline of Tunisia is sometimes seen? Would the Italian soldiers of tomorrow die fighting on the soil of their homeland? Or, like the conscripts whom Cavour sent to the Crimea, would they become soldiers of an invading army—in Africa, Albania or Greece? Queen Victoria had recently assumed the title of Empress of India. Could the dream of an Italian Empire and a gaudy title seduce a descendant of Victor Emmanuel?

After his return from the Montecitorio Palace, the King stepped onto the other balcony of the Quirinal Palace with the Queen and with several royal princes. Among them was the Crown Prince Frederick, son-in-law of Queen Victoria and heir to the first German Emperor. To him belonged the privilege of an active command in the war against France. There was renewed jubilation in the square when this Teutonic warrior lifted up the King's son—a sickly and timid boy eight years old—and showed him to his future people.

The traditions which the Crown Prince Frederick inherited were military, but his sympathies were liberal, and Bismarck was not alone in wondering what would happen to Germany when he succeeded his now octogenarian father. No one foresaw that, in ten years' time, he would ascend a throne when he was already dying of cancer. Both his own son—the last German Emperor—and the boy whom he showed to an exuberant Roman crowd were to spend their last years in exile: the one in Holland, and the other in Egypt.

From the same balcony—on June 17th, 1846—Pius had blessed a Roman crowd for the first time. He was then almost a stranger. None could foretell what his reign might bring or how it might end. Now he was dying of old age. He survived the first King of Italy by only one month.

The people who had seen their dead sovereign in the Quirinal Palace flocked to St. Peter's, where the Pope's body lay in state in the Chapel of the Sacrament. The feet protruded through the rails, and incessant kissing made the soles of their red shoes shiny. The figure in the Quirinal Palace, so some Romans declared, had been a wax image, and not the King at all. But Pius they recognized, and even in death he was smiling. Pope's men or King's men: it made little difference. Many who once detested papal rule were grateful to Pius for having stayed in Rome. They gave him an affectionate, and sometimes tearful, farewell.

If they wept, they also chattered. Whom would the Cardinals elect? A new Pope meant more to the Romans—and more to most Italians —than a new King.

CHAPTER NINE

THE SECOND PRISONER

FROM THE moment of a Pope's death to the election of his successor, the presiding member of the Sacred College is the Camerlengo, and not its Dean. The holder of this office was Cardinal Vincenzo Gioacchino Pecci, who had been Archbishop of Perugia throughout the old Pope's long reign. He was tall and thin, and he looked fragile. He was, none the less, alert as well as shrewd and clever. The smile was broad and the eyes kindly; but many remarked on his facial resemblance to Voltaire.

He was born—on March 2nd, 1810—in Carpineto, a pleasant hill-town village in the heart of Latium and overlooking the old coach road from Rome to Naples. Though his father, Colonel Domenico Pecci, had served under Napoleon, the family traditions were solidly papal. From the entrance to his home, the child saw the distant sky-line of Anagni, where two Popes—Innocent III and Boniface VIII— were born, and where a proud Colonna humiliated Boniface VIII by slapping his face.

The house, spacious and well-proportioned, stood immediately above a steep incline, but it was in no way isolated from its humbler neighbours. In Latium, where the scourge of malaria and the fear of brigands drove people to the hills, the houses of the rich and the poor were often huddled together. The Peccis—careful, but not uncharitable —knew that the life of the poor was hard. They knew, too, that in their part of Latium, the men of culture were few. There was no middle class, and most of the people could neither read nor write. Upon the cultured, therefore, fell the burden of leadership. When necessary, they must be the spokesmen of the poor.

With an older brother, Vincenzo Pecci went to the Jesuit college in Viterbo, where he saw the palace and the tombs of the Popes who ruled the Church while they were exiled from Rome. He was fifteen when, in 1825, Rome observed a Holy Year. As part of the celebrations, he led a deputation of students to the city, and Pope Leo XII granted them an audience. Two other young people—Giuseppe Garibaldi and Maria Cristina, future Queen of the Two Sicilies—may have passed him in a Roman street.

His intellectual gifts were formidable, and for many years he continued to compose Latin verses which good judges praised. At twenty-seven he became the Apostolic Delegate in Benevento, a papal city islanded in a Bourbon Kingdom. Four years later, he went northwards to be the Apostolic Delegate in Perugia. This Umbrian capital stands fifteen hundred feet above sea-level and, as in his native Carpineto, Pecci lived again in close proximity to the poor; but Perugia was also rich in churches, palaces and paintings, and many of its families cherished their cultural heritage. Instead of the skyline of Anagni, where two Popes who magnified their temporal power were born, Pecci now saw—far below him in the valley between Perugia and Monte Subasio—the little city of Assisi, birthplace of Francis, the saint who took poverty for his bride.

In 1843, Gregory XVI sent him to Brussels as his Nuncio. If any country made a mockery of that Pope's first Encyclical Letter *Mirari vos* and his emphatic denunciation of the ideas proclaimed by the Catholic liberals, it was Belgium. The Belgians' hatred of rule by a Dutch King who was Protestant and unfriendly brought Catholic and liberal together. Their unity made separation from Holland possible, and in 1831—the year of Pope Gregory's election—there was a new throne to fill. The most likely candidate was Leopold of Saxe-Coburg. Brought up as a Lutheran, he became an Anglican when he married the short-lived and only child of England's Prince Regent; he refused the new throne of Orthodox Greece; and then, as a Catholic convert, he agreed to become the first King of the Belgians. For his second wife, he chose a daughter of Louis-Philippe, King of the French.

Many believed that his Kingdom could not last; the resentment of the neighbouring Dutch was deep, and the racial cleavage between Fleming and Walloon persisted. The strong bond was the alliance between Catholic and liberal, and Leopold was determined to remain a constitutional ruler. In 1848—when Metternich fled from Vienna, Louis-Philippe from Paris and Pius from Rome—his own Kingdom survived the revolutionary shocks. Constitutional rule implied an acceptance of strains and stresses. Leopold agreed with his niece, Queen Victoria, that in a time of danger the last thing which a ruler should do is to run away.

Pecci had spent only three years in Brussels when Pope Gregory recalled him and appointed him to be Bishop of Perugia with the rank of an Archbishop. Instead of hurrying back to the Pontifical State, he spent a month in London, where he saw many signs of political change and tension. In the previous year, the potato crop had failed in Ireland, while rain ruined the harvest in England. Ireland was starving to death, and England could not feed her.

Robert Peel and Gladstone saw clearly that the old corn laws must be abandoned. The day of economic protection was over; free trade must take its place. The two statesmen put the welfare of the people before their own political reputations. Though they won their way, the Tories did not forgive them. Before 1846 was out, both were defeated. Peel never regained office, and Gladstone—just a few months older than Pecci—stayed in the political wilderness for seven years.

Brussels and London gave Pecci an insight into civil and laical government. Indirectly he learned something about the Irish who were starving, but whose Church—as Montalembert long ago discovered—was unfettered by the State. In their thousands, Irish people crossed the Atlantic to find work in a land where 'a free Church in a free State' was a reality. The experience gained in Northern Europe might have made Pecci a Catholic liberal, despite all his personal loyalty to Pope Gregory; but before he went to Brussels, he had spent his life entirely within the theocratic Pontifical State, and mostly in places where the illiterate were many and cultured laymen very few. Government was the responsibility of an élite, not a privilege to be shared with the uninstructed. Though Pecci was genuinely concerned about the condition of the poor, it was unlikely that he cared for their company. He was a lone thinker, and his chief companions were books. A man of the study, he trusted too much in the power of the pen.

The Archbishop was enthroned in Perugia only a few weeks before Gregory died, and once again he surveyed movements and events from an Umbrian—and spiritually almost an Olympian—height. He judged them in the light of the teaching of Thomas Aquinas. All authority came from God, and the Temporal Power imposed on the Pope the duty to give his own subjects justice, security and good government; for every man had the right to life. Government in the Pontifical State ought to have been exemplary. Pecci defended the Temporal Power and treated Victor Emmanuel as the usurper, but he was far from blind to the decadence of the Pontifical State or to the misdeeds of its servants, clerical or lay. On one nightmare occasion, when Garibaldi's volunteers were driven out of Perugia, the papal troops looted the city and killed many harmless civilians. Like the English after the massacre of Peterloo, Pius struck a medal to record their triumph.

Within a year the papal troops retreated from Perugia. The citizens were more than glad to see them go, and they welcomed Victor Emmanuel when he was eventually compelled to visit them. The Archbishop stayed away. He watched over a city and a countryside now under Savoyard rule, and he noted how little was the difference which it made to the people's welfare. The rich might be richer, but the poor were poorer, and young men were compelled to join the army.

The real gainers were the commercial men unknown in a remote village like Carpineto during Pecci's childhood; for Italian unity put many customs' officers out of business. This was the century of the middle classes, and in Italy they were battening on the courage or idealism of the followers of Garibaldi and Mazzini. Wherever Victor Emmanuel acquired new territory and new subjects, those who obtained the right to vote averaged only one out of every fifty. The poor were unrepresented; and Cardinal Pecci was ready to battle for them against their new masters.

He was Camerlengo at a hazardous time. The last Conclave was held in the Quirinal Palace, where not very much was left to show that it once belonged to the Pope. 'Even the most ardent Protestants,' Augustus Hare had written, 'are a little shocked that the famous Quirinal Chapel, so redolent of Church history, should be turned into a cloak-room for balls, and the cloak-tickets kept in the holy water basins.' In 1800, when Rome was a republic and Pius VI had recently died a prisoner of the French, the Camerlengo of the day summoned the Cardinals to Venice for their Conclave. Now, in 1878, Cardinal Manning was urging Pecci, in like manner, to summon the Sacred College to a place outside the Kingdom of Italy.

Word reached Francesco Crispi, Minister of the Interior. He pretended that he cared nothing for what was said or done inside the Vatican, but he had no intention of allowing the Conclave to fall under foreign influence. Accordingly, he told the Camerlengo that if the Cardinals wished to hold their Conclave elsewhere, they would be escorted to the frontier with all the honours due to them under the Law of Guarantees. Neither the new Pope nor any of his Cardinals would be permitted to re-enter Italy. The papal Palaces would be occupied.

Cardinal Manning found his plan frustrated by the powerful Sicilian Minister who had told a new King that he must call himself Humbert I, but his prestige was undiminished, and there were Cardinals who wanted him to be elected Pope. For all his past adroitness in the pursuit of high office, Manning declined the prospect. The next Pope, he was certain, must be an Italian. That, perhaps, was the general view expressed in the Conclave. Hadrian VI—a Dutchman and the last non-Italian Pope— was neither popular with the Romans nor very distinguished. In fact, a succession of Italian Popes unbroken since 1523 has been one of the Church's instinctive tributes to Italy's spiritual unity.

The Cardinals elected Pecci. He was 67, and his fragile appearance may have been an asset. Short reigns are sometimes favoured. Pius had been Pope too long.

When white smoke issued from a makeshift chimney which clung to a wall of the Sistine Chapel, thousands of people in St. Peter's Square began to wonder whether they should stay where they were or go inside the basilica. If the new Pope came to the outer balcony and blessed them, he would show that he was liberal and ready to forgive the loss of his predecessor's Temporal Power; but if he went to the inner balcony and turned his face against the people in the Square, he gave a sign that there was no forgiveness and, perhaps, no real change of papal policy.

Most of the people continued to wait in the Square. Like other discerning observers, however, Matilda Lucas noticed that nearly all the priests were leaving the crowd in the Square and entering St. Peter's. Accordingly, she followed them into St. Peter's, where she soon saw a white-haired old man waving his hand far above her. 'I think, Miss, we shall have an anti-Pope,' said an Italian at her side. 'We have been told,' she wrote, 'that the way to the outer loggia had been blocked by a heavy bit of furniture to prevent his giving the benediction outside, but who knows if this is true?'

The crowd which had waited in the Square went away offended. An opportunity for reconciliation was lost. If Vincenzo Pecci had been more responsive to popular sentiment, he might not have chosen his papal name as a partial tribute to Leo XII: a theocrat who, as the oldest generation in Rome well remembered, not only forced the Roman Jews to listen periodically to a Catholic homily, but also spoilt the pleasures of the Roman Christians by dying, in 1829, in the middle of their carnival.

Unrecognized by the Romans in the streets, Pope Leo XIII crossed the Tiber and collected his papers from the Falconieri Palace. On his return the gates of the Vatican closed behind him for the last time. He made himself the second prisoner of the Vatican because, like Pius before him, he refused to acknowledge the loss of his Temporal Power. As a sovereign, he instructed his Secretary of State to announce his accession to all Christian courts. As a sovereign, too, he was crowned, but in the Sistine Chapel.

This angered the Romans. There was space enough for many thousands to witness a coronation in St. Peter's; but admission to the Sistine Chapel was restricted to certain ecclesiastics, papal officials, the black aristocracy and the representatives of sovereigns and governments other than the Italian. Though the Roman citizens once took part in the election of a Pope, even the pageantry of a coronation was now withheld from their sight.

There were disorders. Resentment, once provoked, fed on other grievances. They tarnished the people's memory of Pius. He had not wanted to be buried, like many other Popes, in St. Peter's. For his burial place, he chose the church of St. Lawrence-beyond-the-Walls because it stands close to the vast *campo santo*, to which the Romans bring their dead. Through all his tribulations he had loved them; and each Sunday they had come to him, parish by parish, to hear him expounding the Gospel. Even as a prisoner, he was Bishop of Rome.

Death is reconciliation, and a mournful crowd would have watched the funeral procession a week or a few days after Pius had died. Yet grief is transitory, and more than three years went by before a special chapel was prepared as his final sepulchre. Then, through fear of rioting, it was decided to take the body from St. Peter's to the church of St. Lawrence-beyond-the-Walls in the middle of the night. The fear itself created a new grievance. The people, it seemed, were not to be trusted. Stones were thrown.

Leo was distressed and thought of leaving Rome. His links with its people were deliberately severed, and perhaps he had never liked the humid and low-lying city. Its rich musical culture meant nothing to him, since music tired his nerves. 'He will find it tedious in Paradise,' observed the priestly singer, Giovanni del Papa. The Cardinals, when invited to go with him to the top of the Vatican gardens, marvelled at his capacity to walk briskly and well ahead of them to a little Swiss chalet which he had built, and which he called his 'rustic Castel-gandolfo'. He was, after all, a hill-man who had spent more than half his life—first as Apostolic Delegate and then as Archbishop—clambering around the tortuous streets of Perugia.

He granted few audiences and, unlike Pius, he seldom arrived in state. He preferred to give each person an undivided attention. To the first Anglican clergyman presented to him he said: 'I give you my special benediction, my son.' He ate very little, and the servants complained that he lacked the geniality and open-handedness of Pius. He was distinctly less *simpatico*. 'He sits up late, dictating to his nodding secretaries,' wrote Matilda Lucas. 'The other morning, when the servant rapped once or twice at his door, he got no answer. The man called the other servants, and they were all much frightened, thinking he was dead. They broke the door open and found that he had fallen asleep upon the *scrittorio*, with his head on his arms, overcome with sleep while writing to an archbishop, and there had remained all night.

When they roused him, he told them not to mention it, which of course did not prevent their doing so. Padre Giovanni told us this.'

Though Leo saw the cruel side of the industrial revolution which began in England, he did not share Pope Gregory's detestation of material progress. On the contrary, he provided the Vatican with one of the earliest telephonic switchboards and was probably the first occupant of a palace to install a hydraulic lift. In Pius's day, the rooms of the Vatican were softly lit with oil lamps and candles, while torch-bearers led visitors up and down the stairs. At great expense, Leo introduced gaslight and was all too soon converted by Thomas Edison to the use of electricity. He enlarged St. John's Lateran, and some thought it a mercy that the Savoyard usurpation prevented him from becoming the chief builder in the Rome of the late nineteenth century.

Political motives played their part in his enlargement of St. John's Lateran: his Cathedral as Bishop of Rome, and also the Mother Church of Rome and the World. Leo made it the burial place of Innocent III and eventually of himself. Innocent III—mightiest of all exponents of papal dominion and the chastiser of temporal sovereigns—died in Perugia in 1216. Perugia's former Archbishop transferred the remains to Rome with little or no consideration for the feelings of the Umbrians. Nor were the feelings of the Romans considered. The Law of Guarantees enabled Leo to do what he wished with his own Cathedral, but legality has its limits. The letter kills. St. John's Lateran, like St. Peter's, was built with the skill, labour and even the money of the people. No legal fiction could destroy their share of its spiritual ownership.

The mosaic from Leo III's *triclinium* still stands at the summit of the Lateran Hill and proclaims the old Guelph doctrine that Pope and Emperor alike derive their authority from Christ through Peter; but the Emperor, according to Dante's *De Monarchia*, derived his authority directly from Christ, and not through Peter. A King in the Quirinal meant a triumph for the Ghibellines. To avoid political offence, the bones of Innocent III should have been left to moulder in Perugia.

Discourtesies on both sides, however, were constantly blocking the approaches to reconciliation. At one time Francesco Crispi made friendly overtures, while at another he became a rabid anti-clerical and issued harsh decrees. He called himself a Sicilian, though his family was originally Greek and had settled in Albania, where his grandfather was an Orthodox priest. Most anti-clericals were indifferent to the claims of religion, but Crispi's forebears belonged to a religious minority often despised in a Mohammedan country. The Orthodox Church, unlike the Roman, allowed its priests to marry and welcomed laymen as its theologians. Crispi protested often because he was at heart a Byzantine. When, as Mayor of Rome, Prince Torlonia called on Cardinal Parrocchi to express the city's congratulations to Leo on reaching the jubilee of his ordination, Crispi dismissed him from office.

Ernest Nathan, who took Torlonia's place as Mayor, persuaded the municipality to erect a statue of Giordano Bruno in the Campo dei Fiori—the flower-market of old Rome—where he had been burned alive in the Holy Year of 1600. Bruno—born in Nola, not far from Naples—owed his misfortunes partly to the strong influence of a religious reformer of the fourteenth century who became a Cardinal. Nicholas of Cusa, who was once sent to Constantinople in search of union, believed that the religious wars of his day were foolish, since they were fought between men who held fundamentally the same views. He was also critical of Aristotle's sway over Christian thought, and he distrusted all the systematic thinkers. Man was fettered by his own mind. His knowledge of God was intuitive, and not dialectical. Perhaps, if more of his contemporaries had read his writings and understood them, Nicholas of Cusa would have gone to the stake, and not to the Sacred College.

Expelled from his Dominican monastery, Bruno crossed the Alps in search of spiritual freedom. He lectured in Wittenberg and Prague; he made a temporary home in London and visited Oxford, where, he declared, learned men venerated *sancta asinita* ('holy stupidity'), the foe which always stood in the way of man's search for truth. Nearly all the great leaders of the Reformation had once been Catholic priests; and sometimes they clamoured for doctrines which the Church had never repudiated. They lived in a Ptolomaic universe which had the unmoving earth for its centre.

Copernicus, himself a Catholic priest, destroyed that universe. The earth and all the stars moved round the sun. Bruno, who was a poet, discerned that there was not one world, but a plurality of worlds. Each, as a part of infinite nature, expressed the divine unity.

> *Quindi l'ali sicure a l'aria porgo,*
> *ne temo intoppo di cristallo o vetro;*
> *ma fendo i cieli, e a l'infinio m'ergo.*
> *E mentre dal mio globo agli altri sorgo,*
> *e per l'eterio campo oltre penetro,*
> *quel ch'altri lungi vede, lascio al tergo.*[1]

[1] 'Thus I lift wings into the air. I have no fear of any barrier of crystal or glass. I pierce through the heavens and reach the infinite. While I ascend from my globe to others and penetrate into the ethereal sphere, what others see far beyond them I leave behind me.'

Truth was never arbitrarily revealed; the Jewish records had no more validity than the Greek myths. 'One does not know God,' Bruno wrote. 'One becomes God.' The vision of the reformers was in no way more spacious than that of the Catholics. Like men enchained in the cave described by Plato, their backs were turned to the light, and what they saw were shadows. Homesick and in despair, Bruno recrossed the Alps and stayed for a while in Padua, where a number of Greeks were studying at the university without any fear of persecution by the Roman Church. In Venice he was betrayed to the Inquisition.

When brought to Rome, Bruno was kept a prisoner for six years while the Inquisitors examined his writings, and while Cardinal Bellarmine, among others, wanted certain statements clarified. The prisoner claimed that he had never ceased to be a Christian, and when he heard his condemnation, he said: 'Perhaps you are more afraid to pronounce this sentence than I am to receive it.'

Bruno was deprived of his orders and excommunicated. He was then handed to the Governor of Rome for punishment, and an order was given to destroy his books and to burn them publicly in front of St. Peter's. The condemned man showed no sign of repentance. He died willingly as a martyr, he said, and his soul would ascend with the smoke to paradise. The Company of San Giovanni Decollato provided the chaplains needed when a man is about to be put to death; and it summoned two Dominicans, two Jesuits from the Gesù, two Oratorians from the Chiesa Nuova and a priest from San Girolamo to combat Bruno's errors. For all their professional skill, they failed to overcome his 'accursed obstinacy'; 'the brain whirled with a thousand errors and vanities'.

According to the Company's record, Bruno was so persistent in his obstinacy that he was at last led away to the Campo dei Fiori by the ministers of justice: 'there, stripped naked and tied to a stake, he was burned alive, accompanied always by our Company singing the litanies and the comforters urging him right to the last minute to abandon the obstinacy with which he ended his wretched and unhappy life'.

Bruno's writings were often obscure, wayward and cantankerous. Only a few of the top-hatted anti-clericals who witnessed the unveiling of his statue may have read them carefully; but if the chief purpose of the ceremony was to annoy the Pope, it succeeded. Leo almost decided to stay in Rome no longer. He felt the hurt all the more because he was certain that the Church had nothing to fear from a greater knowledge and dissemination of the truth.

His own mind was capacious, but his views were authoritarian.

Time and again his authority was Thomas Aquinas. He lauded the Thomist philosophy in *Aeterni Patris*, the first in his long series of Encyclical Letters; he founded an Academy of St. Thomas Aquinas; and he set aside a large sum for a new edition of the Thomist writings. Nearly all his subsequent Encyclical Letters—from *Arcanum* on the indissolubility of Christian marriage to *Graves de communi* on Christian democracy—provided Thomist answers to contemporary problems. Leo wished to leave the world in no doubt that the Thomist philosophy was the official philosophy of the Church.

The challenge to the modern world was sharpest when, in 1891, he issued the Encyclical Letter *Rerum novarum* on the social rights of the worker: 'a small number of very rich men have been able to lay upon the teeming masses of the labouring poor a yoke worse than slavery'. 'Unhappy workers,' the Pope continued, 'must be rescued from the hands of those speculators who, making no distinction whatever between a man and a machine, abuse their person without measure to satisfy insatiable cupidities.'

Rerum novarum stung the conscience and became a landmark in social history. Lamennais, Montalembert and Lacordaire never wrote sentences more trenchant. They had tried to build a bridge between the Church and the liberals. Now, at a first reading, *Rerum novarum* seemed to indicate the building of a papal bridge between the Church and the socialists. Observers in France, however, knew better. As a young officer, Count Albert de Mun was taken prisoner at Metz. While in captivity, he reflected on the condition of the poor. The Ministry of War made him resign his commission when he founded the Circles of Christian Workers. Later he founded a left-wing party called Catholic Alliance. Leo repudiated it. He expected Catholics to work for the spiritual regeneration of society, but this did not entitle them to form a separate Catholic political party.

Leo gave a final explanation of his attitude to Catholic parties in 1901, when, at the age of ninety-one, he issued his *Graves de communi*. 'The intentions and activities of those Catholics who work for the betterment of the proletariat,' he wrote, 'can never bend to preferring one civil régime to another.' The only lawful Christian democracy was that which had been 'freed from all political significance, and to which is annexed no other meaning than that of beneficent action among the people'. This implied 'the co-operation above all of those who, because of their wealth, their social position, their intellectual and moral culture, exercise the greatest influence over society'.

A systematic philosophy may provide the thinker with a map, but no map remains contemporary if it cannot be adjusted or changed.

The Church may not have needed the perpetuation of an official philosophy, and Leo may not have drawn the fullest nourishment from his study of a single philosopher. Because he lived in close proximity to unlettered people throughout his years in Carpineto and Perugia, it was hard to tell whether his chief handicap was likely to be loneliness or pride.

KING VICTOR EMMANUEL II

POPE PIUS IX
After the portrait by G. P. A. Healy, 1871

FROM COUNCIL TO COUNCIL
Opening of the Vatican Council, December 8th 1869

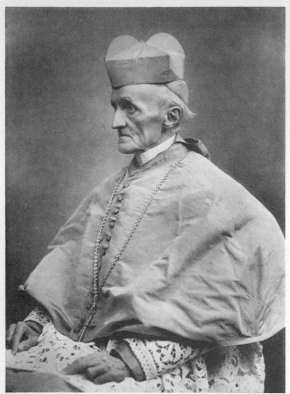

CARDINAL MANNING

Photo Mansell Collection

CARDINAL
NEWMAN

Photo Mansell Collection

Photo Mansell Collection

GIUSEPPE MAZZINI

VIA DEL CORSO (c. 1865-1875)
Palazzo Doria on the left (still lived in by the Doria family);
Palazzo Odescalchi on the right

PANORAMA OF ROME (c. 1870)
Taken from Janiculum hill, now the sight of the Garibaldi monument

Photo Alinari

FUNERAL OF KING VICTOR EMMANUEL II
(from a painting by C. Maccari in the Palazzo della Signoria, Siena)
As the Cortege enters the Pantheon the central figure in the group of State
representatives is Frederick, Crown Prince of Germany, father of the last Kaiser

KING HUMBERT I

QUEEN MARGARET,
HIS CONSORT,
THE FIRST QUEEN
OF ITALY

CHAPTER TEN

THE WILL OF THE PEOPLE

TWO PRIESTS whom Leo delighted to honour were Luigi Tosti and John Henry Newman: one a Benedictine, and the other an Oratorian. Both were his intellectual peers.

Tosti was a year younger than Leo and only eight when he first climbed the hill to the Abbey of Monte Cassino. At eighteen he began to write his history of the Abbey, and he exulted in its fine tradition of praying and working actively for greater harmony in the world. One exemplar of this tradition had been Bruno of Asti, who was the Abbot of Monte Cassino early in the twelfth century, and who tried to foster a spirit of conciliation between Rome and Constantinople. To Benedictines still living on a shore of the Bosphorus he wrote: 'We truly hold, and from the heart firmly believe, that although the customs of the Churches are distinct, nevertheless there is one faith, indissolubly united to the head; that is Christ; and He Himself is one and remains the same in his body.'

The need for reconciliation between Rome and Constantinople persisted through the centuries, but Tosti grew to manhood in Bomba's Kingdom, and he longed to see the people freed from their oppressors. In order to spread Gioberti's idea of Italy united under the presidency of the Pope, he decided that a periodical known as the *Ateneo d'Italia* should be printed in the Abbey, and he obtained permission from the Minister of Police to install a printing press. The Minister was a harsh man called Carretto, and the monks may have deliberately flattered him, for his portrait in full uniform was hung on an Abbey wall.

Gioberti, Manzoni and Rosmini were among the writers eager to contribute to Tosti's periodical, and Monte Cassino might have become the acknowledged birthplace of Italian unity. Unfortunately, Gioberti talked too much about it. In his famous book on the 'Moral and Spiritual Primacy of the Italians', he had criticized the Jesuits and praised the Benedictines. This pleased neither Bomba nor his court, and Monte Cassino was soon said to be a hotbed of irreligion and democracy. The printing press was seized and many monks sent into exile, but Carretto's portrait continued to hang on a wall.

The police in Naples accused Tosti of belonging to a group of stabbers, and he escaped imprisonment only through the help of influential friends. He sought and obtained an audience with Pope Pius, then living in Portici. Though Pius showed little sympathy, he offered the choice between a reduction to the status of a layman or a passport for the Pontifical State. Tosti rejected the first proposal because it was unworthy alike of himself and of the Pope. He chose exile, and, while living in Rome and Florence, he wrote his 'Abelard'.

Renan, who saw him in 1850, was astonished by his close knowledge of the writings of Kant, Hegel, George Sand and Lamennais. Nine years later, Gregorovius found him living in Monte Cassino as though nothing had ever ruffled his serenity. 'In this extraordinary being,' he wrote, 'burns a beautiful and profound spirit. All in him is intuitive, he works and studies little, he creates by himself. When he speaks, he laughs open-heartedly. It is the laugh of a happy nature which has never been tormented by ambition. None the less, there is in his glance something of a superior intelligence which at once reveals the true nature of a Prince of the Church: in him lives the spirit inherited by the Benedictine aristocracy.'

After struggling for some years against banditry in Bomba's old Kingdom, the Italian Government took steps to protect its monuments. One of the richest, alike in historic associations and in its library, was the Abbey of Monte Cassino. On King Humbert's behalf, Tosti acted as its curator. The Abbey was both a shrine and a museum, and this particular relationship between Church and State pleased him. Nor did it prevent Leo from appointing him to be vice-archivist of the Vatican under the immediate authority of Cardinal Hergenroether, a Bavarian. Henceforward Tosti worked in two camps, but if anyone complained that he was too liberal and a servant of the Savoyards, Leo took little or no notice. He believed in a scholar's freedom.

Soon after his accession someone asked the Pope what would be his policy as the Church's ruler. 'You will know my policy,' he replied, 'when you see the name of my first Cardinal.' First of his Cardinals was Newman. 'My Cardinal!' Leo confided in a later year. 'It was not easy. They said he was too liberal; but I had determined to honour the Church in honouring Newman.'

It was, indeed, far from easy; for Manning created in Rome the impression that Newman did not want to be made a Cardinal. The two great English converts were never restful with each other. Newman felt a distrust of Manning, while Manning thought that Newman's publication of his Anglican sermons was 'a literary vanity'. Newman was willing enough to accept the honour which Leo offered him, but he did not want to spend his last years in Rome. He preferred to remain in his Oratory in Edgbaston, a suburb of Birmingham. Manning hid even from himself the bitter truth; he had no wish to share his glory with a second Cardinal in Protestant England.

In the end Leo got his Cardinal, whom he received with the utmost pleasure. Throughout their first meeting, he held Newman's hand. He spoke very slowly, for he knew that many cultured foreigners read Italian with ease, but are often confused when it is spoken at a normal pace. At the close of the audience, Leo said that he wished to show Newman a special honour. He took his arm and led him to the outer door. This was a courtesy which former Popes had reserved for Catholic sovereigns. Nor was it the last courtesy; for Newman was invited to use the Vatican's famous hydraulic lift.

While Leo stayed inside the Vatican as its prisoner, the Cardinals moved with a sagacious freedom through the city and the neighbourhood. In time they forgot to decorate their coaches with mourning drapery. One by one, those who owed their elevation to Pius quitted the earthly stage, though for some years a Cardinal whom he had selected from a princely house of Europe, old or new, might still bear a name familiar to the Romans: for example, Cardinal Gustav Adolph Hohenlohe, who was either too mean or too poor to keep the Villa d'Este in Tivoli in good repair; or Cardinal Lucien Bonaparte, whose inward and unworldly nature transfigured features which resembled those of his great-uncle, Napoleon I.

To the aristocrats in the Sacred College, Leo added Edward Henry Howard, whose grandfather had the luck in 1815 to succeed a third cousin as the twelfth Duke of Norfolk, and whose uncle—later the thirteenth Duke—became the first Catholic to enter the House of Commons since the Catholic Emancipation. Before Wiseman ordained him in the English College, he was an officer in the Life Guards and had served in India. He was tall and magnificently built, and he may have been the handsomest Guards officer of his day. Leo made him Bishop of Frascati and Archpriest of St. Peter's. Both offices were formerly held by Cardinal York, 'the last of the Stuarts', whom political supporters called King Henry IX. If Cardinal York never looked like an English King, Cardinal Howard never ceased to look, or to behave, like a fine English cavalry officer. Ladies were disappointed if they went to St. Peter's on a Sunday morning and found that Cardinal Howard was not in the procession which passed beneath Michelangelo's dome on its way to the apse. 'An Italian built this dome,' someone said, 'but England built the only Cathedral capable of adorning it.'

One of Leo's early Cardinals was his own older brother, Giuseppe Pecci. Nothing else indicates that the Pope was a nepotist, and it may well be true that a number of Cardinals in the Curia pressed him to select Giuseppe, who was once a Jesuit and had a rare independence of mind. His influence over the Pontiff was negligible. So, for that matter, was the influence of most of the other Cardinals resident in Rome. To Cardinals who ruled provinces he listened carefully, and Herbert Vaughan—Manning's successor at Westminster—had the doubtful distinction of helping to stop his overtures to the Anglicans. Leo insisted that all Cardinals in Rome should be honoured, but he preferred not to lean on them too heavily for advice.

This led to an altercation with Cardinal Luigi Oreglia, Bishop of Palestrina. Despite his dislike of Savoyard rule in Rome, Cardinal Oreglia was himself from Piedmont, and he thought that an occasional northern bluntness of speech in the Vatican did no harm. One morning he provoked Leo into saying: 'You forget, Lord Cardinal, that if I make Cardinals, I can also unmake them.' 'Very well!' came the reply. 'Let Your Holiness begin with me, and straight away!' Leo's retort was to make Cardinal Oreglia the Camerlengo.

By naming Newman as his first Cardinal, Leo indicated his desire to bring illustrious thinkers, scholars and men of letters into the Sacred College, thereby demonstrating to the world that the Church had nothing to fear from the truth; but it was not altogether correct to claim that this action revealed his policy. The dictator of his policy was a grand design. Leo was a master of statecraft, and he used it for restoring the prestige of the Holy See as a necessary prelude to winning back the Temporal Power. Three times within a century the Temporal Power had been forfeited—to the French, Mazzini and Victor Emmanuel. Leo saw no reason why this third forfeiture should be permanent. Temporal Power was his by right. In Encyclical Letters he showed his concern for the people, but in political action he showed concern for Heads of States and Governments.

Great movements, Newman once observed, are seldom born of committees, and the ageing Pope was surrounded by old Cardinals. The grand design for vindicating the papal right to Temporal Power took shape in his own mind. It was not something to discuss with any Prince of the Church who had no understanding of statecraft. Leo needed the support, encouragement and skill of younger men. In 1887, he chose the youngest member of the Sacred College—Cardinal Mariano Rampolla, a patrician from Sicily, who was then only forty-four —to be his Secretary of State. Cardinal Rampolla was once Nuncio in Madrid, and through his persuasion the Spanish Government agreed with the German Government to accept Leo's arbitration in a dispute over the Caroline Islands.

Hitherto the Pope's chief foe outside Italy had been Bismarck, whose

Kulturkampf—the 'campaign for civilization'—was directed against the Catholics. When the German Chancellor sent Count Mieczislav Ledochowski, Archbishop of Posen and Gnesen, to prison for two years, Leo retaliated by naming the prisoner a Cardinal. On his release, the Archbishop was summoned to Rome, where he spent the rest of his days as a member of the Curia. Leo seldom, if ever, asked for his advice.

Bismarck appreciated a show of strength, and when he realized that he could not rule the new German Empire without the consent of the Catholics, his hostility to Leo gave place to admiration. The *Kulturkampf* was brought to an end. Leo, however, was not content with this triumph, and he turned his attention to France. She was a Catholic country and, after her defeat in war, she might have become monarchical again, if only the monarchists were not sharply divided between Bourbonists, Orleanists and Bonapartists. All of them raised the cry of 'throne and altar'. So doing, they provoked the republicans and made many of them stridently anti-clerical. The Third Republic was faulty, but it represented the French people. Accordingly, its authority came from God. Leo, therefore, enjoined the French Catholics to give it their loyal support. The pronouncement from Rome shook them. Pious ladies were said to be praying for the Holy Father's conversion. The Pope, declared gossipers in the Boulevards, had joined the anti-clericals.

Inside the Vatican Leo held his elaborate court both as the Pontiff and as a King. He let it be known that he was unable to receive a Catholic sovereign who first visited the Quirinal Palace. His rule even applied to statesmen from Protestant countries. John Morley, for example, went to Rome after Gladstone had given him the old Irish Office. Though an agnostic, he exerted a definite influence in a Catholic country which then formed part of the United Kingdom. In Rome he had something to say and to hear; but because he committed the error of first seeing King Humbert in the Quirinal Palace, Leo did not grant him an audience. Instead, he had a meeting with the General Superior of the Jesuits.

Leo granted far fewer audiences than did Pius. He also made them simpler because he liked to talk with people individually; but for special occasions no splendour or ceremony was ever sacrificed. Humbler Romans were free to enter St. Peter's at all hours of the day. Yet the fine presence of Cardinal Howard—an Englishman put in charge of their greatest church—was a poor substitute for their deliberate exclusion from the ceremonies which marked each anniversary of Leo's coronation. Only the highly privileged received an invitation to be present inside the Sistine Chapel, while the Sala Regia was filled with foreigners and selected Italians who had asked for, and received, tickets of admission.

Among them, in 1892, was Augustus Hare. 'The passage of the Pope to the Sistine on his coronation anniversary,' he wrote, 'was a very fine sight. Leo XIII looked dying, but gave his benediction with the most serene majesty, sinking back between each effort upon his cushions, as if the end had indeed come. Only his eyes lived, and lived only in his office; otherwise his perfectly spiritualized countenance seemed utterly unconscious of the thundering *evvivas* with which he was greeted, and which rose into a perfect roar as he was carried into the Sala Regia.'

Augustus Hare lived in Rome partly on his earnings as a writer and partly on fulfilling services for royal visitors to Rome. He acted as guide to the Forum for the Duke of Connaught, Queen Victoria's youngest son, and he was also tutor to the Prince Royal of Sweden, later King Gustav V. For this tutoring he was given a decoration, which he did not fail to wear on every appropriate occasion, including the anniversary of Leo's coronation. 'The potency of "Orders" here,' he wrote, 'is so great that my Swedish decoration not only gave me the best place, but I took in two young men as my chaplain and equerry!'

Leo needed to have the most ostentatious court in Christendom because he was deliberately impressing the foreigner and relying on his support to vindicate the claim to Temporal Power. This was dangerous. For one thing, it sharpened the conflict between the Kingdom of Italy and the Holy See. One hot-tempered leader from Sicily, Francesco Crispi, fostered an alliance with Austria and Germany, while another Sicilian—the tall and rugged Cardinal Rampolla—sought the friendship of the French. The Romans had resisted the French invader in 1849, and they would resist again. Some of Leo's followers, in fact, argued that war was inevitable. Whoever 'entered Rome with gunshot'—wrote Father Zocchi, a Jesuit, in 1884—'will never leave except for gunshot'. The Pope's independence, he added, would probably be secured only by war, 'which, after all, is the means which Providence has always chosen hitherto'. Crispi was friendly with Cardinal Hohenlohe and talked to him frankly about his fears. 'Let the Pope,' he told him, 'beware of being himself the cause of war, and remember what it cost Pius IX to have had recourse to foreign bayonets.'

Though language was often militant, Crispi's fears of war were not well founded. No country seriously considered going to war in order to re-create a theocratic State. The 'Roman Question', as it was soon called, had the appearance of an international problem. In reality, it was an Italian dispute, and the final settlement depended on conciliation between the Holy See and an Italian Government. Leo himself recognized that the old Pontifical State was never to be restored in its entirety. He wanted Rome. Yet the Rome over which Pius was ruling in 1870 already belonged to history. The city was becoming more metropolitan, and its population during Leo's long reign increased from about 300,000 to more than 470,000. No one could have made so large a city amenable to theocratic rule.

Leo gradually adopted a gentler attitude to Italy, and in 1887 he made a statement which showed his readiness to be at peace with the State, so long as the rights of the Holy See to its own independence were recognized. Loyal to the harmonizing tradition of Monte Cassino, Tosti at once seized the opportunity to write *La Conciliazione*, in which he argued that the last barrier to accord would be swept away when the Holy See renounced its Temporal Power. His views were too bold alike for Leo and for Crispi. Leo, while honouring a scholar, was not prepared to sacrifice the principle of Temporal Power. He gave Tosti a severe rebuke. 'We are not asking for conciliation,' Crispi declared in his turn. 'There is no need for it because the State is not at war with anyone. We neither know nor wish to know what the Vatican is thinking.'

Time, none the less, was on Tosti's side. So were the Italian people. In his statecraft Leo took them too little into account, but he was careful to appoint Bishops who would live in close touch with them and uphold the rights of the poor. One was Camillo Guindani, whom he made Bishop of Bergamo. In 1860, when the Kingdom of the Two Sicilies was destroyed, Bergamo provided Garibaldi with more recruits than any other city, but Bishop Guindani found that its anti-clerical sentiment was weak. The citizens wanted reconciliation. Bergamo, they said, would have settled the dispute between Church and State already.

Pius had told the Catholics to be 'neither electors nor elected': it was illicit for them to take any part in parliamentary activities. Leo softened the ban by stating that their participation was 'not expedient'. Yet the ban remained and became ever more irksome. In 1882, a new law increased the electoral roll from 628,000 to more than two millions. Virtually all the middle classes were enfranchised. Abstention now seemed pointless and even harmful. By his own anxiety to appoint Bishops who understood the people Leo created a new channel of information for himself and the Curia. Statecraft which omitted the human element was doomed to failure.

A diocesan Bishop better known to posterity than Giuseppe Guindani was Giuseppe Sarto, Leo's eventual successor. Born of a poor peasant family near Treviso, Giuseppe Sarto was already a parish priest in his early thirties when the last Austrian official left his neighbourhood and he became a subject of the first King of Italy. He knew how, even under foreign domination, the love of Italy swelled from the hearts of the humblest people. As Bishop of Mantua, and later as Patriarch of Venice, he endured many rebuffs from the Italian Government. Ministers might be Voltairean and anti-clerical, but not the people. The Patriarch loved his people, and he joined them in their welcome when King Humbert went to Venice.

Leo forgot the magic of monarchy. His court was more splendid than Humbert's and he could distribute honours and titles throughout the Catholic world; but while the Pope stayed within the Vatican, the King made himself known to his own people from one end of Italy to the other. He was a soldierly man with a simple manner, and he had at his side an intelligent and spirited woman who loved her Church and her country. Leo was the second prisoner of the Vatican, and Humbert the second King of Italy; but Margaret was Italy's first Queen. Leo sought to win souls. Margaret won hearts.

CHAPTER ELEVEN

HUMBERT AND MARGARET

HUMBERT WAS only eleven when he lost his mother and was condemned to share a Spartan existence with his two brothers, Amadeus and the crippled Odo. At eighteen, when he was a cavalry officer in Milan, he met Eugenia, wife of the Duke Litta Visconti Arese. She was seven years older than Humbert, but the youth's need to love and to be loved quickly found fulfilment.

In many ways, the heir to the Italian throne resembled his father. He was short in stature, though not physically grotesque. He was amorous, fearless, a lover of the open air, and a born soldier who longed to be under fire. His manners were simple and gentlemanly. Titles and distinctions of rank meant almost nothing to him. In part, this was due to family pride. Like his father, Humbert divided the world between members of the House of Savoy and the excluded multitude. This unobtrusive, but implacable, division helped him not only when he moved in the sophisticated circles of Milan which accepted the Duchess Litta as their social leader, but also when he lived in Rome. The black aristocracy could not deny that the Savoyard usurper was the head of the oldest ruling House in Europe. Nor could it deny that Humbert was well-bred.

A royal court needs a Queen, and Humbert's success as a constitutional ruler depended largely on the choice of the right consort. That choice rested with Victor Emmanuel alone.

First the King selected Princess Matilde, a Hapsburg and Humbert's cousin on his mother's side. Shortly after her betrothal, Matilde got ready to go to a ball in Vienna. She was smoking a cigarette when her governess suddenly entered the dressing room. In her confusion, the girl hid the cigarette inside her dress, which caught fire. According to a report, Austrian etiquette forbade anyone not of royal blood to touch the Princess. That night she died in agony. Humbert consoled himself by going back to Milan and to the Duchess Litta.

In his turn, Victor Emmanuel became a victim of etiquette; for he could announce no new betrothal within a year of Matilde's death. When the period of waiting was over, he sent an urgent dispatch to Humbert in Milan. 'Come with me,' he wrote. 'I have found you a wife.' The chosen bride was a first cousin on the paternal side: Margaret, daughter of the eccentric Duchess of Genoa, who had converted her second husband into a chamberlain.

Here was a marriage by royal command, and not a love match. Yet it was a tribute to Victor Emmanuel's common sense. Margaret was both as thoroughly Piedmontese as her husband and as thoroughly Italian. Together they worked loyally for their House and for Italy. As a child, Margaret knew the torment of living under the same roof as the Marquess Rapallo, stepfather and half-servant. Meanwhile Humbert detested Rosina, his stepmother, and was determined to rid Rome of her presence as soon as he became King. Rosina meddled in affairs and incurred the hatred of Cavour and many others. Humbert took care that none of his own mistresses interfered in State matters. He understood the limits of Latin liberty.

Victor Emmanuel did not allow his daughter-in-law the full rank of First Lady of the Land. While he lived, her sojourns in Rome were comparatively few. Yet, gruff-mannered though he was, he increasingly appreciated her sweetness and her tact. Together she and Humbert did what the King was always reluctant to do: they travelled from one end of the Kingdom to the other. Wherever they went, the Princess chose members of the local aristocracy to be her ladies-in-waiting. A few aristocratic families still held aloof in Naples, Palermo or Florence; but in no Italian city were the royal couple without friends and supporters. Humbert had the devotion of the army and the navy, and Margaret insisted that her court should not be confined to aristocrats and state officials; it should be open to all the talents.

With her charm she wrenched Giosuè Carducci from his republican loyalties, and the most revered poet of the day became a full-blooded monarchist. No matter how persistent were the accusations levelled against the House of Savoy as a bulwark of freemasonry and Voltairean sentiment, the Neapolitans were touched when they saw Margaret descend from her carriage and follow a religious procession on foot through the streets. She, at least, belonged to the same royal House as their Blessed Maria Cristina, Queen of the Two Sicilies.

As soon as the court went out of mourning, Humbert and Margaret began their first tour through Italy as King and Queen. On November 17th, 1878, they were driving through Naples with their son, the Prince of Naples, and with Benedetto Cairoli as the Minister in attendance, when a young cook called Giovanni Passanante broke through the police cordon and pointed a dagger at the King. Humbert remained completely calm, but Margaret may have saved his life by pushing her bouquet of flowers straight into the assailant's face. Cairoli leaned forward to protect the nine-year-old Prince and was stabbed. Though Passanante was ignorant and demented, he had gleaned some revolutionary ideas from Mazzini. He wanted to hasten the coming of the Universal Republic. Emperors and Kings stood in its way: 'they eat too much'.

To be attacked by an avowed republican was politically a blessing in disguise. The Romans, however, heard the news without waiting to learn who was the potential killer. Their anger was at once directed against prominent members of the black aristocracy. 'We went down by short cuts to the Palazzo Altieri,' Matilda Lucas admitted, 'to hear the crowd hoot Prince Altieri, who put no lights in his window. He was the man who gave a ball while Victor Emmanuel was lying dead.'

Humbert and Margaret reaped the full benefit of the people's anger when, a week later, they made their state entry into Rome. 'There was an immense crowd of every class,' wrote Augustus Hare, 'from ex-*guardia nobile* to peasants in the costumes of Sora and Aquino, and through them all the vast procession of sixty carriages moved to the palace with flags flying, and cannon thundering, and the one little bell of the royal chapel tinkling away as hard as it could because the other churches would make no sign . . . The little Prince of Naples is quite hideous, but they say well brought up by an English governess.'

The debts which Victor Emmanuel had incurred were enormous, but Humbert was determined to pay them. He closed down a number of royal establishments and introduced economies in the Quirinal Palace. Sycophants of the old King were furious. Since Leo was maintaining the papal court in full splendour, they thought it inappropriate for Humbert to lower the standards of his own court. In actual fact, he raised them. There were fewer officials and flunkeys than in his father's day, but the etiquette was stricter and the contacts with the country were closer. Humbert and Margaret had their childhood memories of what the court in Turin was like before Victor Emmanuel became a widower; it was military and exclusive. The new court in Rome was also military, but it was by no means exclusive; for Margaret liked to be surrounded by men of letters, musicians and painters. The court of Italy must not be divorced from art.

The Queen was frank in her likes and dislikes. Many Italians thought Verdi a greater musician than Wagner, who expected adulation when he visited Rome; but Margaret preferred German music to Italian, and Italian music to French. She also preferred Venice to Rome or Florence, and she stayed in the City of the Lagoon as often as possible. For one thing, she loved the paintings of Gentile Bellini, Carpaccio and Giorgione. For another, Venice was the Italian city least dominated by papal influences. It had a sturdy sense of independence. Daniele

Manin, champion of its freedom and half-Jewish, was chiefly concerned with liberating the city and its neighbourhood from Austrian control. His interests in the House of Savoy were secondary. 'Make Italy,' he told Victor Emmanuel, 'and we are with you; if not, not.'

Victor Emmanuel made Italy, and Venice was grateful. Only a few of its citizens troubled about the Pope's loss of his Temporal Power. Monarchy prevailed, and the *evvivas* which greeted the smiling Queen as her gondola glided through the Grand Canal were all eager and spontaneous.

If Margaret had not been wholeheartedly Catholic, she would have suffered less from the divided allegiances of Rome, the capital city. In private conversation, Humbert nearly always assumed that the Law of Guarantees was generous and offered the basis of a permanent settlement between Church and State. He was prepared to wait. Margaret, on the other hand, saw with her own eyes how the papal estrangement crippled the influence of the Quirinal Palace. The first ball which she attended as Queen was given at the Caetani Palace by the Duchess of Sermoneta. 'The Prince opened with the Queen,' wrote Augustus Hare, 'but *because* the King and Queen were to be there, all the great nobles had to stay away: so for once the Palazzo Caetani did not shine.'

Prince Filippo Doria Pamphili—head of the Roman branch of an illustrious Genoan family which, in more than one generation, was to mix its blood with English—accepted from the King the Prefecture of the Palace; but the black families which shunned the House of Savoy included the Borghese, Barberini, Chigi, Aldobrandini, Salviati and Sacchetti. Year after year, the Lancellotti family kept the main gate of its Palace shut as a token of mourning for the Pope who had lost his freedom. The Massimo family was closely related to the King, but it remained faithful to the Pope. So, too, did those Bonapartes who continued to inhabit Rome, and who were always careful to point out that, even though the Emperor Napoleon III had forfeited his throne, they were still a royal family. Prince Jerome Bonaparte was King Humbert's brother-in-law, but his own kinsmen in Rome chose to regard the pious Cardinal Bonaparte as their head.

Nor were the supporters of the Temporal Power all extremely orthodox in their religious beliefs. During the Vatican Council nearly all the Bishops who had thought that a definition of papal infallibility was 'inopportune' used to meet in the Rospiglioso Palace, where the hostess was Princess Zagarolo. Prominent among her guests were Archbishop Darboy and Bishop Dupanloup. Before his execution by the Communards of Paris, Archbishop Darboy managed to let Pius know that he condemned the loss of his Temporal Power. His view was shared by the Rospigliosi family; for nearly all its members left Rome for Tuscany, so that they might avoid any contact with a Piedmontese court.

To that particular generation of a great Roman family, life in Tuscany may have seemed a life in exile. In 1883, it was also a life in exile for the former Princess Mary of Cambridge, who had rejected Victor Emmanuel's offer of marriage. After marrying the Duke of Teck, she got hopelessly into debt. Queen Victoria, her first cousin, refused to lend any money, and the Duke was compelled to take his family away from England. One was a shy and intelligent girl of sixteen—Mary, later Queen of England—who thought it amusing that the family in exile took the names of Counts and Countesses of Hohenstein, while never ceasing to speak to each other in English. The family stayed in Paoli's Hotel on a bank of the Arno in Florence until it was lent the Villa I Cedri, about two miles outside the city.

The young Princess enjoyed her life in Florence, despite the hardships of living in what she called 'short street', and she visited one museum after another: 'how much nicer,' she wrote, 'than going out to tea and gossip!' Her mother's reactions to Florence are not recorded. Yet the older Princess Mary could never have forgotten that, as the wife of Victor Emmanuel, she would have become the first Queen of Italy and held her court in the Pitti Palace. Destiny, perhaps, was merciful. As a faithful Protestant, she refused to be the consort of a Catholic King. Italy was thus spared the spectacle of a court in which Europe's ugliest monarch stood by the side of a good-natured English Queen who became exceptionally stout and had often to be seated on two chairs. And who would have been the more extravagant: the King or the Queen?

Margaret, in her turn, began to lose her figure, but never her charm. It was more than the cult of royalty which made scholars like Gregorovius eager to go to the Quirinal Palace. Humbert was apt to scoff gently whenever the Queen held a literary salon. He did not share her liking for Carducci. Yet he knew that her work was complementary to his own. If he read the newspapers diligently, he preferred to leave the books in the library untouched. When the Queen turned the conversation to literature, he laughed and told the guests that now he could leave them and go to bed.

Humbert wanted action. He was at a shooting party when, in 1884, the news reached him that cholera was raging in Naples. Without a moment's hesitation he hurried south, where he found the Archbishop of Naples, Cardinal San Felice, comforting the dying and careless of the risk to his own life. Publicly the King and the Cardinal embraced each other. Then they walked together through the stricken districts. They made the conflict between Church and State seem shadowy and unreal. In the past Naples often changed its King. Thanks largely to Humbert, it has never ceased to be royalist.

Doctors from other cities followed the King's example and went to Naples. Among them was Axel Munthe, a Swede, who had set up a fashionable practice in Rome and lived in the house where Keats died. The account of his experiences during the scourge in Naples provided a memorable chapter to his 'Story of San Michele'. He described how the churches remained open all through the night, while rats were seen gnawing at the dead. Hour after hour bodies were thrown into the pits of a vast improvised cemetery. How many, Munthe asked, were thrown into them alive? 'Hundreds, I should say.'

The admiration which Cardinal San Felice felt for a King who wandered fearlessly through the overcrowded hospitals of Naples was shared by some other members of the Sacred College, and notably by Cardinal Alfonso Capecelatro, Archbishop of Capua, who belonged to a noble Neapolitan family. Like Newman, he was an Oratorian, and in his thinking he was deeply influenced by Montalembert and Tosti. Though never polemical, Cardinal Capecelatro did not hide from Pope Leo or Cardinal Rampolla his belief that their policy was wrong. The Church was mystical and should be above politics. In an effort to explain his meaning, he altered the famous Montalembert-Cavour phrase 'a free Church in a free State' and made it 'the free Church with the free State'.

Capecelatro was not only the second Oratorian in the Sacred College; he was also its second man of letters, and he proudly recalled that he had been Manzoni's friend. To his intellectual peers Leo allowed dissent. Newman and Capecelatro alike brought a literary renown to the Sacred College. Rampolla, who might have been his foe, treated the Archbishop of Capua with marked respect and even affection. In their hearts, perhaps, Leo and Rampolla knew that their policy was producing only negative results; for the days of the Temporal Power would never return. Meanwhile a Catholic people which longed for reconciliation was estranged. The Pope had become far too old to change the habits of his mind. More than a prisoner of the Vatican, he was a prisoner of his own statecraft.

Many features of Italian politics were, indeed, dark and repellent. Bribery and corruption became more than ever rampant in the south, where the vicious circle of poverty and ignorance was hard to break. The old claim that no man retired from political life richer than when he entered it lost validity. Yet many Senators and Deputies, distressed by the moral shortcomings of their parliamentary colleagues, strove hard to raise the standards of public behaviour. Their legislation was often far more enlightened than that of other countries. In 1889, for example, they succeeded in abolishing the death penalty.

In reality, the death penalty was already archaic because judges refrained from pronouncing the infernal sentence. Few evils scarred the memory of the old Pontifical State more than its savage record of executions and life imprisonments. As a young artist, Massimo d'Azeglio lived for a while in Rocca di Papa, a small town on the Alban Hills. Its local doctor, Leonido Montanari, found himself selected by lot to kill an informer. The doctor, a generous and imaginative man, stabbed the informer, but failed to kill him. Together with an accomplice, he was sentenced to death, and Massimo d'Azeglio went to the Piazza del Popolo to witness their public hanging. The executions were delayed for hours because the condemned men refused to accept the last rites of the Church. The priests pleaded with them in vain; for theirs was the courage, pride and contempt of Giordano Bruno. Here was one of many incidents which convinced a future Prime Minister of Piedmont that Rome was a 'sewer' and unworthy to become Italy's capital.

Saul of Tarsus approved when he saw his fellow-Jews stoning Stephen to death, but many Italians detested the death penalty because it transformed one among them into a butcher of human flesh. The occupation degraded a man and, so doing, made manhood itself bestial. According to the law before 1889, Giovanni Passanante merited death for his attempt to murder the King in Naples. Yet Humbert agreed with his counsellors that the young cook was mentally unstable and misled by a poor grasp of Mazzini's ideas. As he was more sinned against than sinning, his life should be spared.

The abolition of the death penalty was not the only notable legislative achievement of 1889. In England, four years beforehand, Henry Labouchere persuaded the House of Commons so to amend the criminal law that any homosexual action between men was made a criminal offence. For more than eighty years his amendment tortured innumerable Englishmen, young or old, whom nature had sexed differently from the majority. In 1889, however, the Italian Parliament heeded the ceaseless efforts of Cesare Lombroso, a professor from Turin and a pioneer psychiatrist; it abolished all punishments for sexual offences between men so long as they were not accompanied by acts of violence, infringement of the rights of minors, or outrages to public decency. There was a general agreement that the Code Napoléon offered a sufficient protection to minors.

The parliamentary men had all disobeyed the papal injunction to be 'neither electors nor elected', but the two reforms which they made in a single year showed their spiritual maturity. Like Mazzini, foremost among anti-clericals, they were more Catholic than they knew. One day the barriers imposed by the Roman Church would disappear. Then everything would depend on whether Catholics entered the Senate and Chamber of Deputies as a compact clerical party or individually as left-wing and right-wing members who happened also to be Catholics. Whatever pressure groups may have helped to abolish the death penalty and punishments for sexual offences between men, they were not clerical.

Though Rome had two separate courts, their purposes were different. Leo wished to impress the powers with his supra-national status, while Humbert and Margaret were chiefly concerned to make their own court a symbol of Italian unity. Crowned heads, whether Catholic or Protestant, had been reluctant to offend the Pope by visiting the King and Queen of Italy. In consequence, a whole decade went by before a foreign monarch slept in the Quirinal Palace. First to stay with Humbert and Margaret was the young Wilhelm II, who had recently succeeded his father as the German Emperor.

The protocol of the Vatican forbade him to call on the Pope by driving straight from the Quirinal Palace. In the morning, therefore, he went to the Capranica Palace, then the Prussian Legation, with the Empress Augusta and his brother, Prince Henry. The other important guest at the Legation was Cardinal Rampolla. Together they ate an excellent luncheon with a fine assortment of Castelli wines. Late in the afternoon the Emperor, Empress and Prince Henry entered a carriage driven by four blackish horses and mounted by German postillions. An outrider led the way to the Vatican. Leo received Wilhelm and Augusta alone, but Henry soon interrupted the audience by throwing open the door and declaring: 'A German prince shall not be kept waiting in an anteroom.' Whereupon Leo talked about *la pluie et le beau temps*: in other words, about nothing in particular.

According to protocol, the German royalties should have been driven back to the Legation, but Wilhelm ordered the postillions to return at once to the Quirinal Palace, and he made the Prussian Minister go with him. Members of the black aristocracy were not slow in circulating stories that the German Emperor and his brother had enjoyed the Castelli wines too much. There may have been some truth in their allegation: Castelli wines are deceptively potent.

Five years later the German Emperor and Empress went back to Rome. Their visit coincided with a garden party which Lord Vivian, the English Ambassador, was giving for the King and Queen. All the royalties then staying in Rome were invited, and they included the Duke of York, later to marry the shy daughter of Princess Mary, Duchess of Teck, and to ascend the English throne as King George V. The only royalties who declined the invitation were the German Emperor and Empress, who went to Tivoli for the day. Various reasons were suggested. Some believed that the Emperor disliked the Duke of York, his first cousin, and wished to avoid him. Others thought that the King and Queen were deliberately slighted. Berlin was a more flamboyant capital than Rome.

For a second time the Hohenzollerns exhibited their brash manners to the Romans, but Margaret had taken care that her own son should be well-bred and well-educated. He was born a sickly and undersized child. Whenever the King and Queen were living in the Quirinal Palace, he was driven away in a carriage to spend most of the day in the grounds of the Villa Doria-Pamphili, just beyond the Janiculum Hill, where the altitude was relatively high and the air fresh.

At the age of eleven, his days of childhood ended abruptly, and Lieutenant-Colonel Egidio Osio, formerly military attaché in Berlin, was appointed to take charge of his education. Since Osio was not a full Colonel, he was called the Prince's Vice-Governor, and not his Governor; but the sway was absolute, and although Osio's ideas on education were Spartan, the King and the Queen accepted them. They were allowed to see their son only at breakfast-time on Thursdays and Sundays.

The boy, moreover, was given a Tuscan manservant. Rosmini and Manzoni had won the battle for making Tuscan the normal literary language of modern Italy. No matter how keen was their desire to promote Italian unity, the King and Queen failed to conceal their own Piedmontese accent or to give up speaking the dialect when they were alone. This made them ashamed; for they were unduly influenced by the examples of France and England, where the correct accent was the accent of the governing class. Yet the Italian language is rich precisely because it embraces many vigorous dialects. Language in Italy is a territorial, and not a class, distinction. Why otherwise should a Tuscan have been chosen for the Prince's manservant? Two Italian dramatists of European stature are Carlo Goldoni and Luigi Pirandello. Goldoni's plays have always been hard to understand outside Venice. So are Pirandello's plays outside Sicily. Even in the manner of his speech, the Prince of Naples was separated from his parents.

Exclusive training and a painful knowledge that he lacked physical grace and stature deepened the solitariness of an only child. The Prince was intelligent, well-informed, shrewd and caustic, but he was also unimaginative and, unlike his mother, he cared nothing for music or for painting. If in time he grew sturdy, the excessive burden of his studies left its mark. Yet Egidio Osio was not unkindly, and in later years his pupil showed an affection that was almost filial. In England, the future King George V—five years older than the Prince of Naples —started to collect stamps. In Italy, the heir to the throne started to collect coins, and his first coin was a *baiocco* of Pius IX. It was the smallest copper coin minted in the old Pontifical State and was roughly equivalent to the now defunct English farthing.

At eighteen, the Prince of Naples already possessed one of the finest collections of Italian coins. What did the coins mean to him, or the stamps to George of England? Coins are made to spin. They pass ceaselessly from one pocket to another, but none can tell the whole of their individual history. The *baiocco* or two which hungry and chained papal prisoners begged from Lamennais, Lacordaire and Montalembert when they were making their unrewarded journey to see Pope Gregory: are they now for ever encased in the world-famous collection of coins begun by an unattractive and lonely boy?

With the Prince's approach to manhood arose the problem of his marriage. Like his father before him, he was not free to decide who should be the future Queen of Italy. At the same time, it was hard for anyone to find him a Catholic bride, since Catholic monarchs still hesitated to offend the Pope by even visiting the royal family in Rome. Once Margaret became alarmed when she heard that Lord Dufferin and Ava, the English Ambassador, was calling at the Quirinal Palace. Through the marriages of her numerous descendants Queen Victoria had already made herself the grandmother of Europe. Margaret feared that her own son was about to be caught in the widespread net of English princesses brought up as Protestants. The princess chosen for Italy might make her submission to the Church of Rome; but it would be enforced, and not genuine.

The bride who was ultimately chosen came from the tiny and impoverished court of Montenegro. Princess Helen was the sixth of the eleven daughters of Prince Nicholas, later Montenegro's last King. She had spent a simple childhood among the people of Cetinje, but she often went to Russia, where she stayed with the family of Tsar Alexander II, her godfather. When she returned to Moscow to attend the coronation of Nicholas II, Russia's last Tsar, she met the Prince of Naples.

She was Orthodox, and not Roman Catholic. In Roman eyes, however, the Orthodox Church was schismatic, but not heretical; its orders and sacraments, unlike those of the Protestants, were valid. Princess Helen crossed the Adriatic to Bari, where, in the splendid basilica of Saint Nicholas, she professed the faith of the Roman Church. She then went on to Rome, where—on October 24th, 1896—she married the Prince of Naples in Santa Maria degli Angeli, the church which Michelangelo had created from the baths of Diocletian.

As the cheering crowds watched the bridal procession from the church to the Quirinal Palace, they forgot their original disappointment that the heir to the throne had been given a princess from almost the smallest court in Europe. They also forgot that, two days later, Italian plenipotentiaries must sign the humiliating Treaty of Addis Ababa; for, in the only war waged during the reign of Humbert, a soldier-King, their country had been beaten.

After the unity of Italy was completed, her statesmen began to turn their attention to Africa. Motives were mixed and often dangerous. Some assumed that, since united Italy represented a new Great Power, she ought to behave like one. They were offended because France, though a recently vanquished country, was allowed to establish a protectorate over Tunisia, a land which can sometimes be seen from a region in Sicily with the naked eye.

Others knew that their compatriots were good colonizers and enriched every country in which they settled. Hard experience taught their statesmen that poverty in the south was not due solely to ignorance and mismanagement. The whole country was poor in almost everything save human resources, in which it abounded. Large-scale emigration could not be avoided, but the emigrant to a country in which the writ of his King did not run had to start work at a low wage and often with excessively long hours. He needed time in which to overcome the prejudices of a foreign people and to make good, whereas in an Italian colony he would soon be a master. His pride would not be crushed.

Colonies, however, were seldom developed solely to provide living space for overcrowded people. Prestige was involved, and Italy won her unity at a time when the older Great Powers still scrambled for territory, even outside Africa. In the first year of King Humbert's reign, Bismarck presided over the Congress of Berlin. Russia was given Bessarabia; Austria was permitted to administer the two provinces of Bosnia and Herzegovina; and England acquired Cyprus. 'I have brought back peace with honour,' Disraeli told the English; but Italy—Cinderella of the Great Powers—got nothing.

Prestige and rhetoric are yoked together. Italians were soon told that their country was 'the prisoner of the Mediterranean' and would find the key to its freedom only in the Red Sea. As a first step towards this liberation, a small commercial station was opened in Assab. In 1890, Crispi launched the colony known as Eritrea. There followed various ill-planned schemes for territorial expansion. Lovers of military adventure cast their thoughts on Ethiopia, and they roused the fears of Ras Menelik.

Regular soldiers knew that no military enterprise should be started without enough troops or adequate preparation. Above all, the skill of the enemy should never be under-estimated. Crispi, realizing the dangers, tried to restrain the Governor of Eritrea. The Governor, however, was General Oreste Baratieri, who, as a youth only nineteen years old, took part in Garibaldi's lightning march from the Strait of Messina to Naples. Its speed warped his judgment. If he once had little respect for the old Neapolitan army, he had none now for the Ethiopian foe. He failed to ask for reinforcements in time or in sufficient numbers. At Adowa—on March 1st, 1896—he was beaten.

This was Italy's first foreign war. It brought humiliation not only to herself, but also to the whole of Europe: a backward people living in the heart of Africa had effectively challenged the legend that white-skinned men are racially superior to all others. The King, who always wanted a large army, thought that more troops should be sent at once to Eritrea and so restore the prestige of his country.

Mercifully, other counsels prevailed. The blame belonged to Baratieri, but the defeat brought Crispi's long public career to an end. To Antonio Di Rudini, another Sicilian, fell the task of negotiating the Treaty of Addis Ababa, whereby Italy renounced for ever any claim to establish a protectorate over Ethiopia. Freedom from all entanglements with Ethiopia was the best wedding present which a statesman could have given to the future King Victor Emmanuel III.

Mazzini would have condemned the whole military adventure in Africa, for it caused Italy to deviate from the path of her rightful destiny. According to his philosophy, it would not have been true to claim that she got nothing from the Treaty of Berlin. By giving independence to Rumania, Serbia and Montenegro, this treaty brought Europe yet another stage nearer to her own unity. European unity, however, depended on the rule of the people, not on the rule of their Kings.

No matter how good and conscientious a King might have been, the men who stood closest to him were army officers, aristocrats and bureaucrats. They watched him fraternizing with the people and were probably not dismayed. As a gentleman, he had only one set of manners, whether he was talking with a rich landowner or with a carter; but his ambiance was not plebeian. He belonged to an exclusive set. In a society which was not hierarchic, monarchy would have no meaning.

People, and not Kings, would establish the united Europe of the morrow and make Rome her capital city. So Mazzini believed. He was a prophet, and little more. Many in his own country are still inclined to disregard him. In 1893, John Morley had a long talk with King Humbert about Garibaldi and Cavour. With the King, he found, Mazzini was 'much less in favour'.

CHAPTER TWELVE

OUTCASTS AND SINNERS

ALL ROADS may lead to Rome, but in the days of papal rule few English or American writers passed within its walls unless they were rather well-to-do. John Keats might never have seen Rome but for a friend's desire to save him from untimely death. John Milton, when he left for Italy at the age of twenty-nine, took with him a manservant and a few influential letters of introduction. To see Rome was not enough for him. The poet went on to Naples. He would have also journeyed through Sicily to Greece if news of civil war in England had failed to reach him.

In 1786, Johann Wolfgang Goethe—then thirty-seven and settled in his ideas—cast aside his duties as a Minister in the small court of Weimar and fled to the Brenner Pass. He was in so great a hurry to see Rome that he spared no more than three hours for Florence. Yet he got out of the coach which was taking him from Perugia to Foligno as soon as it reached the crossroad to Assisi. This was because he had read Palladio's account of a very beautiful Temple of Minerva to be found in the centre of the little city. He walked up the hill to Assisi, although a strong wind was blowing.

'With disgust,' he saw on the left 'the enormous structures of churches and bell towers, huddled together in Babylonian fashion, under which St. Francis reposes.' He took no notice. The only church which concerned him in Assisi was Santa Maria della Minerva because it was embedded in the ruined Temple of Minerva. He was delighted with what he saw. The visit was well worth the fatigue of having now to go from Assisi to Foligno—a distance of about eight miles—not by coach, but on foot.

As Goethe began walking down the hill, four rough-looking men surrounded him. Two were armed with guns. Had he forgotten, they asked, to go to the Franciscan convent?

'No!' Goethe lied. 'The building has long been known to me. But I am an architect. This time I wanted to stop and look at Santa Maria della Minerva which, as you know, is a model of architecture.'

The ruffians did not know. They refused, moreover, to believe that anyone—even though a foreigner—would leave the coach before it reached Foligno, if he had already paid the full fare. A man who walked away from Assisi without paying his respects to St. Francis was more likely to be a smuggler than an architect; and the four men said so.

Goethe was a wise traveller. He knew where he wanted to go and what he wanted to see. He wished to taste, and not to devour; and taste is individual and wayward. The painters who adorned the basilica of St. Francis—Cimabue, Giotto, Lorenzetti and Simone Martini—meant nothing to him, and his own favourite painters are all forgotten. As Goethe loved natural scenery, he was not long in Rome before he felt the urge to travel further south and to see the oranges still hanging on their trees.

According to his own account, the weather at the end of February 1787 was rainless and serene. 'The sky resembles azure silk lit by the sun. What will it be in Naples? Vesuvius hurls stones and ashes, and at night its peak is seen enflamed. Let us hope that nature in her bounty offers us a river of lava.' Though he saw no river of lava, Goethe was not disappointed; the spectacle of the smoke billowing from Vesuvius was 'marvellous' and transformed the entire atmosphere. 'We found ourselves to be really in another land.'

The more fortunate travellers were often those who went to Rome not by way of Florence or Civitavecchia, but by way of Naples; and who approached the city not from the north, but from the south. The sea journey from Marseilles appealed to Englishmen whose purses were slender and who needed to travel cheaply. The network of railways—growing in Italy and already large in France—made travelling easier for poets and other writers who, unlike Milton, would never have a manservant. To the newcomer, when the weather is fair, the Bay of Naples looks like the gateway to Paradise. It is actually the gateway to a city which flourished as a Greek colony long before Rome knew greatness.

Among the poor men who, in 1888, saw Naples before they set foot in Rome was George Gissing. Outwardly his life was a tragedy. He was good-looking and oversexed; he stole money, and the theft was discovered; he married a prostitute, and she slowly went mad; he wrote fine prose and never earned a handsome fee. He lived always on the razor-edge of poverty. Yet fortune granted him two long and spiritually rewarding trips to Italy.

He saw at once the splendour of Vesuvius: 'not black smoke, but tinted *pink* like a cloud'. For his first midday meal he bought 'bread and fruit, all for threepence, and a bottle of wine for fourpence'. Never was the sound of a donkey braying, a street organ grinding or a beggar asking for alms out of his ears, but he wandered happily through one noisy alley into another. Soon, however, came the urge to go northwards to Rome. Late on a November night he began the eight hours' journey. The train may have started from a city in the deep south, for it seemed to be carrying many other passengers about to see Rome for the first time in their lives.

'All night long,' Gissing wrote, 'a hundred times one or other was using the phrase *a Roma*. Century after century has this name *Roma* been used, and pronounced doubtless in much the same way. An odd and dangerous thing was the examination of tickets whilst the train was at full speed—the collector going along from door to door outside.'

The train reached Rome at about seven in the morning, and Gissing chose Shelley's grave for his first pilgrimage. He saw the Tiber ' "tawny-coloured" as in Horace's day'; and he admired the teams of oxen which brought from the countryside their heavy loads of fruit, vegetables and casks of wine. 'These fine beasts, with their immense horns, always make me think of the antique. Such animals Virgil saw, and Homer, I suppose. The oxen at Naples were of larger size, marvellous beasts, but they haven't the same long horns.'

As a poor man, Gissing thought twice—perhaps even three times —before paying for his admission to a museum; but the Sistine Chapel he could not ignore. 'You have to obtain tickets of admission from the Pope's Major-domo, but it is a mere formality. Unfortunately, here too one has to give gratuities, sometimes as much as *five* in a morning's walk through the rooms. The Italians are shameless in such matters. After getting my card of admission, I went up to the Scala Regia—a sublime staircase—and, at length, very tired, found myself before a dark little door on which was written *Cappella Sistina*. I knocked and was admitted.'

Like most other discerning visitors, Gissing must have gazed for a long time at the roof painted by Michelangelo. 'What,' he asked, 'are the exquisite figures seated on the beams that divide the nine spaces? I don't find them mentioned either in Murray or in Baedeker.'

Gissing went almost everywhere on foot, as even a rich man should do when he is in Rome. He found the 'glorious walk' which led first from the Pyramid of Cestius to St. Paul's-beyond-the-Walls and then eastwards across unspoilt country to the Via Appia. Once he took a train to the Milvian bridge and tramped along the Via Cassia, so that he might spend a noon-day amid the ruins of the ancient Etruscan stronghold of Veii. 'From the sixth milestone, the road is paved like the streets of Rome, with small diamonds of lava, bordered with diadems of larger size; on either side is a broad walk unpaved.'

Time and again, he may have returned to the Lateran Hill to see the view from the steps beneath the triclinium of Pope Leo III. For him, as for James Bryce and Henry James, this was just about the finest view to be seen anywhere in Rome; it was the view seen by Pope Pius IX immediately after his penitential climb to the top of the *Scala Santa*. 'In front,' Gissing wrote, 'the Sabine and Alban Hills, with just a tip of the Volscian between. In the foreground the fine arcaded city wall, with the gate of San Giovanni and the older Roman gate hidden by trees. Beyond the walls the long stretch of the Acqua Claudia.'

Gissing's tribute to the view from the steps below the triclinium was one of the last to be written by a man of letters. The speculative builder soon blotted it out; for at this time his defiling purpose was fast making Rome beyond the walls, as well as within them, featureless and ugly. Gissing wrote as though the Romans themselves were burdened by an ever-increasing drabness in their surroundings.

'The change in passing from Naples to Rome,' he declared, 'is inexpressible. One is no longer in the same country, no longer among the same people . . . the streets of modern Rome are monotonous and wearisome to an incredible degree, and there is absolutely no picturesqueness in the common life of the people. Rome is very silent. Never a street organ—not one; never a man crying his wares. To be sure it makes it much pleasanter to walk about than in Naples. There you can't go a yard without being importuned on one account or another. Here you are never addressed. The people are grave, decent, sober; very good-natured, but also, it seemed, very dull. No, it is not the same nation as in south Italy.'

Very different, however, were the reactions to Roman life shown by Phil May, a young artist from Yorkshire, who was in Rome at the same time as Gissing. He was the seventh of eight children, and he came from the outskirts of Leeds. It had become one of England's dirtiest-looking cities and was eventually to contain about sixty thousand back-to-back houses. Yet for Phil May, life in Leeds was poetry, and almost his first job was that of a scene-painter for its Grand Theatre. At twenty-one he sailed to Australia to draw humorous sketches for the 'Sydney Bulletin'.

'Couldn't you finish up your drawings a bit?' his chief once asked him.

Phil May knew better. 'When I can leave out the lines I now use,' he replied, 'I shall want six times the money.'

He was only twenty-four when Theodore Fink, a wealthy Australian admirer of his drawings, paid for him to study art in Rome. Phil May went willingly enough; but it was life in the streets of Rome, and not the treasures in its galleries, which held him captive. He saw the ill-clad youngsters—some with the freshness of mountain air from the south still glowing in their cheeks—as they played or slept in a sunless alley, while their father knocked at door after door in search of work. It was not for a father of many children to understand why the failure of a bank had suddenly interrupted a building boom.

Phil May also saw that the ground floor of nearly every house in the older and narrower streets of old Rome hummed with activity throughout the greater part of the day. Each was a workshop in which a family may have worked at its own craft from generation to generation. The Roman was always an artisan at heart, and he loved the individuality of his work. Artisan, craftsman, artist: the differences were mainly linguistic, and Phil May was all three.

'Be it never so crumbly,' he wrote to a brother, 'there's no place like Rome.'

Though fame made him profligate with his money, Phil May went back to Leeds determined to clear off a few small debts contracted with little shopkeepers willing to help him, though he was still a minor. He entered a shop and said that there was an account to be settled. May's friend was dead, but his successor went through the account book. He found no record of the debt.

'Look at an earlier account book,' Phil May suggested. There was again no record.

'Haven't you an even earlier account book?' At last, the record was found.

'Now you must give me a discount.'

'A discount?'

'Yes, discount for a cash payment!'

The new shopkeeper agreed, and Phil May settled the account. He then stood at the counter and, with a few deft lines, made a drawing, which he presented to the shopkeeper. Both knew that it was worth quite a number of guineas.

In Rome there was another brilliant Englishman who, later in life, would have thanked heaven for an opportunity to clear all his commitments and to be free from debt. About a year after George Gissing and Phil May arrived in Rome, a thirty-year-old student entered the Scots College. The younger Scottish students did not know what to make of Frederick William Rolfe, who was born in the City of London; who may have had no Scottish blood; who insisted on an unfettered freedom to make 'afternoon calls' in Rome; who was allowed to wear the black soutane instead of the student's purple one; and whose career, apart from an interlude at Oscott, was strangely unorthodox. They had looked forward to meeting him because he was reputed to be an Oxford man, and they barely hid their disappointment when they heard that he belonged to no Oxford college.

The Scots College endured him for about six months before he was dismissed. Rolfe then went to live in the house of the Duchess Sforza-Cesarini, whose son had been with him at Oxford. By birth, the Duchess was a Colonna, and Queen Margaret was her friend. The Prince of Naples, when a child, used to say that she was the most beautiful woman whom he had ever seen.

The Duchess, whose house in Rome was large, sheltered Rolfe for less than a year. Later, as he struggled in Wales to make ends meet, he called himself sometimes Fr. Rolfe and sometimes Baron Corvo. His image-making faculty was abnormally developed, and he indulged in fantasies. It is less certain that he deliberately told lies. If he misled people by signing himself Fr. Rolfe, he never doubted that he was given the vocation to be a Catholic priest. It is also possible that the Duchess Sforza-Cesarini or another member of her family transferred to him the title deeds of a small property. With it, as with many other properties in Italy, may have gone the proprietor's right to a courtesy title. While he held the deeds, Frederick Rolfe may have been Baron Corvo.

Even the claim that he was once at Oxford may also have been genuine. In 1868, eighteen undergraduates matriculated at Oxford as 'unattached students'. At that time the cost for three years' residence in a college was about one thousand pounds. This was more than many hard-working professional men were willing to pay for a son's university education. Frederick Rolfe would have reached the age for matriculation when the number of 'unattached students' at Oxford had greatly increased, and when their name had been changed to that of 'non-collegiate students'. They suffered from the frequent snobberies and snubs of other undergraduates more expensively educated in a college. They were poor men's sons and known contemptuously as 'toshers'. When an effort was made to secure the University church of St. Mary's for their corporate Sunday service, the Vicar—J. W. Burgon—'refused on the ground that all the oxygen which could be got into the church was needed for the services already held there on Sundays'.

Many 'non-collegiate students' left Oxford without taking their degree. In the early years, in fact, about half of them failed in their first examination, known as Responsions. Rolfe, who left school at fourteen, may not have been a good self-teacher. And who could have made him a zealous reader of Xenophon's *Anabasis*? He was, perhaps, too proud and sensitive to explain his lowly condition and record at

Oxford to Scotsmen in Rome; but, even without a college or a degree, he would have honoured Oxford with his command of a lorldy language.

'Hadrian the Seventh', first published in 1904, won renown long after poverty had killed Rolfe, its author. The novel is his apologia. George Arthur Rose is Rolfe himself: tired in mind, 'worn out by years of hope deferred, of loneliness, of unrewarded toil'; certain of his priestly vocation and at last rescued from a relentless quagmire of poverty and debt by a chain of capricious circumstances which led to his election as Pope. Though Rose is presented as a Pope of this century, the liveliest pages in 'Hadrian the Seventh' are those which reveal the Rome known to Rolfe when he walked through its streets in a black soutane.

In those days many Romans still vividly remembered incidents like the breaching of the wall at Porta Pia and the devastating flood of the Tiber just three months later. When the great Pope Leo I dared to meet Attila face to face, he made the 'scourge of God' submissive to his will. What might Pius IX not have achieved by meeting the soldiers of Victor Emmanuel when they were at the gates of Rome, or by moving among the Roman people when their homes were flooded? The letter of the law kills. It also lies.

Rolfe would often have heard the story that, immediately after his election, Leo XIII wished to bless the people in St. Peter's Square and found that the way to the outer balcony was blocked. 'Who knows if this is true?' So wrote Matilda Lucas at the time. Rolfe gave the story the ring of truth. He did more; for he made it a moment for turning the wheel of history.

'The Supreme Pontiff beckoned Orezzo.

"Lord Cardinal, this balcony looks into the church?"

"Into the church, Holiness."

"Which window looks out over the city?"

"The window on the left."

"Let the window on the left be open."

The Sacred College swung together as to a scrum . . .

"Holiness, that window was bricked up up in 1870, and has not been opened since."

"Let it now be opened."

"Holiness, Pope Leo had wished to have it opened on the day of his own election; but it was impossible. Impossible! *Capisce?* The rust of the stanchions, the solidity of the cement—"

"All that We know. The gentleness of Pope Leo was persuaded. We are not gentle; and We are not to be persuaded by violence . . ."

. . . At a sign from the Pope, the master-mason came forward and fell on his knees. Hadrian stooped.

"Son, open that window!" '

While Phil May watched the humbler Romans at work or play in the streets and George Gissing counted the *lire* he was able to spend, a twenty-four-year-old Italian was invading the fashionable bars and salons. Gabriele D'Annunzio was clearly not his real name. He came from Pescara, an Adriatic seaport, and his origins were commonplace. It was his luck, or misfortune, to be encouraged in egocentric and boastful behaviour by an indulgent father, who sent him, when a boy of eleven, to a Jesuit college in Prato. He stayed there for seven years and was splendidly instructed in the Latin and Greek languages. Once, when serving Mass for a priest whom he did not like, he recited all the responses in faultless Greek.

Gabriele D'Annunzio may have gone to Prato too late for the Jesuits to mould his mind. He was impenitently a sensualist and a pagan. At twelve he began an unabashed career as a seducer of women, and at sixteen he published his first volume of exotic verse. He was small, slim and curly-haired. A scoffer called him 'the amusing little Pomeranian'. Yet he had flashing eyes and a musical, almost feminine, voice. After he had shaken Roman society by eloping with the daughter of a duke, the fascination which he exerted over women grew all the stronger.

He was 'the poet without sentiment'; the lover without a heart. He craved to be made a prince, and in Mussolini's day he at last became the Prince of Montegranate. By that time he knew that the title was a bauble. To be acclaimed throughout his world as D'Annunzio the Poet was enough.

In Rome he was first a gossip-writer and then a Deputy in Parliament. Neither occupation satisfied him. He needed a bigger stage. No doubt readers laughed when they read his description of the way in which French residents listened to a famous preacher in their church of San Luigi dei Francesi. 'Another lady, famous for having the smallest and prettiest feet in Rome, comes hopping in like a bird, filling the church with a suave fragrance of sin. She does not hear the preacher. Her eyes are fixed on a young man who is standing with his back to a statue by Lorraine. When the preacher has finished, she falls to her knees and plunges her nose into a great bouquet of violets which she has bought. She inhales the fragrance voluptuously, then she rises . . . '

If D'Annunzio was often amusing, his humour was neither warm nor generous. The 'little Pomeranian' found it easier to snarl and to snap. He cared nothing about the debts which he was incurring, and when he grew bored with Rome, he went to Naples to live with a Sicilian princess. He knew that his pretensions did not deceive the aristocrats, 'so devoted to good manners and the arts of gentility that they have been gradually losing the right to live'. He was an outsider still.

Gossip-writing gave D'Annunzio too limited a field. Rome was a capital with a twofold contingent of Ambassadors; and although papal displeasure prevented the Catholic monarchs from making any state visit, the Grand Hotel was often filled with minor royalty. Yet the Italian capital was not a vast web which, like Paris or London, enticed and entangled the largest number of artistic people and drained away the talents of the provincial cities. Neither Turin nor Florence sacrificed an iota of its own cultural greatness when the Government and Parliament settled themselves finally in Rome. Between 1871 and 1901, Rome's population almost doubled, but it was still only the third largest city in Italy. Naples came first with a population of 563,000; Milan, second with 493,000; and Rome, third with 462,000 inhabitants.

The singer in Naples, the writer in Milan and the painter in Venice had seldom a particular need to go to Rome in search of fame. Regional pride in its own artists was strong, and all the former capital cities of the once fragmented Italy took care to preserve their old cultural standards and traditions. No great publisher has ever moved away from Milan, and the journalist in Rome has no Fleet Street. The national newspaper, as the phrase is understood in England, does not exist in Italy. Each Italian newspaper, however national or international in its coverage of news, is rooted to a region. The *Nazione* was founded in Florence in 1859. A year later, Garibaldi's triumph in the south was marked by the founding of the *Roma* in Naples. Each, as its title showed, anticipated the day of Italian unity. The *Roma* chose for its motto 'Monarchy and Democracy, Religion and Liberty'. Though unity was soon achieved, the *Nazione* is still published in Florence, and the *Roma* in Naples. The great newspaper of Turin—the *Stampa*—was founded in 1867, when the city was no longer a capital. The *Corriere della Sera* was founded in Milan in 1876. Rome's *Messaggero* did not appear until 1878.

As a capital city, Rome needed an opera house, but it has never dimmed the prestige of the Scala in Milan or San Carlo in Naples. The last three decades of the nineteenth century, for example, witnessed the first productions of a number of Italian operas which have stood the test of time: in Milan, Boito's *Mefistofele*, Verdi's *Otello* and *Falstaff*, Leoncavallo's *Pagliacci* and Giordano's *Andrea Chénier* and *Fedora*; and in Turin, Puccini's *Manon Lescaut* and *La Bohème*. Rome was chosen only for the first productions of Mascagni's *Cavalleria Rusticana*, *L'Amico Fritz* and *Iris*. Otherwise the Italian capital saw no first production until, in 1900, Puccini's *Tosca* was presented; and the libretto had already made it a Roman opera.

Through his Roman journalism Gabriele D'Annunzio made little stir north of the Arno, or even in his native Pescara. Society itself was provincial, and most of the titled people whom he described or mocked in Rome were unknown figures in Venice or Palermo. It was through their journeys from one city to another that King Humbert and Queen Margaret helped to make the monarchy national and popular. A court which never moved away from the Quirinal Palace would soon have become atrophied.

Except as a poet or novelist, the only national field offered to D'Annunzio in Rome was political. Accordingly, he became a Deputy. He had no use for party politics or discipline. One day he wandered by accident into the room where the Socialist Deputies were conferring together. They greeted him with ironical cheers. His response was immediate. He announced that he was now himself a Socialist; he was 'issuing from Death and going towards Life'. The word was little known at the time, but D'Annunzio was a proto-Fascist.

The more Rome changed its outward appearance, the more it seemed to remain essentially the same. Young men and boys bicycled out to the harbour and shore at Fiumicino and then raced each other home—as did the charioteers of long ago—over a flat and bumpy road. One morning excited onlookers watched the first motor-car which throttled its way through the mile-long Corso, but sentimental Englishmen still knew it as the street in which Shelley was living when he composed 'The Cenci' and 'Prometheus Unbound'. If inspiration came to Shelley in Rome, why not also to them? One 'budding poet' whom Matilda Lucas met in 1896 was Edward Marsh. 'I fancy his poems are more in the future than written, he looks so very young and timid.'

However much, in 1888, Gissing had lamented the ugliness of Rome's new streets, he was back nine years later to feast his eyes once more on the ancient glories. 'Christian art,' he wrote, 'has not the unspeakable charm that I find in pagan relics and memories.' For this reason, and despite the natural beauty of its surroundings, Florence failed to appeal to him as much as Rome, or even Naples. 'Florence is the city of the Renaissance, but after all the Renaissance was only a shadow of the great times, and like a shadow it has passed away. There is nothing here that impresses me like the poorest of Rome's antiquities.'

Gissing had recently formed a close friendship with H. G. Wells, and he was anxious that the novelist—young, but already a money-maker—should join him in Rome and bring his wife. He found a hotel where, if they lunched out each day, the cost for the two would be 98 lire a week. Then came the haunting fear that Catherine Wells might not like Italy. 'The fact is,' he told her, 'I always feel it is a terrible country; its unspeakable beauty is inseparable from the darkest thoughts; go where you may, you see the traces of blood and tears. To be sure, this will apply to the whole world; but here one remembers so much more than in other countries.'

The decision to go to Rome, however, rested with Herbert Wells, and not with Catherine. Herbert had dipped into the guide books, and they roused his innate historical imagination. 'The more I see of these Murrays the more I settle to Rome. Naples seems to me too much volcano and scene painting—a jaunt—a place where loafing is impossible because of the *lazzaroni*, and as to Florence! I'd sooner Winchester any day.'

Gissing's fear that Catherine Wells would not like Italy must have persisted, for his letters frequently mentioned some tribulation. 'I had a roast fowl the other day (after my fever), and the landlady (good, beastly creature) *tore it up* before me with her fingers—never touching knife or fork . . . No, no; I must go back to the Europeans. These lower-class Italians are Oriental in their savagery.' Whatever warnings Gissing gave to Herbert and Catherine Wells, they made no difference. Herbert set his heart on Rome and meant to stay there a whole month. 'Dull, cold and wet days will do for churches, galleries and such. But the spring sunshine will be about and on such days the open air.'

The letters which passed between Gissing and his friends cast one more light on the unchanging character of Rome. Damask and silk trail in the dust and the dirt. Castelli wine is drunk by peasants, and peasants' dishes still furnish the narrow repertory of a Roman kitchen. Roast fowl, soaked in oil, may still be torn and eaten without knife or fork. Yet the ills of life are forgotten in the spring sunshine; and what Herbert Wells called 'loafing', the Italians call *il dolce far'niente*: 'the delight of doing nothing'.

Towards Christmas 1897, and a few weeks after Luigi Tosti had died, Gissing went to the Abbey of Monte Cassino. Many other visitors who climbed the steep path from the town below had the sensation that time stood still in the monastery. From its windows were seen range after range of mountains and hills. They existed long before man made his mysterious appearance on the earth, and they may continue to exist long after his departure. But if nothing was hurried in the monastery, time did not stand still. Through prayer, thought and study, the followers of St. Benedict carried on their work of reconciliation in a troubled world.

While the train was taking him back from Cassino to Rome, Gissing overheard the conversation of three Americans:

'How long do you think of staying here?'

'Today's Wednesday, how does Saturday morning strike you?'

'So long?'

'How does Friday strike you? We've got to see Rome.'

'Well, that gives us one clear day.'

The three Americans who found that they could spare a day for sightseeing in Rome were no more foolish that Goethe when he hastened through Florence or ignored the Franciscan monastery in Assisi. The world is too large to be seen in a lifetime. Travel is wasteful when it is not enjoyed.

Swift Atlantic liners and increasing networks of railways were changing the scope and the style of the traveller. In turn, they began to change the cities which he visited. Even if Victor Emmanuel II had not transferred his capital from Florence to Rome, the city of the Popes could hardly have reached the closing years of the nineteenth century without some large hotels or tramlines. Their usefulness would be acknowledged when, in 1900, Rome observed a Holy Year. Then, if he lived long enough, Pope Leo would be ninety.

He was far too fond of modern inventions to accept the statement of Pope Gregory XVI that a railway should be called a *chemin d'enfer*: 'a road to hell'. On the contrary, he knew that it had become a main road to Rome. In the Holy Year of 1825, Pope Leo XII received pilgrims from all parts of Italy. In the Holy Year of 1900, another Pope Leo, or his successor, would receive them from all parts of the world. There might be no blessing bestowed on the people of Rome from the outer balcony of St. Peter's, but Queen Margaret—most faithful of Catholics—promised that 1900 should be a quiet year for the court at the Quirinal Palace.

As his years advanced, Leo became increasingly reluctant to devote his time to audiences. Pius had received each family of the black aristocracy separately. He was human and sympathetic, and at times he made a pun or uttered a *bon mot*. Leo, when he received a black family, had a few words to say to each member, but his manner was stiffer, and he was not a born conversationalist. Younger members often dreaded a family audience.

This was true of Vittoria Colonna and her sister, whose father shared with Prince Orsini the hereditary distinction of standing near the papal throne as a Prince Assistant. 'The Pope,' wrote Vittoria Colonna,

'looked scarcely human in his emaciation and parchment-like colour-
ing and was incredibly ugly. He wore mittens, and his shrivelled
fingers emerging from them looked like forks. He asked my father
whether he destined either of us to be a nun, which prejudiced me
against him.'

When he reached the age of eighty-six, Leo ended his separate
audiences for each black family. In their place, he held a New Year's
reception for all the faithful Roman patricians who kept away from the
Quirinal Palace. Yet, even if his burden of audiences was lightened, he
meant to be active during Holy Year, when many hundreds of non-
Italian ticket-holders would behold with their own eyes the splendour
of the ceremonies within the Vatican. Among the pilgrims from beyond Italy was Oscar Wilde.

English society had punished him severely, and after the 'Ballad of
Reading Gaol' and 'Salome' he wrote little more. The lyre was almost
broken. Passion and loneliness drove him back to a fleeting and hollow
companionship with Alfred Douglas in Naples, but he loved his two
sons and his wife. The sons were given the name of Holland. Everything was done in a vain attempt to prevent them from knowing even
the name of the father who used to play with them so gaily in their
childhood.

'Let me have one glance of my husband.' So Constance Wilde
pleaded after his release from prison. It was not to be. In 1898, when
only forty, Constance entered a nursing home in Genoa and submitted
to an operation to correct a spinal injury. The operation killed her.
Ten months later, when he could afford to make the journey, Oscar
Wilde went to look at her grave at the famous hillside cemetery in
Genoa. 'It was very tragic seeing her name carved on a tomb—my
name not mentioned of course—just "Constance Mary, daughter of
Horace Lloyd, Q.C." and a verse from Revelations.'

In earlier years Oscar Wilde would have been welcomed at the
British Embassy and at other Roman houses. James Rennell Rodd—
'true poet and false friend', with whom he once spent a holiday on
the Loire—had been the Second Secretary at the Embassy and was
later to return as Ambassador. But now Wilde was outcast and in
perpetual need of money. He even thought it useless to make any
attempt to get a ticket, so that he might see the Pope on Easter Day.
To his surprise, he was offered one by the hall porter at the Hotel de
l'Europe. 'When I tell you that his countenance was of supernatural
ugliness, and that the price of the ticket was thirty pieces of silver,' he
wrote to Robert Ross, 'I need say no more.'

The Pope was 'wonderful as he was carried past me on his throne, not of flesh and blood, but a white soul robed in white, and an artist as well as a saint . . . I have seen nothing like the extraordinary grace of his gesture, as he rose, from moment to moment, to bless—possibly the pilgrims, but certainly me.' Thereafter Wilde spent his money getting tickets from the hall porters who made a lucrative business out of robbing the pilgrims. When he found that the Vatican gardens were open to the Bohemian and Portuguese pilgrims, 'I at once spoke both languages fluently, explained that my English dress was a form of penance, and entered that waste, desolate park with its faded Louis XIV gardens, its sombre avenues, its sad woodland . . . One Philippe, a student, whom I culled in the Borgia room, was with me: not for many years has Love walked in the Pope's pleasaunce.'

Each time he went to the Vatican, Wilde found that Leo was wearing a different robe. On the last occasion, 'I gave a ticket to a new friend, Dario. I like his name so much: it was the first time he had ever seen the Pope: and he transferred to me his adoration of the successor of Peter: would I fear have kissed me on leaving the Bronze Gateway had I not sternly repelled him. I have become very cruel to boys and no longer let them kiss me in public.'

Yet the Vatican was not Rome, and Leo was not the only sovereign for whom, even in the Holy Year, the people cried *evviva*. Wilde was drinking an iced coffee outside the Caffé Nazionale when he saw King Humbert driving past. 'I at once stood and made a low bow, with hat doffed—to the admiration of some officers at the next table. It was only when the King had passed that I remembered I was *Papista* and *Nerissimo*! I was greatly upset: however, I hope the Vatican won't hear about it.'

Before the year was out both King Humbert and Oscar Wilde were dead. In May 1898, there had been rioting in the streets of Milan, and the regional military commander, General Fiorenze Bava-Beccaria, restored order through action that was too harsh and costly in human life. Army officers were loyal to the King, and he to them. For this reason, a group of Italian anarchists in the United States decided that the King must die. They sent an emigrant called Bresci back to Italy to do the deed. The King was always heedless of danger, and on July 29th he met his death in the grounds of his own palace at Monza, a few miles from Milan.

Republicans seldom hid their belief that the King was surrounded by army officers and others who hated the ideas of Mazzini and distrusted democracy. None the less, the murder shocked them quite as much as it shocked the royalists. They did not want rule by violence.

The dead King was brought back to Rome. Like his father, he was buried in the Pantheon. It was Christian burial, but the Bishops stayed away.

Four months later—on November 30th—Oscar Wilde died in a little Paris hotel. He had spent his last Easter in Rome. Perhaps, it was the only happy one since the torment of his trial and condemnation in 1895. Almost at the last hour a Passionist Father received him into the Catholic Church. About half a dozen friends followed the coffin—on foot and in the heavy rain—to the cemetery at Bagneux. Reburial among his peers at Père Lachaise came later.

> And alien tears will fill for him
>   Pity's long broken urn,
> For his mourners will be outcast men
>   And outcasts always mourn.

Rome is much older than the Papacy, and some of the religious men who entered the city in the Holy Year of 1900 were not particularly concerned with the baroque ceremonies within the Vatican or St. Peter's. Both at the beginning of the year and at its close, two major writers in the English language—William James and James George Frazer—found themselves staying at the same time in the Hassler Hotel above the Spanish Steps. Ten years beforehand, Frazer had seen the publication of his 'Golden Bough'. The mastery of this scholarly young Scot over the English language was soon widely acknowledged, and the 'Golden Bough' was read aloud to Alfred Tennyson—Queen Victoria's Poet Laureate—while he sat for his portrait by George Watts. Its opening chapter described the fearsome life of the god of the oak as he waited in the wood around Lake Nemi for his successor and slayer.

In the mid-nineteenth century, American travellers to Nemi—high above the lake and about twenty miles to the south of Rome—discovered that the village had only one inn. The inn itself had only one bed, but it was large enough for six people. Now the fame of Frazer's 'Golden Bough' had made a visit to Lake Nemi almost as obligatory as a visit to the graves of Keats and Shelley in the Protestant Cemetery. English visitors wished to see for themselves 'the calm, the burnished surface of the lake, Diana's mirror'. 'There, among the green woods and beside the still waters of the lonely hills, the ancient worship of the god of the oak, the thunder and the dropping sky lingered in its early, almost druidical form, long after a great political and intellectual revolution had shifted the capital of the Latin religion from the forest to the city, from Nemi to Rome.'

On Christmas Day 1900, William James described another lake.

This was Rome itself: 'the most satisfying lake of picturesqueness and guilty suggestiveness known to this child. . . . Just a FEAST for the eye from the moment you leave your hotel door to the moment you return . . . such a geological stratification of history! I dote on the fine equestrian statue of Garibaldi, on the Janiculum, quietly bending his head with a look half-meditative, half-strategical, but wholly victorious, upon St. Peter's and the Vatican.'

Nor could William James allow the year to end without looking at the inscription on the statue erected in the Campo de' Fiori to Giordano Bruno; for the Holy Year 1900 also marked the tercentenary of his martyrdom: ' "*il secolo da lui divinato qui dove il rogo arse*"—"here, where the faggots burned!" It makes the tears come, for the poetic justice; though I imagine B(runo) to have been a pesty sort of crank, worthy of little sympathy had not the "*rogo*" done its work on him. Of the awful corruptions and cruelties which this place suggests there is no end.'

Like most other religious people, William James pondered deeply on the mystery of death. He made a solemn pact with Frederick Myers that the one who died first would do his best to send a message back to the other. Myers had written his 'Human Personality and Its Survival of Bodily Death', but he knew that he would no longer be alive when it was published. He went to Rome to die. Axel Munthe, who was his doctor, described the last hours in 'The Story of San Michele'.

' "I know I am going to die," he said. "I know you are going to help me. Is it today, is it tomorrow?"

' "Today"

' "I am glad, I am ready, I have no fear. Tell William James, tell him."

' His heaving chest stood still in a terrible minute of suspense of life.

' "Do you hear me?" I asked bending over the dying man, "do you suffer?"

' "No," he murmured, "I am very tired and very happy."

' These were his last words.

' When I went away, William James was still leaning back in his chair, his hands over his face, his open note-book still on his knees. The page was blank.'

There is another side to the story, and many years later it was told by Bernard Berenson. In the afternoon he met James, who said that he had just seen Myers die. The last thing for which the dying man asked was the morning newspaper.

'Yes,' Berenson commented in his old age, 'I too would wish to live to the following day, so as to see what was happening before I left this realm of being.'

Holy Year and the nineteenth century passed into history, but pilgrimages to Rome were never ended. In 1901, a bearded medical doctor from Vienna was seeing Rome for the first time; he was born the same year as Oscar Wilde, and only a very few yet realized that he was a revolutionary newcomer in William James's own field of psychology. As a married man with five children to maintain, Sigmund Freud was thirty-nine before he felt able to afford a week's holiday with his brother in Venice. Thereafter he visited Italy almost every year. In 1897, he went as far south as Orvieto, where he pondered deeply on Signorelli's frescoes of the 'Last Judgment' in the Cathedral. Yet he waited until he was forty-six before he felt himself to be emotionally prepared for a first pilgrimage to Rome. He loved the city whole-heartedly. 'Rome'—so he wrote to his friend, Wilhelm Fliess—'has been an overwhelming experience for me . . . one of the summits of my life.'

Goethe, whom Freud revered, left Weimar determined to be in Rome in time for All Saints' Day. Since Catholics venerate the saints, he imagined that there would be some spectacular ceremony in St. Peter's. He was wrong, and the first great ceremony took place on the following day—All Souls' Day—when he found himself admitted to the splendid chapel inside the Quirinal Palace. There he saw Pope Pius VI, a 'very beautiful and venerable figure' surrounded by Cardinals 'of different ages and stature'. The enchantment vanished when Goethe realized that he was assisting at a Mass which, as a Protestant of the day, he neither liked nor understood.

In the same year that Freud arrived in Rome, Hilaire Belloc resolved to walk all the way from the Valley of the Moselle to the Eternal City. As a Catholic, he knew why he wanted to be in Rome on a particular day. 'I will start from the place where I served in arms for my sins; I will walk all the way and take advantage of no wheeled thing; I will sleep rough and cover thirty miles a day, and I will hear Mass every morning; and I will be present at High Mass in St. Peter's on the feast of St. Peter and St. Paul.'

Belloc belonged to two countries. He was born near Paris in 1870 while the Bishops were assembled in Rome for their Vatican Council; and, like the proclamation of the decree of papal infallibility, his arrival occurred during a violent thunderstorm. He went to the Oratory School at Edgbaston, where the boys took the presence of Cardinal Newman so much for granted that, among themselves, they called him 'Jack'. After completing his military service in the French Army,

Belloc began a fine career at Balliol College, Oxford. Later he became a naturalized British subject. Nothing, however, could have made him either wholeheartedly English or wholeheartedly French. Belloc was European. For him, Rome was the true centre of a Catholic Europe.

'I wish money would not drive me so.' He knew fame, but never wealth. The walk to Rome could not have been done by a man who failed to practise the utmost frugality. There was no sense of hurry until he realized that Rome was near, and then the 'small square paving of the Via Cassia rang under my feet'. At the foot of the last hill, he prepared to enter the city. 'There was an open space; a tramway: a tram upon it about to be drawn by two lean and tired horses whom in the heat many flies disturbed. There was dust on everything around.'

Belloc was present at High Mass in St. Peter's on the feast day of St. Peter and St. Paul; he saw Cardinal Rampolla, 'a fine man, like a great horse'; but Pope Leo, now ninety-one, was too sparing in his audiences to receive a Catholic writer then little known, even though Newman—'my Cardinal'—had instructed him in Latin.

Two years later King Edward VII troubled the Foreign Secretary, Lord Lansdowne, by his anxiety to see Pope Leo during a visit to Italy. England was still one of the countries which had no official representative at the Vatican, and Lansdowne insisted that the call on the Pope should be informal. King Edward first went to Naples, where he startled his entourage by walking through the slums with Queen Amelie of Portugal and Mrs. Cornelius Vanderbilt. When he got to Rome, he told his suite exactly how they should behave in the Pope's presence. They were free to bow as often as they liked, but they were not to kneel before him or to kiss his ring.

To emphasize the private character of the audience, which took place on April 29th, 1903, Cardinal Rampolla was not present. The Pope was sprightly and the encounter very cordial. It was one of Leo's last audiences. Within three months—on July 20th—he was dead.

CHAPTER THIRTEEN

WHERE ALL ROADS MEET

FOR A SECOND time since the fall of papal Rome the Cardinals got ready for their Conclave. Giuseppe Sarto, Patriarch of Venice, left his house which nestles close to St. Mark's and went by gondola to the railway station, where he bought a return ticket to Rome.

'Come back soon, Your Eminence!' someone shouted.

'Living or dead,' the Patriarch replied, 'I shall return.'

If Cardinal Sarto hoped that the Conclave would be brief, it was partly because he loved Venice and felt homesick whenever he went to Rome.

Most papal reigns are short. There were twelve in the seventeenth century, and eight in the eighteenth century. Together, however, the reigns of Pius IX and Leo XIII spanned fifty-seven years; and both were dominated by political issues. Pius fought a losing battle in defence of Temporal Power, and Leo schemed for its restoration, at least in an attenuated form. The one Pope was served by Antonelli, and the other by Rampolla. Each of the two Cardinals was a master of diplomacy; but whereas Antonelli was little more than a layman in scarlet clothing, Rampolla was deeper-visioned. For one thing, he shared Leo's belief that the Church had nothing to fear from scientific discovery or scholarly investigation.

Many who admired Leo looked on Rampolla as his obvious successor. Yet Leonine policy had been limping sadly behind the times. For too long, it assumed that the loss of Temporal Power in 1870 was no more permanent than its loss when Napoleon made Europe his chessboard. When Italy relied on support from Bismarck, Leo cultivated the friendship of republican France; but now the anticlericals were at the helm in Paris, and they were determined to separate the Church from the State. Temporal Power was not an international issue. The problem could be solved only by agreement between the Holy See and an Italian Government.

Leonine policy towards Italy, however, was particularly negative and self-destructing. So long as loyal Catholics were told to be 'neither electors nor elected', the Italian Parliament could not faithfully reflect the true opinion of a Catholic country. The gainers were the Socialists, whose views were revolutionary and anticlerical. They taught the

workers that their trade union was a better instrument of power than
a parliamentary vote, which at the moment they did not even possess.
It was bad enough that Rome should have two separate courts; but
it was worse that the city should be the centre of two separate, and
actually divergent, foreign policies. The Holy See should at least be
neutral. So the Italian Government believed; and it was anxious to
prevent the election of Cardinal Rampolla.

Leo, like Pius, reigned too long. It followed that Rampolla, though
only sixty, had been too long the Secretary of State. Some personal
friends regarded his candidature with disfavour because they knew
that, like Leo, he was bound to be political. They believed that the
days of a political Pope were over. The times demanded a Pope who
was primarily pastoral. One who shared this view was Cardinal Alfonso
Capecelatro, Archbishop of Capua. Another was Cardinal Domenico
Svampa, Archbishop of Bologna.

Rampolla the Sicilian and Capecelatro the Neapolitan were aristocrats who had much in common. Their families had served the old
Kingdom of the Two Sicilies well. In the days before Italy was united,
the claim was sometimes made that the best Bishops came from the
two former Kingdoms: Piedmont and the Two Sicilies. On the whole,
these Bishops were princely men and willing to be frank alike with
their monarch and with the Pope.

Cardinal Domenico Svampa did not belong by birth to a charmed
circle, and his training in Rome was conventional. Unlike Capecelatro,
he was not altogether a man of letters, but he admired intellectual
courage. Before becoming Archbishop of Bologna, he was Bishop of
Forli, and in the neighbouring village of Predappio he may have seen
a small and pugnacious boy called Benito Mussolini. All his experiences
in turbulent Romagna made him realize that the priestly training in
Rome bore no relation to the urgent social problems of his day. The
Church must be forward-looking if it seeks reconciliation with a
hot-blooded people easily provoked to violence. A first essential step,
so Svampa believed, was the election of a pastoral Pope.

Not every aristocratic Cardinal was forward-looking. Luigi Oreglia
was an aristocrat from Piedmont, but he ignored the King, and for
about twenty years he avoided any contact with Leo. He detested
modern ideas, and he condemned Catholic Democracy as wholeheartedly as Gregory XVI had done in the reply to Lamennais and
his friends. He had been the Nuncio in various countries before
Pius IX made him a Cardinal, and now the sheer weight of seniority
brought him his rank as Dean of the Sacred College. This meant that
the Monsignore selected to be secretary to the Conclave would have

to be acceptable to him. The choice was expected to rest between Pietro Gasparri and Giacomo Della Chiesa. Cardinal Oreglia, however, wanted Raffaele Merry del Val, then thirty-seven, to be the secretary, and he won his way.

Raffaele Merry del Val was born in London, trained at Ushaw College and ordained for Manning's diocese of Westminster. As the son of the Spanish Ambassador in Rome, all the palaces of the black aristocracy were open to him. His mother, though an Englishwoman, identified herself with the black aristocracy so completely that she once refused an invitation to preside at a *thé de bienfaisance*. As she explained in the hearing of Vittoria Colonna, 'I cannot preside over the tea-table, for if a lady of the white world comes up, I couldn't possibly offer her a cup of tea.' The young secretary of the Conclave was voteless, but he was already a titular Archbishop, and no man endowed with intelligence and social grace is without influence. Merry del Val had good reasons for wanting a pastoral Pope to be elected.

In order to prevent the election of Cardinal Rampolla, the Italian Government sought a foreign ally. It found him in the most Catholic court of Europe. The Emperor Francis Joseph of Austria-Hungary came to his throne in Vienna in the revolutionary year of 1848, and he readily assumed that socialism was synonymous with anarchy. He wanted no more Encyclical Letters on social order or the rights of workers. In past centuries, the Holy Roman Emperor claimed, like the King of Spain, the right to 'exclude' a candidate to the papal throne, even though the Cardinals may have given him the required number of votes. In 1605, for example, Spain used her right of 'exclusion' and thus prevented the election of a great Oratorian, Cesare Baronio.

The successful candidate needed for his election two thirds of the Cardinals' votes and one extra vote. A count showed that Cardinal Rampolla wanted only another ten votes to secure his election. Whereupon Cardinal Puzyna, Archbishop of Cracow, read a Latin statement that expressed the objections of the Emperor Francis Joseph to the candidature of Cardinal Rampolla. The Emperor claimed the right of 'exclusion'.

Cardinal Oreglia—abrupt alike with Popes and Kings—stood no nonsense from an Emperor. 'This message,' he declared, 'has no place here, either officially or unofficially. We will not take the least notice of it.'

A later count showed an increase in the votes cast for Cardinal Rampolla, but they did not reach the number required for his election. The Cardinals believed that they were taking no notice of an Emperor's veto. Indirectly, however, it damaged Rampolla's chances. The Cardinals had invoked the aid of the Holy Spirit, and now they were troubled by a political farce. Was it not better to elect a Pope who made no claim to statecraft and whose concerns were almost entirely pastoral?

Then, to his unutterable dismay, Giuseppe Sarto found that he was likely to be the favoured candidate. He wept when he realized that he might never see Venice again. Merry del Val saw him kneeling near an altar; he comforted the stricken Cardinal and gave him the courage to await his fate. Sarto accepted the election, but only as a cross; and he called himself Pius because that was 'the title of him who suffered most'.

Capecelatro of Capua and Svampa of Bologna both voted for him, though Rampolla was their friend. A pastoral Pope was at last to sit again on Peter's throne, but whether he was the Pope whom the two forward-looking Archbishops were seeking, time alone could tell. It was a good sign that Pius X wanted to bless the people from the outer balcony; but Cardinal Oreglia was adamant and said 'no'. The Pope was saintly, and he lacked the arrogance of Rolfe's mythical Hadrian the Seventh. Already Vatican officials had been moving among the crowd in St. Peter's Square and inviting gentry to enter the basilica. Within its walls they at last saw a figure whose head was amply crowned with silvery hair, and who waved from a balcony high above them. As he blessed, his back was turned against the city.

Yet a new Pope still meant more to the Roman people than a new King. Nothing ever made Victor Emmanuel III glamorous, for he paid the physical penalty for being the son as well as the grandson of first cousins. In an effort to remove the impediments of excessive inbreeding, a Princess from tiny Montenegro was chosen to be his bride. The new King was short, and his Queen towered above him. Sometimes guests at a crowded reception saw only the Queen as she walked the length of a room, for the King at her side was hidden from their view. Margaret, now the Queen Mother, had been ashamed of her own inability to speak with a refined Tuscan accent, and she took care that this fault should be corrected in her only child. Queen Helen, on the other hand, learned Italian as a foreigner. Often when she was alone with the King, they spoke together in French.

The King did not like the Quirinal Palace with its elaborate furniture and fittings. He wanted a homely place where he could knock nails into a wall without causing any costly damage. He moved into the Villa Ada, a mile or two away from the Porta Pia, and gave it the name of the Villa Savoia. The Quirinal Palace—which an earlier generation of Italian statesmen wrenched away from Pius IX—was used for state occasions. While the King collected coins and felt free to knock nails into a wall, the Queen often cooked a meal and preferred to run her own house in a simple way.

By all accounts, the royal couple were admirably suited to each other. In her childhood days in Cetinje, the Queen had lived very close to the people, and in its harbour she learned to fish. Throughout her life, and despite the wealth of dialects which confuse most foreigners in Italy, she retained her fondness for talking to passers-by and listening to their woes. Few claimed that she was ever elegantly dressed, but she was warm-hearted, and her ladies-in-waiting—notably Vittoria Colonna—were proud to render service to her.

The widowed Margaret—Italy's first Queen—was a formidable mother-in-law. King Humbert had looked to her constantly for support and advice. She knew the world, and it was to her salons that academicians and men of letters continued to flock. Once she had seen a Minister stabbed in her carriage, and the threats to King Humbert's life were numerous enough to prepare her for the shock of his eventual assassination. Experience as well as temperament made her increasingly conservative.

What the Queen Mother never lacked was the Savoyard gift of putting humble people completely at their ease. On returning to Rome after King Humbert's death she lived in a modern palace on the former grounds of the demolished Villa Ludovisi, which Stendhal had loved. The palace—later to become the American Embassy—ran alongside the Via Veneto, then a quiet street. It was thus within easy reach of the large park of the Villa Borghese, in which Margaret liked to stroll. One fine spring evening, the Queen Mother and her lady-in-waiting did not hear the park keepers when they shouted: '*Si chiude! Si chiude!*'—'We are closing! We are closing!' They reached the gates and found them shut.

While they waited for someone to come along, they saw a poorly dressed girl sitting on a bench. 'May we sit here with you?' asked the Queen.

'It's not my park,' the girl said pertly. Soon she began to talk about herself. 'I'm waiting here for the park keeper. He has promised to marry me so that I can give a name to my baby. He was the friend of my little boy's father. Now the father is dead, and I'm in despair.'

'But why,' asked the Queen, 'are you here when it has got so late?'

'Because the keeper is still on duty, and he asked me to wait here for him. For that matter, why are you both here?'

'We are here,' the lady-in-waiting explained, 'because Her Majesty and I found the gates shut.'

'Why has she called you Her Majesty?' asked the girl. 'Who are you?'

'My name is Margaret, and I am the mother of the King.'

The girl sprang to her feet. There was a fleeting look of fear in her eyes. Then she knelt down, kissed the Queen's hand and said:

'You are just like me, Your Majesty. You, too, are a widow.'

Queen Margaret's son maintained the father's traditions, and he revered the army. If his manners were simple, he never forgot that he was the head of the oldest ruling House in Europe. Just as his grandfather regarded Napoleon III as a *parvenu*, so he resented any vulgar display when the last German Emperor visited him. His arrival with an escort of tall Pomeranian Guards was not forgiven. Nature had given Victor Emmanuel few inches, but he did not lack dignity. He had a caustic tongue and his attitude to the Church was decidedly anti-clerical. Yet he upheld the image of a constitutional ruler.

The Constitution had not been changed since his great-grandfather, Charles Albert, granted it to the people of Piedmont in 1848. It allowed the King very substantial powers, and no one could tell how he might use them in a time of major crisis. Would he act firmly on his Ministers' advice? What contrary influences would be near his throne?

If the King was not glamorous, neither was Giovanni Giolitti. More often than not, this statesman, who came from Piedmont, was Prime Minister during the first fifteen years of the King's reign. The way in which Giolitti governed the country showed how wrong was Cavour in thinking that he had introduced the English parliamentary system into Piedmont and the Kingdom of Italy. Giolitti managed Deputies; he rigged elections; and when things became too difficult for him, he discreetly retired. Then, as a crisis receded or was forgotten, he returned to the helm.

Meanwhile the English had been witnessing a fierce party warfare between Conservatives and Liberals. David Lloyd George divided them by a people's budget which not only introduced death duties and a sharply scaled income tax, but also led to profound social changes. The vote in the British Isles meant power, and women began to fight actively for their own right to vote. They sought imprisonment and went on hunger-strikes; but in Italy the party system was marred by a 'transformism' which made it difficult to tell whether a particular measure was favoured by reactionaries or progressives. Politicians spoke a language which the people were often unable—or unwilling—to follow.

If Italian politics were hard for ordinary Italians to understand— and most were voteless until Giolitti enlarged the franchise in 1913—

the foreign visitor to Rome usually ignored them completely. He found a city in which the past and the present were so wrapt together that they gave contemporary time a different perspective. Sigmund Freud may have lost his heart to Rome at first sight, but Rainer Maria Rilke admitted that the city had 'an oppressingly sad effect for the first few days'. Its pasts were too abundant. Though Rome was beautiful, this was only because 'there is much beauty everywhere'.

Rilke was twenty-eight when—on October 29th, 1903—he wrote to a young poet, Franz Zaver Kappus, and explained the true nature of his liking for Rome. 'Waters unendingly full of life move along the old aqueducts into the great city and dance in many squares over white stone basins and spread out in wide spacious pools and murmur by day and lift up their murmuring to the night that is large and starry here and soft with winds. And gardens are here, unforgettable avenues and flights of stairs, stairs devised by Michelangelo, stairs that are built after the pattern of downward-gliding waters—broadly bringing forth step out of step in their descent like wave after wave. Through such impressions one collects oneself, wins oneself back again out of the pretentious multiplicity that talks and chatters there (and how talkative it is!) and one learns slowly to recognize the very few things in which the eternal endures that one can love and something solitary in which one can quietly take part.'

'I am still living in the city,' Rainer added, 'on the Capitol, not far from the finest equestrian statue that has come down to us from Roman art—that of Marcus Aurelius; but in a few weeks I shall move into a quiet simple room, an old flat-roofed summerhouse, that lies lost way deep in a large park, hidden from the town, its noise and incident. There I shall live all winter and rejoice in the great quiet, from which I expect the gift of good and industrious hours.'

Nearly three years later—in the height of the summer of 1906—James Joyce, then barely twenty-four years old, left Trieste in the hope of securing a better fortune in Rome. He arrived with his wife and one-year-old son, Giorgio; took rooms at the Via Frattina; and found a cheap little Greek eating place. He was employed in the Italian correspondence branch of an Austrian Bank, and his salary was 250 lire a month. In the evenings, he gave English lessons.

'There are two great patches on the seat of my trousers,' he wrote to his brother, Stanislaus, in Trieste, 'so that I cannot leave off my coat in the office and sit stewing for hours.'

The only prominent figure whom James Joyce saw in Rome seems to have been Cardinal Rampolla: 'a tall strong man with a truculent face' wearing 'a red beretta stuck anyhow on his head'. Rome was like 'a man who lives by exhibiting to travellers his grandmother's corpse'. It was clearly not the city for the future writer of 'Ulysses'. 'I wish someone was here to talk to me about Dublin.'

Poverty oppressed James Joyce—bank clerk and family man—too much. Otherwise he might have joined the throng of visitors who, evening after evening, threw small coins into the Trevi fountain as a token that they wished to return to Rome. For the writers who returned were many. William James was back again in 1905 to attend a Philosophical Congress. He agreed to speak in French on 'Does Consciousness Exist?' and he was surprised to find that he wrote French more rapidly than English. Moreover, he was uninhibited in Italian—'the awful gibberish I try to speak'—and thus conversed with Giovanni Papini and other Italian pragmatists.

At the time, they were publishing a monthly called *Leonardo*. These men, William James wrote, 'show an enthusiasm and also literary swim and activity that I know nothing of in our own land, and that probably our damned academic technics and Ph.D.-machinery and university organization prevents them from ever coming to birth'. They 'are none of them Fach-philosophers (specialists in philosophy), and few among them teachers at all. It has given me a certain new idea of the way in which truth ought to find its way into the world'.

This visit in 1905 pleased William James all the more because his younger friend, George Santayana, was staying in Rome at the same time. The disadvantage was Santayana's love of wandering round the city; for it was rare to find him in his hotel. At first, Santayana gave his devotion to Florence, but he noticed that a friend, when caught up in the life of the Anglo-American colony in neighbouring Fiesole, no longer lived with his old simplicity. In the end, he expressed his preference for Rome: 'larger, nobler, more genuinely alive, and more appealing to wide reflection. In Florence it is rather the quaint, incidental and hopelessly archaic that people feed their imagination upon.'

Meanwhile Henry James was still his brother's rival as a lover of Rome. In 1909, he re-appeared in the city as an affluent writer in possession of a motor-car. He enjoyed the experience when his car was ferried across the Tiber from Ostia to Fiumicino, 'which the age of the bicycle has made, in a small way, the handy Gravesend or Coney Island of Rome'.

For William James, however, the visits to Rome were ended. He was now mortally sick, though he mustered enough strength to listen to a lecture which Freud gave in German at Clark University. The trip to the United States and the lecture were both signs that the academic world had at last begun to realize that Freud's contribution to psychology might be serious. 'The future of psychology,' William James told him, 'belongs to your work.'

What James actually thought of Freud's work is scarcely known, for he was too ill to keep his diary up-to-date. The two men went for a walk together. Suddenly James stopped, handed Freud a small bag, and asked him to walk on. He would follow his companion as soon as he got over an imminent attack of angina pectoris. 'He died of that disease a year later,' Freud wrote in his 'Autobiographical Study', 'and I have always wished that I might be as fearless as he was in the face of approaching death.'

In 1911, Freud was back again in Rome, where he paid daily visits to Michelangelo's statue of Moses in the church of San Pietro in Vincoli. No work of art—not even Leonardo da Vinci's 'Last Supper' in Milan—impressed him more. He thought that he would write 'a few lines' about it. The statue became the theme of one of Freud's most important essays, but the writer did not finish it without returning once more to Rome. 'I have visited the ancient Moses again'—so he told Ernest Jones, later his biographer—'and I am convinced that my interpretation is right.'

Another writer who returned to Rome was Hilaire Belloc. His 'Path to Rome' sold more than one hundred thousand copies and made him famous; but he was a widower with a family to educate, and the need for money continued to drive him hard. None the less, he stood for Parliament as a Liberal and scorned the notion that, as a Catholic, he had little chance of winning enough votes. 'Gentlemen,' he announced at an election meeting, 'I am a Catholic. As far as possible, I go to Mass every day. This is a rosary (taking it out of his pocket). As far as possible, I kneel down and tell these beads every day. If you reject me on account of my religion, I shall thank God that He has spared me the indignity of being your representative.' His was the Lancashire constituency of South Salford. Blunt-spoken people admired his courage, and he entered the House of Commons as a valiant, if unconventional, back-bencher.

Belloc saw Rome again in March, 1914. Nearly thirteen years had passed since he began his walk from the Moselle Valley to the Eternal City. Yet 'Rome goes on astonishingly the same! Little growth and the same people of all nations and the same irritating backwardness and one-horsedness about all its arrangements.'

CHAPTER FOURTEEN

THE FEAR OF FREEDOM

ROME, IN Belloc's phrase, was still 'astonishingly the same' even to many who thought that liberating changes might have followed the election of a pastoral and saintly Pope. There were, indeed, reforms in liturgical worship as well as reforms aimed at making the work of the Roman Curia more expeditious, but people waited in vain for some sign that Pius X no longer wished to be regarded as the prisoner of the Vatican. At one time there were hopeful reports that he intended to make a pilgrimage to the Abbey of Monte Cassino. No conciliatory gesture could have been more eloquent, but someone prevented it.

On December 28th, 1908, an earthquake killed fifty thousand people in Messina and twelve thousand in Reggio Calabria. The Pope was anxious to leave at once for the stricken areas, but Raffaele Merry del Val—now a Cardinal and Secretary of State—forbade the journey. Cardinal Rampolla's days of commanding influence were ended. The young Anglo-Spaniard who took his place barely slackened the diplomatic war against the Kingdom of Italy.

For this continuance of the struggle, Cardinal Rampolla might well have forgiven him. What he did not forgive was the way in which Merry del Val and his group of supporters within the Curia waged war against every known scholar—priest or layman—who applied scientific methods to his studies, and particularly if his studies were Biblical. In a brief decade the new iconoclasts shattered the Leonine image of a Church in which the textual scholar, the philosopher and the historian may find a full exploratory freedom. The priest who makes war on the prophet has always some abstraction to denounce. Once it was Liberalism or Democracy; then Socialism; now it was Modernism.

The Church needs prophets as well as priests. In the twelfth century, Gioachino da Fiore, a monk from Calabria, foretold a rule of the Church by the Holy Spirit. Though his ideas were condemned, they exerted for a while an influence over Dante. There have always been some faithful Catholics who believe that the Holy Spirit makes the Church dynamic, and not static. In the last century, the idea of development in doctrine received a powerful impetus from Newman, who was gifted with the historical imagination, and whom Pope Leo made his first Cardinal.

Biblical criticism was even older. Its origins, in fact, can be traced to the arguments of two French priests of the seventeenth century— Richard Simon and Nicholas Malebranche—who were Oratorians. Simon believed that the Bible ought to be interpreted as freely as any other book, and Malebranche denied that miracles were possible: it was blasphemous to claim that the Author of nature was willing to break a law which He had Himself made.

The second half of the nineteenth century witnessed a changed attitude to history. As the servant of truth, history became far more than the relating of a story. Benedetto Croce was later to call it 'the only concrete form of philosophizing'. Every historical fact of happening might be re-examined and revalued in the light of its contemporary significance. Historians became not only interpreters, but also textual critics. They needed both imagination and a capacity for exactitude.

In the middle of the last century, Charles Kingsley—a polemical clergyman who wrote romances—was chosen to be the first Regius Professor of History at Cambridge. At its close, the Regius Professor was Lord Acton. The more scientific methods of studying documents were bound eventually to find favour with open-minded Biblical scholars and Church historians. Among them was Louis Duchesne— later the writer of a luminous 'History of the Church'—who presided over the Institut Catholique in Paris until Pope Leo called him to Rome. In 1880, he founded the *Bulletin Critique* for the study of Church history.

In the next decade, one of the workers in the Institut Catholique was Alfred Loisy, who had been Renan's pupil at the Collège de France and was now a priest. He pleaded that the critical methods which Duchesne applied to Church history should also be applied to the Biblical records. An article which he wrote on the inspiration of the Biblical writers caused him to be expelled from the Institut Catholique.

Although Loisy was deprived of an influential teaching post, he refused to be silenced, and when, in 1900, Adolf Harnack, most learned of all German theologians, published his 'Essence of Christianity', the French priest replied with *L'Evangile et l'Eglise*. Harnack wrote as though the Church, once it was founded, became degenerate and distorted, but Loisy assumed that it had ample capacity for spiritual renewal and development, for Christ Himself worked through the Church. Loisy so obviously accepted the critical approach to documents and institutions that his defence of the Church led to his own condemnation.

Another victim was George Tyrell, an Anglo-Irishman who had been an Anglican clergyman and became a Jesuit at the age of thirty-seven. He liked to express his views in anonymous writings, and he wrote a 'Letter to a Professor of Anthropology', which was translated into Italian without his knowledge. Extracts were published in the Milan newspaper, *Corriere della Sera*, and, in 1907, he was expelled from the Society of Jesus.

Two years later, he died rather suddenly and without having formally retracted his errors. Accordingly, he was denied Catholic burial. Yet, as soon as Henri Brémond—once a Jesuit and now a secular priest—heard that Tyrell was sick, he went to the bedside. Later he recited the funeral prayers, delivered an oration and faced without flinching the ecclesiastical penalties imposed on him. Loisy and Tyrell knew that their views might provoke censure, but in Italy the lash of the anti-Modernists fell on many humble priests who did not even know that they were being judged until they heard of their condemnation.

Prominent among laymen who recognized the need for a new and critical approach to Biblical texts was Friedrich von Hugel, a religious thinker who exerted a deep influence on younger men. In Italy, perhaps, there was no serious alarm until Tomasso Gallarati Scotti and other laymen in Milan published a review that was frankly critical. Laymen, in other words, were claiming the right to be interpreters of Biblical texts.

They did not call themselves Modernists. The word was coined by their foes, and it seemed to have been used for the first time when the Bishops in Piedmont issued a collective pastoral letter for Christmas, 1905. There was no doubt that their pastoral letter had the approval of the Vatican, where six Cardinals were leagued together for the suppression of Modernism.

One of the six Cardinals was the young, but powerful, Raphaele Merry del Val. The others were Francesco Segna, who left his teaching post in the Apollinare to avoid expounding the Thomist philosophy, which Pope Leo favoured; Benedetto Lorenzelli, who was Nuncio in Paris before France renounced her Concordat with the Holy See; Gaetano De Lai, whose clerical career was spent entirely in Curial offices; Giuseppe Vives y Tuto, an erudite Capuchin, who was confessor to the Pope; and the ultra-conservative Luigi Oreglia. Five of the Cardinals were members of the Roman Curia. Though Lorenzelli was Archbishop of Lucca, his visits to Rome were very frequent. Eventually he became himself a Curial Cardinal.

Between them, the six Cardinals held the key offices in the Curia. On their side, too, was Father Lodovico Martin, a Spaniard, who had been the General of the Jesuits—the 'black Pope'—since 1892. Against their combined influences, forward-looking residential Archbishops like Cardinal Capucelatro and Cardinal Svampa were almost power-less. Yet they did their best to protect individual priests and scholars who were accused of Modernism.

Pope Leo had founded a Biblical Commission to which he wished to attract the best scholars of the day. After his death, insidious changes in its membership turned the Commission into a mouthpiece of the militant group of Cardinals. In 1905, it asserted that the books of Holy Scripture have a character which is absolutely historical; in 1906, it upheld the Mosaic authenticity of the Pentateuch; and, in 1907, it declared that St. John was the author of the Fourth Gospel. A month later, the Pope issued the decree of *Lamentabili*, which condemned Loisy's offending *L'Evangile et l'Eglise*. There followed the Encyclical Letter *Pascendi dominici gregis* and the *Motu proprio sacrorum antistitum*. The three documents showed that the Vatican refused to be in any way accommodating with the Modernists.

Loisy was still undaunted, and he published his own comments on the decree of *Lamentabili* and the Encyclical Letter *Pascendi*. The Holy Office retorted by pronouncing against him the major sentence of excommunication.

The six Cardinals were all undoubtedly sincere. With the utmost sincerity, for instance, Cardinal Lorenzelli was later to claim that the earthquake in Messina and Reggio Calabria had been a divine affirma-tion of ecclesiastical authority. Cardinal Vives y Tuto was deeply respected for the holiness of his character. Cardinal Merry del Val already knew the words which he wished to have carved on his tomb: *Da mihi animas coetera tolle*—'Give me souls, take away everything else'. All the six Cardinals acted in the knowledge that the Pope supported them. As Pius X lacked scholarship, he did not understand the part which doubt and speculation play in the search for truth. Truth, after all, had been divinely revealed; and the Pope detested the thought that the faith of simple people all over the Catholic world might be under-mined by the progressive ideas and critical methods of more learned men.

As writers, Loisy and Tyrell were well able to defend themselves. Like Lamennais, they were free to continue their speculations even after the Church had condemned them. The real tragedy of the drive against the Modernists was that the six Cardinals and the 'black Pope' set in motion a new variant of the old Inquisition. Apostolic Visitors were sent from one Italian diocese to another to conduct exhaustive enquiries. They encouraged all sorts of people to be the 'mercenaries of orthodoxy'. Whenever these people wanted to denounce someone whom they suspected to be a Modernist, they were given an assurance that their own name would not be made known. The espionage was all the more deadly because it was anonymous.

One sufferer whom Cardinal Svampa befriended was Michele Fabri-Pulignani, Vicar-General at Foligno. As his Bishop was old and infirm, the Vicar-General carried almost the full burden of administering the diocese. Yet he was a very active town councillor, and he founded a small weekly journal. In his writings he referred to the human viscera which the Franciscan monks of Assisi carefully preserved in the basilica of Santa Maria degli Angeli. It was not true, Fabri-Pilignani claimed, that the viscera were those of St. Francis.

At almost a single stroke of the pen, Fabri-Pulignani incurred the wrath of the priest chosen to be the Apostolic Visitor in Foligno. This was Gianmaria Santarelli, who was a Franciscan born in Assisi, and who had always resolutely maintained that the viscera preserved in Santa Maria degli Angeli were taken from the body of the great saint. Soon after his appointment, Santarelli announced that he would go to Foligno and begin his investigations. Fabri-Pulignani replied that his Bishop was indisposed; it would be better, therefore, to postpone the visit for a few days, so as to enable the Apostolic Visitor to be appropriately received. Santanelli was furious. Without a moment's hesitation, he left Assisi in a hired carriage and reached Foligno at two o'clock in the morning. He avoided any meeting with the Vicar-General as he listened to complaints against him.

A particular grievance of priests and laymen accused of Modernism was a confusion of heretical thought with private action. Salvatore Minocchi published a translation of the 'Prophecies of Isaiah'. In a rather too long preface, he argued that the Prophecies were written by three different people. The Archbishop of Florence refused to give the translation his *imprimatur*. Whereupon, Minocchi sought and obtained an *imprimatur* from Cardinal Svampa, the Archbishop of neighbouring Bologna. As a writer and translator, Minocchi could defend himself as easily as did Loisy; but why was he rebuked for calling on Tolstoy during a visit to Russia?

In actual fact, unconventional conduct was condemned just as ruthlessly as heretical writing. A glaring example was the fate of Francesco Salimei, who was a member of the Noble Guard. He had married a daughter of Friedrich von Hugel and attended George Tyrell's funeral. Both actions indicated that his sympathies were with the Modernists, but he was left unmolested until, in 1910, Theodore Roosevelt paid a visit to Rome. The former President of the United States naturally desired to have an audience with the Pope. Merry del Val prevented it. Ernest Nathan, who had offended Pope Leo by erecting the statue to Giordano Bruno in the Campo de'Fiori, was still the Mayor of Rome, and he decided to give a banquet in Roosevelt's honour. Among the invited guests was Salimei, who, as a former member of the Rome municipality, felt bound to accept. Merry del Val had him expelled from the Noble Guard.

Cardinal Svampa was openly a protector of priests suspected to be Modernists, and when he died in 1907, an Apostolic Visitor was sent to Bologna to purge the diocese before handing it over to a successor. The new Archbishop was Giacomo Della Chiesa. He belonged to a patrician family from Genoa, and his education was completely secular. He had even taken a degree in civil jurisprudence before he decided to enter the priesthood.

When Rampolla went to Madrid as Nuncio, he chose Della Chiesa to be his secretary. The advantages of a legal training were soon shown in the young priest's clarity of expression, for he seldom needed to delete or alter a single word in his letters. Rampolla brought him back to Rome when he became Secretary of State. He had wanted Della Chiesa, and not Merry del Val, to be the secretary for the Conclave. Giacomo Della Chiesa was sent to Bologna as Archbishop because he was Rampolla's friend; his new office was really a sentence of exile from Rome.

Whether or not Romagna appealed to him, Della Chiesa soon put simple people at their ease as he rode on horseback from one village to another. Unfortunately, he was small and slightly deformed, and the citizens of Bologna had expected a more impressive-looking Archbishop. They called him *il Piccoletto*: 'the little one'. Their strong civic pride was hurt as the years passed without the conferring of a red hat. Not until Pius X held his last Consistory was the Archbishop of Bologna admitted to the Sacred College. For once, it was claimed, the Pope overruled the objections of his Secretary of State.

Many others suffered during this inquisitional period which Rampolla called a 'dark and deep night'. Theodore Roosevelt was a religious man, and he had been popular with the American Catholics during his days at the White House. He bore the refusal of a papal audience without any rancour. In private, however, he expressed his sorrow that the Pope did not have better advisers.

For Louis Duchesne the refusal of a papal audience had harsher consequences. His 'History of the Church' was a scholarly achievement, and when he heard that it was placed on the Index, he demanded to see the Pope. Merry del Val prevented the audience, just as Antonelli had tried to prevent Rosmini from seeing Pius IX when he was about to be driven out of Gaeta. The Pope of the day was more than a prisoner of the Vatican; he was also the prisoner of a few Curialists.

As the Church was hierarchical in its structure, it stressed the virtue of obedience. Bishops were submissive to orders from the Vatican. In turn they expected submissiveness from their own clergy. Rosmini had been right to condemn the way in which, in the old Venetian Republic, Bishoprics went to the cadets of wealthy or influential families; but he also demanded a better education for the seminarists. They were still trained to be men of memory rather than men of thought.

Pius X, a poor man's son, appointed many Bishops who were of humble birth. One of the few exceptions was Giacomo Radini-Tedeschi, whom he made Bishop of Bergamo. If this Bishop appointed a peasant's son—Angelo Roncalli—to be his secretary, he knew that the stocky young priest from Sotto-il-Monte had rare gifts of sympathy and judgment. The complaint that the attack on the Modernists was launched by Bishops and priests who came from homes bereft of culture was not altogether just. Oreglia and Merry del Val were both patricians.

None the less, the inquisitors, aristocratic or plebeian, exploited the spirit of fear which hovers over the poor and the needy. Priests felt dependent on their superiors, just as their fathers had often depended on a patron for their livelihood. They were not required to be adventurous in thought or action. Only a few were historians, or even theologians. In consequence, they had imperfect ideas of the exacting demands which the search for truth makes on the scholar and the thinker.

These seekers after truth were anxious to remain within the Church: 'to work a reform within it, and not against it'. In the words of Giovanni Semeria, a Barnabite monk who exerted great influence on Cardinal Svampa, they were Christians 'who wished to remain faithful to Christ, who felt the powerful mysteries of the Church, but who did not want to abandon the scientific methods which had illuminated so much of their work and that of others in the secular field; they wished to live an abundant life in Christ, a life of thought, love, art, democracy'.

Some Bishops and priests chose to be silent; but they, too, felt the wound. The Vatican Council of the last century had achieved almost nothing beyond declaring the Pope to be infallible when he speaks *ex cathedra*. Were Bishops to be merely executants of orders issued by the Curia in Rome? Had they no collective rights of their own? If another Pope called them to Rome for a new Ecumenical Council, would they not forthrightly demand a recognition of their collegiality? Why should the bureaucrats of the Holy See keep them at so great a distance from the Bishop of Rome?

The élite were few, and the conformists were many. It was thus possible to impose an anti-Modernist oath on teachers in the seminaries. If this conformist spirit prevailed in the Italian Church, how could the Italian State be immune? 'To believe, to obey, to fight': that might have become a slogan attractive to crusaders against Modernism. It was actually a slogan which, in a later decade, Mussolini devised for his Fascists.

War on the Modernists was all the harder to accept because Pius X had begun his reign under the most promising conditions. He was eager to reform the Curia, the seminaries, the structure of the dioceses, and the Canon Law. On many who were fortunate enough to talk with him he left an indelible impression of human warmth and goodness. In 1905, he received Charles Augustus Briggs, a close friend of Friedrich von Hugel, and one of the best Biblical scholars in the United States. In former years Briggs had been a Presbyterian Minister, but his methods of Biblical criticism were condemned by his Church. Thereafter he joined the Episcopalians.

The Pope and his Protestant caller spoke together with a disarming frankness. With a few more encounters between them, perhaps a sad chapter in this century's history of the Roman Church need not have been written. Pius X wanted guidance. This might have come from Briggs or from Duchesne. Instead, it came from a few resolute Cardinals too close-minded even to perceive what priests like Salvatore Minocchi and laymen like Friedrich von Hugel were trying to do.

Another non-Roman clergyman received by Pius X was Lonsdale Ragg, an Oxford scholar who was then the Anglican chaplain in Venice. During the audience, the Pope spoke almost entirely about a beloved city lost to his sight for ever. He was ready to go back to Venice, 'even in a packing case'. The Anglican chaplain may have had fewer pastoral burdens than the former Patriarch of Venice. Some of his flock were rich, and others were living in retirement after spending their lives as officials in India or elsewhere in a far-flung Empire on which the sun never set. They were a relatively closed community of class-conscious —perhaps almost caste-conscious—English residents. Their social leader was Lady Layard, the tall, regal and alarming widow of Sir Henry Layard, a Victorian celebrity who excavated some of the ruined palaces of Nineveh.

The community nearly always had an outcast. In the last century, he was the well-to-do John Addington Symonds, who employed the handsomest gondolier on the Lagoon. In the early years of this century, he was Frederick Rolfe. Proud, penniless and doomed to a shortish life by anxiety and malnutrition, the Catholic author of 'Hadrian the Seventh' sought help from the Anglican chaplain and then, when he had received it, reviled him. The chaplain's wife, Laura Ragg, was herself a scholarly writer, and she was recognized as an authority on both Jane Austen and Alphonse Lamartine. She agreed with her friends that Rolfe was not a gentleman and, on her own unquestioning authority, she asserted that he was not even a decent writer.

Lonsdale Ragg preferred not to endorse harsh judgments on a beach-comber of the canals. Yet he was astonished and put to shame when long after his chaplaincy in Venice was ended, Rolfe sent him a letter and made a partial repayment of the money which he had borrowed. In 1913—the year in which Thomas Mann published 'Death in Venice' —Baron Corvo took to his grave both the sense of priestly vocation and a passionate desire to be freed from the tyranny of debt.

For all the crusading against the Modernist, Pius X was ready to come to terms with a new century. Except to a few over-zealous foreigners like Madame Merry del Val, the old Roman distinctions between the black and the white aristocracies were wearing thin. Friend-ship and humour pierced many barriers, and in 1901 Vittoria Colonna married Leone Caetani, Prince of Teano and eldest son of the Duke of Sermoneta. Gone were the days when a Colonna slapped the face of the mighty Pope Boniface VIII, who was a Caetani. Pius X kept up the New Year's reception which Leo had introduced for the Roman patricians, but he invited all members of their family to attend. Thus Vittoria Colonna could still go with her father to the Vatican, though her husband was the grandson of the blind Duke of Sermoneta who delivered to King Victor Emmanuel II the results of the Roman plebiscite in 1870.

Circumstances, if not personal inclination, made the Pope amend the 'non expedit' which was intended to prevent all faithful Catholics from voting or standing for Parliament. Individual Bishops were given the right to decide whether the Catholics in their particular diocese should take any part in parliamentary life. The Vatican wanted a Catholic party: cattolici deputati si, ma non deputati cattolici—'Catholic deputies, but not just deputies who happen to be Catholics'.

It recognized the need for a Catholic party too late. Already an extremely able priest, Romolo Murri, had founded the National Democratic League. He studied at the secular University of Rome as well as the Gregorian University. This double training convinced him that it was possible to be both a good Catholic and a good democrat. The Vatican might want cattolici deputati, but the country needed *deputati cattolici.* The age-long struggle between Guelphs and Ghibellines—Pope's men and Emperor's men—was taking a new form. Caesar, according to Dante, does not derive his authority from Peter. The *deputati cattolici*, therefore, would think and act without ecclesiastical control and without ever betraying their Catholic consciences. The Vatican did not accept Dante's doctrine. Romolo Murri was reduced to silence, but not for long. In 1909, he entered the Chamber of Deputies as a Radical. There followed excommunication.

None the less, his ideas began to spread among good Catholics. They influenced not only Luigi Sturzo, a priest from Sicily, but also Giorgio Montini, who edited a newspaper in Brescia and who was convinced that if enough genuine Catholics entered the Chamber of Deputies, they could heal the breach between Church and State in Italy. They needed freedom, not directives from their Bishops. Giorgio Montini liked the play of ideas, and he encouraged his two sons, Lodovico and Giovanni Battista, to discuss political and other issues openly with him. His second son—one day to become Pope Paul VI—inherited from his father a fondness for the word 'dialogue'.

With more *deputati cattolici* in the Chamber, parliamentary rule under Giovanni Giolitti might have been less prosaic and less bellicose. Among them might have been a few far-seeing men who worked not only for reconciliation between Church and State, but also for closer European unity. Mazzini had pointed the way to Italy's true future. Rome should be more than the city of the Pope, and more than the capital of Italy; for the Risorgimento was but a stage towards the re-ordering of a people's Europe. Instead, the spokesmen of popular opinion in Italy looked southwards to Africa, and particularly to Libya.

The defeat which General Baratieri, a hero of the Risorgimento, met at Adowa should have made the country wary of any new colonial adventure. It should also have shown that heroes belong to their own age, and not to others. Yet, if heroes belong only to their own age, why did Italy have to wait until 1911—a full forty years after the breaching of the Aurelian walls—before Giuseppe Sacconi's colossal monument to Victor Emmanuel II was at last completed? In the heart of Rome a giant King with a plumed helmet strides a giant horse in full military splendour. Was the sword, which he claimed that he often drew, to be sheathed for ever? Italy must be worthy of Germany and Austria-Hungary, her military allies.

In the last century, France had offended Italy by annexing Tunisia, and there was now a danger that she might extend her North African territories eastwards. There was also the Italian's longing to cultivate his own land. In the south, fathers encouraged one son or more to emigrate, partly because the successful emigrant sent money back to the needy home, but also because they wanted to avoid any further fragmenting of the family land. In a colony, the land-hungry peasant might soon cultivate his own hectares, but when he emigrated to the United States or to Canada he became a wage-earner, a town-worker, a 'factory hand'. Libya appealed strongly to Sicilian peasants with large families to feed. They fancied that the climatic conditions of a country sometimes visible from their own coast were similar to those in Sicily. Giolitti believed that policy should keep pace with popular opinion; but it was not without anxiety that he launched Italy into a war for Libya.

A strenuous opponent of this war was Benito Mussolini, now a Socialist leader of the extreme left wing. The partisan spirit he inherited from his father, Alessandro Mussolini, who was the blacksmith in the village of Predappio. A blacksmith's life can suit a man with the philosophical temperament. For a while, Thomas Masaryk—a Czech boy who was only a little older than Alessandro Mussolini—worked for a man who was blacksmith, farrier, bone-setter and teeth-extractor in the Moravian village of Hodonin. The forge pleased him.

'I liked working as a blacksmith,' Masaryk wrote. 'It's a job which calls for strength and quickness, and it doesn't need a lot of talk. In the summer we were often hard at it from three in the morning till ten or eleven at night. But it's fine work; the smith at the fire and anvil overcomes the stubbornness of matter.' In later years Thomas Masaryk became the founder and first President of the Czechoslovak Republic; but his fingers, twisted and gnarled at the anvil, stamped him for ever as one who had been a manual worker.

Alessandro Mussolini did not possess the philosophical temperament. His smithy was the village centre for political agitation. He named his son Benito as a tribute to Benito Juarez, the Mexican revolutionary who, in 1867, ordered the shooting of the Emperor Maximilian. In former years, Romagna was the most turbulent region within the Pontifical State, and its proneness to violence did not end when the King's Ministers took the place of the Pope's. Mussolini was sent to a school run by the Salesians, who promptly expelled him when he knifed a fellow-student. Thereafter he was almost entirely self-educated.

Mussolini wrote well, spoke with a fiery eloquence, and craved for action. One of his first books was a short study of Jan Hus, the Czech reformer who died at the stake convinced that he was not a heretic. He gave it the title of 'Jan Hus the Truthful'. 'In giving this little book to the press,' the author stated in his preface, 'I express the hope that it rouses in the mind of the readers hatred for every form of spiritual and political tyranny: whether it is theocratic or Jacobin.'

Unlike Thomas Masaryk, Mussolini was not a systematic reader. He took from other writers—Nietzsche, Sorel, Bergson and Machiavelli —only the ideas which were useful to him. He may never have read Marx. A dominant idea he borrowed from William James: 'belief in the truth of a proposition tends to bring about its truth in fact'. He distorted this idea into a belief that propaganda, when flamboyantly directed, can make any desirable proposition become truthful.

Despite an admiration for William James, there is no certainty that Mussolini heard about a famous address which, in 1906, this exponent of pragmatism delivered on the 'Moral Equivalent of War'. Although, as James admitted, human history was 'a bath of blood', he believed that war could be outlawed without losing any of the martial virtues of 'intrepidity, contempt of softness, surrender of private interest, obedience to command'. This could be done, however, only by finding 'moral equivalents for war'. People of different nations might combine for the conquest of nature or for the building of a better society. Young men, instead of being enrolled for compulsory military service, could join a civilian corps devoted to a particular form of social service.

Two years later, nearly all the Indians then living in Johannesburg entered the grounds of a mosque, where a Hindu lawyer stood near an enormous cauldron. They had undertaken to register themselves as Indian residents under certain conditions. These conditions, they affirmed, were ignored by the Government's leader, General Jan Smuts. In protest, the Indians threw their certificates of registration into a cauldron. At a given signal, the Hindu lawyer set the certificates on fire. The lawyer was Mohandas Gandhi, and this burning of his countrymen's certificates became his first experiment in *satyagraha*: a passive resistance which, as he explained, was made active by the spirit of love. Gandhi, at least, found one 'moral equivalent of war'.

William James showed how a man endowed with all the martial virtues might yet adopt some 'moral equivalent' for war. Mussolini loved action and detested the Libyan War. He had the gift of leadership. With his imagination and drive, he could have striven to keep Italy out of every suicidal war; helped to displace an expensive and cumbrous conscript army with a peace corps designed to rescue southern Italy, Sicily and Sardinia from their agricultural backwardness, poverty and ignorance; and brought the liberating influence of the Risorgimento a stage further by championing the cause of national self-determination throughout Europe.

Mussolini might have been the right man of action to carry on

Mazzini's work. He read Mazzini, however, no more thoroughly than he read James. If he preached the importance of duty, he forgot Mazzini's assertion that the duties of man can be fully assumed only by those who are themselves free. He opposed the Libyan War only for party and tactical reasons; he was not opposed to all wars. Despite his ceaseless playing with ideas, Mussolini put action before thought. His nature was coarse-grained. He wanted power, and only for himself.

Within less than a year, the Libyan War was brought to an end. It gave Italy *de facto* sovereignty not only over Libya, but also over Rhodes and the Dodecanese Islands. On the surface, Turkey was the loser; but she expelled about fifty thousand Italians resident in her areas. She also boycotted all Italian goods, and Rhodes ceased to be a flourishing commercial centre. The results of the Libyan War, moreover, mocked the spirit of the Risorgimento. If it was right for Victor Emmanuel II to rescue Italians from Austrian rule, it was wrong for his grandson to consent to Italian sovereignty over a group of islands in which nearly all the people were Greeks. Nationalism led to the creation of united Italy, and now men like Thomas Masaryk in Prague were preaching Mazzini'a ideas of freedom to the Slavs. The Libyan War, in fact, served to hasten the day of a general conflagration in Europe.

Meanwhile the pressure on Italian soil persisted. In 1913, the annual number of emigrants from Italy rose to 872,000: one out of every forty Italians was leaving the motherland, and this at a time when Giolitti had increased the size of the electorate from three and a half million to eight million voters. No matter how intensive might become the cultivation in the sandy wastes of Libya, the new adventure could never have solved the problem of Italy's abundant man-power: children of the sun and the comeliest of all the European races.

War for Libya, however, taught Giolitti a few lessons which he never forgot. He realized that Italy was ill-prepared for any martial enterprise. Its military machine was too inelastic to assure victory. The statesman from Piedmont was resolved, therefore, to keep Italy out of a major war. If this war began and he was still her Prime Minister, Italy would be neutral.

In the early summer of 1914, the Archduke Francis Ferdinand committed the error of going to Bosnia for the military manoeuvres. At Serajevo he was shot dead, together with his morganatic wife, the Duchess of Hohenburg. The aged Emperor Francis Joseph, when he heard the news, treated it as God's judgment on a sinful heir. He did not know that the tragedy would hurl the world into its greatest war and tear away a mask of civilization.

On August 2nd, Pope Pius X issued an exhortation to all Catholics. His words expressed the profoundest grief. In a war between Catholic Austria and Orthodox Serbia, the sympathies of the Vatican might have been wholeheartedly on the side of Austria. Nearly all the political troubles which afflicted Pope Pius IX could be traced back to the refusal to make Austria his foe. But the issue was not clear-cut; for Belgium, a most Catholic country, had been shamefully invaded.

The Austrians were confident that right was on their side, and the Ambassador to the Holy See made a bold approach to the Pope. 'Holy Father,' he declared, 'thousands of Catholics will march in the armies of Austria and Germany. Through me, His Majesty the Emperor of Austria asks that Your Holiness bless his armies in this struggle.'

The Pope refused: 'I bless peace, not war.'

For about three years his health had been failing. Sometimes gout gave him excruciating pain. War he could not endure. On August 20th, he died.

CHAPTER FIFTEEN

BLIND WARMAKERS

AMID UNEXPECTED difficulties and vexations, Cardinals who lived outside Italy made their way to Rome to elect a new Pope. French or German, English or Austrian: each was a Prince of the Church which, he believed, had been founded by the Prince of Peace; and each owed loyalty to a belligerent modern Caesar, regal or republican. The prospects of the war—in the late August and early September of 1914—changed from day to day, and almost from hour to hour. Catholic was fighting against Catholic, and anti-clerical against anti-clerical. Not since the election in Venice of the long-suffering and charitable Pius VII had Cardinals held a Conclave under similar conditions of strain, anxiety and unnatural reticence.

Among the Cardinals who arrived from Italian sees was Giacomo Della Chiesa of Bologna: *il piccolo*. He was not yet sixty, and he had been a Prince of the Church for less than three months. At the last Conclave, Cardinal Rampolla failed to secure enough votes. A pastoral, rather than a diplomatic, successor to Pope Leo was favoured; but now the gifts of Rampolla's friend and pupil were appreciated. To the world's surprise, and to his own, the most recent Cardinal and the smallest in physical stature became Pope. Hurriedly the papal tailor hemmed and shortened the smallest of the three robes which he had prepared for the successor of the saintly Pius.

The new Pope chided him. 'Carlo, Carlo! You forgot all about me.'

Giacomo Della Chiesa took the name of Benedict because the last native of Bologna to become Pope was Benedict XIV. This was Prospero Lambertini, a child of the eighteenth century, who enjoyed exchanging letters with Catherine the Great, Frederick the Great and Voltaire. The new Benedict had far more serious things to do. In a world gone mad, he must be a peacemaker. The Vatican's neutrality must have nothing in common with indifference. Benedict did not give his first blessing from the outer balcony of St. Peter's. Like Leo, though for a markedly different reason, he decided that his coronation must take place within the Sistine Chapel. For the first time since 1870, the papal tokens of mourning were appropriate. Peter's successor blessed peace, not war.

As a peacemaker, too, Benedict wished to end the persecution of the Modernists. If he upheld the former condemnation of Modernism, he insisted that the utmost care should be taken before any priest or layman was accused, or even suspected, of holding Modernist opinions. An early step was the reinstatement of Francesco Salimei, whom Cardinal Merry del Val had driven out of the Noble Guard.

Cardinal Merry del Val's days of dominance in the Roman Curia were ended. The new Secretary of State chosen by the Pope was Domenico Ferrata, who had gallantly fought a losing battle for the Church when he was the Nuncio in Paris. Many outside Rome approved the choice. Cardinal Ferrata, however, died only a few days after his appointment. His place was taken by Cardinal PietroGasparri, who, in younger years, had lived in Paris as a Professor of Canon Law at the Institut Catholique.

Benedict and his Secretary of State asked for a ban on all aerial action outside the war zone; for a periodical truce to enable fighters to bury their dead; and for a truce at Christmas. Their requests were seldom granted. The spirit of hatred grew ever stronger and moral judgments coarsened. Benedict tried to prevent the war from involving other countries, and for a time he pinned his hopes on the United States. He wanted that great democracy to work actively for peace, and never to join the warmongers. In the Easter Week of 1915, he granted an audience to an American journalist.

'Convey my greeting and my blessing to the American people,' he said. 'Tell them that my sole desire is to work conscientiously and unselfishly for peace, so that this horrible massacre may be ended as soon as possible. Tell them this, and you will render a great service to God, to humanity and to the world . . . The eyes of the entire world are fixed upon America, and the entire world awaits from her an initiative in favour of peace. Will the American nation know how to seize the favourable moment? I pray to God they will.'[1]

In the same Easter Week, Benedict granted an audience to Matthias Erzberger, a leader of the Central Catholic Party in Germany. 'If the war lasts much longer,' he told him, 'there will be a social revolution such as the world has never before seen.'

Benedict made these two statements at a time when Italy was speedily becoming involved in the European slaughter. He knew the laical mind better than any of his recent predecessors, and his natural clear-sightedness enabled him to see that a small group of leaders were about to impose on the country a war which the people did not want and

[1] Quoted by Nazareno Padellaro in his 'Portrait of Pius XII', translated by Michael Derrick (London, Dent, 1956).

Photo Mansell Collection

THE ASSASSINATION OF KING HUMBERT IN THE
ATHLETIC GROUND OF MONZA, JULY 29TH 1900

Photo by courtesy of H. Montgomery Hyde

HENRY JAMES AND WILLIAM JAMES

Photo Mansell Collection

GEORGE GISSING 1897

Photo Mansell Collection

HILAIRE BELLOC

POPE PIUS X

Photo Giordani

CARDINAL MERRY
DEL VAL
ecretary of State to Pope Pius X

Photo Giordani

POPE BENEDICT XV

Photo Giordani

POPE PIUS XI

Photo Giordani

MUSSOLINI (c. 1920)

Photo Radio Times Hulton Picture Library

GIACOMO MATTEOTTI
Murdered by Fascists in 1924

Photo O. Restaldi

POPE PIUS XII

Photo Giordani

ALCIDE DE GASPARI
IN 1947
Prime Minister

Photo ANSA

Photo Felici

POPE JOHN XXIII WITH PRESIDENT
AND MR. AND MRS. JOHN EISENHOWER

POPE PAUL VI

which, even if they happened to fight on the winning side, would bring them no lasting advantages. Both as Pope and as a patriot, he wanted Italy to keep out of the war.

Here he shared the views of Giolitti, an impenitent anticlerical. Church and State, the old statesman once declared, are 'two parallels which ought never to meet'. All too soon, however, he must have wished that the King had a political sagacity equal to the Pope's. Italy, he knew, might gain far more by skilful diplomacy than by joining either side in a war.

Giolitti was the victim of his own tactics. Just when the country most needed his leadership, he had put himself out of office. The launching of the war for Libya taught him that the generals were inept and the army's equipment quite inadequate. Though he renewed Italy's increasingly unpopular alliance with Germany and Austria, he knew that its terms were merely defensive and did not bind her to join in any war of aggression. At the moment of danger he would keep his ill-prepared country neutral. In March 1914, however, he made one of his periodic retirements from office and, on his advice, the King chose Antonio Salandra to be President of the Council. Giolitti thought that Salandra was his own puppet. It was a cardinal error. Salandra was ambitious and set out to please the King, who liked Giolitti no better than his grandfather had liked Cavour.

In July—and without warning Italy or Germany, her allies—Austria sent a war-making ultimatum to Serbia. Giolitti, who was in London, hurried to tell Salandra that the ultimatum did not commit Italy; she must remain neutral. The country wanted neutrality, but a number of political leaders also wanted territorial gains. Some had an eye on Trento, Southern Tyrol, Trieste—Austria's main gateway to the Mediterranean—and the Dalmatian coast, so that they might give Italy a better strategic frontier in the north and convert the Adriatic into an Italian lake. Others had an eye on Nice, Corsica and Malta. The first group favoured war against Austria, while the second favoured war against Austria's foes. A third group tried to put Italy's neutrality up to auction; it might be bought at a price. Each of the three groups was Machiavellian and immoral. The blind were leading the blind.

For a short time, Mussolini found himself in the same camp as Pope Benedict and Giolitti; he wanted Italy to keep out of the war. Then, like Benedict, he realized that the longer the war lasted, the greater was the probability of social revolution. Unlike the Pope, he was impatient for revolution; and so war suited his purpose.

Others, too, longed for war. Professional soldiers were not content to man frontier posts or to strut around in uniform. Generals contemptuously rejected a civilian notion that they were inept. The King's training was military, and so was his entourage. Like his martial grandfather and father, he played the role of a constitutional monarch; but the Constitution, granted by Charles Albert in 1848, was itself based on the French Constitution of 1830. It was outdated and required reform. The royal prerogatives were too ample. For one thing, the Ministers were responsible to the King, and not to Parliament.

Parliament, in fact, was almost a cipher. What Cavour and his successors failed to learn from England was the importance of an active opposition within the Chamber. In the House of Commons at Westminster the arch-debaters of the last century—Disraeli and Gladstone—made their most memorable speeches sometimes as Prime Minister and sometimes as Leader of the Opposition. In the present century the Leader of the Opposition holds a full-time post and receives a regular salary. Giolitti, on the contrary, retired to his estate in Piedmont whenever he was out of office. There he lived far from Rome, just as the King and his court in Rome were far from Milan and other northern cities in which the political opinion of Italy was mainly formed. Yet, even if Giolitti had been in Rome at the time, he would probably have heard nothing about the secret negotiations which Salandra and the Foreign Minister, Giorgio Sonnino, had started with England's Foreign Secretary, Edward Grey.

The auctioneers won their way, and on April 26th the three Entente Powers—England, France and Russia—signed with Italy the secret Treaty of London. It promised Italy military assistance, an extension of territory to the Brenner Pass, and enough gains on the Dalmatian coast to ensure her dominance in the Adriatic; it also promised to exclude the Holy See from an eventual Peace Conference. In return, Italy undertook to enter the war on the side of the Entente within a month.

What had happened in London was known to almost no one in Italy beyond the King, Salandra and Sonnino. Not until May 4th—eight days after the signing of the treaty—did Salandra tell Berlin and Vienna that Italy was renouncing her old alliance. He waited yet another day before telling the High Command that Italy would fight against Austria. All its plans had been based on the assumption that if Italy went to war, England and France would be her foes. A contrary war was now to start in less than three weeks.

The Entente Powers bought an ally and a vast amount of human cannon-fodder in exchange for promises which might be difficult, if not impossible, to fulfil. In any event, the promises concerned areas in which England had no vital interests. Leading members of the Government in London—for example, Herbert Asquith the Prime Minister, David Lloyd George and Edward Grey—considered themselves to be good Gladstonian Liberals. Yet they allowed a secret treaty to bind the Italian people to the chariots of war without the knowledge—still less the approval—of their Parliament. At this time there was no English statesman who possessed Gladstone's knowledge and love of Italy.

Certainly the rhetoricians raised their voices in the market places and penned articles for the newspapers, including Mussolini's new *Popolo d'Italia*. How, they asked, could Italy remain a Great Power if she stayed out of the war? Or be faithful to Garibaldi's memory and the spirit of the Risorgimento if she ignored the opportunity to liberate compatriots who in Trento and Southern Tyrol were still living under Austrian rule? Who, in fact, could doubt that Italy's prestige was at stake?

Prince of the rhetoricians was Gabriele D'Annunzio. A few years before the war his extravagances and debts drove him out of Italy, but he was welcomed back to proclaim the glories of war and sacrifice. Thus he was chosen to be the principal speaker at the King's unveiling of a monument at Quarto, close to Genoa, where Garibaldi and his thousand volunteers embarked for their conquest of Sicily and Naples. An advanced copy of his speech was sent to Rome. In the absence of Sonnino, the Foreign Office decided that the King ought not to hear such an inflammatory pronouncement. A telegram was sent in the King's name to the Mayor. 'If affairs of State,' it declared, 'change my desire to regret and prevent me from taking a personal part at the ceremony, they do not keep me away in my thoughts.'

D'Annunzio was untroubled. He alone was at the centre of the stage at Quarto, and Milan's *Corriere della Sera* had already published his speech. The telegram to the Mayor, moreover, enabled him to pay a tribute to 'His Majesty the King, absent but present'. He journeyed triumphantly from Genoa to Rome, where he delivered a fiery address in the Capitol. 'Italy,' he announced, 'is no longer a *pension de famille*, a museum, a horizon painted Prussian blue for international honeymooners—but a living nation.' Queen Margaret listened to his speech behind a screen.

The poet spoke at Quarto on the day after Italy denounced her alliance with Germany and Austria. On the day before this denunciation, German and Austrian troops began a successful offensive against the Russians. Within the three weeks of Italy's entry into the war, many thousands of Russian soldiers had been captured. The auctioneers, it seemed, miscalculated. Bernard von Bülow—once Germany's Foreign Minister and now, for a second time, Ambassador in Rome —tried hard to break the new alliance. He let it be known that Germany, when she won the war, would restore the Temporal Power to the Pope; he also warned Giolitti that the old alliance had been broken.

Giolitti belonged to a leisurely age, and he did not trouble to reach Rome before May 9th, when he heard officially that the German-Austrian alliance was repudiated. He saw the King as well as Salandra, and he spoke to each with the authority of a political leader who had the largest following in the Chamber of Deputies. Parliament, he told them, would oppose Italy's entry into the war.

As Parliament was not in session, Giolitti asked that it should be summoned as soon as possible. No less than three hundred Deputies showed their support for him by calling at his Roman residence and leaving their visiting cards. Salandra, however, postponed the date for the opening of Parliament from May 12th to May 20th. He played for time.

By slow stages Giolitti found out what were the terms of the Treaty of London. Yet a few precious days went by before he knew that there was a clause which committed Italy to go to war not later than May 26th. The clause was a fatal error and an affront to Parliament. Yet—so Giolitti believed—it marked an irrevocable decision. If Parliament successfully opposed the entry into the war, the King, who had signed the secret treaty, would be compelled to abdicate. Neutrality as well as war might lead the country to revolution.

D'Annunzio spoke bitter words about Giolitti, and the crowds shouting for war grew denser. Giolitti could not let the full truth be known, but he would have nothing to do with Italy's belligerency. He went back to Piedmont. It was the statesman, and not the King, who abdicated. Leaderless and confused, and with 407 votes against 74, the Deputies accorded full powers to the Government 'in the event of war'. On May 23rd, war was declared against Austria. Declarations of war against Germany and Turkey came later.

The Commander-in-Chief bore a glamorous name; for Luigi Cadorna was the son of the general whose troops breached the wall at Porta Pia in 1870. The King, like his grandfather, believed that he must be always with the army in time of war. He donned uniform, left for the front, and soon got so used to a camp bed that he would sleep on no other. When, more than thirty years later, he went into exile, he took his old camp bed with him.

Kings might abdicate and statesmen go into the wilderness, but one steadfast worker for peace was Pope Benedict. He knew that if Germany's foes won the war, the Holy See would be excluded from the Peace Conference; he also knew that if Germany won, his Temporal Power might be restored. It made no difference. The Pope was too clear-eyed to trouble himself with the threats or promises of war-mongers. The war was evil and suicidal. How could it be halted?

Men who saw Benedict spoke of his simple earnestness. A member of the Foreign Office in London suggested that Hilaire Belloc, who had acquired new fame as a war commentator, should go back to Rome and talk with the Pope.

'I had a long, long talk with him,' Belloc wrote to Charlotte Haldane. 'He is a *thoroughly good man*, which is not what I had been led to expect! I had thought to see one of those subtle and very *bornés* Italian officials—*bureaucrates*. Instead of that he has something like Holiness in his expression and an intense anxious sincerity. He spoke of individual conversion as opposed to political Catholicism in a way which—with my temperament all for the Collective Church—profoundly impressed me.

'He talked about Poland—"the key after the war"—which presupposed that the Allies would win the war.

' "But do you think they will, Mr. Belloc?" '

Another visitor was Henry Herbert Asquith, England's Prime Minister when she entered the war. He listened politely as Benedict spoke of the necessity of ending it. All the Pope drew from Asquith, who had little love for the Catholic Church, was the occasional repetition of a phrase spoken with a very English accent: *Nous irons au bout, nous irons au bout*—'We shall go on to the end.'

Yet Benedict kept on seeking paths to peace. He drew encouragement from the discovery that Charles, the new and young Emperor of Austria, wanted peace and was sending his brother-in-law, Prince Sixtus of Bourbon-Parma, on a barely secret mission to the Allied capitals. What Benedict needed was a closer official contact with Berlin, where there could be no Nuncio. Catholic Bavaria, however, was still a Kingdom. In May 1917, therefore, the Pope chose Eugenio Pacelli to be Nuncio in Munich. Sooner or later, he hoped, the Nuncio would talk frankly with German statesmen, if not with the Emperor.

Roman by birth and richly Roman in his speech, Eugenio Pacelli belonged to a black family which had served the Popes for generations. His grandfather, Marcantonio Pacelli, followed Pius IX to Gaeta. On the Pope's return to Rome, he was given the thankless task of dismissing all those who could no longer be retained in the papal service. In 1861 —the year in which the Kingdom of Italy was proclaimed—he helped to found the Vatican's official journal, the *Osservatore Romano*. Eugenio

Pacelli's father and elder brother were both lawyers. An uncle, Ernesto Pacelli, had been head of the Vatican bank, the *Banco di Roma*.

The Pacellis, in fact, produced more lawyers and financial administrators than priests, but Eugenio himself could have seldom doubted that it was his vocation to enter the priesthood. When five years old, he heard about the Christian martyrs, and he said to an older sister:

'I want to be a martyr, too—but without the nails.'

Like Pope Benedict, Eugenio Pacelli was given a secular education, and he passed from the former Collegio Romano to the University of Rome. The Collegio Romano had been founded by Ignatius Loyola, and it remained a Jesuit stronghold until 1870—six years before Pacelli was born. Then, renamed the Liceo Ennio Quirino Visconti, it became a secular stronghold. Pacelli heard class-mates hissing when he read an essay aloud and mentioned the genius of Augustine. He was not dismayed; he went on reading.

At eighteen, Pacelli left the University of Rome and entered the Capranica, which is the oldest of Rome's theological colleges. A year later, an illness caused him to leave the Capranica. For a man of his sensitive temperament, the studies may have been too narrow and the discipline too rigid. Thereafter he lived at home, while studying at the Apollinare. Life at home encouraged him to be solitary. He liked to be alone and to walk alone.

Pope Leo sent for him on the day of his graduation. The aged Pope and the youthful ordinand differed in their mental equipment. Pacelli was not a speculative thinker and set little store by the gaining of academic honours. No one in the next decade was likely to accuse him of Modernism. If his gifts of judgment and political acumen were acute, he preferred to use them as a militant and orthodox worker for the Church in its perpetual struggle with secular authority. Leo and the ordinand were both born diplomatists. They were also both lone workers. Pride was their strength—and, perhaps, their weakness.

The Nuncio met the German Emperor in the small town of Kreuznach, and he made a favourable impression. 'Pacelli,' the last Kaiser wrote in the days of his exile in Doorn, 'is an attractive and distinguished man, of high intelligence, with very fine manners: he is the perfect model of an eminent prelate of the Catholic Church.' A favourable impression on the German Emperor, however, was not enough. Nor was the mission of Prince Sixtus of Bourbon-Parma. With the advent of the war, power had passed from the palace to the High Command. The time was ripe for the Pope to address all the belligerents. At the third anniversary of the war, he was completing an appeal to end the 'useless carnage'.

'If months or, worse still, years are to be added to these three years of bloodshed,' he declared, 'no one can imagine the accumulations of suffering to mankind. Is the civilized world to be only a field of death? Is Europe, so glorious and flourishing, to rush into the abyss as if stricken by a universal madness and commit suicide?'

Since peace without a military decision implied compromise, the Pope included some proposals in his allocution. Germany, for instance, was to evacuate Belgium and the occupied areas of France, while the Allies were to restore the German colonies.

The belligerent leaders were in no mood to listen. Georges Clemenceau called Benedict the 'German Pope'—*le pape boche*. Heinrich Ludendorff called him the 'French Pope'. The Italian newspapers wrote as though he was deliberately betraying the country's war effort. All Italy, it was claimed, supported the war. 'This war will make us one nation': so H. G. Wells was often told during a return visit to Italy. Yet soldiers were fighting seven thousand feet and more above sea level, and those who came from the far south were seeing snow for the first time. Home leaves were few and short. Many Italian soldiers could neither read nor write, and it was impossible for them to describe their experiences on a perilous mountain front. They knew nothing about the Pope's appeal for peace. The war continued because the generals on each side believed that they might yet deliver the knock-out blow.

Earlier in this revolutionary year of 1917, belief in the knock-out blow had been strong among the French. On April 6th, the United States entered the war against Germany. Ten days later, General Robert Nivelle launched a major offensive which was intended to bring military victory within a few hours and at a trifling cost of life. His plans were known to too many people. Among them were the German generals, Ludendorff and Hindenburg.

French troops moved over scorched and heavily mined land. They reached the front line of their enemy only to find that he had withdrawn methodically to a second line. In less than a fortnight more than one hundred thousand French soldiers were killed. Nivelle retired disgraced, and when Philippe Pétain took his place as Commander-in-Chief, he found that the failure of the offensive had led directly to a mutiny. Soon it affected half the French army.

Pétain acted boldly. He wrung from the Government in Paris a promise that there should be no appeal from any death sentence which he himself confirmed. Yet his death sentences did not exceed twenty-six. He was far more concerned with remedies than with punishments, and he laid more than half the blame on the officers who did not show enough consideration for their men. The barrier between them and the ordinary soldier was too rigid. The soldier was a man of flesh and blood and nerves. There was a limit to his powers of physical and moral endurance. His periods under fire should be shortened; his periods of leave made more regular; and his rest camp placed well beyond the sound of gunfire. Pétain was convinced that if there had been less indifference to the welfare of the fighting soldier, the mutiny might never have occurred.

Even so, the soldiers drew their own distinction between revolt and treason. 'At the front,' said their spokesman, 'we resist. The *boches* shall not pass. But we will not have another offensive.' The mutiny was, in fact, so well disciplined that Ludendorff knew nothing about it until his opportunity was over. The manner in which Pétain ended the mutiny, he wrote, 'was more important than a great victory'.

Yet, even without the mutiny, the French could not have launched another major offensive in 1917. With the French put on the defensive and with the resistance of the Russians broken by their revolution, Ludendorff set out to defeat, one by one, the countries which were actively fighting against the Austrians. First Serbia crumbled, and then Rumania. In the early hours of October 24th, Ludendorff attacked the Italians at the Alpine salient of Caporetto. By midday they were in full retreat. Town after town, and village after village, fell to the enemy. Venice itself stood endangered.

The legendary link with Garibaldi and the Risorgimento helped Cadorna at Caporetto no more than it had helped Baratieri at Adowa. Both, indeed, were the architects of their own misfortunes. Cadorna worked to plans which were not altered, even when it became almost a certainty that Ludendorff would turn his crack troops southwards. The King felt the humiliation of defeat almost as much as his great-grandfather, Charles Albert, had done in 1849. For a while he thought seriously of renouncing the throne.

With defeat came a fuller knowledge of the way in which Cadorna treated his officers and men. He cared little or nothing for the rights of the individual, and his justice was too rough. More than once men were shot for offences committed in areas in which they had not set foot. Among the men shot for desertion were volunteers from the United States.

Born and bred in Piedmont, Cadorna inherited some of the bad traditions of the former Piedmontese army, which was excessively disciplined and disregarded the welfare and education of its troops. The maxim at the old War Ministry in Turin—'Books make a soldier unlearn his trade'—still influenced the military mind. None of the fifteen thousand soldiers whom Cavour sent to the Crimea could have known why they were fighting on Russian soil. Nor did the soldiers of Piedmont's mightier allies. 'I stood,' Florence Nightingale declared, 'at the altar of murdered men.'

Wherever Victor Emmanuel II acquired new territory, his Ministers ordered the holding of a plebiscite. Outwardly the new Kingdom of Italy was based on the consent of the people. Yet it condemned the youths and men of military age to a barrack-life patterned by the Piedmontese—a frontier people once surrounded by potential enemies. In the old Kingdom of the Two Sicilies—bounded in the north by the Pontifical State and elsewhere by the sea—army discipline had been gentler. Officers understood their men. For all his faults, King Bomba seldom signed a death warrant. The speed with which Garibaldi conquered Sicily and marched on Naples magnified the illusion that the Bourbon army was effete and useless, but it had very much to teach northern commanders about the flexibility of discipline and the need for welfare.

Now, in an hour of crisis, Cadorna was dismissed. Armand Diaz, a Neapolitan of Spanish descent, took his place. Like Pétain in France, the new Commander-in-Chief realized that there was a limit to the endurance of human flesh and nerve. He also realized that a man is a better soldier when he knows why he is fighting, and he soon organized services of information for the troops. As Italians and Slavs were fighting against the same foes, Diaz urged Sonnino to abandon his own anti-Slav attitude. Italy had become involved in a conflict of ideas, and they were making nonsense of some of the territorial aims expressed in the secret Treaty of London.

In 1915, the reasons for the war against the Austrians were calculative and rhetorical. After Caporetto, they were patriotic: the enemy was on Italian soil and must be driven out. Italians felt that same love of the motherland which in France made mutiny in the army a disciplined affair. Giolitti recognized the changed condition of the war, and henceforward he was an active supporter. At last, it seemed, the Italians had become one nation.

Under a more enlightened military leadership, the Italian soldier regained his resilience and showed once more his intrepidity and resourcefulness. In June 1918, Pietro Badoglio checked a new enemy offensive on the Piave. On October 24th—exactly one year after the disaster at Caporetto—Italian troops began an advance. A week later they reached the village of Vittorio Veneto and had taken an enormous number of prisoners. Austria-Hungary was beaten, and she soon asked for an armistice.

The war took a toll of about six hundred thousand Italian lives. More than that number of men were crippled. Sorrow mingled with jubilation; for 'the war to end war' was over. From century to century Italians, like the Slavs, lived under the domination—or the threat of domination—by the Hapsburgs and their puppets. The war brought Italian and Slav closer together, and in April a Congress of Oppressed Nationalities had approved a Pact of Rome. One of its signatories was Benito Mussolini.

Now the structure of the Austro-Hungarian Empire was broken. Vienna—so long the chief citadel of Catholic Europe—was reduced to poverty and islanded in a small State. Before the war the Emperor Francis Joseph had more than fifty million subjects, but republican Austria would have no more than six million citizens. What could Italian statesmen not achieve if they were clear-visioned and saw the true consequences of Vienna's fall? 'Italy's position,' Carlo Sforza observed, 'is what France's position would be if Germany had suddenly vanished from the map.'

Mazzini had predicted that freedom for Rome would mean freedom for the world. Now came the opportunity to recognize the freedom of all the people who, like the northern Italians in the last century, cast off the Hapsburg yoke. Their political centre of gravity might thus shift from the old authoritarian Vienna to a new liberating Rome. 'Out of the nationalities,' wrote Mazzini, 'would grow the United States of Europe, the republican alliance of the peoples . . . that great European federation, whose task is to unite in one association all the political families of the old world, destroy the partitions that dynastic rivalries have made and consolidate and respect nationalities.'

Though the United States failed to keep out of the war, Pope Benedict had been right to pin his hopes on her moral leadership. For two years her President, Woodrow Wilson, maintained the attitude that he did not know what the war in Europe was about. If his sympathies were more Anglo-French than Austro-German, he nursed no friendly feelings towards Tsarist Russia, and he longed to see her autocratic system overthrown. A load dropped from his mind when the Tsar abdicated. Kerensky, the new Russian ruler, was a fellow-liberal. If America were to enter the war, she must have no autocrat among her partners.

The Kerensky revolution proved to be no more than a breathing-space between one tyranny and another. Meanwhile America had joined the conflict; but she did so as an Associated Power, and not as an ally. No allied treaty, open or secret, fettered her discretion. As from an eminence, Wilson watched the struggle and worked out a plan for peace. If he had any political heroes, they were Edmund Burke and Gladstone: the one, an Irishman who saw that the American colonists had justice on their side, and who pleaded at Westminster for conciliation; and the other, an Englishman of Scottish descent who fought for the principle of nationhood throughout Europe and who yet failed gloriously in his battle for Irish home rule.

For both Burke and Gladstone, true government was government by consent. Wilson, their pupil, went further. He wanted democracy; and democracy was government by discussion. The cure for defective democracy, he was certain, was more democracy; the more arguments are thrashed out, the more right opinion is likely to prevail.

Wilson was not ready—nor was the time yet ripe—for Mazzini's idea of the United States of Europe. None the less, he saw the basis for a future world order in a community of free nations leagued together to preserve the peace. He learned willingly from others— even from Theodore Roosevelt, a predecessor at the White House and a thorn in the President's flesh because he was constantly urging the administration to make a greater war effort. Roosevelt had given the idea of a league of free nations a fresh impetus when, in 1910, he received the Nobel Peace Prize. 'It would be a master-stroke,' he said in his speech, 'if those Great Powers honestly bent on peace would form a league of peace, not only to keep the peace themselves, but to prevent—by force, if necessary—its being broken by others.'

The President crossed the Atlantic to be acclaimed as a saviour of civilization. For more than three years the Quirinal Palace had been a military hospital, to which Queen Helen and the Queen Mother paid regular visits, but rooms were got ready for the reception of the President and his wife. The portals of the Vatican—once barred to Theodore Roosevelt—were opened to them. Wherever the President went in Rome, the crowds were rapturous. Perhaps no foreign visitor to a capital city in Europe had received such a welcome since, in 1864, the Londoners shocked Queen Victoria and Archbishop Manning by their delirious greeting to Garibaldi. A league of nations, open diplomacy, and national self-determination: what more could the war-weary Italians want?

First of their wants was a statesman with vision: one who saw the changed shape of Europe and who knew that it was favourable to Italy. All the new succession States could be her friends and partners —and particularly Jugoslavia, her neighbour on the Adriatic with twelve million inhabitants. Ideas know no frontiers, and liberation from the Hapsburg yoke was but a stage in the European revolution begun south of the Alps by Mazzini, Garibaldi and Cavour. Nationhood alone is not enough. Fundamentally, Wilson's ideas were Roman. The time had arrived to give Europe a new version of the *Pax Romana*. Mazzini once firmly believed that this leadership would come from Rome.

That may have been his cardinal error. No one escapes from the influences of early childhood, and as his mind was more Catholic than he realized, Mazzini gave to Rome an almost mystical significance. So did Garibaldi and Cavour, though the Capitoline Hill stood too far from the industrial and enterprising cities of the north. Turin was always on guard against a potential invader, whether French or Austrian. A Government still located in such a martial city might have recognized the true consequences of Austria's defeat. Vienna was no longer to be feared. Woodrow Wilson was willing enough to give Italy a better Alpine frontier, though it meant the incorporation of Southern Tyrol, where the people spoke German. An Italian who grasped Wilson's ideas and recognized their affinity with Mazzini's might have spoken ably at the Peace Conference in Paris alike for his own country and for its newly liberated neighbours.

The statesmen who governed Italy at the end of the war, however, lacked fullness of vision. Their sights were set on the coastline of Dalmatia, and they demanded the honouring of the Treaty of London as clamorously as Shylock in Venice demanded his pound of flesh. They wanted the Adriatic to be an Italian gulf, not a sea to be shared in fair partnership with Jugoslavia. These statesmen did not come from Piedmont or Lombardy; they all lived close to the Mediterranean. Salandra belonged to Puglia, and Sonnino to Pisa. Vittorio Orlando, who led the Italian delegation in Paris, was a Sicilian. Francesco Nitti, who succeeded Orlando as Prime Minister, came from Lucania. Except for Salandra, they were southern men. They thought of more gains in Africa, full sovereignty over the distant Dodecanese Islands, and the occupation of Smyrna. These were territorial ambitions, and each mocked the new doctrine of national self-determination.

Italy's spokesmen in Paris pursued only the shadows of greatness. Their methods were not flexible, and they soon lost influence at the conference table. At one point they left Paris. Then they returned, lest they be compelled to make a separate peace.

They quarrelled chiefly over the seaport of Fiume. Though most of its citizens were Italian, the hinterland was almost entirely Slav. Wilson reminded the delegates that if Fiume was Italian, so also was a large area of New York. The Italians could not invoke self-determination for Fiume if it was to be denied to the German-speaking people of Southern Tyrol. Fiume, he decided, should be declared an open city.

From that moment Rome's hero of yesterday became the most reviled man in Italy. D'Annunzio poured scorn on a President whose mouth was 'full of false words and false teeth'. Spectacular solo flights during the war had given new wings to the poet's fame. Once he showed his contempt for Parliament by flying over the Montecitorio Palace in Rome—seat of the Chamber of Deputies—and dropping a chamber-pot filled with carrots.

D'Annunzio's answer to the Treaty of Versailles, which Orlando had signed, was to occupy Fiume and to establish a so-called Regency of Carnara. 'Fiume or death!' he cried, but there was no resistance when he entered the city with a number of once high-ranking officers and others who were disgruntled with the stark realities of peace. Money flowed chiefly from wealthy men in Trieste or Venice who were eager to see the rival port of Fiume commercially destroyed. The poet knew that his action suited the bitter public mood of Italy. He relied on encouragement in Parliament, in the Government, and even at court. Yet his Regency made a potential foe of Jugoslavia, who should have been Italy's friend, and it alienated the sympathies of other countries. After fifteen months D'Annunzio was compelled to retire. He was probably glad to go. For one thing, he suspected that the people around him cared little for his poetry. As with his mistresses, so with Fiume: D'Annunzio soon got bored.

Once again Italy was tripped by her legendary Risorgimento. If King Victor Emmanuel II said little or nothing when regular officers leagued with Garibaldi, his grandson said nothing when they connived at D'Annunzio's occupation of Fiume. Where was the difference between D'Annunzio's assault on Fiume and Garibaldi's on Sicily? 'Rome or death!' once shouted Garibaldi. 'Fiume or death!' came a parrot's cry.

Rome is Italy's, while Fiume now lives under the name of Reka and belongs to Jugoslavia. Yet Rome is itself legendary. There was sound common sense in the reluctance of the King's grandfather to leave Turin first for the banks of the Arno and then for those of the Tiber. Originally, Mussolini's Fascist movement was confined to Milan. Its violence might have been contained far more effectively if the Italian Government still had its capital in the north.

None the less, Rome had been the capital for half a century. Though it had no major industries, its population rose from 244,000 in 1871 to 691,000 in 1921. In this half-century, the population of Naples rose from 448,000 to 772,000. The largest rate of expansion was in Milan, where the population rose from 199,000 to 718,000. Garibaldi's march on Naples was all the more glamorous because he gained the largest

Italian city for his King. Soon Mussolini was to march on Rome. He travelled in comfort by train. Here, too, he was no innovator. It was by train that Garibaldi completed the last five miles of his march on Naples.

The Risorgimento was itself traditional. Mazzini was a lay Savonarola; Garibaldi a soldier of fortune, a *condottiere*; and Cavour a Machiavelli in thought and action. Yet each had a quality seldom found in the men who stood closest to D'Annunzio and Mussolini. Queen Victoria discerned the same quality in the ungainly and almost tongue-tied Victor Emmanuel II, who, as King of Sardinia, visited her at Windsor. This quality was chivalry.

CHAPTER SIXTEEN

FLIGHT FROM REASON

ON HIS walk from the Moselle Valley to Rome in 1901, Hilaire
Belloc caught his first view of Lake Bolsena when the evening
was cool and moonlit. He sat on the coping of a wall, drank a
little wine and ate a little bread and sausage. At that moment he
needed song and companionship more than landscape. 'Please God, I
had become southern and took beauty for granted.' Accordingly, he
stopped a small cart driven by a smiling and contented old man.

'We raced down the hill, clattering and banging and rattling like a
piece of ordnance, and he, my brother, unasked began to sing. I sang
in turn. He sung of Italy, I of four countries: America, France, England,
and Ireland. I could not understand his songs nor he mine, but there
was wine in common between us, and *salami*, and a merry heart, bread
which is the bond of all mankind, and that prime solution of ill-ease—
I mean the forgetfulness of money.'

Twenty years later Belloc was back again in Bolsena, and what he
wrote of Rome in March 1914, he might now have written of the whole
Italian countryside: it 'goes on astonishingly the same'. 'A good bed
in Bolsena,' he wrote to Mrs. Raymond Asquith, 'is one English shilling.
A good dinner of soup and macaroni and ham and eggs and a bottle
of wine is one shilling and threepence.'

To a returning visitor very little in Italy seemed to be changed by
her three years of war. Where Belloc once saw a little cart guided by
an old peasant he might now have seen an ageing motor-car driven
by a young commercial user. Yet the sight was rare: 'they promise
me carriages of petrol and of horse—or of the Gods—perpetually,' he
complained, 'but *none* matured.'

The war had vanished like a brutish dream, but the peace which
followed was embittering. The soldier returned to his village without
a gratuity and often without a welcome. Many war-time industries
came swiftly to an end, and among industrial workers at least one out
of every ten was soon unemployed. As wages did not keep pace with
the ever-rising prices in the cities, there were constant strikes and
displays of violence. Bolsena might be quiet and cheap, but not
Milan.

Despairing voices were heard in the Vatican. An old fear that

Constantinople, when ceded by the Allies to Tsarist Russia, would increase the power and influence of the Orthodox Church gave place to the new and more deadly fear of a revolutionary Russia suddenly becoming Communist and atheistic. Marxist ideas knew no frontiers, and Cardinal Gasparri believed that the new succession States would be too weak to defend themselves. Like the statesmen in Rome, he failed to see that Italian partnership might give them strength.

It was hard for the older Cardinals to associate strength with the Italian Kingdom. In their youth they imagined that one day Rome would be restored to the Pope; if necessary, with the aid of foreign bayonets. Its occupation by the Piedmontese, they had been told, was evil, and evil does not endure. Pope Benedict, however, had ignored all hints from Berlin that the Germans, when victorious, would give back his Temporal Power. He wanted peace; and when it came, he saw that Italian unity should be made permanent and stable. For this reason, he revoked the '*non expedit.*' In Italy's first post-war election—in November, 1919—Catholics were everywhere free to vote and free to stand for Parliament.

No less important was the tacit consent which Pope Benedict gave to Luigi Sturzo when he formed a separate Popular Party. This formidable and big-nosed Sicilian priest designed his party to be independent of all control by the Bishops and to be as non-sectarian as any political party in the United States or in England. In particular, it was to meet the needs of industrial workers and peasants, about whom—so Sturzo believed—their actual rulers knew almost nothing. Somehow or other, the social cleavage must be bridged.

Sturzo took care never to claim that the Popular Party was the only one which a good Catholic could join. He recognized that there was a wide and healthy diversity of political views among Catholics. At the same time, he was convinced that a non-sectarian party based on a few fundamentally Christian principles was the one most likely to mirror the true Italian mind and to heal the discord between Church and State.

The first post-war election brought one hundred Popularists into the Chamber of Deputies. Among them was Sturzo's friend from Brescia, Giorgio Montini. Soon afterwards a newcomer to the Chamber of Deputies was Alcide De Gasperi. He belonged to Trento and, as a member of the Austrian Catholic Party, he had sat in the Parliament in Vienna. The Peace Treaty made him a subject of the Italian King. Henceforward he worked for Italy. Though a stranger to the Roman arena, he was already enriched with parliamentary experience. He had also an ample knowledge of the old Hapsburg Empire.

The life of that Empire might have been spared if the rulers in Vienna had applied the right surgery in good time and created for its multi-racial people—Poles, Czechs, Slovaks, Magyars and Austrians— a democratic federation. Instead the Hapsburg court acted as though every condemnation in Pius IX's Syllabus of Errors was vibrant with truth: democracy and Catholicism were foes. Like Carlo Sforza, how- ever, De Gasperi saw that the death of an Empire gave Italy a sudden chance to exert a truly European influence. He also saw that democracy and Catholicism should be allies. Where an older generation looked beyond the sea for national greatness, De Gasperi looked northwards to the peoples with whom he had once lived and worked. Catholic democracy and European unity should also go together.

For the moment the Popularists faced many difficulties. The Chamber of Deputies had been too long an anticlerical enclave. Throughout the war, moreover, the Ministers ruled the country chiefly through the issue of decrees. Parliament seldom met. In consequence, its prestige was low and, in 1919, only about half the electors troubled to record their votes. If one hundred Popularists entered the Chamber, so did one hundred and fifty-six Socialists. Unlike the Popularists, they were in no mood to show respect either for the King or for Parliament. While the King was reading his speech at the opening of Parliament, they shouted: *'Viva la Repubblica socialista!'*—'Long live the Socialist Republic!' They then walked out of the Chamber, singing the Italian version of the 'Red Flag'.

A King who signed a secret treaty which committed his country to war may have had little use for Parliament. Now the Socialists had mistakenly turned his disregard to contempt. Instead of giving strength to Parliament, they chose to swell the ranks of the agitators in the market place. Perhaps D. H. Lawrence was right when, in his 'Twilight in Italy', he observed that 'an Italian only cares about the emotion. It is the movement, the physical effect of the language upon the blood which gives him supreme satisfaction . . . Which is why D'Annunzio is a god in Italy.'

The Popularists knew that they must answer unreason and sheer rhetoric with reason and thus give proof of their own political maturity. This was far from easy. Most of them had entered the Chamber of Deputies for the first time. If their Church was authoritarian, they were themselves strongly individualistic: some ultra-conservative, and others almost Socialists. As a team, they were hard to lead and could never be driven. In addition, their leadership had one perilous flaw. Luigi Sturzo was a priest. He was imaginative, resourceful and coura- geous. Under better conditions he would have shown his parliamentary skill to far greater advantage. He was, in fact, a born parliamentarian; but he was also a steadfast priest. The Church came first.

Benedict understood Sturzo's motives. They were Dante's in modern dress. The Pope derives his authority from Christ through Peter, while the statesman's authority comes from Christ directly. Dante, however, was only a layman, and not a Doctor of the Church. In the Vatican there were Cardinals who held a contrary view, and this had been mirrored for more than eleven centuries in the mosaic of the Lateran *triclinium*, wherein Peter is shown bestowing the pallum on Leo III and giving a banner to Charlemagne.

As Pope Benedict was physically deformed, his life-span was unlikely to be long. After him might come a Pope who lacked his sympathy with the laical mind. The successor's ban on a priest's membership of a political party could at once deprive the Popularists of their leader. Faced with the alternatives of politics and priesthood, Romolo Murri had chosen politics and braved excommunication. Sturzo, however, knew that priesthood was his vocation. When faced with the same alternatives, he would submit and remain a priest.

Because the general election of 1919 had given no party a clear majority over the others, there was a succession of short-lived Governments. To the King's annoyance, even Giolitti returned to his old office for a time, although he was approaching eighty. Giolitti still saw problems very largely as he had seen them when, nearly thirty years beforehand, he became Prime Minister for the first time. Labour disputes were best left alone, for—as he discovered during the general strike of 1904—violent men soon gave up their violence. Thus he was calm and almost inactive when, in 1920, about six hundred thousand workers occupied factories all over northern Italy. One industrial magnate insisted that he must order the troops to shoot on the factories which the workers had occupied. Giolitti offered to begin the operation by first ordering them to shoot on the magnate's own factories.

The general strike came inevitably to an end, and Giolitti presided over a meeting in Rome between employers and workers. Once again, he believed that he had settled a major dispute through masterly inaction. The episode, he wrote, was 'analogous to the general strike of 1904 which had aroused so much terror and then revealed its inanity'. What he forgot was that wealth had largely shifted from his own landowning class to that of the industrial magnates; and it was their property which the strikers seized. If the war made the many poorer, it made some of the few much richer; and the new rich were haunted by the spectre of revolution. So were the King and his court. Russia's revolution had been a blood-bath; a deliberate decimation of the landed, intellectual and professional classes. The deposed Tsar and all his family had perished. The son of murdered King Humbert would have been less than human if he remained entirely free from fear. So would have been the inmates of the Vatican. Communism, wherever it appeared in Lenin's day, was persecuting and godless. The country began to yearn for a strong and resolute leadership.

Italy was seldom freed from tribulation; nor was she ever for long denied laughter and song. The sun shone alike on the factory roof and on the lakes and fields. Each village held a festival on the day of its patron saint, and few were the Communists who, except through poverty, failed to give their little boy or girl a present on the *giorno onomastico*, the feast day of the saint after whom the child was named at baptism. Vittoria Colonna—now a Caetani by marriage and the Duchess of Sermoneta—may have lamented a loss of elegance in post-war Rome; but, on the whole, the Romans retained both their lack of punctuality and their reluctance to take anything too seriously. Throughout the country the love of pageantry still ran deep and, three years after the war had ended, Italians forgot the tumults of the market place as they ceremoniously re-buried their own Unknown Warrior.

On October 28th, 1921, the bodies of eleven nameless soldiers who had died on different battlefields were brought to the Cathedral in Aquileia. A woman who lost her son in the war entered the Cathedral and dropped a white flower on one of the biers. The Duke of Aosta—cousin to the King and the war-time Commander of the Third Army—stepped forward and replaced the flower with a bronze wreath. The other biers were left to rest permanently within the Cathedral, but the one with the bronze wreath was taken by devious routes to Rome and then conveyed to the church of Santa Maria degli Angeli to be blessed by the leading army chaplain. On November 4th—the third anniversary of Italy's victory—it was given a final journey to the Altar of the Country, which stood above the main steps of the Vittoriano and immediately beneath the gigantic equestrian statue of King Victor Emmanuel II.

Simplicity and pompousness, humility and arrogance: these contrary strains mingled together in the honours shown to Italy's Unknown Warrior. Eleven biers were brought to Aquileia Cathedral, loveliest of all the ancient churches which Italian soldiers wrested from the Austrians in an early month of the war. The bereaved mother came with her flower from Trieste. The bier on which the flower fell was taken to the Roman church in which the heir to King Humbert was married to a princess from Montenegro. The Altar of the Country—

last resting place of the Unknown Warrior—stood embedded on the Vittoriano, to which Romans and foreigners alike had already given the mocking name of the 'Wedding Cake'.

Where else could the patriots have re-buried an Italian soldier who was almost certainly a Catholic by baptism and upbringing? Three of the four arch-basilicas—St. Peter's, St. John's Lateran and Santa Maria Maggiore—were extraterritorial: by the law of the Kingdom, they belonged to the Holy See, which had been neutral throughout the war. More suitable for the soldier's re-burial might have been the Pantheon, which, since its first building by Agrippa, has never ceased to be a place of worship; in the year 399, it received, and still bears, the Christian name of the church of Santa Maria ad Martyres. Within its circular walls are buried Raffaelo and the first two Kings of Italy. The Unknown Warrior might have kept company with them, just as another Unknown Warrior lies with dead Kings and once famous men in Westminster Abbey.

Official Italy, however, chose to follow the French example, and not the English. In Paris the soldier's grave is shadowed by Napoleon's Arc de Triomphe; in Rome, by Victor Emmanuel's statue and the towering white marble walls of the Vittoriano. Had the war and all the suffering of the Italian people produced no deeper vision even of their own Risorgimento? The men who lay dying on a battlefield often wept for their mother, their children and the plot of land which they had tilled. Many may have thought of a village church in which they were baptized or made their first Communion. Or was the Catholic religion little more than a palimpsest written over the heart of a tradition-loving and still pagan land? The Vittoriano would never have been designed or approved except at a time when German influences over the minds of Italy's rulers and savants were strong. In a city crammed with shrines and churches, a nameless Italian soldier was given a tomb with a Teutonic setting. The enemy, it seemed, was not yet conquered.

Nor was the State yet reconciled with the Church. The ceremony of re-burying the Unknown Warrior, like the funeral of King Humbert more than two decades beforehand, was marked by the absence of the Bishops. This time both sides felt the hurt more keenly, for both wanted reconciliation. Benedict was clearer-sighted in his attitude to the State than had been Pius X under the influence of Cardinal Merry del Val, a non-Italian; but his search for peace and emphatic warning that war was suicidal incurred the wrath of the warmakers, and notably the Italian. Clear-sighted, too, was his willingness to let Sturzo lead a non-sectarian party in the Chamber of Deputies. It was not Benedict's fault

—nor, for that matter, was it really Sturzo's—if the party's discordant voices helped to destroy any belief that the country might find a deliverer within the ranks of Parliament.

This longing for a deliverer enabled Mussolini to blaze his path to power. He was actually the promoter of two Fascist parties. The first was small: republican, revolutionary, anti-capitalistic and anti-religious. The second came into existence—at first, imperceptibly—when bankers, industrialists and large landowners grew afraid of revolution and were willing to hire Fascist bands for the protection of their own property. Giolitti was right when he thought that he had settled a major industrial dispute through masterly inaction. The danger of revolution from the Left—if it ever existed—was overcome. What Giolitti had never experienced—and, therefore, never expected—was revolution from the Right.

A systematic thinker seldom changes his course. Mussolini, however, was not systematic. He chose or repudiated ideas according to his need. Since his overwhelming need was personal power, he was only too ready to jettison all former ideas which still barred his path. He could be monarchist, capitalist and outwardly religious: King's man and Pope's man. As King's man, he might please the court. As Pope's man, he might calm the Curia. On the very day that the Unknown Warrior was re-buried above the steps of the Vittoriano, Cardinal Achille Ratti allowed the Fascist banner to be brought into Milan Cathedral.

In the end reactionary influences within the Vatican might have become too strong for Benedict to resist, thus causing Sturzo to lose his tacit support; but those who believed that the Pope had not long to live proved to be right. On January 22nd, 1922, Benedict died. The task of electing a successor was far from easy. Thirteen times during the Conclave a crowd gathered in St. Peter's Square and then went away disappointed because the smoke which issued from a makeshift chimney above the Sistine Chapel was black. Only after the fourteenth count did white smoke show the people that a Cardinal had at last obtained the necessary majority of two thirds and one extra vote.

There was a mighty cheer when the new Pope—Achille Ratti, who took the name of Pius XI—went to the outer balcony of St. Peter's and gave his first blessing *urbi et orbi*: to Rome and the world. Not since Pius IX stood on the balcony of the Quirinal Palace in 1846 had the Roman multitude received a Pope's first blessing. This action, the new Pius explained, was 'an augury of that peace for which the world sighs so much'.

He had done what Pius X and probably Benedict XV wished to do.

All three were northerners and understood the traditional longing of the people to be rid of foreign tutelage. Thus they differed from Pius IX and Leo XIII, who were born and reared in the old Pontifical State, and who genuinely believed that its destruction was sacrilegious. Achille Ratti, however, had been Archbishop of Milan and a Cardinal for only a few months before his election as Pope. He was still little known to the Italian people. If his first blessing from the outer balcony of St. Peter's indicated that his reign might be liberal, he had spent the greater part of his life in a conservative ambiance. For almost a quarter of a century he worked in the Ambrosian Library in Milan, and when Italy entered the war, he was living in Rome as Prefect of the Vatican Library.

Greatest of all librarians may have been Antonio Panizzi, the Italian exile who persuaded his new English compatriots to build the vast domed reading room of the British Museum, and who insisted that even the poorest man had the right of full access to knowledge. Panizzi would not have thought it strange to see the God-fearing Gladstone and the atheistic Karl Marx sitting close to each other in his reading room; but he was more than a great librarian. Without a death-warrant issued against him, he would never have become a librarian and, perhaps, he would never have left Italy. Achille Ratti, on the other hand, was a librarian to his finger-tips.

For one thing, he loved to give help and advice to readers. On his first visit to the Ambrosian Library, Angelo Roncalli—then a young priest and secretary to Giacomo Radini-Tedeschi, Bishop of Bergamo —saw thirty-nine volumes of old parchment labelled: *Archivio Spiritual —Bergamo*. He began to explore them and soon found that they contained a first-hand account of the visitation of the diocese of Bergamo which Cardinal Carlo Borromeo made in 1575. Convinced of their importance and prompted by his Bishop, Roncalli sought the advice of the Prefect of the Ambrosian Library. Ratti received him in his private study and promised to examine some of the volumes. When Roncalli returned to the library, the Prefect greeted him warmly and agreed that the editing of the volumes would be a work of undoubted importance, though likely to become the task of a life-time.

'Certainly,' he said, 'to annotate these manuscripts in a critical way and to present them within their historical framework would be a fine thing to do. An admirable work for a young man.'

Ratti also agreed that all the pages and documents of the thirty-nine volumes should be photographed, so that their editor could work outside the library. The photographing of documents was still in its infancy, but the Prefect undertook to supervise the photography himself. Wherever Roncalli happened to be living—in Bergamo, Rome, the Balkans, Paris and Venice—he found time to continue his editorial work. When the eighth and last volume was published, he had become known throughout the world as Pope John. According to its title-page, however, the editor was still Angelo Roncalli.

The Prefect of the Ambrosian Library may have felt a special sympathy with the intelligent and historically minded priest who, like himself, was a Lombard of lowly origin. Roncalli had the good fortune to begin his priesthood under an aristocratic Bishop who loved the open air, talked freely with the people, defended them whenever they were the victims of social injustice, and treated his young secretary as a son. Together they were gay and seemingly care-free workers. They never became the slaves of a fixed routine. If their hours were irregular, they were often uncommonly long. Roncalli reached maturity at ease with the world.

As a librarian, Ratti spent many years in close contact with distinguished, if often old-fashioned, scholars. He knew Oxford well and liked to visit the Bodleian Library; and Bodley's Librarian never forgot that, as Prefect of the Ambrosian Library, Ratti was the custodian of a library almost contemporary with his own. His host in Oxford was Wickham Legge, a courtly physician who was once tutor to Prince Leopold, Duke of Albany—Queen Victoria's son, to whom the royal scourge of haemophilia had been transmitted. Another English friend was Henry Masterman Bannister, an Anglican clergyman and liturgiologist who lived in Rome for twenty years. During the war, some pro-German influences within the Vatican proved too strong for Bannister's liking, and he returned to Oxford, where he spent the closing years of his life as Sub-Librarian of the Bodleian.

From Legge and Bannister, Ratti heard often of plans for Anglican reunion with the Roman Church. He knew one or two of the men who participated with Cardinal Mercier, the Belgian Primate, in the Malines conversations. It was natural, therefore, that when he became Pope, he authorized Masses for the conversion of Anglicans. He also liked to talk with learned Jews, and he often insisted that the Old Testament formed an integral part of the Scriptures, on which the authority of the Church is based. Each non-Christian religion had to be judged at its highest level, and not at its worst.

Despite his Anglican friendships, Ratti did not doubt that it was God's plan to bring the whole world into the fold of the Roman Church. As Pope, he did not allow Catholics to take any part in the assemblies of non-Catholics. 'There is but one way in which the unity of Christians may be fostered,' he declared, 'and that is by furthering the return to the one true Church of Christ of those who are separated from it.' This conviction made him a staunch promoter of missionary work. He decided that a missionary exhibition, already approved by Pope Benedict, should be made a main attraction for pilgrims to Rome during the Holy Year of 1925, and he required each of the religious orders to send its missionaries to heathen or non-Catholic lands. When he consecrated six Chinese Bishops to work in their own country, he took a bold and, indeed, revolutionary step towards freeing the Church from its European dominance.

In his politics Ratti was not adventurous. Anglican friends like Legge and Bannister were beautifully mannered, but they clung to a pre-war order and resented change. Ratti became still more conservative when, as Nuncio in Warsaw in 1920, he heard the firing of the guns as Polish patriots hurled back the Red Army of Communist Russia, which had advanced almost to the gates of the city. He detested the cruelties inflicted upon helpless people in the name of World Revolution. The Fascist banner which he admitted into Milan Cathedral was that of crusaders against Communism. Their leader had a strong man's bearing.

It was not long before the new Pope announced that priests must abstain from political activities. Luigi Sturzo promptly obeyed. The Popularists lost their pilot when the waters were increasingly turbulent. For those who knew the Pope well, the decision was inevitable. He had no liking for Christian Democracy, and Dante himself would have frowned on a priest whose activity, however laudable, was more becoming to a layman. Sturzo might have forestalled the papal decision by a timely retirement in favour of a man like De Gasperi; but this energetic lieutenant from Trento had still to win confidence. His background, manner of speech, and style of writing seemed too Austrian. Within the Popularist camp reigned 'confusion worse confounded'. It made Mussolini the chief beneficiary of the papal decision.

Rome, none the less, continued to give a smiling welcome to its visitors. Once again Hilaire Belloc found the city spiritually unchanged. 'Were you not impressed in Rome,' he wrote to Mrs. Reginald Balfour on June 28th, 1922, 'by the much greater position of Religion and the tiny dimensions to which the official world has been reduced? The most striking contrast was the procession of St. Philip Neri. Something like half Rome was blocked to traffic by enormous crowds following the Saint, all the rest of the City was empty, and meanwhile the King, the Ministers and a handful of Free Masons were officially playing the fool unveiling a Mazzini monument which no one cared about and which no one goes to see.'

Playing the fool, indeed! Mazzini died an impenitent republican, and now the King was troubled about his own future. Mussolini claimed to uphold the Church and the monarchy, but one monarch can be deposed in favour of another. What if the strong man's candidate was the Duke of Aosta—the King's first cousin, who was a far more glamorous figure, and whose father had once been King of Spain? The King had an intimate knowledge of the long history of his own House of Savoy. He was well aware that contemporaries often condemned his great-grandfather, Charles Albert, for an inability to make up his own mind. Some called him Hamlet, and others called him King Wobble. The one decisive action had been his abdication. King Victor Emmanuel III wished neither to abdicate nor to be called another Hamlet. On the day of decision he would be resolute.

For all his shrewdness, simple way of living and kindly attitude to humble people, the King had the pride of his dynasty and held the views of a caste. If he lived away from the Quirinal Palace, he was still the prisoner of his own environment. Later, when an exile in New York, Luigi Sturzo wrote that although the republican tradition in Italy was kept alive by only a small group from 1860 to 1922, 'the feeling was fairly widespread, even among members of other parties, that Italy would never know true democracy under the monarchy, given the coalition round the throne by powerful forces representing the upper bourgeoisie, the old aristocracy, the army and the bureaucracy'. Members of the caste declared among themselves that a choice must soon be made between Fascism and Communism. They preferred Fascism because it appeared to offer protection to property and status. Within the royal circle Mussolini had an active champion in the now ageing Queen Margaret.

There was, however, at least one influential landowner in Venetia who refused to accept the view which prevailed in his caste. Giacomo Matteotti was eloquent, outspoken and fearless. He had also a sound knowledge of economics as well as a deep understanding of the real needs of the peasantry; and he entered the Chamber of Deputies as a Social Democrat. If disorders were rampant among workers in the factories and in the fields, they were deliberately fomented by Fascist bands. Matteotti was anxious, therefore, that his constituents in Rovigo should not answer violence with violence. Otherwise they would get themselves entrapped. The Government, Matteotti insisted, had enough police at its disposal. They should be told to do their duty.

The police acted under command. It was also under command, as Matteotti and many others were shocked to discover, that they ceased to act. The revolution of the Right was in full swing.

CHAPTER SEVENTEEN

DUCE

T HE DAY of decision for the King arrived on October 28th, 1922—exactly one year after a bereaved mother from Trieste dropped her flower on one of the eleven biers brought into Aquileia Cathedral. Many thousands of Fascists were then marching on Rome. The challenge was extremely grave. The Government, led by Luigi Facta, agreed to proclaim a state of siege. The King, however, rejected the advice of his Prime Minister and refused to sign the proclamation. On the evening of the following day, he sent for Mussolini. Fascist bands continued their march on Rome, while their leader travelled from Milan in a *wagon-lit*.

For the first time in his life, the fiery agitator of other days was wearing a top hat and frock coat when he went to the King with his list of Ministers and Under-Secretaries. They were not all Fascists. Prominent in the list was Giovanni Gentile—philosopher, Senator and a Liberal—who collaborated with Benedetto Croce in editing *La Critica*, and to whom fell Croce's former office of Minister of Public Instruction. Among the Popularists in the list was Giovanni Gronchi, a young Tuscan schoolmaster, who was chosen to be Under-Secretary at the Ministry of Public Instruction. This show of moderation and willingness to include non-Fascists in the Government pleased the King. 'The excellent and well-balanced composition of the list,' he told his new Prime Minister, 'could not have been happier.'

Moderation, however, was only a pose. Mussolini knew that Parliament was not bound to accept him as Prime Minister. He resolved, therefore, to use some threatening words when he addressed the Senators and Deputies at a joint session and demanded their votes. 'With three hundred thousand young men armed at every point, fully decided and almost mystically ready to obey my command,' he said, 'I can chastise those who have defamed me and have tried to besmear Fascism. I can turn this deaf and grey hall into a straw-carpeted bivouac. I can bolt the door on Parliament and create a Government formed exclusively of Fascists. I can; but—on the first occasion, at least—I do not wish to do so.'

By 306 votes to 116, Parliament gave Mussolini his authority to be Prime Minister. Socialists, Communists, and republicans voted against him; but the men who cast their votes for him included Giolitti, Salandra and De Gasperi. They even included Facta, whose advice the King had unconstitutionally rejected. The vote cast by Salandra caused no surprise. By negotiating a secret treaty which required the King's signature, he had already caused the King to act unconstitutionally.

For a second time, perhaps, Giolitti voted against his conscience. In 1915, he agreed with the majority in Parliament to give full powers to the Government because the alternative would have been the King's abdication. In 1922, if Parliament refused to accept Mussolini as Prime Minister, the King's position would again be compromised. Yet if Parliament still retained the right to reject a Prime Minister and his colleagues, it had no longer the power to impose its will. Whether the King stayed or went, Mussolini would have bolted the door.

He soon asked for full powers. The Parliamentary Commission, over which Salandra presided, approved. In the Chamber 275 Deputies consented, and 90 opposed. In the Senate 171 Senators consented, and 33 opposed. In vain, men argued that there had been no parliamentary surrender. Nearly two years later, Croce was still giving a cautious support to Fascism. He wrote:

'Fascism was, and could be, nothing else than a temporary bridge for systematizing a stronger liberal régime. Fascism has met serious needs, and it has done much good, as everyone knows. It advanced with the consent and amid the applause of the nation, so that, in one sense, there is in the public spirit the desire not to return to the weakness and inconclusiveness which preceded it. There are votes cast without hesitation; and there are other votes which are given after long deliberation on the "pro" and the "con". Votes of enthusiasm and votes of duty.'

Those words were hard to reconcile with Croce's better-known judgment that authoritarian régimes, 'whatever their name or disguise, are not conservative. They impoverish the social forces, rouse inefficiency and apathy, open the way to weariness and disorder, and provoke revolutions.' The idea of the Corporate State—later to be expounded by Mussolini himself in the justly famous *Enciclopedia Italiana*—was not altogether uncongenial to the Latin mind. If this type of State was avowedly authoritarian and hierarchic, so also was the Church.

Very few foreigners abstained from visiting a country which had sacrificed its parliamentary freedom. There was, for example, no postponement of a state visit already arranged to be paid by King George V and Queen Mary. During her youthful years in Florence, the future English Queen lived so much in 'short street' that her family could never afford a trip to Rome, through which she once passed in the middle of the night. Now she was a resplendent figure as she bowed from the royal box to the people inside Rome's Opera House. To Lina Waterfield—a life-long English resident in Florence and a regular contributor to the 'Observer'—an Italian onlooker said: 'It is surprising how she can look such an aristocrat while wearing such a quantity of jewels.'

King George and Queen Mary were, in fact, the first state visitors to Fascist Rome. Their arrival compelled the Italian King and Queen to forsake the Villa Savoia for a few days. Though King Victor Emmanuel had reigned for about twenty-three years, he was so little familiar with the Quirinal Palace that, when he escorted Queen Mary to the banqueting hall, he went to the wrong door. He was annoyed when Queen Mary laughed.

Armed with a list prepared by her son-in-law—Lord Lascelles, a former member of the British Embassy in Rome, and later the Earl of Harewood—the English Queen devoted her scantily available time to examining treasures in Roman palaces, museums and galleries. The people did not know what she thought of the Corporate State, but it pleased them to see how much she liked their city. Croce might console its critics with the comment that Fascism was only 'a temporary bridge'. Rome, on the other hand, was the Eternal City.

The Italian version of the Corporate State, however, was soon making its appeal to casual visitors from other countries.

They experienced a sense of orderliness and discipline. Trains 'ran on time'; passengers who rested a foot on the seat of a railway carriage were fined; strikes became illegal; many glaring abuses were checked. Mussolini, moreover, knew how to give Fascism a striking, even if illusory, public image. He could claim that one of his political forebears was Garibaldi, who shared his contempt for Parliament. On unveiling a statue to the amazonian Anita Garibaldi, he said: 'I would like to think that if a miracle could happen and the statue of Garibaldi could take life, he would recognize in the blackshirts the successors of the redshirts of his day.'

At first, few foreign residents troubled to take Fascism and its claims too seriously. 'Here in Rome'—George Santayana wrote to Henry Ward Abbot on January 16th, 1924—'the world is pleasing: it seems always to have cared for things worth having; it is congenitally beautiful, born to enjoy itself, and straightforward in its villainies and sorrows. I walk about, knowing no one and speaking to nobody, and I feel that everybody understands me; and what is more and greater, that everybody is at work for the sake of the very things that I am inwardly at work about, human liberty and pleasantness breaking through the mesh of circumstances and laughing at it.'

If in the opening month of 1924, Santayana found the Roman world 'straightforward in its villainies and sorrows', the year was later marked by a crime which opened many eyes to the true nature of Mussolini's rule. According to an Electoral Law, which was the Fascists' first deliberate change in the Constitution, the party obtaining the largest number of votes in the whole country at a general election was to receive two thirds of all the seats in the Chamber of Deputies. Henceforward Italy would have no more debilitating coalition Governments.

The first general election under the Fascist régime was held on April 6th. The results showed that there had been no need to introduce the Electoral Law; for the Fascists received nearly five million votes and gained 268 seats, while together their opponents—Socialists, Liberals and Popularists—gained only 160 votes. There was no longer an opposition party which the Fascists had to fear. Yet one strong Deputy refused to be silenced. This was Giacomo Matteotti, Socialist and landowner. In a speech lasting for two hours and frequently interrupted, he showed how the Fascists acquired innumerable votes through bribery, corruption, intimidations and ruthless violence. They had lost any moral right to represent the Italian people.

Matteotti knew that he had signed his own death warrant. As he left the Chamber, he said to a fellow-Deputy: 'And now prepare my funeral oration!'

On June 10th—the day on which Mussolini received the award of the Dante Alighieri Society's medal for services to Italian culture— Matteotti was kidnapped during a walk along an embankment of the Tiber. Week after week went by without a trace of the missing Deputy. Convinced that he had been killed, his wife called on Mussolini and asked that his body should be handed to her for burial.

'*Signora*,' he said, 'I trust that I may return your husband to you alive.' He then told his secretary to escort the lady downstairs.

'Please do not trouble,' she replied. 'Matteotti's widow can leave alone.'

On August 16th, the body was found in a culvert off the road between Rome and Lake Bracciano. There was every sign that the murder had been brutal. The country seethed with anger, and many threw away their Fascist badges. For weeks the pavement from which Matteotti had been kidnapped was covered with flowers, and near the spot people were seen to kneel and pray. The one tribute which the opposition ought to have paid to Matteotti was a firm demand for Mussolini's dismissal. In the end, the King and his court might have felt themselves defiled by their tacit support of Fascism. Rightly or wrongly, thousands of people assumed that it was Mussolini himself who ordered the killing. It was said that he spoke of Matteotti as 'the corpse at my feet'.

The opposition, however, was not resolute. Instead of insisting on Mussolini's dismissal, many of its members decided to leave the Chamber. They included Salandra, Orlando and Giolitti. In the Roman phrase, they 'retired to the Aventine'. It was the clerisy, and not the King, who abdicated. One who never again crossed the threshold of the Chamber was Giorgio Montini. Later he closed down his newspaper in Brescia. Its publication would not be renewed, he said, until Italy was free.

Negative indignation is seldom productive. In time, the Romans forgot Matteotti's murder as they prepared for a Holy Year which, in 1925, brought about one million pilgrims into their city and into its churches and shops. They were nearly always impressed by what they saw in Fascist Italy. Black shirts and gay uniforms suited the Mediterranean looks of brisk or smiling youths. Mussolini himself was a great showman as he sat at the far end of a vast room in the Palazzo Venezia and watched a visitor advancing nervously towards him. In January, 1927, Winston Churchill gave a gladsome account of his own interview with the Fascist leader. He wrote:

'It is quite absurd to say that the Italian Government does not rest on a popular base or that it is not kept in office by the active consent of the great majority of the population. I could not but be fascinated, as so many people have been, by Mussolini's courteous and simple bearing, by his calm and serenity in spite of so many burdens and dangers. It is easy to see that his only thought is for the welfare of the Italian people.'

'If I were Italian,' Churchill added, 'I would don the Fascist black shirt.' It took a Gladstone to enter the cells of a ghastly gaol in Naples to find out for himself how the political prisoners were treated and how numerous they were likely to be.

Showmanship was not synonymous with open diplomacy. Very secretly Mussolini began negotiations with Cardinal Gasparri, the papal Secretary of State, to end the 'Roman Question' and to reconcile the State with the Church. Both sides wanted conciliation: Mussolini, because he knew that it would please the people and strengthen his hold over them; and the Pope, because it would also make possible an advantageous Concordat with the Italian State. For legal advice the Pope relied on Francesco Pacelli, who—like his younger brother, Eugenio—combined skill and acumen with an unyielding conviction that the rights of the Church were formidable and sacred. On February 11th, 1929, Mussolini and Gasparri met in the Lateran Palace, where they solemnly signed three separate pacts—a Treaty, a financial convention, and a Concordat.

The Treaty marked the Holy See's recognition of the Kingdom of Italy and Italy's recognition of an independent Vatican State, of which the Pope was sovereign; the financial convention bound Italy to pay 750 million lire in cash to the Holy See and also to transmit one thousand million lire in Italian consolidated stock, which yielded five per cent each year; and the Concordat granted a large number of privileges to the Church. The Pope wanted the Concordat and conceded the Treaty. Mussolini, on the other hand, wanted the Treaty and conceded the Concordat. The pacts were an agreement between two hierarchs: the one spiritual, and the other secular.

When their signing became known, there was immediate jubilation in Italy and throughout the Catholic world. By acknowledging the Pope's full sovereignty over scarcely a square mile of Roman soil, the Italian State vindicated his claim to the exercise of Temporal Power. Mussolini solved a problem which had baffled Italian statesmen for nearly six decades. He solved it, moreover, without any aid or compulsion from foreign powers. Thus he showed that the problem had all along been Italian, and not international. At the same time, its solution greatly increased the Duce's prestige outside Italy. The Pope uttered the casual, but long unforgotten phrase that he was a 'man sent by Providence'.

To perpetuate the memory of the day on which the pacts were signed, Mussolini decreed that February 11th should displace September 20th—the anniversary of the breaching of the wall near Porta Pia—as a public holiday. He also decided to open a new thoroughfare stretching from St. Peter's Square to an embankment of the Tiber and to call it the Via della Conciliazione. It meant nothing to him that the new thoroughfare destroyed the charm of the old Borgo and marred the harmony of St. Peter's Square with the gash of an exaggerated vista.

The Pope, in turn, busied himself with new buildings inside his tiny Vatican City State. They included a high-masted wireless station, a railway station and a prison. Yet Pius XI delighted chiefly in the older buildings brought once more under his acknowledged sovereignty. 'When a piece of territory,' he declared, 'can boast that it contains Bernini's colonnades, Michelangelo's dome, all the treasures of literature and science and art to be found in the archives, libraries, museums and art galleries of the Vatican; when, above all, there is to be found within it the tomb of the Prince of the Apostles—one has every right to say there does not exist anywhere else in the world a territory so great and so precious.'

In law, the precious territory was papal. In spirit, it was still Italian; and so was the bulk of its treasures. The Vatican City State, in fact, could not be completely divorced from Italy. Nor did its sovereign want an absolute divorce. On the contrary, the financial convention and the Concordat gave the Vatican an influence hard to resist. The bonds which it received from the Italian State represented about £20 million in the currency of the day. As more than one observer pointed out, they made the Vatican a preference shareholder in the Fascist régime.

Even tighter was the grip which the Concordat imposed on the State and the people. 'The Treaty and the Concordat,' Pius XI insisted, 'stand or fall together.' Two articles which belonged more strictly to a Concordat were embodied in the actual Treaty. Article 1 stated that 'Italy recognizes and re-affirms the principle consecrated in Article 1 of the Consitution of the Kingdom of March 4, 1848, according to which the Catholic Apostolic Roman Religion is the religion of the State.' The Constitution which Charles Albert granted to his subjects in the old Kingdom of Sardinia, however, never contained an article so harsh as Article 23 of the Lateran Treaty. This read: 'The judgments and provisions of the ecclesiastical courts, when officially communicated to the civil authorities, concerning ecclesiastical and religious persons and spiritual or disciplinary matters, will have automatically full juridical efficacy, even in regard to the civil effects of them.'

In plainer words, the ecclesiastical courts were given the right to punish priests, monks and nuns for heresy and other ecclesiastical offences. They could imprison them in cell or cloister without any hindrance from the State. There was no concession to the idea—sponsored first by Montalembert and then by Cavour—that there should be a free Church in a free State. Article 23 was based more on the theocratic principle that there should be an authoritarian Church in a fettered State.

By the terms of the Concordat, the Church was permitted to teach religion 'according to traditional Catholic formulae' in all primary and secondary schools. No one could teach religion or select the religious books to be used without the Church's approval. A priest who had returned to the lay status could be, and often was, refused permission to teach any subject at all in a state school. The State, moreover, had to follow the Church's marriage laws, and Italian judges lost the right to rule on the validity of religious marriages, even if they were con-

tracted in violation of civil law. Only through an ecclesiastical and—
as it proved—an expensive process could an unconsummated marriage
be annulled.

No doubt the great majority of Italians believed that there should be
religious instruction in all the schools and that marriage was binding
until a partner's death. Yet the refusal to let an ex-priest teach in a
state school was by no means the only illiberal feature of the Concordat. The civil magistrature could not even arraign a priest without
an approach to the ecclesiastical authorities for permission. Nearly a
century beforehand, Rosmini wrote 'The Five Wounds of the Church'.
If the Church did not pay its share of the taxes in a modern State, he
argued, the burden would fall on other citizens. The Concordat,
however, freed ecclesiastics from the payment of income tax and other
direct taxes.

There was one ban on the dissemination of Bibles produced by
Protestant societies and another ban on evangelical meetings in private
houses. The Italian Government was also obliged 'to prevent in Rome
anything that can be in contrast' with the sacred character of the city.
Did Mussolini seriously believe that Rome was more sacred than
Milan?

The best features of the Lateran Treaty—and the ones which the
world applauded—were based on the far-seeing Law of Guarantees
which a liberal-minded Parliament passed in 1871. The Concordat,
on the other hand, was a document which never came under any serious
parliamentary scrutiny. Mussolini was no longer concerned with Parliament. Its once outspoken members had nearly all 'retired to the
Aventine'. Nor were there enough professors and teachers within
Italy to make an effective protest. They were compelled to be Fascist
conformists or else to sacrifice their jobs. This only a few could afford
to do.

Freedom demanded a champion. Benedetto Croce knew now that
he had been wrong in regarding Fascism as 'a temporary bridge'
towards 'a stronger liberal régime', and he did not shirk his duty. He
was a man of ample wealth and, as he sought no university chair, he
was also a man of ample leisure, which he used to the fullest advantage.
No one could deprive him of his livelihood. He belonged to Naples,
and he was proud to uphold the intellectual integrity of its greatest
thinkers, from Aquinas to Vico. As a Senator, therefore, he spoke his
mind in Parliament. He said:

'Apart from men who think that Paris is well worth a Mass, there
are others for whom not to hear a Mass is worth infinitely more than
Paris, because it is an affair of the conscience.'

For this comment, the irreligious Mussolini never forgave Croce. Carabineers stood outside his house in Naples. His letters were censored, and once Fascists raided his library. Yet no one dared to hand a cup of hemlock to a philosopher of international fame. Croce blamed Mussolini for approving the Concordat. Later he blamed him still more for not observing its conditions. 'Much of the Concordat remains a dead letter,' he told Lina Waterfield. 'Yet, in one sense I am relieved at this; I was against the Concordat being made in the first place, but once signed, it is a serious thing for a great country not to carry out its obligations. . . . It seems very wrong to me for Mussolini to make political capital out of the Church, and then to show he did not mean to keep to its articles.'

Mussolini remembered, or forgot, the terms of the Concordat to suit his own convenience. By June 1931, his violations of the Concordat had become so flagrant that Pius XI issued his first serious protest in an Encyclical Letter called *Non abbiamo bisogno*: 'We have no need'. To ensure its world-wide publicity, Eugenio Pacelli arranged that Francis Spellman—later Archbishop of New York and a Cardinal—should take copies of the document by air to Paris and circulate them to the press outside Italy.

About that time, too, a man barely thirty years of age was planning his own spectacular protest against Mussolini's régime. His father was Adolfe de Bosis, admired for his translations from the works of Shelley and other English poets; his mother was the daughter of an American Methodist missionary and had spent most of her life in Italy. Lauro de Bosis came under the strong influence of Mario Vinciguerra, who thought that, for the moment, patriots should forget old republican and anticlerical aims and concentrate on compelling the King to remember his constitutional duty. For this reason, the young man became Secretary of the Italo-American Society in New York, which formed a rallying point for a steadily increasing number of Italian exiles. He was on a holiday in Paris when he heard that his mother and Vinciguerra had both been arrested.

Lauro de Bosis reacted promptly. He addressed a pamphlet to the King and had many thousands of copies printed. His next step was to buy an aeroplane, which he called *Le Pégase*. After about five hours of flying experience he left Marseilles for a pamphlet raid on Rome. As Air Minister, Italo Balbo might do his worst.

'Fascism,' Lauro de Bosis wrote, 'will not fail unless there are a score of young men who will sacrifice their lives to cleanse the minds of the Italians. In the days of the Risorgimento there were thousands of young men ready to give their lives, but now there are very few.

Why? It is not that their courage or their faith is less than that of their fathers: it is that nobody takes them seriously. All of them, from their leaders downwards, foresee its early end, and to them it seems out of all proportion to give their lives to put an end to what will fall by itself.

'That is wrong. We must die. I hope that after me many others will follow and that they will succeed in shaking public opinion.

'If my friend Balbo has done his duty there will be those who are awaiting me. So much the better. I shall be worth more dead than alive.'

On October 3rd, 1931, his aeroplane disappeared. Rome spelt death for the airman-pamphleteer. A few weeks later it also spelt a period of internment and political eclipse for a lean and bald-headed Indian who walked through its streets clad only with a loin-cloth, a shawl and sandals. As spokesman of the Indian National Congress, Mohandas Gandhi had gone to London for a Round Table Conference in St. James's Palace. Many years beforehand, when a young law student in London, he sought and obtained an interview with Cardinal Manning. The love of talking about religion with men and women whom he believed to be good and sincere grew upon him. On this new—and, as it proved, last—visit to London, he had made friends with George Bell, Bishop of Chichester, and with Hewlett Johnson, Dean of Canterbury.

Now he was passing through Rome on his way back to India. He told General Mario Moris—one of Italy's chief pioneers in aeronautics, who met him at Termini station—that he wished to talk both with the Pope and with Mussolini. Neither audience had been arranged, and General Moris was uncertain what to do. There followed telephone calls to the Vatican and to the Palazzo Venezia. Mussolini would receive Gandhi at six in the evening. The Pope had not been warned of Gandhi's arrival, and as his visit to Rome was very brief, it was not possible to grant him an audience during the normal period.

There was a striking contrast between the life-histories of Achille Ratti and Mohandas Gandhi. Less than a fortnight after Ratti had allowed the Fascists to bring their banner into Milan Cathedral, Bombay marked the arrival of the Prince of Wales in India with a complete *hartal* of silent and inactive protest. Twenty-four hours later, however, this gave place to savage mob-violence within the city. As a penance, Gandhi began a five-day fast. 'With non-violence on our lips,' he wrote, 'we have terrorized those who have differed from us. The Swaraj that I have witnessed during the last two days has stunk in my nostrils.'

In February 1922, when Cardinal Ratti became Pope, Gandhi knew that, sooner or later, he would be arrested and tried for disaffection. His trial took place on March 18th, and he pleaded guilty. 'Non-co-operation with evil,' he told Judge Robert Broomfield, 'is as much a duty as is co-operation with good. But in the past, Non-co-operation has been deliberately expressed in violence to the evil-doer. I am endeavouring to show to my countrymen that violent Non-co-operation only multiplies evil, and that as evil can only be sustained by violence, withdrawal of support of evil requires complete abstention from violence.

'Non-violence implies voluntary submission to the penalty for Non-co-operation with evil. I am here, therefore, to invite and submit cheerfully to the highest penalty that can be inflicted upon me for what in law is a deliberate crime and what appears to me to be the highest duty of a citizen.'

The judge, whose courtesy matched Gandhi's, sentenced the offender to a total of six years' imprisonment: 'and I should like to say in doing so that, if the course of events should make it possible for the Government to reduce the period and release you, no one will be better pleased than I'.

Within two years Gandhi underwent an operation for acute appendicitis, and the remaining period of his sentence was remitted. Otherwise he might still have been a prisoner when the man who blazed his path to power through violence signed the Lateran Pacts with Cardinal Gasparri.

Nor were political reasons and sympathies the only ones likely to make Pius XI unwilling to receive Gandhi. His own sincere longing to hasten the day when the whole human family might be brought within the fold of the Catholic Church conflicted with an old Hindu doctrine, dear to Gandhi: 'If a man reaches the heart of his own religion, he has reached the heart of the others too.' In later years Gandhi told his American biographer, Louis Fischer: 'I am a Hindu, a Muslim, a Christian, a Jew, a Parsi.'

Though the Pope did not receive him, Gandhi found that the Vatican Galleries were open to him. He was free to walk into the Sistine Chapel alone and to treat it as a place dedicated to prayer. 'I saw a figure of Christ there. It was wonderful. I couldn't tear myself away. The tears sprang to my eyes as I gazed.'

Then, as six o'clock approached, he walked down the great hall of the Palazzo Venezia with his secretary, Mahadev Desai, and with Madeleine Slade, daughter of an English admiral, who had joined his *ashram* near Ahmedabad under the Indian name of Miraben. At the other end of the hall sat Mussolini. He rose to greet them, and when the interview had ended he walked with them to the door. Next morning Mussolini sent Gandhi a list of the buildings—clinics, hospitals and schools—which he ought to see before he left Rome. Gandhi, however, chose only to see Maria Montessori and her Roman school.

In the evening, as he sat spinning and talking to a daughter of Tolstoy, Princess Maria, the King's daughter, entered the room with her lady-in-waiting, who carried a large basket of figs. 'They are Indian figs,' said the Princess.

'Her Majesty the Queen packed them for you herself,' added the lady-in-waiting.

The following day was the Mahatma's weekly day of silence. In silence, therefore, Gandhi travelled from Rome to Brindisi and embarked on the ship 'Pilsna' for Bombay. Rome had pleased him all the more because he decided to give no interviews to the press while he was journeying back to India. He refused to discuss the results of the Round Table Conference until he had talked in India with Jawaharlal Nehru and other members of the Congress Working Committee. Thus he was all the more surprised when, as the 'Pilsna' sailed southwards through the Red Sea, the ship's wireless told him that he had given an interview to Virginio Gayda, editor of the *Giornale d'Italia*, in which he made it known that he intended promptly to revive India's campaign of resistance to English rule.

This interview was never given, but the words which the *Giornale d'Italia* attributed to Gandhi created a bad impression in England and in the governing circles of the old British India. The words of a Fascist editor were still preferred to those of an Indian who believed that falsehood was a form of violence. This was one of the reasons why his re-arrest soon after his return from London was taken so quietly in England. Gandhi himself did not doubt that the falsehood originated with Mussolini.

'I looked into his eyes,' he said to a follower, 'and I could tell that he was lying.'

Why did Mussolini invent the lie? Did he imagine that it would please the Government in London? Or was he already dreaming of an Empire which might exist side by side with the world's largest Empire —the British? Perhaps he had begun to think of bringing Ethiopia under subjection.

There were various moral and other reasons why many Italians became increasingly impatient with the Fascist régime. Yet one non-Italian admired Mussolini's method so wholeheartedly that he wished to emulate them. He was Adolf Hitler, a former Austrian house-painter.

CHAPTER EIGHTEEN

GALE AND TORMENT

'THE MONARCHY is the sacred symbol—glorious, traditional, millenary—of the nation. We have strengthened the monarchy and made it more august. Our loyalty is perfect.' So Mussolini declared on the first anniversary of the Fascist march on Rome. More than seventeen years later, when the once admiring Hitler was his senior partner in warfare, he spoke openly to Galeazzo Ciano, his son-in-law, about his attitude to monarchies. He said:

'They are like those thick and strong trees, very flourishing on the surface, but hollowed by insects from within. All of a sudden they are struck down by lightning, and there is no human power that can set them up again.'

In outward appearance, Mussolini had, indeed, 'strengthened the monarchy and made it more august'. If the Fascist song *Giovinezza* was sung on all public occasions, so also was the Royal Anthem. Portraits of the King and Queen were seen in every school. The children prayed first for the Pope and then for the King and Queen. Their prayers for the Duce came third.

Throughout England and her Empire November 11th was known popularly as Armistice Day, and a huge throng gathered in Whitehall to observe a two-minutes' silence. Everywhere in Italy, however, November 11th was celebrated as the King's birthday. Schoolchildren acclaimed him as 'Victor the Victorious': 'the last Great War was fought and won under his high command'.

When the half-crazy Giovanni Passanante tried to kill King Humbert as he drove through the streets of Naples with Queen Margaret and the boy-heir to his throne, no one—from the King downwards—wanted him to hang, and it was in Humbert's reign that Parliament abolished the death penalty. Mussolini not only brought back the death penalty; he also established it for attempts on the King's life. The mildest insult to any member of the Royal Family was severely punished.

Outwardly, too, the people approved the close alliance between the Crown and the Fascists. Before Mussolini's advent to power, there had been enough republicans to form a separate party. Perhaps the majority of Socialists were also republicans. In the days when Victor Emmanuel II

—the *Re Galantuomo*, who faithfully observed the Constitution granted by his father—ruled over Italy, Humbert and Margaret travelled on his behalf from one city to another, and they were always assured of a welcome; but, with the extension of the franchise and the growth of a free press, the sentiments of the people became more pronounced. There were cities which the *Re Galantuomo*'s grandson dared not visit until Mussolini imposed a political conformity. Then all was changed. The symbol of monarchy became truly 'sacred'. Republicans and Socialists were silenced: it seemed, for ever.

Queen Margaret had given unstinted praise to Mussolini. At her death in 1926, it was found that she named him as the executor of her will. Her son, however, was not fooled. He knew the history of his own House of Savoy too well not to realize what he had surrendered to a formidable Minister. Though the new régime provided him with more adulation and popular prestige, he suffered a loss of power alike for himself and for his heir. Mussolini gave the young Crown Prince Humbert the title of the Prince of Piedmont, and he intended it to be a demotion of royal rank. The Prince's right to succeed his father as King of Italy was subordinated to the approval of the Grand Council of Fascism. The monarchy, in fact, was made a Fascist institution.

Twice the King had violated the Constitution of 1848 and thus forfeited any claim to be another *Re Galantuomo*. The first violation was his signing of the Treaty of London without the knowledge—still less, the approval—of Parliament. The second violation was the refusal to accept his Prime Minister's advice and proclaim a state of siege. For each a heavy price had to be paid by himself and by his people. With the second violation the King got himself trapped. How could he escape?

In the critical days of October 1922, he was determined not to behave with the uncertainty of his great-grandfather and thus risk hearing himself called Hamlet or King Wobble. Yet temperamentally he had far more in common with Charles Albert than with Victor Emmanuel II. In reality, he played Hamlet to the end of his long reign. Mussolini was Claudius: the unjust, though not incestuous, usurper of his throne. The longer the Duce's rule endured, the more surely it seemed that Fascism and the monarchy must stand or fall together. Already the monarchy was being 'hollowed by insects from within'.

The style of the royal household was bound to change when Queen Margaret became a widow. She was just as Italian as King Humbert. The tie between them was not marital fidelity, to which King Humbert made no claim. On the contrary, it was a close blood-relationship. First cousin worked harmoniously with first cousin, Piedmontese with

Piedmontese. The King had his soldiering, and the Queen her literary salon. The one never invaded the chosen field of the other.

Helen, the new Queen, could not completely take Margaret's place. For one thing, the Queen Mother had a widowhood which lasted for more than a quarter-century; for another, she retained her salon and, very largely, her social influence. She was religious and thoroughly at home within her Church. Queen Helen was also religious, but she was reared in a Church which made few, if any, concessions to Rome. Her submission to the Roman Church was required for reasons of State. It could hardly have been made unreservedly.

Slav succeeded Latin as First Lady of the Land. The Church, language and literature of the Italians became Helen's at one remove. She felt nearer home when speaking with the King in French and cooking simple meals within the secluded Villa Savoia. It may even have pleased her that the King's anticlerical views made visits from the Roman clergy comparatively rare. The Orthodox clergy in her native Cetinje were more plebeian in their style. They mingled freely with the people.

Helen also felt nearer home when she was fishing from a river bank in the heart of the Italian countryside or from a boat beyond the desolate beach at Castel Porziano, a royal estate not far from Ostia. The art of plying the rod, which she learned almost as a child from fishermen in the harbour at Cetinje, she soon taught to the King.

What made the King a fisherman? Was it solely the desire of a man who had been lonely and ill-shaped in boyhood to share a pleasure with his wife? Or was there also a deeper need to escape from the artifices of kingship and from an accusing sense of failure? Did he not in some ways resemble Russia's last Tsar, who was the conscientious and Orthodox godfather of Queen Helen? Nicholas II loved his wife and his children. Milan Stefanik—a Slovak who tried to win his support for the cause of Czechoslovak independence—admired the Tsar for his natural courtesy, but regarded him as a well-bred cavalry officer too weak to order his court aright, let alone control events.

Nature is seldom primogenitary, and like the Tsar, the King of Italy was not cast in a mould of greatness. He was intelligent, but not forceful or visionary. Calculators persuaded him to sign the secret Treaty of London, and his country's true interests would have been better served by a strict neutrality. Again calculators believed that Fascism was the only alternative to Communism. Matteotti had been almost alone in seeing that a few straightforward and timely police measures might have prevented the revolution of the Right. 'The multitude,' wrote Machiavelli, 'is more constant and more wise than any monarch.' He added:

'It appears to me that they who condemn the tumults between the nobles and the plebs are condemning just those things which were the first cause of Rome winning any freedom; and that they give more weight to the rumours and noise which sprang from such tumults than to the good effects which they brought to pass.'

By giving too much weight to the tumults, rumours and noise of workers and workless, a grievous error was committed by the King, the court, the lay clerisy, and at last by the Senators and Deputies, whose function was to represent the will of the people. If Mussolini hungered for personal power, he was none the less astonished by the ease with which he compelled others, step by step, to surrender their old authorities. It made him contemptuous.

Unlike his father, the King was a family man, and the family cultivated the more homely virtues. Transitions from the Villa Savoia to the Quirinal Palace were transitions from the home to the office, where managers and workers must often mask their actual feelings. The etiquette of the court was stiff, and the Queen hated false poses. She made friendships, and they were lasting; she also spoke readily with humble people, and she had a shrewd knowledge of how they lived and what they endured. Her beneficence may not always have been prudent, but it was genuine. If the family came first, that was no fault in the eyes of the Italian poor.

The literary salon died with Queen Margaret. Its revival by her daughter-in-law would have been out of character. Yet if ever the royal court needed to become a beacon of intellectual light, it was when Mussolini imposed the Fascist oath on all teachers and turned even the universities into mental barracks. The King was one of the few well-read monarchs left in Europe. In his own field of numismatics, he was a master. The teachers whom the Fascists drove from the universities and the schools still belonged, like the King himself, to the Common-wealth of Learning. A royal acknowledgment of this fellowship might have had a sobering effect on the power-drunken Duce who, when he wrote his early book on Jan Hus, expressed the hope that it would rouse in the minds of readers 'hatred for every form of spiritual and intellectual tyranny'. No intellectual light came from the Quirinal Palace or from the Villa Savoia. Instead, the fisherman let propaganda turn him into a demi-god.

Meanwhile his children were growing up. Eight months after the signing of the Lateran Treaties, he announced the betrothal of the Prince of Piedmont to Princess Marie-José, daughter of the reigning King of the Belgians. That the wedding took took place in the Quirinal Chapel—once the scene of Pius IX's election as Pope and later used for a cloak room whenever Victor Emmanuel II held a reception—betokened the changed relations between the Holy See and the House of Savoy. At the age of eleven, Princess Marie-José had been sent to a convent school in Florence, and for a long time it was widely recognized that she might be chosen as the bride for the Italian heir, who loved his army life and charmed many with his youthful looks and good manners.

To those who wanted the court both to be less military and to give Italy a stronger cultural leadership the choice seemed admirable. The bride's father, a valiant defender of his invaded country, descended directly from the first King of the Belgians—Queen Victoria's 'Uncle Leopold'—who was the model of a constitutional ruler and who managed to stay on his throne in the revolutionary year of 1848, when Metternich fled from Vienna, Louis-Philippe from Paris, and Pius IX from Rome. Her mother, Queen Elizabeth, was a Wittelsbach and thus belonged to the same gay-spirited, unconventional and sometimes eccentric family as the Empress Elizabeth of Austria and Maria Sofia, last Queen of the Two Sicilies.

The bride inherited from her mother a deep love of music, and from her father a serious devotion to historical studies. Among King Albert's parting gifts was a French translation of Benedetto Croce's recently published 'History of Italy from 1871 to 1915'. A more useful present could hardly have been given to an intelligent Princess who—if the Grand Fascist Council approved—might one day become Italy's third Queen.

Even without the crippling influence of a dictatorship, the Princess from Brussels might have found the court in Rome hard to endure. Her mother had an abounding interest in the political and cultural movements of the day. When an Immortal of the French Academy died, Queen Elizabeth longed to know who would be elected to take his place. If the successful candidate was a favourite writer, she wished to be in Paris when he presented himself beneath the cupola. Behind the closed doors of the little church in the Alsatian village where Albert Schweitzer was born, she listened to his organ-playing of a fugue by Bach. Later she became the first royal lady from Western Europe to visit either Communist Russia or Communist China.

Queen Helen of Italy was not Queen Elizabeth of the Belgians, and the Villa Savoia was not Laeken. In the Villa Savoia beneficence was almost the sole guiding principle of royal action, and the Princess of Piedmont found herself isolated from the main streams of a living European culture. Her husband inherited the military traditions of the House of Savoy, but not his grandmother's fondness for music. Few, indeed, are the great musicians who came from Piedmont.

In Naples, which became the birthplace of her children, the Princess of Piedmont was more fortunate. The San Carlo Opera House, which immediately adjoins the Royal Palace, is far comelier than the Opera House in Rome. The musical appreciation of the people is livelier, and the Princess may often have heard them talking of their most celebrated tenor, Enrico Caruso, whose funeral procession in 1921 was watched by more than half the citizens. In more normal times the Princess might have forgotten the slower tempo of life in the Villa Savoia as she moved among the sharp-witted and song-loving Neapolitans.

The times, however, were not normal. In reality, Naples was no more free than when the regicides from Paris set up their brief Parthenopean Republic. When the Princess of Piedmont wished to meet Benedetto Croce, there arose difficulties which seemed to be insuperable. Croce could not call on the Princess, nor she on Croce; for his house was always guarded by Fascist police. The meeting, if arranged at all, had to be secret.

At first, Croce thought that he might talk with the Princess in the large room of the Museum which contains the pictures taken from Pompeii, but other visitors would have noted the encounter. Apart from the virtual certainty of a report reaching Mussolini in Rome, a serious conversation would have become impossible. Eventually a friend engaged in archaeological work arranged a meeting in a small office used by the Superintendent at Pompeii. On the appointed day Croce carried a roll of plans and designs under his arm and walked with his friend to the small office, where he awaited the Princess.

She began the conversation by speaking of her father and by showing Croce her treasured copy of his 'History of Italy', which she wanted him to sign. After Croce had talked freely about the intellectual climate in Italy, the Princess asked him what he thought of the monarchy. Croce, though discreet, was far from silent. 'I did not believe, I told her, that the monarchical spirit was dead in Italy. It was smouldering under the ashes and would burst into flame if the King made some resolute gesture.'

Did the philosopher's message reach the ears of the King? Every Hamlet, perhaps, has a warning ghost.

If it was a bad day for Italy when the King sent for Mussolini, it was a worse day for Europe and the world when—on January 30th, 1933—the aged President von Hindenburg sent for Hitler. The new German Chancellor had very much in common with the Italian Duce. Both were violent and dictatorial, and both were skilful propagandists and eloquent. There was, however, one deep difference between them. The Italian loved personal power for its own sake; he used it for brilliant improvisation and for cutting a dazzling figure. The German leader who came from Austria was excessively imaginative and cruel; but he used personal power in order to carry out a diabolical master-plan. That plan was fully explained in the pages of *Mein Kampf*, which he dictated to Rudolf Hess during a period of imprisonment. It was thus laid bare for all to read.

The people who read the evil book from cover to cover included two shocked foreign observers in Berlin. One was the French Ambassador, André François-Poncet. The other was the Nuncio, Eugenio Pacelli, later to become a Cardinal and to succeed Pietro Gasparri as Pius XI's Secretary of State. Both were certain that Hitler meant every word that he had written in *Mein Kampf*. Now a wild genius was given his power to change the face of Europe.

André François-Poncet hurried to Paris in an effort to convince members of the French Government that Hitler could not be driven out of office. The only way of controlling his activities, therefore, was to enter into a convention with him. 'You are wasting your time,' André Tardieu, Minister of State, told the Ambassador. 'Hitler won't last much longer. His fate is sealed. Any convention with him would consolidate his power. Should war break out, not a week would elapse before he would be deposed and replaced by the Crown Prince.'

Military opinion was no less emphatic. 'You will see,' said the Chief of the General Staff, 'how long it will take Germany to catch up with the twenty millions we have spent on armaments.'

Cardinal Pacelli's ideas on how to curb the activities of the German Chancellor were not dissimilar to those of François-Poncet. Only a few months later Hitler sent Franz von Papen to Rome to negotiate with Pacelli a Concordat between Germany and the Holy See. Mussolini gave the German emissary full encouragement. 'The signing of this agreement with the Vatican,' he told him, 'will establish the credit of your Government abroad for the first time.'

Together with Cardinal Pacelli, Franz von Papen signed the Concordat on July 8th, 1933; and it was the first to be signed between the Holy See and a German Reich since the days of Martin Luther. Pacelli did not regret having signed this Concordat with a country led by the Jew-baiting author of *Mein Kampf*. 'I have never regretted that agreement with Germany,' he told François Charles-Roux, former French Ambassador to the Holy See. 'If we had not had a Concordat, we should have had no legal standing in our protests.'

No legal standing, perhaps; but moral standing was the more important. Some observers saw a lowering of Christian standards when the Holy See negotiated with a Government which did not intend to forgo its persecution of the Jews. When the Christian mysteries began to penetrate into pagan Rome, the citizens regarded Christians and Jews as members of the same sect. Most of the early Roman converts to Christianity may have belonged to the Jewish race. Later the Christian majority often persecuted the Jews. Time and again a Pope was their abettor. During each Conclave the fear prevailed within the Roman ghetto that the Cardinals might elect yet another intolerant Pontiff.

Even as late as 1825, the Roman Jews could not leave their ghetto after dark. Pius IX tore down the walls of the ghetto. It was an act of moral courage; so also was his refusal to go to war with Austria. 'We seek and embrace all races, peoples and nations,' he told the Cardinals, 'with an equal devotion of paternal love.' Here was doctrine which gave the Holy See its moral standing in all protests against injustice, whether the sufferers were Catholics, Protestants or Jews.

Cardinal Pacelli was extremely sensitive as well as highly intelligent. He had lived among the German people in the days of their military defeat and severe economic adversity. Sorrow at their plight made him all the more indignant that they should turn aside from former liberal traditions to treat the Jews like lepers who were not even made in God's image. His gifts were diplomatic, and he used them with the utmost skill; but if the first step in the relations with Hitlerite Germany was a Concordat which gave the Holy See a legal standing in its protests, when and how could the moral standing be asserted?

A Concordat reached with the Holy See would have meant little more to Hitler than the convention which François-Poncet wanted to establish between Germany and France. Not for the first time would a solemn agreement have been treated in Berlin as a 'scrap of paper'. The day for an emphasis on legal niceties was over. The Concordat was meant to safeguard the rights of the Church in Germany; but if the Romans were once mistaken in regarding Christians and Jews as members of the same sect, they were not wrong in seeing that the new religion had its roots in the old.

The kinship between Christian and Jew is unbroken, though brother has often slaughtered brother. To this day the Jews in Naples are called *parenti della Madonna*: relatives of the Virgin Mary. Their persecution disquieted the consciences of many German Catholics taught always to be obedient to authority. Ambiguity of statement may have an occasional value in diplomatic warfare, but there are times when the juridical response to a challenge is not enough. The great Pope Leo I met Attila, 'scourge of God', face to face; and the Christian world was grateful whenever Pius XI—in intellect and emotions a simpler man than the papal Secretary of State—expressed his own views in a few blunt words. Once he said: 'We are all Jews spiritually.'

What foreign statesman other than a diligent French Ambassador, or what Prince of the Church other than Cardinal Pacelli, had really troubled to read *Mein Kampf* from cover to cover? Statesmen, like soldiers, treated with disdain a demagogue who never rose beyond the rank of corporal in the Great War. Above Hitler there was Hindenburg, whom the German people had twice freely elected to be the President of their Republic: a monarchist and a soldier vested with power to dismiss and to choose a Chancellor. He could dismiss his new Chancellor whenever it became expedient to do so. Hindenburg, however, was already nearing the age of eighty-six when he sent for the Nazi leader. On August 2nd, he died. Hitler then assumed all the functions of the President; he was Fuehrer as well as Chancellor. No one stood above him any more.

In many other ways, 1934 was a crucial year for Europe. June 30th was Hitler's night of St. Bartholomew. On July 25th, Austria's Chancellor, Engelbert Dollfuss, was murdered. Mussolini reacted sharply and ordered a mobilization of troops along the Brenner frontier. It was the right thing for him to do. By looking northwards to guard the freedom of Austria and the new Succession States, Mussolini had a long-term chance to help in creating for Europe a new *Pax Romana*; but now this required the containment of a military Germany, whose swift re-arming could no longer be kept secret.

The deepening German menace drew the statesmen of England, France and Italy closer together. In May 1935, they met at a conference in Stresa to discuss measures of security. Mussolini gave Italy the fleeting image of a peace-loving power. Yet he wanted more than security. He craved for greater prestige and military glory. Not content with looking northwards, he looked southwards as well. In exchange for the agreement in Stresa with England and France, he expected to be given a free hand in Ethiopia. Earlier he had sponsored Ethiopia's admission to the League of Nations, but now he wished to avenge Baratieri's defeat at Adowa in 1896. Like countless other Italians, he was enslaved by the twisting and magnified legend of the Risorgimento.

Man has ill-treated the Italian countryside. In his ignorance he cut down virgin forests, destroyed innumerable water-courses and eroded the soil. In later centuries he made vast tracks of Roman Africa untenable for human habitation. Whoever wishes to see what the face of nature was like before man's arrival on the earth needs to go to Ethiopia, where the population is sparse and its wants are few. There was a mocking truth in Fascist propaganda: Italy, a people without a land; and Ethiopia, a land without a people.

Before the war the flow of emigrants from Italy to the United States had been unceasing. A grave social difficulty arose for a work-hungry nation when Washington imposed its quota-system on immigration. At first, Mussolini built his hopes on irrigation and other economic developments in Libya. Yet in 1930 the number of Italian settlers barely exceeded two thousand, and the Duce grew tired of collecting deserts. He found it more convenient to remember Adowa. Accordingly, he turned his gaze to a country ruled by a Christian Emperor with a gentle bearing and a courtly manner.

If Mussolini had been less bombastic, he could have got everything he wanted. So Marjorie Lady Warwick told the Duchess of Sermoneta; and her brother was Anthony Eden, the English Minister who, in an effort to avoid the war, offered Ethiopia a corridor which passed through British territory to the sea if, in exchange, she surrendered part of Ogaden to Italy. What made Mussolini scorn the deal was far more than bombast; it was a ruthless determination to wage war. He told Carlo Sforza that, unless there was a war, he would not accept Ethiopia, even as a gift.

His own people felt the lust for war. They resented the attitude of the English, who had been the veteran scramblers for territory in Africa, and whose modern Commonwealth and possessions overseas outstripped the old Roman Empire in size, wealth and power. Why did a satisfied nation oppose the will of a people in need of more land? The answer was not simple, for the English held conflicting views on the future of their own Empire. Many talked about the equality of status between one member of the Commonwealth and another. Even in the colonies which had not reached Dominion status, there was a devolution of authority. The main burden of the discussions at a Round Table Conference which Gandhi attended in London was when and how to establish a federal and independent Government in India. Yet when Gayda faked his interview with Gandhi for the *Giornale d'Italia* English rulers in India seized on their chance to discredit the Congress leader, whom they quickly sent back to prison. Empire-building is seldom, if ever, a clean business. In Italian eyes, the English were hypocrites.

The charge was not altogether just. As in Italy, so in England; it was often necessary to distinguish between governors and governed. The English people went willingly to war against the Kaiser's Germany because she had invaded Belgium. Theirs was a moral response. Germany was pledged to uphold Belgium's neutrality, and Italy had introduced Ethiopia to the League of Nations. One invasion was as wrong as the other. By arguing in this way, the English people forced the pace for their own bewildered Government. A war in Ethiopia seemed to them so wrong morally that many were puzzled to know why the Pope made no protest.

In vain, Arthur Hinsley, the new Archbishop of Westminster, offered an explanation. This outspoken Yorkshireman of humble birth had been a formidable Rector of the Venerable English College in Rome. He knew how to get things done. When he decided that the English College must move its summer seat from Monte Porzio— beloved by Westminster's first Archbishop, Nicholas Wiseman—to a site overlooking Lake Albano, he acquired a house which Queen Margaret wanted for herself. He was already sixty-three when Pius XI chose him to be Apostolic Delegate in Africa and thus a key-worker in the papal effort to bring the pagan world into the fold of the Roman Church.

Few knew better than Hinsley how Mussolini's war would be regarded in the Vatican, in the mission field, and in England. The Pope, he said, 'is a helpless old man with a small police force to guard himself, to guard the priceless archaeological treasures of the Vatican, and to protect his diminutive State which ensures his due independence in the exercise of his universal right and duty to teach and guide his followers of all races'.

The explanation was neither skilful nor convincing. The Pope might be 'a helpless old man', but one of the Lateran Pacts had made the Holy See a major bondholder of the Italian State. It could have exerted a strong influence against a war on a country ruled by a Christian. The Pope, however, was eager to bring back to the Roman Church all who had been separated from it. The Coptic Church to which the Emperor of Ethiopia belonged was schismatic, if not heretical.

With some notable exceptions, the Italian clergy supported the war. They saw nothing sacrilegious in Mussolini's call on married women to surrender their wedding rings and thus provide the country with a gold reserve for its war needs. At eight o'clock one morning, Queen Helen went to an urn close to the tomb of the Unknown Warrior. Into the urn she threw her wedding ring. Then she watched while other women followed her example. Meanwhile Cardinal Schuster, Archbishop of Milan, blessed women as they dropped their wedding rings into an urn outside his Cathedral. When the war began, he said:

'The Italian flag is at this moment bringing in triumph the Cross of Christ into Ethiopia, so as to free the road for the emancipation of the slaves and, at the same time, to open it to our missionary propaganda.'

Many Italians were furious when they heard that the wife of Prince Filippo Doria-Pamphili, a rich Roman landowner, refused to cast her wedding ring into an urn. Among friends, however, the Queen spoke in her defence; for the Princess was a Scot, and it was natural that she should share the feelings of her compatriots. The Queen, a Slav; the Princess of Piedmont, a Belgian; and Princess Doria-Pamphili, a Scot: the Roman aristocracy had often married into the Catholic families of other countries. The most conspicuous example was the Prince Borghese who married Gwendoline Talbot, daughter of the sixteenth Earl of Shrewsbury. The Romans adored her, and when she and her three children died from scarlet fever in 1839, thousands of poor people followed the funeral procession to the basilica of Santa Maria Maggiore.

There was a custom that whenever the body of an illustrious Roman was lowered into its grave, the chamberlain went to the church door and told the coachman in charge of the family carriage that his master or mistress did not need his services any more. The coachman then broke his staff of office and drove mournfully away. When this was done at the funeral of the young and lovely Princess Borghese, 'the whole of the vast crowd waiting outside the basilica broke into tears and sobs, and kneeling by a common impulse, prayed aloud for the soul of their benefactress'.

The Romans could take a foreigner to their hearts because the traditions of the city had long been cosmopolitan: 'a bare three millions of our subjects,' said Pius IX, 'possess two hundred million brothers of every nation and every tongue'. Now, however, most of the brothers were turning against Rome; for when Mussolini started his war against Ethiopia, the representatives of fifty-two nations agreed in Geneva to apply sanctions against Italy.

Defiance was the immediate response. The people willingly made sacrifices. The war went forward, and Italy became more united than ever before. The people applauded when Mussolini chose an old Fascist comrade, Emilio De Bono, to take the Army into Ethiopia; they applauded when Galeazzo Ciano led the first flight of the Italian Air Force over the invaded country; and many even applauded when they heard that the invaders had used poison gas against their primitively armed foe. Yet the applause was not unanimous. Some high-ranking professional soldiers were anxious. Why was Mussolini's young son-in-law chosen to lead the first flight over Ethiopia? And why did it take so long before the Duce removed De Bono and put Pietro Badoglio, a professional soldier, in his place? The Army, they insisted, must be kept free from political intrigues and influences.

The shame of the war against Ethiopia was not one-sided. As a psychological weapon of warfare, sanctions were a failure; as an economic weapon, they became a farce. They were imposed by the League of Nations, to which the United States did not belong. Germany deliberately ignored them. The Suez Canal was not closed to Italian shipping, and sanctions did not apply to coal and petrol. Otherwise the Italians could never have completed their mastery of Ethiopia. If Mussolini and his minions exposed their cruelty, Governments exposed their weakness, and commercial magnates their selfishness and greed. Collective security was a mirage.

On May 5th, 1936, sirens sounded all over Rome and sent people hurrying to the Piazza Venezia. There rose a mighty cheer when Mussolini walked onto the balcony and made his few words a secular utterance *urbi et orbi*: 'I announce to the Italian people and to the world that the war is over. We are a satisfied nation—so now to work.'

Mussolini was himself far from satisfied. The King was delighted to be acclaimed Emperor of Ethiopia and to ride with Badoglio at his side from the Colosseum to the Piazza Venezia. The Duce stayed away. His military glory was still insufficient, and he felt aggrieved that Italian losses did not exceed two thousand men. Italians were not thorough-going warriors. They disliked cruelty too much. The Duce wanted toughness.

Many an Italian soldier saw an African country with fresh and admiring eyes. In a later decade young people who went to a holiday camp in Italy found themselves sleeping not under canvas, but in a conically shaped hut known as a *tukul*. The *tukul* is an Ethiopian hut made entirely of bamboo stems. In the same decade, too, a foreign visitor walking through the streets of Trastevere might often have been struck by the lustrous beauty of a child whose features were half-Mediterranean and half-Ethiopian. Love is still the world's conqueror.

Mussolini was determined that the Italian should be less *simpatico*. Yet it was precisely his intuitive sympathy which would have made him an admirable colonizer. He arrived in the old colonial Africa too late. African blood, however, has long coursed through the people of southern Italy, Sicily and Sardinia. One day they may take the lead in creating harmony between Europeans and Africans.

Though Mussolini waged war in the teeth of sanctions officially imposed by fifty-two countries, he did not intend to be permanently estranged from London and Paris. Without their help, he could not prevent Hitler from annexing Austria. Outwardly the British Empire and Commonwealth represented world leadership and power. War was still raging in Ethiopia when—in January, 1936—King George V died. Flags were flown at half-mast in Rome. The King and Queen attended a memorial service in the Anglican church of All Saints. So did Mussolini. If a major war recurred, he was not going to join the wrong side.

England and France revealed the full weakness of their statesmanship only when, in March, Hitler defied the Treaty of Versailles by sending troops into the Rhineland and the Saar. In its initial stage, this remilitarization was no more than a bluff. Hitler would not even have attempted it unless Mussolini was deeply committed to his African adventure. The German troops were little more than a token force. Those who goose-stepped from Saarbruecken station to a parade ground numbered less than one hundred, and most were recruits. On the other side of the frontier stood many French troops awaiting orders. They had only to advance, and the German soldiers would have been at once withdrawn. Even if Hitler survived the blow to his prestige, he would have found it hard, and perhaps impossible, to make Mussolini an ally. To François Charles-Roux, the Pope said:

'If you had promptly mobilized two hundred thousand men, you would have rendered an immense service to the entire world.'

Instead, the fabric of security in Europe was smashed. Though Mussolini had attended the memorial service in Rome for King George V, he allowed no Italian official to be present when a new King was crowned in Westminster. His excuse was that an invitation had been sent to the Emperor Haile Selassie, now an exile in England. In reality, he no longer believed that friendship with England was worth while. Her leaders, he eventually told Ciano, were 'the tired sons of a long line of rich men, and they will lose their Empire'.

Only a few months after the coronation of King George VI, Mussolini was rapturously welcomed in Germany. Eight hundred thousand Germans—the largest visible audience which the Duce ever addressed —cheered as he spoke in their own language, though he knew it indifferently. The military manoeuvres which he witnessed at Mecklenburg convinced him that an inevitable war would be won by Germany.

Hitler still admired Mussolini. It did not follow, however, that he admired Italy. He sent his troops into the Rhineland while Italians were fighting in Ethiopia. The civil war in Spain created another dispersal of Italian strength. At first Mussolini sent only Fascist volunteers to fight for General Franco against a legitimate republican Government. He imagined that the war would soon be over and that he would gain a new and speedy triumph as a crusader against Communism. In actual fact, the civil war lasted for nearly three years, and the Fascist volunteers had soon to be augmented by regular soldiers. This suited the Fuehrer.

He could now forget the promptness with which Mussolini sent troops to the Brenner after Dollfuss had been murdered. In March 1938, he was the master of all Austria. To the Pope's grief, Cardinal Teodore Innitzer, Archbishop of Vienna, joined in the general cry: *'Heil Hitler!'* The same cry was raised by soldiers guarding the new frontier of the German Reich as they looked southwards to Italy: a cockpit of the morrow.

Within two months of his entry into Vienna, Hitler paid a state visit to Italy. First he went to Florence. The city was decorated in impeccable taste, but the Fuehrer's arrival coincided with the making of new drains in various parts of the city. A prison sentence was imposed on the wag who said:

'You can see the Germans are coming. We are digging trenches.'

The paintings in the Uffizi Gallery fascinated Hitler, but they bored Mussolini, who reluctantly accompanied him. The Duce wished to lead a race of bull-doggish pugilists, not a nation of artists. Accordingly, it meant something that Hitler was now able to see Italian soldiers goose-stepping in the same way as the Germans. This deliberate imitation annoyed Italo Balbo and many others among Mussolini's earliest supporters, but the Duce insisted that the goose was an Italian animal. Was it not the cackling of Roman geese which once awakened the defenders of the Capitol and thus prevented its capture by the Gauls? The goose-step became known officially as the *passo romano*.

On May 3rd, Hitler reached Rome. As a lady-in-waiting, the Duchess of Sermoneta stood with the Queen and other ladies looking from a window of the Quirinal Palace. Some may have been watching the *passo romano* for the first time. As soon as they saw the leading carriage in Hitler's procession, the Queen and all her ladies raced towards the drawing room. Not everyone in Rome, however, was so light-hearted. The Pope, outraged by the state visit, ostentatiously retired to Castelgandolfo. Hitler had looked forward to seeing the Vatican Galleries and entering the Sistine Chapel, but his entourage was told that these had all been 'closed for repairs'. The persecutor of the Jews and the foe of the Church must not see the 'Last Judgment' painted by Michelangelo, though it shows the damned sinking to perdition. Nor must he enter the tiny chapel of St. Lawrence to look at the delicate paintings by Fra Angelico.

The people—and not the Church—gave to the Dominican painter the name of *Beato* Angelico. From century to century, the process for his canonization has remained in abeyance. The needed evidence of any miracle is lacking. Suppose Fra Angelico performed a miracle belatedly by calling to repentance a wicked man who stood entranced before his paintings? Since the miracle would be unrecorded, it could not hasten the day of Fra Angelico's canonization. Yet allowing Hitler to enjoy the Vatican Galleries and the Sistine Chapel as much as he had enjoyed the paintings in Florence might have led to happier results for Europe and the world than did the policy of appeasement blindly pursued in London by Neville Chamberlain and Lord Halifax.

For while the Pope stayed in Castelgandolfo and the Vatican Galleries were ostensibly 'closed for repairs', Hitler induced Mussolini to commit a crime. Not content with the *passo romano*, the Fuehrer wished Italy to imitate the Nazi racial laws as well. This was the price to be paid for Italy's new status as a Nordic country worthy of partnership with pure-blooded Germany.

In all probability, Italian Jews never numbered more than fifty thousand, though many were eminent as doctors, lawyers and writers. To please Hitler, Jewish officers were deprived of their commission, even if they had reached the rank of a general or an admiral. Henceforward no Jew could be a lawyer, a teacher, or a journalist. Mussolini himself had to change his dentist. When Hitler first came to power, many German Jews sought refuge in Italy, for her dictator had openly expressed his disapproval of the Nazi racial laws. Now all the non-Italian Jews were compelled to leave Italy.

Father Agostino Gemelli, first Rector of the University of the Sacred Heart in Milan, might speak of a 'deicide' people tragically unable to belong to Italy 'because of their blood and because of their religion', but this view was not shared by the Pope or by Cardinal Pacelli. Thousands of Italians, in fact, felt the shame of the racial laws, and they were nearly always negligently applied. To those who were able to watch the Fascist rulers at close quarters, the introduction of the racial laws was one more sign of Mussolini's moral decline. Some attributed this decline to the growing influence of his beautiful mistress, Claretta Petacci, and others to a disease which ought to have been cured.

Mussolini claimed to be a political realist. Instead, he became increasingly an escapist. As journalist, he expressed ideas with the utmost lucidity; as improvisor of policy, he acted with boldness and with an astonishing flair for the good effect. He could not fail to win the approval of the Nazi leader who was waiting impatiently for his chance to seize power. Then Hitler, his willing pupil, reached office and thus acquired human and material assets far beyond the grasp of the Fascist who led a country much poorer than Germany.

The war in Ethiopia had been won too easily against Africans who were brave, but ill-armed, and the triumph gave Mussolini an inflated idea of his own capacity. He succeeded where Baratieri, a hero of the

Risorgimento, had failed. An amateur himself in the art of government, Mussolini distributed posts to other amateurs who happened to be staunch party men. Ciano, his son-in-law, became Foreign Minister at the age of thirty-four. Though he was intelligent, the young Minister cared almost nothing for the advice of civil servants.

Key-posts were given to party men even in Ministries concerned with the country's defence. They told the Duce only what he wished to hear. In turn, they became the victims of excessive flattery. Many members wanted to be seen talking with Ciano and his wife whenever they went to the Golf Club. Some were descendants of Stendhal's Roman ladies who knew only the handsome, the debonair, the wealthy and the illustrious. Perhaps there was no fundamental change; for Edda Ciano's father was the Duce, of whom even the King stood in fear: 'to see some of my friends fawning on her and calling her "darling",' the Duchess of Sermoneta complained, 'makes me sick'.

While many rich or well-born Romans cultivated friendships with Fascist leaders, Mussolini himself grew increasingly hostile to people of rank and social influence. If he showed an unfailing deference to the King, he no longer wore a top hat or frock coat on formal occasions; and as his doctors put him on a special diet, he had a ready excuse for keeping away from all receptions and banquets. He used the Palazzo Venezia as his office, but he no more wished to live in it than the King or the Queen wished to live on the Quirinal Hill. Instead, he lived in the Villa Torlonia without troubling to improve its amenities. In the war years, when he heard that Goering intended to stay with him, he was afraid that the German visitor—an indefatigable amasser of works of art—would despise the modest style of his home. He was glad, therefore, when he heard that Goering had been stricken with dysentery which, according to Field Marshal von Mackensen, did not 'permit him to leave his throne, even for ten minutes'.

Not a few Romans avoided Fascist circles because they had an aristocratic disdain for the newcomers who were destroying the last vestiges of the easy-going society which Stendhal described a century beforehand. Yet the men most likely to have shown a silent scorn for Mussolini were senior officers and civil servants who knew the harm done by Fascist amateurs within the Ministries. Month by month, Mussolini drew closer to Hitler, who ruthlessly followed his own plan for reversing the military decision of 1918. Germany was re-arming at a colossal speed. Was Italy, now her immediate neighbour, keeping pace?

Piedmont transmitted her military traditions to the new Kingdom of Italy, and almost every able-bodied young Italian was made liable for military service. Conditions were severe and unimaginative. They shocked officers accustomed to the gentler methods of the old Bourbon army in the south. The treatment to which the younger Cadorna submitted officers and men fighting in the First World War contributed not a little to the disaster at Caporetto. Army leaders seldom moved easily with the times; but, at least, they were not corrupt. They had their own stiff code of honour, and it made them resent the intrusion of corrupt outsiders and political schemers. Some would have endorsed the view expressed in an intercepted letter by François-Poncet who, in 1938, became the French Ambassador in Rome. He wrote:

'In Germany I had to deal with real gentlemen; here, instead, I have to deal with servants who have become masters.'

Mussolini was happiest when addressing the crowd. He started to prepare a mammoth exhibition to commemorate, in 1942, the twentieth anniversary of the march on Rome. An exhibition on so grand a scale would be costly. So were armaments. Which came first in Mussolini's mind? A glorious display, or the serious business of making proper preparations for war? To send Italians into a war before they had enough tanks, cannons and aeroplanes would be to bring the Duce and the whole Fascist episode into contempt. The air force was attracting young men who loved and understood machines. What if the military aircraft in which they were compelled to fight were far outclassed by the aircraft of their foe? They would be in a position similar to the Ethiopian, who pitted his personal bravery against superior arms. His own war in Ethiopia should have taught Mussolini that bombast is not gunfire. Before long he was wishing that he had died in 1937. Posterity might then imagine that his Fascist rule had been clothed in splendour.

Within a few months of his visit to Rome, Hitler met Mussolini again. Their meeting place was Munich, where they signed with Neville Chamberlain and Edouard Daladier a warrant for the strangulation of an independent and democratic Czechoslovak republic. Chamberlain went back to London convinced that he had won 'peace for our time'. Mussolini was applauded in Rome as an arbiter of peace. Daladier and Hitler alone behaved as though they discerned the truth: Daladier, unsmiling because he knew that the Munich agreement was shameful; and Hitler, exultant because once more, even though for the last time, his blackmail had succeeded. Almost for a certainty, a new World War lay less than a year ahead.

Pius XI, now eighty-one and slowly dying, had no illusions about the Munich agreement. He envisaged an Italy turned into a battlefield for the benefit of the Germans. In his heart, perhaps, he regretted the

Church's failure to oppose the war in Ethiopia as well as its failure to understand the real nature of the civil war in Spain. These failures had been conspicuously his own. In one of his last audiences he said:

'Late, too late in my life, I have discovered that the dangers which threaten religion do not come only from one side. They come from the other side as well. From now on, I consecrate what remains to me of life to aid my children to share with me my discovery.'

On January 13th, 1939, he received Neville Chamberlain and Lord Halifax. Chamberlain was Unitarian, and Halifax was the son of Cardinal Mercier's Anglican friend, who strove hard for reconciliation between Rome and Canterbury. For the moment, Pius XI was concerned only with their political leadership in London. By all accounts, he turned the audience into a monologue. There was so much he wished to say about the authoritarian régimes and the persecution of the Jews. The English statesmen listened. If they, too, had spoken frankly, they might have made a better impression. Instead, they saddened the Pope. He thought that intellectually they were sluggish. They did not grasp what was happening to Europe.

In an effort to warn Italians against the peril of identifying themselves with the Nazis, he summoned all their Bishops to Rome. He intended to speak to them on February 11th, which was the tenth anniversary of the signing of the Lateran Pacts. 'Keep me alive at least until February 12th,' he told his doctor.

The address to the Italian Bishops was not delivered. Early on the morning of the 10th, the Pope had died.

CHAPTER NINETEEN

FALLEN CAESAR

CARDINAL PACELLI bent over the body of Pius XI, now lying in the Sistine Chapel, and kissed the forehead and the hands. His duties as Secretary of State ended at the moment of the Pope's death; but his other duties as Camerlengo were increased and would remain exacting until the Conclave for a new Pope was over. The Camerlengo was determined that all the traditional procedures of a Conclave should be scrupulously followed. Afterwards he would go to Rorsbach, in Switzerland, for a holiday, and he renewed his passport. Whatever the future might bring him, he had no wish to become Secretary of State again.

Fourteen scrutinies had been needed before Achille Ratti was elected in 1922. Two alone were sufficient for the election of Eugenio Pacelli. If he had failed to obtain the required majority at the second scrutiny, he might never have become Pope. He was taken completely by surprise, and when the Cardinal Dean asked what his name would be, he replied: 'Pius'. With a little more reflection, he would almost certainly have chosen a more distinctive name.

The Conclave was both the first to be held since the march on Rome and the shortest for more than three hundred years. The Fascists controlled all the newspapers, save the *Osservatore Romano*. Their editors were told 'to greet the new Pope, whoever he may be, with words of deep respect, and to refrain from indicating any preference for one or another'.

The Fascist press might be respectful or feign indifference, but the Romans were jubilant when Pius XII came to the outer balcony of St. Peter's to give his first blessing *urbi et orbi*. Rome had always been his city, and now he was the first Roman to become Pope since the election of Innocent XIII in 1721. Frequent visits abroad, moreover, had made him a memorable figure outside Italy. Among the first foreigners to call at the Vatican were Eamon de Valera of Ireland and Joseph Kennedy, the wealthy American Ambassador in London, who presented each of his numerous children to the Pope.

To mark the reconciliation between the Church and the State, the Prince and Princess of Piedmont attended the coronation in St. Peter's. So did Ciano, and he was furious when he found that he was not seated in the same row as the representatives of sovereigns. Even more important than reconciliation between Church and State, however, was reconciliation between Pope and people, and the news that the actual crowning of the Pope with the triple tiara would take place on the outer balcony brought an unprecedented crowd into St. Peter's Square.

However wrathful Hitler and Mussolini may have been—and neither expected the once condemnatory Secretary of State to be elected—few Popes ascended Peter's throne amid more displays of popular good will. Yet the brief prospect of peace and harmony between Peter and Caesar—the dream of Dante—was illusory. Three days after the coronation, German troops entered Prague. On the following night, Hitler slept in Hradcany Castle. The former papal Secretary of State had been right when he told Chamberlain and Halifax that the agreement reached in Munich was worthless.

Hitler sent his troops into Prague without first warning Mussolini. On Good Friday—and without warning Hitler—Mussolini sent troops into Albania. Fuehrer and Duce did not trust each other. Yet, in May, Ciano went to Berlin to sign with Joachim von Ribbentrop a Pact of Steel. Mussolini and his son-in-law knew quite well that Italy had very little steel to offer her mighty neighbour. Factories for munitions were far too few; aircraft, tanks and guns were mostly outdated; and all talk of 'eight million bayonets' ignored the fact that Italy was unlikely ever to mobilize more than three million men. These were the men whom Hitler wanted: if not as cannon-fodder, then as forced labourers.

What Italy needed was peace. According to the official propaganda, Ciano and Ribbentrop signed the Pact of Steel 'to assure a peace founded on justice'. Ribbentrop led Ciano to believe that a major war still lay about three years ahead. None the less, the pact committed Italy to be on Germany's side whenever hostilities began. At that very moment German plans were far advanced for an autumnal invasion of Poland.

At a late hour on August 21st, Ciano received the staggering message that Ribbentrop was about to sign a Russo-German Pact in Moscow. The Duce's immediate public response was a claim to be himself the originator of the idea of a pact between Germany and Russia. The claim made nonsense of the part played in the Spanish Civil War by volunteers and regular soldiers from Italy; for why fight against Communism in Spain if Hitler seeks a Communist endorsement of his war on Poland?

On hearing the news, millions of Europeans became convinced that there was no escape from a new major war. Pius XII decided to broadcast an appeal for peace. Speaking from Castelgandolfo, he said:

'Nothing is lost through peace. All can be lost through war.'

The crisis deepened. Mussolini, angered by the way in which Hitler pushed Europe towards war without consulting him, let it be known that he was not sorry 'to watch from the window'. The black-out was imposed on the Italian cities. An imaginative man of letters like Mario Praz might walk through Rome in the darkness, delight in the moonlit Travertine stone of princely palaces and listen, as though for the first time, to the sound of water cascading from a fountain in the street. Yet he had spent some of his best years lecturing in Liverpool and Manchester before accepting the chair of English literature at Rome University. To those who knew the two countries as intimately as Chaucer or Milton had known them, the thought of war between Italy and England was always intolerable.

So to others was the thought of war between Italy and France. No one described the Roman society of his day more faithfully than did Stendhal. Emile Zola—novelist of France and champion of Alfred Dreyfus—was born an Italian. Rome and Paris had often been called twin sisters. Now the cultural unity of Europe was barbarously threatened.

Even greater was the anxiety among ordinary citizens who had never read a foreign book nor crossed a frontier. They longed for a leader who was not content, even for a moment, idly 'to watch from the window'. Peace-making is often a strenuous activity, and most Italians who remembered the Great War wanted their country kept out of a new war altogether.

The Pope was not thinking of Italy alone. Since all could be lost through war, he begged for time. On August 31st, he asked Germany and Poland for a fifteen days' truce so that an international conference might meet. Here was a direct appeal to Hitler. This strange demon—a murderer and an adorer of fine paintings who made the boasted wicked-nesses of Benvenuto Cellini seem trivial by comparison, and who had been pointedly denied access to the Vatican Galleries and the Sistine Chapel—would he heed the Pope's request and halt his time-table for war on Poland? It was like asking for a miracle; but when the Nuncio delivered the papal note in Berlin, he received a reply which led him to believe that Hitler was prepared to accept a truce. That evening the streets in Rome were lit again. Before dawn, however, the German Army was on the march. The hour which Hitler chose for Poland's 'elimination' had struck.

By signing the Pact of Steel, Ciano gave Hitler a blank cheque. The time for presenting it was still to come. Hitler had made his deal with Moscow, and he needed no other helper in the rape of Poland. The French and the British were on the defensive. For them it was a 'phoney' war. Hitler allowed Italy to be neutral; but as neutrality was a word alien to the Fascist vocabulary, Mussolini declared Italy to be 'non-belligerent'.

His compatriots received one shock after another: first, the swiftness of the lightning war on Poland; then her partition between the Germans and the Russians; and finally Russia's war on Finland. Neutrality, after all, would have been a more suitable word than non-belligerence. Mussolini's reputation suffered. The King hated the Germans and wished to escape from their clutches. Not a few were hoping that he would seize his chance to dismiss a powerful Minister who understood propaganda, but not warfare.

Few dreaded the prospect of a new war for Italy more than did her Queen. In November she prepared a letter addressed to the reigning Queen of the Netherlands, the Queen of Bulgaria, the Queen of Denmark, the widowed Queen Elizabeth of the Belgians and the Grand Duchess of Luxembourg. The letter recalled that, in 1529, two Princesses of the House of Savoy—Margaret of Austria and Louise of Angoulême, mother of Francis I, King of France—worked so strenuously for peace that the Treaty of Cambrai became known as the *Paix des Dames*. Queen Helen now invited her five 'dear sisters' to join in an appeal for an international conference to end the war. The letter was submitted to Mussolini as President of the Council. Politely the Duce imposed his ban.

The letter was long, and someone familiar with Savoyard history —almost certainly either the King or the Princess of Piedmont—must have assisted in its drafting. Six years had passed since Cardinal Pacelli arranged with Archbishop Spellman to smuggle the Encyclical Letter *Non abbiamo bisogno* out of Italy. What if the Queen had not submitted her letter to Mussolini? There was no Constitution of 1848 left to violate. The constitutional error, even if it existed, could not have been greater than the King's signing of the Treaty of London or his refusal, in 1922, to sign the decree for a state of siege. If the letter had been published outside Italy without Mussolini's consent, there would have been an immediate crisis in the relations between the court and the Duce. The time was ripe for Mussolini's dismissal. Neither materially nor morally was Italy prepared for war.

Fear is man's great oppressor. The King and his court were afraid of Mussolini, and Mussolini was afraid of Hitler. As Fulke Greville, friend of Giordano Bruno as well as Philip Sidney, wrote:

> For Power can neither see, work or devise
> Without the people's hands, hearts, wit and eyes:

So that were man not by himself opprest,
Kings would not, tyrants could not make him beast.

On December 21st, the King and Queen visited the Pope. A week later the Pope returned their call. He was the first Pontiff to enter the Quirinal Palace since the days of Pius IX's voluntary imprisonment, and the Roman crowd cheered him as he crossed from one bank of the Tiber to the other in a rainstorm. For all his anticlerical feelings, the King showed the Pope the utmost deference and escorted him to the foot of the stairs when he was leaving. Soon afterwards the Pope's three nephews—Carlo, Marcantonio and Giulio Pacelli—were made hereditary Princes of the Kingdom of Italy.

Pope, King, Queen and people all wanted peace. So in his heart did Mussolini; for though the prizes of war may glitter, defeat is shameful. Italy, he soon told Hitler, could not, and would not, become involved in a long war. On March 10th, Ribbentrop arrived in Rome and arranged for Mussolini to meet Hitler on the Brenner. The Pope granted the German Foreign Minister an audience and read aloud a documented account of Nazi atrocities in Poland. According to one version, Ribbentrop almost fainted and was assisted to a chair by Cardinal Maglione, the Secretary of State. According to another, he saluted stiffly and left the room before the Pope had finished reading the account aloud. Whatever happened, he let the Pope know that eighty million Germans were determined to win a total victory within the year. Before long, he declared, France and England would sue for peace.

Within a week Mussolini met Hitler on the Brenner, and his fear that the war in the west might be long was overcome. He was jubilant when he heard that Norway had been invaded. On May 10th, German troops poured into Holland, Belgium and Luxembourg. The Pope sent messages of sympathy to the rulers of these three countries only to be sharply reminded that he had infringed a clause of the Lateran Treaty. When the *Osservatore Romano* published the messages, the Fascists reacted by attacking the boys who were delivering copies. Ciano realized that this conduct was improper, and he ordered Dino Alfieri, Ambassador to the Holy See, to offer an apology. 'Your Government,' the Pope later told Alfieri, 'has the power to put us in a concentration camp if it wishes, but we shall do nothing against our conscience.'

It required only five days for the Dutch resistance to collapse. On May 26th, German tanks took Boulogne and raced towards Calais. Next day the Belgian Army laid down its arms. On the night of June 3rd, the Germans reached the harbour of Dunkirk, and the beaches from which British soldiers were being evacuated came directly under their fire. Nine British divisions were lost. So were thirty French divisions, the entire Dutch and Belgian Armies and vast supplies. The Germans now faced the French with a superiority of three to one in manpower and five to one in armoured units.

Only then did many high-ranking Italian officers even know on which side their country would be fighting. All their plans had been made for defensive warfare. As in the east, so in the west; Germany did not need an Italian ally. Mussolini, however, was completely convinced that Germany must soon win the war, and he dreaded the prospect that it might end before Italian blood had been shed in battle. He had already personally assumed the high command of the armed services. He did not trouble to consult the Fascist Grand Council, the Council of Ministers or the Fascist Parliament. Only Hitler counted. On June 10th—the sixteenth anniversary of Matteotti's assassination— he brought Italy into the war.

Mussolini persisted in the belief that the war would soon be over; it could not be prolonged into the winter. Before November he demobilized about three hundred thousand men. Work was restarted on the great exhibition to mark, in 1942, the twentieth anniversary of the Fascist conquest of Italy. Yet Mussolini had seen wars won with a fatal ease, and now—encouraged by Ciano and without telling Hitler—he planned a new war of his own. He did it with Hitlerite guile, but without Hitlerite genius. His intended victim was Greece.

On October 25th, King George of the Hellenes attended the inaugural performance of Puccini's *Madame Butterfly* in the newly constructed State Theatre in Athens. The Greek Government invited Puccini's son and daughter-in-law to be present, and their visit was arranged by the Italian Minister for Popular Culture. On the following evening a reception was held in the Italian Legation. Barely thirty hours later—at three o'clock on the morning of October 28th—an ultimatum was handed to the Greek Prime Minister, General Metaxas. Italy was at war with Greece. Every Greek knows that the climate in his country deteriorates towards the end of October and that a rainy season begins, but Mussolini had chosen the date deliberately. October 28th was the eighteenth anniversary of the Fascist march on Rome.

Hitler was furious. The last thing he wanted was a British base on the Continent. The Greek morale was splendid. Until Hitler came to Mussolini's aid by sending some of his own well-equipped troops southwards, there was no hope that the Greek resistance could be broken.

The chief enemy of the Italian airman or soldier was his wretched equipment. Italian fighter aircraft were massively outgunned by the

Liberator or later the Flying Fortress. An order to attack the enemy's speedier and more heavily gunned aircraft was virtually a death sentence. This story of faulty or inadequate equipment could be told wherever Italians were fighting: in Greece, Libya or Somalia. On the Gondar plateau in Ethiopia, for instance, twelve thousand Italian soldiers who had no Air Force to support them, no anti-aircraft defences and no tanks, resisted for 193 days before surrendering. They were then near starvation, and their uniforms were in rags.

The 'short' war in the west had already lasted for a year when Hitler launched his offensive against Russia. He gave Mussolini no warning, but the Duce fulsomely praised his action. This second war in the east was, in turn, bound to be short. Without consulting any of his generals, Mussolini insisted on being allowed to send 200,000 Italian soldiers to the new front. He went to Verona to review the first division on its way to Russia. Over the telephone, he told his son-in-law that the review was perfect. 'Be that as it may,' wrote Ciano in his diary, 'I am concerned about a direct comparison between our forces and the Germans. Not because of the men, who are, or who may be, excellent, but because of their equipment. I should not like to see us play the role of a poor relation yet again.'

Once more Mussolini faced the prospect that the fighting might end before there had been a sacrificial shedding of Italian blood; but Hitler also forgot that if the fighting in the east was not soon over, the victory might go to 'General Winter'. Most of the Italian soldiers were born and bred south of the Alps. Ill-equipped and ill-clad, they were treated with contempt by the better armed and more warmly clothed Germans. Within eighteen months their numbers were reduced by half. Countless thousands went back to the homeland with a foot or a hand lost or permanently maimed through frost-bite. If, in the summer of 1941, these two hundred thousand men had been well equipped and sent to North Africa instead of Russia, the subsequent story of the Second World War might have been differently written.

They were already enduring their first winter in Russia when, on the night of December 7th–8th, the Japanese attacked Pearl Harbour and, according to Fascist propaganda, broke the naval power of the United States. Mussolini, once more jubilant, declared war on the United States simultaneously with Hitler, and he spoke to the Romans from the balcony of the Palazzo Venezia. This time they were not particularly demonstrative. 'We must not forget,' Ciano wrote, 'that it was three o'clock in the afternoon, the people were hungry, and the day was quite cold.'

It was not Mussolini alone who had expected the war to be short.

In June 1940, people all over Italy spoke of *questa guerretta*: 'this little war'. Just as economic sanctions once stiffened their resolve to bring the war in Ethiopia to a successful conclusion, so the blockade and the air raids made them more than ever determined to resist the foe. Whether the bombed city was London or Naples, Liverpool or Genoa, the cry of the people was virtually the same: 'We can take it!'

Italians suffered not from any lack of physical courage, but rather from a corrupt and amoral leadership. Mussolini despised them, but only because he had become himself despicable. War against France and Britain; against Greece; against Russia; and finally against the United States: each time, he expected a quick and spectacular return for the expenditure of Italian blood. Airmen, soldiers and sailors might have little precise knowledge about corruption or ineptitude in high places, but they were its sufferers. Experience made them cynical and bitter. Thousands were the soldiers who surrendered because they had no ammunition left. There was hardly an Italian family which did not count a prisoner of war among its members.

Death did not spare the Duce's family. In August, Bruno Mussolini had been killed near Pisa while experimenting with a new type of aircraft. His father meant to be stoical, but he hated the approach of Christmas and he wanted the festival to be abolished altogether; for it 'only reminds one of the birth of a Jew who gave the world debilitating and devitalizing theories, and who especially contrived to trick Italy through the disintegrating power of the Popes'. The newspapers were instructed to make no mention of Christmas.

Early in 1942, it was the turn of the Royal Family to go into mourning; for the Duke of Aosta, Viceroy of Ethiopia, died a prisoner of the Allies. A Requiem Mass was held in the church of the Sudario. Only members of the court were invited; but, as each wearer of the Collar of the Annunziata became the 'cousin' of the King, Ciano was present. No sooner had the ceremony begun than a woman dressed in mourning entered the church. Ciano saw that she was Donna Rachele Mussolini, his mother-in-law. She 'took the first seat she could find and wept throughout the entire ceremony. . . . She came on foot and she left on foot.'

No matter how many court invitations she might receive, Donna Rachele stayed nearly always in the background. The Duce was thus amazed to hear that she had gone to such an intimate royal ceremony. 'This is the first time such a thing has happened,' he said. Yet, while she wept in the church, Donna Rachele had no thought of herself as the wife of a great leader. Instead, Ciano wrote, 'she was simply the mother of a lieutenant of twenty, killed in his aeroplane'.

The admiration which Hitler once felt for Mussolini gave place long since to contempt, and he sometimes humiliated the Duce by rousing him from his sleep with a telephone call in the small hours of the morning. Italy became increasingly dependent on German support. Field Marshal Albert von Kesselring set up his headquarters in the imposing Villa Aldebrandini at Frascati, a bare twelve miles from St. John's Gateway. The Gestapo began actively to function within the city, and one macabre visitor to Rome was Heinrich Himmler. With biting sarcasm, the King began referring to Mussolini as the Gauleiter for Italy.

No less humiliating was the greater apathy of the people. They had scarcely noticed that the newspapers made no mention of Christmas, which—in unheated apartments and with little appetizing food—they tried to celebrate in traditional fashion. In the middle of August came *ferragosto*, the feast of Augustus: the festival which, in pre-Christian Rome, was held in the Emperor's honour, and which the Church has turned into the feast day of the Assumption of the Blessed Virgin Mary. On that day in 1942, Ciano looked out of the window and saw that the city was empty. As in the pre-war years, the people who were not Roman in origin spent the day with kinsfolk in towns or villages, near or far, 'The war? They want to forget it.'

In February 1943, Ciano lost his post as Foreign Minister and became Ambassador to the Holy See. His demotion was part of the price to be paid for incurring the hatred of Claretta Petacci and her family. Mussolini had sacrificed not only a son-in-law, but also a man who— for all his vanity and impetuous ideas of Italian expansion in the Balkans—wished to be loyal to him.

Meanwhile the campaign in North Africa was drawing to its close. On July 10th, the Allies invaded Sicily. On the 19th, while Mussolini was having an uncomfortable meeting with Hitler at Filtre, the Americans bombed Rome for about two hours. On the 24th, Mussolini summoned the Fascist Grand Council to the Palazzo Venezia. He behaved like a broken man as he listened for ten hours and through the night to the charges which its members made against him. Their chief spokesman was Dino Grandi, architect of the march on Rome and formerly Ambassador in London. He was reported to have said:

'You have imposed on Italy a dictatorship that is historically immoral. You gradually, day by day, have suppressed our liberties and robbed us of our rights. Your dictatorship willed this war. Your dictatorship has lost it. The chief we loved has disappeared . . . Take from your cap that ridiculous Marshal badge that you so inelegantly awarded to yourself. Try to become again the Mussolini of olden days.

But you cannot. It is too late. By your folly and by our weakness we have come to see the destinies of a great people treated like private affairs.

'Among the phrases which you have ordered to be written on all the walls of Italy there is one which you pronounced in 1924: "Perish all factions, even our own, provided the nation survives." Today the moment has arrived. The faction must perish.'

By 19 votes to 7 the Grand Council condemned Mussolini and his dictatorship. It required him to restore all the former functions of the Crown and the Government. He was to ask the King to assume the supreme command of all the armed forces and to take 'the highest decisive initiative' to save Italy. The majority who voted against the Duce included his son-in-law and General De Bono.

According to Mussolini, the functions of the Grand Council were purely deliberative. He had little doubt that, when he saw the King on the following afternoon, he could persuade him to arrest the opponents. For once, the King outwitted his Minister. News of the Grand Council's nocturnal verdict reached him at six o'clock in the morning, and he promptly interpreted it as a dismissal. Before midday he confirmed the appointment of Marshal Badoglio as President of the Council. At the appointed hour, the Duce arrived at the Villa Savoia.

'Your Majesty,' said the aide-de-camp, 'Signor Mussolini askes to be received.'

The King spoke with him for twenty minutes, accompanied him to the outer door and then retired. Mussolini looked in vain for his secretary and his car. Instead, he saw a military ambulance. An officer of the Carabineers stepped forward.

'I am Colonel Fragnani,' he said. 'I am here to protect you. Will you please step into this car?'

The prisoner was first taken to the barracks of the Carabineers, then to a cadet school, and eventually to Gaeta. There a corvette under the command of Admiral Franco Maugeri, a Sicilian, was waiting to transport him to the island of Ponza. His words to Admiral Maugeri were as bitter as those uttered by Garibaldi to Admiral Persano when he was being escorted out of the harbour at Naples. He said:

'We created an empire, conquered perhaps at too little cost—only 1,537 dead. I gave Albania to the Crown. It would have been greatly to my advantage if my complaint had got worse in 1937 and I had died then. They will regret the days of Fascism. No other régime has done what Fascism did for the workers.'

In Ponza, Mussolini read the 'Life of Jesus Christ' by Father Giuseppe Ricciotto. When August 7th—the second anniversary of the death of his son, Bruno—drew near, he sent a letter to the island's parish priest. 'Will you please say a Mass for his soul? I enclose 1,000 lire for you to dispose of as you think best.'

The Government in Rome feared that the Germans might discover where the prisoner was confined and attempt to rescue him. Accordingly, Mussolini was soon moved from Ponza and brought to the island of Maddalena, which lies off the north-east coast of Sardinia and neighbours Caprera, where Garibaldi spent his last years. A priest began to re-train him in the Catholic way of life and arranged for him to attend Mass on the following day. Instead, the prisoner was ordered to leave the island.

His next place of internment was a hotel which stood on the Gran Sasso nine thousand feet above sea-level. 'Is the funicular safe?' he asked. 'Not for my sake, because my life is over, but for those who accompany me.'

The hotel looked unassailable. By the time the prisoner arrived, Badoglio had signed an armistice with the Allies. On the evening when its terms were broadcast, Mussolini wrote a note to the officer in charge. He wanted his revolver.

CHAPTER TWENTY

HUN AND ROMAN

THOUGH PIUS XII strove hard first to avoid the war and then to keep Italy out of the conflict, he also made plans well in advance for the strictest observance of the Holy See's neutrality. Ambassadors like D'Arcy Osborne of Britain and Wladimir d'Ormesson of France were allowed to lodge within Vatican City, but only on condition that they never went outside it while Italy was a belligerent. The same rule applied to refugees like Alcide De Gasperi, who was at work on a catalogue of the Vatican Library. To prevent espionage, all the lodgers—Ambassadors to the Holy See or refugees—were forbidden to enter St. Peter's.

There were refugees elsewhere on the territory of the Vatican City State. In the Lateran Palace lodged Pietro Nenni, the Socialist leader. He was grateful for the Pope's protection, but he forthrightly refused to attend Mass. 'I am a revolutionary,' he explained. Several hundreds of refugees, escaping from religious or political persecution, were encamped in the papal villa and its grounds at Castelgandolfo. The same basic rules were applied in the Vatican, the Lateran and the Villa at Castelgandolfo: no fires were to be lit in the winter months, and there was to be no central heating. The Pontiff and all who lived on the territory of his neutral State were to share the discomforts of the Roman people. The *Osservatore Romano*, moreover, was to publish no Allied bulletins.

While the Pope insisted on having a large bomb-proof shelter for many rare books from the Library, he wanted no air-raid shelter for himself. No matter how many bombs might be falling around him, he wished to stay in his study by day and in his bedroom by night. Except as a prisoner, he would never leave Rome.

In some ways, his task might be easier than had been Pope Benedict's in the previous war; in others, it was far more difficult. Pope Benedict lacked a precise yardstick of rights. The 'Roman Question' was unresolved. The Germans hinted that they would restore the Temporal Power when they had defeated Italy, while the Allies promised Italy that they would exclude the Holy See from the Peace Conference. As an institution, the Holy See stood to gain by German victory, and Austrian influences within the Vatican were strong. Benedict, however, cared little for the political consequences of German or Allied victory. He wanted to halt the war in midstream because the struggle had become useless and suicidal.

His chief representative in Germany was Eugenio Pacelli, who acquired a deep knowledge of the German people and who, for the rest of his life, included Germans in his very restricted circle of intimate friends and spiritual advisers. He knew a Germany that was not, and never became, Nazi and Jew-baiting. As a Roman born and bred, he also knew an Italy that was not pro-Nazi and anti-Jewish. Indirectly, he knew a Russia that was never persecuting and irreligious.

In Benedict's day, there had been no need for a political heretic or Jew to seek shelter in the Vatican. A bare generation later, innumerable anti-Fascists were glad that a square mile of Roman soil lay under the Pope's sovereignty.

Armed with the experience gained in Benedict's day, the Vatican Relief Organization kept pace with the demands which steadily increased as the areas of the conflict widened and became global and as the camps for prisoners of war multiplied. Everything was done to keep prisoners in touch with their families and to assist them in their needs. In 1943, in fact, the Vatican radio succeeded in transmitting nearly a quarter-million messages in many languages. Once again it was recognized that, as the visible head of the Catholic Church, the Pope stood above the conflict. By his work for prisoners, he could earn the gratitude and support of all belligerents. Yet he was not Pontiff alone. He was also Bishop of Rome and Primate of Italy. In his heart, Pius could not be neutral.

Venice had been the only major Italian city seriously threatened with destruction or capture in the First World War. Lest the enemy should wrest the four bronze horses from the façade of St. Mark's and take them to Berlin or Vienna, as Napoleon once took them to Paris, they were shipped across the Lagoon in a barge and brought eventually to the garden of the Palazzo Venezia in Rome. Then Rome was safe; but now no city in Italy—perhaps not even Vatican City—was freed from the dangers of an air raid. As the Duce's office, the Palazzo Venezia was a potential target for attack.

At the end of 1942, Cardinal Maglione was telling Sir D'Arcy Osborne that the Pope, as Bishop of Rome, could not calmly witness the destruction of the Holy City. In terms of human life, however, Rome was not one whit holier than Coventry or Cologne, and Osborne pointed out that the city was also the headquarters of the Italian High Command and a large German command. Around it were many air-fields, and it was a focal point for the railways. Anthony Eden wanted the King and every member of the Government to leave Rome. He also wanted Swiss officials to supervise their departure. Mussolini was prepared to remove the High Command; for, according to Ciano, he did not wish anyone to say that he was remaining in Rome 'under the big umbrella of Catholicism to protect himself from British bombs'.

Yet he did not move away from Rome. President Franklin Roosevelt gave the Pope no promise to refrain from bombing the Eternal City, and the first raid took place on July 19th, 1943. The Pope watched from a window and prayed. He told Monsignor Montini to bring him all the available cash in the Vatican bank, and he let D'Arcy Osborne know that whenever there was another raid, he would share the dangers with his people. The raid was scarcely ended when he hurried to the scene. Some wrathful citizens recalled that the day marked the anniversary of Rome's burning by Nero in the year 64. The chief targets were the railway yards near the vast cemetery of the Campo Verano, but the adjoining basilica of St. Lawrence-beyond-the-Walls was gravely damaged. So were many monuments inside the Campo Verano. Their desecration brought a more private grief to the Pope and other members of the Pacelli family.

On the same day the Pope sent a protest to Roosevelt, who did not reply. About three weeks later there was another raid, when bombs fell not far from St. John's Lateran, and the Pope was soon kneeling among the wounded. Next day—August 14th, the eve of *ferragosto*—news reached the people that Rome had been declared an open city. In gratitude to Pius, they began crowding into St. Peter's Square.

However much Pius had resented the first air raid on Rome, it hastened the day of Mussolini's fall. This took the Germans completely by surprise. So, unfortunately, it did the Allies. 'Italy will be true to her word,' Badoglio announced. 'The war goes on.' The Germans were not deceived, and the Allies were distrustful. Forty-four precious days went by before an armistice was signed, and when Allied soldiers disembarked in Calabria and at Salerno, Field Marshal Albert von Kesselring at once marched on Rome.

On hearing that an armistice had been signed, the Prince of Piedmont drove from Anagni to the Quirinal Palace only to find that the King was preparing to leave Rome together with the Queen and Badoglio. Though the Prince did not want to go away, he obeyed his father and accompanied him to Ortona. In Rome stayed the King's son-in-law, General Calvi de Bergolo. Though Commander of Rome, he was powerless to defend the city effectively against German attack. With no King and no head of the Government in their midst, the Romans were gravely dispirited. There seemed to be no one to remind the

Royal Family of Queen Victoria's firm belief that if King Louis-
Philippe had remained in Paris throughout the revolutionary troubles
of 1848, he could have kept his throne. It was quite a time before the
King realized that he was never to see Rome again.

Nor were the King and Queen ever again to see their daughter,
Princess Mafalda. She had gone to Sofia to attend the funeral of her
brother-in-law, King Boris of Bulgaria, who, according to many
reports, had been poisoned by the Germans. On her way back, she
heard that an armistice was signed. It was dangerous to return to
Rome, but she wanted news of her three small children, whom she
found staying in the Vatican. The Germans said that her husband,
Prince Philip of Hesse, wished to see her urgently in Germany, and an
aeroplane was put at her disposal. She knew neither that her husband
had been arrested nor that she was being sent to Buchenwald, where,
on pain of death, she was ordered never to reveal her identity. Two
years went by before her father and her mother heard of her fate. In
August 1944, Buchenwald was bombed. The Princess had a badly
damaged arm, and the gangrene, which soon set in, killed her.

Kesselring treated the Romans like conquered people, and when six
German soldiers were shot, he ordered General Calvi de Bergolo to
deliver six thousand citizens as a reprisal. Thereupon the General
wrote down his own name and that of his aide-de-camp, Colonel
Montezemole. All Italy north of Salerno, in fact, was soon under the
German military heel. So, too, was Mussolini. Far too many people
had known about his involuntary journeys to Ponza and Maddalena;
and with a skilful use of gliders he was rescued from his eyrie on the
Gran Sasso. The guards ignored Badoglio's order that they must shoot
their prisoner if the Germans tried to take him away. Instead, they
shouted: 'Duce! Duce!'

Mussolini was brought in triumph to an airport where Hitler waited
to greet him. For a brief moment, the old swagger returned to the man
so recently oppressed with thoughts of suicide. He declared that the
monarchy no longer existed, and in the north he established his 'social
republic', soon to be known as the Republic of Salò. Claretta Petacci
was with him once more. Yet, in mind and in body, he was broken.
Henceforward the Germans treated him as their puppet.

Italy was split into two camps. South of Naples there was military
rule by the Allies, tempered by the recognition that Victor Emmanuel
was still King and Badoglio the President of his Council. North of
Naples there was military rule by the Germans, though many things
were done in the name of the Duce. In other words, Italian was pitted
against Italian. There was civil war.

In the last days of September, the Neapolitans rose in anger against the Germans, and on October 1st, the Allies entered the city while Vesuvius was in eruption. They found the streets strangely deserted—for what Neapolitan is not afraid of Vesuvius, a slaughterer of human life?—and the port totally wrecked by heavy bombing. Yet they had not chosen Italy for the major assault on the enemy, and thereafter their advance was maddeningly slow. The destruction of the Abbey of Monte Cassino helped them not at all.

Rome had nine months to wait for its delivery. The sufferings of the people deepened. Men were stopped in the streets and driven away to become forced labourers in Germany. First among the persecuted were the Roman Jews. The Nazis demanded that they should provide fifty pounds' weight of gold. Otherwise they would all be sent to concentration camps. As the Jews were mostly poor people, they could not meet this demand. When the Vatican came to their aid, the Nazis promised to leave them alone.

The promise was worthless. At dawn on October 16th, Princess Enza Pignatelli Aragona was roused by a telephone call. A friend told her that the Nazis were dragging the Jews out of their tenements in the ghetto and driving them away. The Princess at once asked a member of the German Embassy to go with her to the Vatican where, with the least delay, she saw the Pope. Pius lifted the telephone and began enquiries. A note from Cardinal Maglione soon reached the Ambassador for transmission to Berlin. The Ambassador, Ernst von Weizsacher, was a humane man, and he believed that he could offer the Jews more effective help if he acted at 'the local level'. He succeeded in halting the evacuations from the ghetto. The Nazis had intended to take eight thousand Jews away from Rome. The actual number was about two thousand, of whom only a few lived to see Rome again.

From a window of the Palazzo Orsini, which stands immediately above the Teatro Marcello, the Duchess of Sermoneta saw the Jews being hounded out of the ghetto. Soon she was herself under house arrest, but she escaped with her English maid through a little-known passage and took refuge in another palace. For weeks on end, it was said, Prince Doria lived in his own labyrinthine palace on the Corso, where the Germans were never able to find him. No one—rich or poor, exalted or humble—was free from the fear of imprisonment, torture or deportation.

While the Romans endured their own hardships and terrors, they were constantly hearing about savageries elsewhere. To those who still frequented the Golf Club came the shock that Mussolini had allowed his son-in-law to be ignominiously shot with his face to the wall.

General De Bono, who was seventy-eight, and three other members of the defunct Grand Fascist Council shared his fate. They had been summoned to the Palazzo Venezia to give advice, and in voting against Mussolini they committed a crime called treason. In Verona they were tried and sentenced to death.

Ciano was not a faithful husband, but all his faults were forgotten by the wife who, for his sake and for her children's, pleaded with her own father that a life might be spared. It was not injured vanity alone which made Mussolini refuse to give way. Hitler was his master, and Germans were present at the executions outside Verona.

Thirty-two men of the Italian Black Brigade formed the firing squad. Each of the five victims was tied to a school bench, but not until Pareschi had given his overcoat to a sergeant. 'It is brand-new,' he told him, 'and should not be riddled with bullets. Keep it for yourself. There's no chance of my catching cold now.' To De Bono, Ciano said: 'Don't worry. It won't hurt, and it will all be over in a few minutes.'

Execution was not quite so swift for Ciano. He felt the indignity of having his back to the firing squad, and at the crucial moment he wrenched himself free from the ropes. He was not killed outright. The finishing shot had to come from Verona's chief of police.

Little more than two months later, Rome was afflicted with a mass reprisal. A carefully laid time-bomb had exploded while German military police were doing their daily march through the Via Rasella. Thirty-three men were killed. When the news reached Hitler, he gave an order than ten Italians must be shot for every German killed in the street. The executions, moreover, must take place within twenty-four hours. Intelligent members of the German High Command knew that the order was harmful as well as cruel. They wanted to play for time, and one anxious officer suggested an alternative: compel the citizens, he said, to watch a solemn funeral procession and then charge them with its expenses. Yet none dared defy Hitler's order. There began the grim business of compiling a list of the doomed.

Before dawn on March 24th, 1944, no less than 335 men and youths were marched to the Fosse Ardeatine, which were ancient caves close to the catacombs of St. Callistus. Among the forced marchers were many Jews, a priest and General Calvi de Bergolo's aide-de-camp, Colonel Montezemole. The firing squad had to be well supplied with liquor before they were trusted to do their evil work. The butchering went on for hours. When it was over, the caves were dynamited.

Who knows how many consciences were stricken by this deed? Or how many comforted themselves with the thought that they were

obeying superior orders? In varying degree, obedience to orders raised
a moral issue for all combatants. Allied airmen had the strictest orders
to avoid bombing Vatican City, but there was blind bombing elsewhere, and when bombs fell on the papal villa at Castelgandolfo,
about five hundred refugees were killed. Reprisals occurred in many
villages, and some were so remote that news of their ordeal seldom
reached Roman ears. In Filetto, a tiny village not far from L'Aquila,
a partisan killed a German soldier. Captain Mattias Defregger received
an order to shoot all the male villagers. He did his best to mitigate the
order. When he could do no more, he left the duty of carrying out
the order to a younger lieutenant. After seventeen men were shot, the
lieutenant stopped the firing. Outside the province of L'Aquila the
martyrdom of Filetto was little known until Mattias Defregger had
become a Bishop.

For Germany, like every other country, had her saints and devils,
her rebels and conformists, her men of sensibility and her morons.
German soldiers might often walk among Rome's ruins or pray in an
ancient church. To students of letters among them it made little difference that Keats and Shelley were an enemy's poets. Sometimes
Germans, when they saw the Keats-Shelley memorial house at the
foot of the Spanish Steps, knocked on the door. They did not know
that, as a war-time measure, the house had been put under the care of
the Swedish Institute in Rome. To each caller, Vera Signorelli said:
'It is closed.'

'That's strange,' one of them replied. 'There always seems to be
someone cleaning on the second floor.'

The sensitive German was well aware that the Romans hated his
presence in their city. The Allies advanced too slowly, and the hopes
raised in January by landings at Anzio, only thirty-five miles away, were
quickly dampened. The Pope himself stood in danger of deportation,
and he summoned the Cardinals to the Sistine Chapel, where he released
them from any obligation to share his fate. In April Kesselring told the
Pope that he would not defend Rome. Yet the Romans had to wait
until the warm Sunday of June 4th before the first Allied troops
passed through the Porta Maggiore, greatest of the city's gateways.
At first, the people were shy, not knowing how the battle-wearied
soldiers would treat them. Then came a shower of roses and many
offerings of wine.

Mario Praz was among the citizens who watched the Germans
while they were still leaving the city. 'Both morning and afternoon,'
he wrote, 'continuous files of German soldiers, tired, sweaty, but armed
to the teeth, along the Lungotevere, between people, standing in rows

along the streets, people in shirt-sleeves, dirty and silent. They don't laugh, they don't jeer, they don't show pity. The ancient Roman crowd, among the ancient monuments, sees once more an army in rout, understands and is silent.'

The American soldier, foe turned ally, took the place of the German, ally turned foe. As an individual, the American soldier might be little different from the German. In company, however, the different patterns of behaviour became striking: 'When the Americans got drunk,' Mario Praz observed, 'they did ridiculous things, but the thought of the army never remotely occurred to them, whereas the Germans when drunk started doing the goose-step and mimicking the difference between the listless slovenly-looking Italian soldier and the stiff, up-right German.' At heart the German was nearly always a soldier born to his trade; the American and the Englishman were civilians who happened to be in uniform, and their more carefree attitude helped to create in Roman minds the impression that the war was over.

Yet nearly a year went by before the enemy at last capitulated. Meanwhile the people awaited their own hour—or, more likely, days —for scourging and liberation: scourging, because liberation could not come to them before the slow advance of the Allies brought their town or valley into the immediate fighting zone. At one time or another, almost every Italian had war close to his own doorstep. Iris Origo sheltered a number of refugee children from bomb-scarred Genoa on her Tuscan estate, La Foce. In an illuminative diary—'War in Val D'Orcia'—she described how the people upheld each other in their tribulations. Between them was 'the simplest of all ties between one man and another; the tie that arises between the man who asks for what he needs, and the man who comes to his aid as best he can. No unnecessary emotion or pose.'

There was, none the less, a clash of loyalties. When the war began, many an Italian shared the patriotic sentiment of the Frenchman or the Englishman: 'my country, right or wrong'. Mussolini ordered that a youth who failed to report for military service should be shot in full daylight in the Colosseum. Now the war had become fratricide, and Iris Origo recalled that a boy of nineteen called Coletti refused to report for military service and was sentenced to death in Florence. At midnight he heard that he had been reprieved. Three hours later the reprieve was cancelled. Throughout the night, whether reprieved or condemned anew, he continued to comfort a young peasant and a Neapolitan lieutenant who had to die. While facing the firing squad unbound, he recited the Lord's Prayer.

On the following Sunday, the Prior of San Miniato referred to the endurance of the three young men. Though arrested, he refused to take anything back. As a priest, he said, it was his duty to point out examples of a Christian death.

'Five miles' progress': 'eight miles' progress'. So, day after weary day, the London radio might report. As the dragons of war crawled northwards, members of a family got separated one from another, and friend from friend. No one in Rome could tell what was happening in Florence. There was a time when the Bostonians who resided in Italy bantered freely with each other. Santayana, who was critical of Berenson, had asked: 'If he were a real poet, would he turn away from the evening sky to see, by electric light, how Veronese painted it?' Now horizons were altered. Throughout the war, Santayana stayed with the Blue Sisters in their hostel on the Celian Hill. 'They are reconciled to my seeming a bad Catholic,' he wrote, 'and look forward to my deathbed repentance.'

Meanwhile Berenson—a Catholic convert born a Jew—lived on the outskirts of Florence as a hunted man. A few Germans knew where he was hiding, but they kept their secret. Some others took care not to know, lest they show weakness under torture. In the days of affliction Berenson was often consoled by the calm grandeur of an evening sky. 'What a paradise this Italy,' he wrote, 'and how kind to its children if only inky tongued agitators with their belching rhetoric did not whip them up to run amok at Abyssinia, at Spain, at Albania, at Greece, against England, Russia and America!'

Mussolini, chief of the 'inky tongued agitators', lived until the afternoon of April 28th, 1945. Bedraggled and unshaved, he was wearing the uniform of a German soldier and making his way to the Swiss frontier. With him was Claretta Petacci, who for days had never left his side. He believed that the man who found them intended to ensure their escape, and he said: 'I give you the Empire.' In the village of Mezzegra by the shore of Lake Como, the man—known to partisans as Colonel 'Valerio'—shot both Mussolini and his mistress. Their bodies were brought to Milan and, in the Piazza Loreto, they were strung by the heels from a lamp post.

Not all delighted in this disregard for human dignity. Monsignor Montini had often incurred the wrath of Fascist leaders, but when he heard that Mussolini was dead, he urged those around him to pray for his soul. The ugly record of the brief Republic of Salò is in part redeemed by the steadfastness of two women: Edda Ciano, a wife and mother fighting desperately for her husband's life; and Claretta Petacci, a once scheming mistress faithful to her lover unto death. Women are often near the seat of power, and Queen Helen was not altogether wrong when she thought that her appeal, when supported by five Queens, might produce another *Paix des Dames*. Her effort to keep Italy out of a second war was well worth while.

The Queen longed to see Rome again. She was ready to go back, she once admitted to a friend, even if it was only to be a flower-seller of the Spanish Steps. The simple style of the royal couple impressed the English occupiers of southern Italy, where Field Marshal Lord Alexander was Military Governor and Harold Macmillan the Minister of State. At their first meeting, Macmillan asked the King if there was anything he wanted. 'The Queen,' he replied, 'has been unable to get any fresh eggs. Is it possible that we could somehow get a dozen eggs?' The King asked nothing more: 'so with a dozen eggs,' the English statesman commented, 'we sealed our concord with the thousand-year-old House of Savoy.'

Yet, for all his simplicity of manner, Victor Emmanuel never forgot that he was a King and the head of Europe's oldest ruling House, and he refused to comply with a request that he should move away from the Villa Rosebery in Naples when King George VI, the English monarch, arrived to stay at the neighbouring Villa Emma. Harold Macmillan omitted to tell the Commander-in-Chief of the Mediterranean Fleet that the King of Italy was still in the Villa Rosebery. In the early hours of the morning, a picket boat arrested a 'suspicious-looking couple' who were fishing just off the Villa Emma. The noise woke up the English King.

'Says he's the King, sir.'

'What King?'

'The King of Italy, sir.'

The Queen, Harold Macmillan narrated, gave an 'enormous visiting card' to the naval lieutenant. This the English King kept as a souvenir. The time was far distant when Queen Victoria decorated the *Re Galantuomo* with the Order of the Garter and thought him 'more like a knight or King of the Middle Ages than anyone one knows nowadays'.

The King is a person, and the monarchy is an institution. Benedetto Croce was not alone in thinking that the monarchy might be saved if the King were sacrificed. He said that no one could trust a man who, like the King, had put a wreath 'on the grave of Mussolini's father, a drunkard at the best'. It was agreed that, as soon as the Allies entered Rome, the Prince of Piedmont should become the Lieutenant-General of the Realm. Nearly two years later—on May 9th, 1946—the King abdicated. As a proud lover of his royal House, he deliberately copied the formula used by his great-grandfather, Charles Albert, when he abdicated in 1849.

Victor Emmanuel took to his exile in Egypt neither his library nor his collection of coins. The coins he gave to Italy. 'Throughout my whole life as King,' he told Alcide De Gasperi, 'I have never spent a single *lira* for a caprice: all that I have been able to spare I have invested in this collection. By leaving it to the Italian State, I restore all that the State has spent on me and my family during these forty-six years.' As the boat sped southwards to Alexandria, the ex-King stood on deck and watched his native Naples receding in the distance. The inclusion of Januarius among his baptismal names brought him little reward in his earthly life. Perhaps he drew comfort from the thought that the Neapolitans once treated their patron saint as, like him, a scapegoat.

His son, King Humbert II, reigned for only thirty-four days. On June 2nd, a referendum was held to decide whether Italy should be a monarchy or a republic. Twelve million voters wanted a republic, and ten million voters wanted a monarchy. North of Rome, the voting showed the popularity of the republicans; south of Rome, it showed the popularity of the monarchists. The percentage of votes in favour of a republic was: in the north, 64.8; in the centre, 63.5; in the south, 32.6; and in the islands of Sicily and Sardinia, 36.0. The temperamental cleavage of the country is persistent. Never, it seems, has Naples ceased to be royalist. Yet it was a Neapolitan, Enrico De Nicola, who became Italy's first President.

In the Encyclical Letter in which he indirectly condemned the teachings of Lamennais, Gregory XVI wrote that it was wrong, in particular, to attack 'Our dearest sons in Jesus Christ, the princes', but Pius XII lifted not a finger to save the Savoyard dynasty. Like the Germans, the Savoyards entered Rome as conquerors. Now the 'ancient Roman crowd' knew that they, too, had gone. Mazzini's republican dream came true. Yet only partially; for the Pope still lived in the Vatican Palace. Like Pius IX, who became Pope exactly a century beforehand, Pius XII was the dominant Roman figure. He did not allow it to be forgotten that he was also the Primate of all Italy.

CHAPTER TWENTY-ONE

THE EUROPEAN IDEA

LITTLE MORE than two months after the Americans had entered Rome, the Pope lost his Secretary of State. Cardinal Luigi Maglione, a Neapolitan, had been ill for a long time. During this illness, Pius XII resumed duties which were once his own as Cardinal Maglione's immediate predecessor at the Secretariat of State. He did not want to abandon them now that the war was turning swiftly in the Allies' favour and offering the chance that he might help Franklin Roosevelt to produce a just settlement at the peace conference. There was no Allied commitment, as in 1915, to exclude from this conference any Vatican representative. Diplomacy was needed. It happened to be Eugenio Pacelli's most conspicuous gift.

The office of Secretary of State, therefore, remained in abeyance. In other words, Pius XII became his own Secretary of State. Henceforward the two Substitute Secretaries—Domenico Tardini and Giovanni Battista Montini—worked directly under an autocratic Pope, who made it clear that he wanted executives, and not advisers.

For both Substitute Secretaries the relationship must have been a constant strain. Monsignor Tardini, who had charge of foreign affairs, belonged to working-class Trastevere, and his manner was sometimes rough and abrupt. Like Pius X, he was born poor, and he wished to remain poor. Whatever money came his way, he devoted to an orphanage. Monsignor Montini, who had charge of home affairs, was the son of a Deputy and newspaper owner. The years which he spent as chaplain to the students of Rome University may have made him *persona non grata* with Fascist authorities, but they deepened his love of dialogue and discussion. He knew how to keep his ear to the ground, though the régime stifled the intellectual life of Rome and other Italian cities.

With clock-work regularity, Pius XII walked into his study at ten minutes to nine in the morning. Exactly nine minutes later, he pressed a button, and Monsignor Tardini entered. At fourteen minutes past nine, the bell sounded for Monsignor Montini. Fourteen minutes later, Monsignor Montini left the study. There was a two minutes' pause. Then, at half-past nine, the first private audience of the day began.

This rigid system was not without its merits. Achille Ratti had the

Italian's disregard for time. Almost every day someone was kept waiting to be received, often long after the appointed hour. With Eugenio
Pacelli, his successor, time was sacred. Each minute must serve its
purpose. Nor were the Pope's evening encounters with the Substitute
Secretaries often relaxed. Together the two priests entered the study
at half-past six and presented all the documents which required the
papal signature. If the Pope asked a question, one of the priests replied
as directly as possible. He had never to give an answer which bore the
semblance of advice, and he was not permitted to ask questions.

When the style of a document did not please him, the Pope sent it
back to a Substitute Secretary, often without explaining why the
presentation was faulty. No letter bore his signature if it contained a
single error in the typing or if the opening word of a paragraph were
incorrectly spaced. Many establishments have their martinets, but a
war-stricken generation was looking to Rome for spiritual leadership.
It might have come more copiously from a man with a stronger sense
of collegiality in the search for truth and justice. Though not Roman-
born, Monsignor Montini knew the mind of war-time Rome better
than did the Pope. He had spoken with Ciano shortly before the fateful
meeting of the Grand Fascist Council which deposed Mussolini. Like
the Pope, he must have hoped that a separate peace could be secured
for Italy without turning the whole country into a battlefield. This was
no time for withholding confidences from a priest who stood so near
the papal throne.

Two wars were waged simultaneously in Europe. One was a war
between States. The other was a maniac's war against the Jews. In the
war between the States, the Vatican was neutral. It could not be neutral
in the war against the Jews. When Hitler began his racial war in 1933,
he imperilled the lives of rather more than half a million Jews in
Germany. The number of persecuted Jews increased when he annexed
Austria, when he made Mussolini an abettor of his racial laws, and
when he disrupted Czechoslovakia. Later, as Europe's war-time master,
he imposed on the Jews the blackest persecution known in history.
However many of them may have died in extermination camps—and
the figures vary from four millions to six millions and more—an
entire race came near to destruction. To the vocabulary of crime was
added a new word: genocide.

Innumerable convents and monasteries willingly obeyed the Pope's
command that they should shelter the men, women and children
afflicted because of their race. At his bidding, too, the Vatican provided
gold as a ransom for the Jews who lived in Rome. When American
soldiers and airmen first crowded into the Vatican, Pius XII pro-

nounced a blessing in Hebrew for those who were Jews. The Roman
Rabbi thanked him for what he had done for his community. Later
the Rabbi became himself a Catholic.

What else should the Pope have done? Just how profound was his
grief and anxiety may have been known only to his confessor, Augustin
Bea: a Jesuit and a German born of humble parents near the Black
Forest. For many years he was Rector of the Biblical Institute in Rome,
and perhaps no other priest of his day had a deeper knowledge of
Jewish history. The past century in Rome witnessed many occasions
when boldness would have reaped benefits. Reconciliation between
Church and State might have come sooner if Pius IX had gone out of
a Roman gateway to meet the soldiers of King Victor Emmanuel II,
or forsaken his voluntary imprisonment when, at the end of 1870,
the Tiber flooded Rome; if Leo XIII had appeared on the outer balcony
of St. Peter's on the day of his election; or if Pius X had hastened to
Messina and Reggio Calabria after the earthquake of 1908. And was
the Nazi expulsion of the Jews from their Roman ghetto completed
so expeditiously that no robed Cardinal or Bishop was able to give
a visible token of the Church's disapproval?

All institutions tend to be slow-footed; and whatever Pius XII said
or did in condemnation of Hitler's racial war, he would have brought
suffering to others. For one thing, the concentration camps sometimes
contained even more Catholic priests than rabbis. For another, a few
residential Archbishops were convinced that sterner methods would
do more harm than good. When, in 1570, Pius V excommunicated
Queen Elizabeth Tudor, the English intensified their persecution of the
Catholics. What might have been the effect of Pius XII's excommunication of Hitler? For that matter, what had been the effect of Pius IX's
excommunication of Victor Emmanuel II?

The war-time generation passed through a crisis of obedience. Many
guards at Dachau, Buchenwald and other slaughter-camps must have
come from Catholic homes in which they were taught that obedience
is a Christian virtue. That virtue had long been caricatured by Prussian
military discipline; now—in Italy, as in Germany—it was caricatured
by party discipline. The Corporate State could hardly have been
fashioned by men with a Protestant background. Fascism was hierarchic, and it had a church-like structure. At its head was the Duce,
a fallible man and bad. Pius XII was prayerful and good; but had he
not insulated himself too much from advice?

Many documents revealed his hatred of persecution and the cruelties
of modern warfare. They were, however, couched in excessively
diplomatic language. The lay reader often found them ambiguous or

lacking in depth until he had given each word its due weight. When, for example, atomic bombs had fallen on Hiroshima and Nagasaki, protests reached the Vatican from all over the world. Some complained that one day an enemy might use them against Rome or New York. They were boomerangs.

The official comment in the *Osservatore Romano* could scarcely have been briefer. 'The use of atomic bombs in Japan,' it stated, 'has unfavourably impressed the Vatican. This incredible means of destruction remains a temptation for future generations.' Each word counted. There was no need to make the comment longer. Soon would come the peace conference. All the Pope's diplomacy and skill in understatement would then be used for the sake of a just and lasting peace. It is not his fault that no full-scale peace conference has yet followed the Second World War.

The fault was the victors', for the lines at which their armies halted soon hardened into ideological frontiers. Politically Europe was to become two separate continents, and Germany two separate States. Franklin Roosevelt was dead, and Winston Churchill had been driven from office by the votes of his countrymen. Almost alone among steersmen in the West whose names were household words, there remained the Pope. He understood beaten Germany more thoroughly than any of his predecessors. His voice, many believed, would still be heeded; and as if to enhance the Vatican's international prestige in a second and more perilous post-war era, he named many new Cardinals. At long last, non-Italian members of the Sacred College outnumbered the Italian. For the first time since Manning's exceptional day it became a possibility that the future Pontiff would be a non-Italian.

Yet, while making the Sacred College more international and relatively less Italian, Pius XII knew that Communism was not without its appeal to a people who had lived near to starvation and whose youths had been herded to Germany for forced labour. If Italy was at war with the Allies for two years and three months, she was also Germany's foe—and Russia's friend—for more than eighteen months. During this second period, about one hundred thousand Italian soldiers and partisans lost their lives. Many belonged to a partisan group known as the Garibaldi Brigade. At its head was Luigi Longo. Later he became the chief lieutenant of Palmiro Togliatti, ablest of all the Communist leaders outside Russia.

A common struggle against Fascism had brought together men and women who were once openly Communist or Fascist, Popularist or Liberal. It seemed natural, therefore, that the members of Italy's first post-war Government should be recruited from the main anti-Fascist parties and that Palmiro Togliatti should sit with Carlo Sforza, Benedetto Croce and Alcide De Gasperi at the same council table. Sforza and Croce represented the liberal and anticlerical traditions of Cavour and Giolitti, but De Gasperi was a militant Catholic. Once he had been distrusted as a former member of the Austrian Parliament, but four years of imprisonment under the Fascists gave him the nimbus of a patriot; and now millions were accepting his view that an Italian could be both a good Catholic and a good democrat. Officially the Church frowned no more on democracy. Lamennais' dream was at last fulfilled.

Elsewhere in Europe arose Christian Democrats. Like De Gasperi, their leaders came from border regions, where men look on frontier posts with both fear and contempt. In France, there was Robert Schuman, an ascetic Catholic who was born in Luxembourg and had many links with Alsace when the province was under the German eagle. In Germany, there was Konrad Adenauer, who belonged to the Rhineland and first achieved fame as the Burgomaster of Cologne. All three bordermen—De Gasperi of Italy, Schuman of France and Adenauer of Germany—wanted to transcend nationalism and to make Europe 'our country'. Let her be, De Gasperi explained, 'a kind of Switzerland, which includes Italians, French and Germans: all her people peaceful, hard-working and prosperous'.

De Gasperi became the new republic's first Prime Minister, and the non-Fascist parties were soon framing a Constitution. The Christian Democrats agreed with the Communists and the Socialists that 'sovereignty belongs to the people'. In return, Togliatti agreed with the Christian Democrats that the Lateran Pacts should not be repudiated. If De Gasperi argued that an Italian could be both a good Catholic and a good democrat, Togliatti was willing to show that he might also be a good Catholic and a good Communist. It did not matter to him if religious education were excluded from Russian schools and imposed by the Concordat on Italian schools; nor did it matter if divorce were permitted in Russia and banned in Italy. Togliatti wanted Catholic votes.

To Croce, however, the issue of intellectual and moral freedom was fundamental. Once again he was ready to defend the rights of those for whom not to hear a Mass 'is an affair of the conscience'. Though the signing of the Lateran Pacts in 1929 produced a blaze of popular approval, they were prepared secretly and never submitted to a proper parliamentary scrutiny. The Treaty which created the Vatican City State may have represented a legitimate development of the Law of Guarantees which Parliament approved in 1871, and this miniature

State need have impaired Italy's unity no more than does the miniature and independent Republic of San Marino. What caused concern, however, was the linking of the Treaty with a Concordat which contained a number of illiberal clauses. In the words of Gaetano Salvemini, the Concordat created a double sovereignty: 'that of the secular government and that of the Pope, and the Italians became twice subject to authority'. It could not have been accepted by a Cavour, who believed that there should be 'a free Church within a free State', nor by a Giolitti, who said that Church and State were 'two parallels which ought never to meet'.

Liberal statesmen from Cavour to Giolitti wanted to curb the political power of the Church. Even Luigi Sturzo, a priest, tried to make the Popularists a party of Catholics rather than an official Catholic party. All of them belonged to a pre-Concordat age. It would have been more laical and democratic to repudiate the Concordat as a legacy of the Fascist régime and, if necessary, to negotiate a new one. When freely negotiated between the Vatican and a Government responsible to a popularly elected Parliament, a new Concordat could be sealed with the consent of a sovereign people. The retention of the old one, however, turned the solemn declaration that 'sovereignty belongs to the people' into an almost meaningless rhetorical flourish. Sooner or later, events would make the burden of an unrevised Concordat intolerable.

On New Year's Day, 1948, the Constitution of the Italian Republic came into operation. In the following April, the people went to the polls. As the fateful day drew nearer, Pius XII freed Monsignor Montini from his more routine duties as a Substitute Secretary of State, so that he might mobilize clerical support for the Christian Democrats. In the Pope's eyes, they were more than a clerical party; they alone might prevent the Communists from seizing power.

The Italian Communists, however, were ill-served by the Kremlin. Only a few weeks beforehand, Moscow engineered a *coup* in Prague and thus forestalled a Czechoslovak general election which, under democratic control, the Communists would have had almost no chance of winning. Though very little blood was shed, the *coup* involved the death of Jan Masaryk, son of Czechoslovakia's first President. His broken body was found beneath the windows of his fourth-floor flat in the Czernin Palace. According to the official announcement, he had committed suicide. Many in Prague refused to believe that this was true. Suicide or murder, the act was deliberate; and as Jan Masaryk fell to his death, he took away from the new Communist triumph its claim to a liberator's name.

Thereafter the Communist advance westwards was halted. The general election in Italy gave the Christian Democrats a clear majority over the Communists and the Socialists. None the less, it showed that the Italian Communist Party was the strongest in Western Europe. Alone the Christian Democrats could not control a parliament which contained a stone wall of avowedly anti-parliamentary opposition, and De Gasperi was compelled to bring into his Government a few Liberals, Republicans and Social Democrats. He tried hard to rebut the charge that he was solely the leader of a clerical party.

His relations with Pius XII were not always smooth. Once he asked that he might be received at the Vatican with his family on his wedding anniversary. The request was not granted. It was doubtful, moreover, whether Pius XII took him into his confidence before deciding to excommunicate all Catholics who supported Communism. On July 1st, 1949, came a formal announcement from the Holy Office, of which the Pope was the Prefect. It read:

'Catholics who profess, and particularly those who defend and spread, the materialistic and anti-Christian doctrine of the Communists, *ipso facto*, as apostates from the Catholic faith, incur excommunication.'

Hitler died without incurring the penalty which once all Christendom dreaded. While hesitating to use this weapon against the man who brought genocide into the vocabulary of crime, Pius XII did not omit to use it against the ordinary Communist voter in Italy. Something was wrong with the papal scale of values. The few Archbishops who begged the Pope to be careful in any condemnation of Hitler may have been right. Whether or not his excommunication would have increased the people's suffering, it was certain that the excommunication of ordinary Italian Communists in no way weakened their party's power and influence. In a census held in 1931, the returns showed that 966 Italians out of every thousand declared themselves to be Catholics. Less than two decades later, however, the Communist voters were numbering millions. The equation, if it existed, was not mathematical.

While De Gasperi and his colleagues struggled to restore Italy's economy and to heal the ravages of war, the Vatican was busily preparing for the Holy Year of 1950. Never before, it seemed, would so many pilgrims have made their way to Rome: not even when Boniface VIII proclaimed the Holy Year of 1300, which brought Dante to the Lateran Hill and the banks of the Tiber. For the first time since 1870, many tents were pitched on the slopes of Monte Mario and on other open spaces beyond the walls of Rome, but the people sleeping under canvas were civilians, and not soldiers. Many were very young and had 'hitch-hiked' from somewhere north of the Alps. Others were old and, like their forebears, believed that it was meritorious to see Rome at least once before they died.

Monsignor Montini made a special point of helping the English pilgrims. In the buildings which surround the English church of San Silvestro is a long upper room. Knowing that the English feel undernourished if they cannot drink a cup of tea in the afternoon, Monsignor Montini turned this upper room into a tea-centre. On most days throughout the Holy Year, he said an early Mass in San Silvestro and them climbed the stairs to the upper room for his meagre breakfast. To this day the tea-centre of San Silvestro is a haven for young English-speaking people who arrive friendless in Rome.

No matter how many thousands of English-speaking people went to Rome for the Holy Year, they were far outnumbered by the pilgrims of all the other countries; and each Sunday Pius XII faced a vast multi-lingual crowd when he stood at a window of his private apartment to pronounce a midday blessing. Yet this Pope who was seen by more people than anyone else in the world loved solitude. When he walked in the Vatican gardens or through the narrow and elongated grounds of Castelgandolfo, he had to be alone. Gardeners were bidden to hide behind their bushes as he passed. Was he not too solitary to know what other people might be thinking? And how did the Bishops respond when he invited their comments on his wish to promulgate—in the Holy Year of 1950—the dogma of the Assumption of the Virgin Mary?

It so happened that 1950 was also the year when Rome was chosen to be the headquarters of the Food and Agriculture Organization of the United Nations. This special agency of the United Nations—known everywhere as FAO—owed its origin to the drive and imagination of two men Scottish in their blood. One was F. L. McDougall, an economist from Australia. The other was John Boyd Orr, a doctor and farmer from Aberdeen. He was once wandering round the slums of Glasgow when he realized that the wretched physical condition of their inhabitants was due to bad or inadequate feeding. McDougall soon convinced himself that the peace of the world depended on its food supplies. He envisaged a world-wide food organization comparable in strength and efficiency to the International Labour Organization, which has its headquarters in Geneva. One of his earliest converts was Eleanor Roosevelt, who enabled him to discuss his project with the President and to rouse his sympathy. FAO held its first conference in Quebec, elected John Boyd Orr to be its Director-General, and set up temporary headquarters in Washington. Denmark, proud of her own agricultural standards, wanted FAO to be installed in Copenhagen.

The final vote, however, favoured Rome, and a vast white building close to the Baths of Caracalla became FAO's headquarters. Originally Mussolini had planned this building to be his Africa Office.

In other ways, too, Rome became more international; for whenever an international organization wished to hold a conference, the city was often chosen for the meeting. This was due partly to the advantages of air travel, and partly to the excellent conference halls to be found in EUR— the centre which Mussolini started to build for a spectacular exhibition to mark, in 1942, the twentieth anniversary of his Fascist Revolution. Chiefly, however, Rome was chosen because Pius XII was invariably willing to grant the delegates of an international organization an audience and to deliver a brief, if authoritative, address. He kept Monsignor Montini and others busily providing him with information about his callers, whether individuals or groups. Whatever their conference was about, most delegates left the Vatican astonished by the Pope's grasp of their problems.

There was, however, a limit to the work which he could do. The more he opened his arms to the lay world, the more he was disposed to keep the clerical world at a distance. 'Too many trousers and too few cowls': so complained a French Cardinal as he watched a horde of lay people walking past the open bronze door of the Vatican. Apart from public and private audiences, there were those which the Pope conceded regularly to the Prefect or Secretary of each Congregation or department of the Curia. He grew tired of these regular audiences and reduced them to a minimum. In the end, Princes of the Church found that they must make appointments through Monsignor Montini, who was not even a Bishop. The Substitute Secretary, someone said, should be called the Substitute Pope. Later, together with Monsignor Tardini, he was given the rank of Pro-Secretary of State, but the relationship with offended Cardinals was still embarrassing.

At the end of August 1954, he broke the news to the Pope that Cardinal Alfredo Schuster had died. They spoke together for an hour, and Monsignor Montini left the study with the knowledge that he was to succeed the dead Cardinal as Archbishop of Milan. 'Promeatur ut amoveatur': 'let him be promoted in order to be removed'. So an earlier generation of Cardinals murmured when, in 1907, Giacomo Della Chiesa left the Vatican to become Archbishop of Bologna.

Just a fortnight before Cardinal Schuster died, Alcide De Gasperi was stricken by a heart attack, which soon proved fatal. He had been proud to work closely with two Catholics—Adenauer and Schuman —in the task of building united Europe. This, he believed, was an inevitable development of the Italian Risorgimento. The frontiers of the former Italian States had been broken by the will of the Italian people. Now the national frontiers within Europe would be transcended by the will of the Europeans. To the end, De Gasperi insisted that the European idea was an idea of the people, and not of their Governments.

His friend, Schuman, was certainly not alone among distinguished Frenchmen who worked for the fulfilment of the European idea. If Schuman gave his name to the plan on which was based the frontier-destroying European Community of Coal and Steel, Jean Monnet became its first President. René Pleven, in turn, gave his name to a plan for the European Community of Defence. This was designed to strengthen the North Atlantic alliance by creating a supranational European army, in which the troops of Western Germany would be incorporated.

Despite its French authorship, the Pleven plan was rejected by the French Government. De Gasperi was deeply disappointed, although he realized that the European movement could not now be permanently halted. Many wished that he had lived to see the day when—on March 25th, 1957—the statesmen of six States met on the Capitoline Hill and signed the Treaty of Rome, which brought to birth the European Economic Community or, as most Western Europeans prefer to call it, the Common Market. This offered the prospect that, in 1970, the six States would belong to the same customs union and within it establish a free circulation for their capital and manpower.

Some among the spectators of the ceremony on the Capitoline Hill may have recalled Mazzini's prophecy that a future European authority would sit in Rome, the city freely chosen by the European people for their 'true General Council'. The prophecy had now been partly fulfilled, but it was not enough. To Mazzini the cities of Warsaw, Prague and Budapest were as much European as Paris, Vienna and Berlin. Now Berlin was a city cut in two; Warsaw and Prague were under the heel of faceless bureaucrats; and Budapest had recently witnessed the crushing of a people's revolt by the massing of Russian tanks and wholesale imprisonments.

Italians needed far more than partnership in a Common Market with France, Western Germany and the three Benelux countries of Belgium, Holland and Luxembourg. Mazzini and De Gasperi alike had proclaimed that Europe must belong to the people and be governed according to their wishes and their needs. Italy is poorer than either France or Western Germany, but her population roughly equals that of the United Kingdom. For this reason, Italians wanted the British to enter the Common Market. In Europe of the States, their own country would be handicapped by its relative poverty, but, in a people's

Europe, fifty million Italians could count as much as fifty million Britons.

Yet, if united Europe had once been Churchill's idea, it was still to become an idea of the British people. In their attitude they lagged behind their rulers. 'England no longer an island!' So declared a popular London newspaper when, in 1909, Louis Blériot flew across the English Channel in a monoplane equipped with an Italian engine. The lesson that England was no longer an island had still to be learned more fully even after her people had endured a second and more terrible ordeal by aerial warfare. The names of battles fought since Napoleon's day can be thickly strewn on a map of Italy. England, on the contrary, has known no successful invader for nine centuries. Behind her shores the European idea takes root slowly and painfully.

One supranational institute survives the buffeting centuries: the Church of Rome. Pius XII might threaten with excommunication all Italians who voted for Communist candidates, but eastwards of the 'Iron Curtain' drawn across Europe were at least two countries still fundamentally Catholic. Poles and Magyars showed their capacity to be Communist with the State and Catholic with the Pope. If Communism was a challenge, dialogue might prove to be a weapon more effective for Catholicism than any threats of excommunication. The time was approaching when the criticism once made of Pius IX and Leo XIII would be made of Pius XII: he reigned too long. In the last two or three years the decline of his powers became marked. On October 9th, 1958, and at the age of eighty-two, he died at Castelgandolfo.

The Roman crowd watched the baroque funeral procession from St. John's Lateran to St. Peter's. It passed through some of the streets where—on September 19th, 1870—another crowd had seen Pius IX making his farewell drive from the Lateran Hill. No Roman over the age of thirty-five remembered a time when Eugenio Pacelli, as Secretary of State or as Pope, was not a commanding figure. Once again, however, the citizens were soon keenly discussing whom the Cardinals would elect as the new Pope. They heard about the prophecy made by St. Malachia, the Irish friend of St. Bernard of Clairvaux. After the twelfth Pius, he had foretold, there would be a Pope who was *pastor et nautus*: 'pastor and fisherman'; a Pope coming from the sea. Perhaps, a non-Italian?

That the Cardinals would not find their choice easy to make was shown by the Latin sermon which Monsignor Antonio Bacci delivered in St. Peter's immediately before their Conclave began. 'A learned Pontiff,' he said, 'is not enough. It is not enough to have a Pontiff who knows the sciences, human and divine, and who has explored, and experimented with, the subtleties of diplomacy and politics. This is, indeed, necessary; but it is not enough. What is needed above all things, most eminent Fathers, is a saintly Pontiff because a saintly Pontiff can also obtain from God that which the natural gifts do not give.'

The elected one, Monsignor Bacci added, should have strength of mind. He should be a master, but, above all, a pastor. He should be a bridge not only between all nations, but between those who were persecuting the Catholics. Finally, the preacher asked that the elected one should be ready to receive the Bishops.

A few months before his own death, Pius X insisted on bringing Giacomo Della Chiesa, Archbishop of Bologna, into the Sacred College. Otherwise the world might never have heard of Pope Benedict XV. Pius XII, however, died without making the Archbishop of Milan a Cardinal. 'If I did not need a Cardinal's hat to keep out the sun in Rome,' Monsignor Montini told a friend, 'I do not need one to ward off the rain in Milan.' The lack of a red hat was, none the less, an injury to the Ambrosian Church and the great Lombard city of Milan. The Cardinals, too, felt the hurt. In their Conclave of October 1958, the Archbishop of Milan—the 'papable' Giovanni Battista Montini—was the conspicuous 'excluded'.

CHAPTER TWENTY-TWO

THE SECOND REFORMATION

S T. MALACHIA was right. The new Pope was *pastor et nautus*: 'pastor and fisherman'. He came from the sea. Yet few outside the Conclave imagined that the elected Cardinal would be the Patriarch of Venice. For the greater part of his life, Angelo Roncalli had lived far from Rome, and now he was within a month of reaching his seventy-seventh birthday. His reign was almost certain to be short.

To add to the general surprise, he took a name which the Popes left dormant for more than five centuries. Vincenzo Pecci chose Leo because, at the age of fifteen, he led a delegation of students whom Leo XII received during the Holy Year of 1825; Giuseppe Sarto chose Pius because that was 'the title of him who suffered most'; and Giacomo Della Chiesa chose Benedict because the last native of Bologna to become Pope was Benedict XIV.

Angelo Roncalli explained his choice at greater length. 'I am called John,' he told the Cardinals at the moment of his election. 'This name is sweet to us because it is the name of our father. It is pleasing to us because it is the title of the humble parish in which we received baptism. It is the solemn name of innumerable cathedrals scattered through all the world, and in the first place of the sacred Lateran basilica, our cathedral.'

If St. Peter's is the basilica of the Popes, St. John Lateran is the Cathedral of the Bishops of Rome. To the discerning, the new Pope showed that he meant to be the Bishop of Rome in the fullest sense, and not merely by title. He also meant to exalt the Bishops' office. He would most willingly receive them.

To the historian, however, the chosen name was the more surprising because 1958 was not the first year in which the Romans hailed Pope John XXIII. By this title was also known Baldassare Cossa, once a powerful Legate in Bologna. It was the time of the great Schism, and Baldassare Cossa's claim to be the true Pope was challenged by Gregory XII, a Venetian; and by Benedict XIII, a Spaniard. The Emperor Sigismond was determined to end the scandal of three rival candidates to the throne of Peter; and, in 1414, he compelled John XXIII to agree to an Ecumenical Council and to take part in it himself.

Though welcomed in full state at Constance, Baldassare Cossa was required to take an oath that, if Gregory XII and Benedict XIII abdicated, he, too, would abdicate.

Later, when he heard the gravest, and largely false, charges levelled against him, he fled to Sciaffusa. The Emperor's men brought him back to Constance, a prisoner. The Council of Constance deposed him as well as Gregory XII, and Benedict XIII abdicated. The way was then clear for the Council Fathers to elect a new Pope, whose authority must not be challenged. The choice fell on Cardinal Otto Colonna, who took the name of Martin V.

The new Pope pitied the prisoner and begged for his release. Baldassare Cossa went back to Rome, made his submission and became Bishop of Frascati, and once more a Cardinal. He died in Florence, where visitors to the Baptistery still admire the tomb which Cosimo de' Medici commissioned Donatello and Michelozzo to carve in the memory of Pope John XXIII; but Rome excludes his name from the list of Peter's lawful successors, and calls him an anti-Pope. Why, then, did Angelo Roncalli revive his title? Was it to accentuate a firmly held belief that the authority of an Ecumenical Council is superior to the Pope's?

A lifelong love of Church history might have made Angelo Roncalli cling to the age of the Counter-Reformation and the Council of Trent. From Cesare Baronio, a zealous Church historian who belonged to that age, he borrowed the motto *oboedientia et pax*—'obedience and peace'—and made it his own. Three centuries separated the Council of Trent from the Vatican Council of 1869–70. Many imagined that the Council called by Pius IX must be the last held in the West; for the dogma of papal infallibility seemed to exclude the holding of another. There was, for example, its decree that 'definitions are irreformable of themselves and not from consent of the Church'.

It was thus not merely the choice of an unexpected papal name which now puzzled Rome. To Peter's throne had come a man whose background differed from that of all his predecessors in the past century; it differed even from that of Giuseppe Sarto who, like him, was born a peasant and had been a greatly loved Patriarch of Venice. Sarto was a product of the seminary; he was narrowly educated, and his whole life had been spent in Italy. Roncalli was a product of the army as well as the seminary; for twelve years he was the devoted secretary of an aristocratic and socially-minded Bishop of Bergamo, Giacomo Radini-Tedeschi; and thereafter most of his working days were spent outside Italy, and often in the lonelier outposts of the Roman Catholic world. He had the historical imagination, and he knew that somehow the

Church must be made contemporary. Without a touch of holy madness, he liked to declare, the Church cannot live.

Though Eugenio Pacelli was born six years after the Italian troops entered Rome, his family continued to regard them as intruders. By contrast, Angelo Roncalli was compelled to interrupt his theological training in Rome at the age of twenty and to become a 'year's volunteer' in the Italian army. He was enrolled as an infantryman. Before his year's service ended, he was wearing not only a fine moustache, but also a sergeant's stripes.

In 1915, when Italy joined the Allies in the First World War, he wanted to be a military chaplain. Regulations, however, stipulated that priests, when drafted into the army, must first serve in the medical corps. Once again Sergeant A. Roncalli wore three stripes on the right arm of his tunic, and he began to grow a moustache even more vigorous than the old. Constant contact with ordinary people pleased him, and he thought few gifts more precious than speech which enabled a person to communicate freely with others. As Pope, he chose November 4th, 1958, for the date of his coronation because it was the feast day of St. Charles Borromeo. Yet he cannot have forgotten that it was also the fortieth anniversary of the Italians' final victory over the Austrians. The seminary in Bergamo had been turned into a military hospital. On that memorable and distant day, Don Angelo Roncalli comforted more than one lad who had survived the war, but might return home maimed for life.

The ending of the war gave Don Angelo the time for completing a biography of Giacomo Radini-Tedeschi, who had died two days after Pius X. 'There was in his mind,' he wrote, 'something of the military spirit; a love and eagerness for the struggle, for the good, for the Church, for the Pope, for the rights of the Christian people. He did not like a war of pin-pricks: when he waged war, he preferred the firing of cannon; and his taste for battles was that of the true cavalier —under a clear sky and in open country.' Here, perhaps, was more than a touch of self-portraiture. Benedict XV, who had been one of Radini-Tedeschi's closest friends, read the book. With his full approval, Cardinal von Rossum called its author to Rome to work for the Congregation for the Propagation of the Faith.

Don Angelo arrived in January 1921. A year later Benedict XV was dead, and life did not always run smoothly for the priest from Bergamo. Someone with a hidden influence seems to have suspected that he was a Modernist, for an appointment to be Professor of Patrology at what is now the Lateran University lasted only for one term. Pius XI wished to make a Missionary Exhibition a dominant feature of the Holy Year of 1925, and he put Angelo Roncalli in charge of its preparations. Yet the Holy Year had barely begun and the pilgrims who reached Rome were still few when the Pope sent him to Sofia as Apostolic Visitor in Bulgaria. Monsignor Roncalli expected soon to return to Rome. In actual fact, he did not live in Italy again until 1953, when he was already seventy-two and had become Patriarch of Venice and a Cardinal.

The Catholic communities in Bulgaria were few and scattered; and although the Apostolic Visitor had been consecrated a Bishop and given the title of Archbishop of Areopolis, Sofia did not greatly esteem a servant of the Vatican. He had no credentials to present to the court, and in a non-Roman world he had chiefly to rely on his own virtues of courtesy, patience, a genius for friendship and a radiant goodness. Prejudices were not overcome in a day; sometimes not even in a century. To remove them, Roncalli said, was 'ant's work, bee's work', and he was fond of quoting a Latin tag: *gutta cavat lapidem*—'the drop of water hollows the stone'. Orthodox Sofia, he knew, was as religious as Catholic Rome. The tragedy was their spiritual separateness. The Byzantine curtain should have been gently lifted long ago.

After spending nearly ten years in Bulgaria. Monsignor Roncalli was sent to Turkey as Apostolic Visitor. He was proud to enter Constantinople, now called Istanbul. The first Christian Emperor chose to build the capital of his Empire on the shores of the Bosphorus. Four of the Church's Ecumenical Councils were held within the walls of the city. Among Rome's Legates in Constantinople was Anicius, who was born about the time that St. Sophia was consecrated and later became the great Pope Gregory I. Monsignor Roncalli set foot in a twice imperial city neither as Legate nor as Patriarch, for it now contained less than twenty-five thousand Catholics. Twice that number were non-Catholic Armenians. Four time that number were Greeks, and more than half a million citizens were Mohammedans.

Monsignor Roncalli's task was all the more difficult, because he had been simultaneously made Apostolic Delegate in Greece. Between Greek and Turk there was enmity. After a recent conflict came the cruel operation of cutting the Greek element out of Turkey and the Turkish element out of Greece. A million Greeks were forced to leave Turkey, and half a million Turks were forced to leave Greece. The wholesale transfer of populations was not yet ended when Monsignor Roncalli assumed his duties in the two opposing countries. He had learned to live harmoniously with members of the Orthodox Church. Now he had to live at peace with Mohammedans as well. He knew that they, too, could be deeply religious, and he began to regard good will as the strongest bond between men. Constantly he insisted that the things which unite men are more important than those which divide them.

Soon after his arrival in Istanbul, he heard that Kemal Ataturk had banned the wearing of a religious habit. Mullahs and priests alike must dress like laymen. The religious orders wanted the French Ambassador to lodge a protest, but the Apostolic Delegate saw no particular reason why the Turkish decision should be opposed. He invited the Catholic clergy to meet him in the church of St. Anthony and there to don suitably dark clothes. As a biographer put it, Monsignor Roncalli left the church dressed 'like a Broad Church English Vicar'.

The first Anglican Bishop whom Angelo Roncalli met was Harold Buxton, whose vast diocese of Gibraltar embraced Southern Europe and half the Mediterranean world. An early friend in Istanbul was its Anglican chaplain, Austen Oakley. Later, when the Exarch of the Western United States left Los Angeles to become the Ecumenical Patriarch of Constantinople, there quickly developed one of the most fruitful friendships in Roncalli's career. Patriarch Athanagoras had loved the expansive freedom of American life, and his tall and commanding figure seemed to be at odds with the cramped conditions of the Phanar, in which the second Bishop of Christendom has long been compelled to live. He accepted his plight and, though born a Greek, set out to be an exemplary Turkish citizen. In their talks together, Athanagoras and his Catholic friend readily agreed that the things which unite men are more important than those which divide them. Could the nine centuries' breach between Rome and Constantinople be healed?

Towards Christmas in 1944, the Apostolic Delegate was alone in Istanbul when a coded message arrived. He deciphered it himself and could not believe what his eyes were telling him. 'Come immediately,' it stated, 'Transferred Nuncio Paris'. The telegram was signed by Monsignor Tardini. Roncalli at once left for Rome, where he saw Monsignor Montini.

'There must be a mistake,' he insisted. 'I am not the right man for France. The country is too sophisticated.'

'But you speak French?'

'Everyone speaks French.'

The Substitute Secretary arranged for the new Nuncio to see the Pope, but he let him know that everything was already settled. 'If I were in your position,' he said, 'I would thank the Holy Father for wanting to send me to Paris.'

General de Gaulle had asked the Pope to recall the former Nuncio, Valerio Valeri, who was not forgiven for having followed Marshal

Pétain to Vichy. Some thought that the Pope, offended by this request, had deliberately chosen a successor about whom he knew little and who was not yet distinguished. Whoever succeeded Valerio Valeri as Nuncio in Paris would have found his task difficult and delicate. As Monsignor Roncalli expected, General de Gaulle soon handed him a dossier prepared at the Quai d'Orsay. It contained a list of thirty-three Bishops who collaborated with the Vichy régime and should be removed from their sees.

For a minute of two, the Nuncio glanced at the dossier. Then he said: 'I see nothing here save newspaper cuttings. I must ask you to let me have the actual documents on which the accusations against the Bishops are based.'

He played for time, but he won the General's respect. In addition, he won a battle for justice. With the approval of the Quai d'Orsay, he reduced from thirty-three to three the number of Bishops who must vacate their sees.

The Nuncio represented the Holy See, and not the French hierarchy. Yet before he laid down his office, he had visited all but three of the eighty-seven dioceses in France and Algeria. He listened to the Bishops as they discussed the priest-worker movement, the Mission of Paris, the Mission of France and other bold measures designed to bring the French people back to the Church. The French Bishops wanted greater freedom from Vatican control. Yet the Nuncio was the Vatican's servant. Like Monsignor Montini in Rome, he had often to let supplicants know that the Pope had made an unwelcome decision. If he informed the Pope that Philippe Pétain, imprisoned on a lonely Atlantic island, wanted at least one word of consolation from Rome, no response was ever made.

Just as the Nuncio won the affection of France's Bishops, so he gained the approval of her statesmen. When he first met Edouard Herriot, hitherto an uncompromising anticlerical, he said:

'Nothing stands between us but our political opinions. Are they not of little consequence?'

Herriot agreed. Before long, he was saying: 'If only all the other Nuncios in Paris had been like Roncalli, there would have been no anticlericalism in France.'

Meanwhile Robert Schuman was admiring him for his detachment. 'Just look at him,' he said. 'He is the only man in the whole of Paris who carries peace with him wherever he goes. As soon as you are near him, you can breathe it. Indeed, you can almost touch it.'

If it was sometimes his duty to transmit harsh decisions made in Rome, the Nuncio himself was said to have received a papal rebuke for going too often on foot through the streets of Paris. These walks he enjoyed. Even after twenty years of exile from his homeland, he had lost nothing of the Italian's love of movement under an open sky. *Oboedientia et pax*: Angelo Roncalli obeyed the Pope. He still obeyed him when, as Patriarch of Venice, he spoke against any coalition between the Christian Democrats and the Socialists. Pius XII had instructed all the Italian diocesans to do so.

Obedience is too often made synonymous with docility, and it was with other motives that the Cardinals elected Angelo Roncalli to succeed Pius XII. For one thing, he was a comparative stranger to the Vatican, while knowing well how irksome could be the methods and procedures of a distant Curia. For another, he was old. His would be a stop-gap reign. At a fateful meeting in the Villa Malta, a few days before the Conclave, Jesuits and Dominicans let it be known that they wanted a young Pope capable of giving the Church a dynamic leadership. In a few years' time, perhaps their wish would be granted.

Yet if the new Pope was too old to live much longer, he was also too old to change the habits and mental outlook of a lifetime. The elected one, Monsignor Bacci had pleaded in his Latin sermon, should have strength of mind; and this—as the French Cardinals, who knew him well, fully expected—he was quick to display. 'To be Bishop of Rome,' he said, 'is for me not merely a title.' Before the end of the year he had left Vatican City more often than Pius XII left it throughout the nineteen and a half years of his reign. Within three months of his election, too, he went to the monastery of St. Paul's-beyond-the-Walls to tell the astounded Curial Cardinals that he was calling a new Council of the Church 'as an invitation to the separate communities'.

Hitherto his decision to call a Council was known only to Domenico Tardini, whom he had made a Cardinal and his Secretary of State. Later he confessed that as soon as he confided his secret, no one could have been more astonished than he was himself. None the less, his long years away from Rome had been subtly preparing him for entry into the ranks of the great conciliar Popes.

His career had a late flowering; but so also had the career of Augustin Bea, who was born only a few months before him. At the head of his first list of new Cardinals, the Pope put the name of Giovanni Battista Montini. He also included the name of Augustin Bea because he had been the confessor of Pius XII. At that time, it was said, he knew little about the German Jesuit, who was soon to prove a powerful supporter of the call for a Council. It was the Cardinal's idea that there should be a special Secretariat for the Union of Christians. The Pope promptly approved and made Bea its Secretary.

The new Cardinal did not doubt that almost the whole of his own past career had been the preparation for a momentous task; but it was within the Vatican that he often encountered his greatest difficulties. He arranged the private audience which, at the end of 1960, Pope John granted to Dr. Geoffrey Fisher, the first post-Reformation Archbishop of Canterbury to enter Rome. No photograph was taken of the Pope and the Anglican Primate standing together. That morning Vatican officials turned away all press photographers from St. Peter's Square. Their gesture merely made the Romans' curiosity all the greater. Already Pope John had opened the floodgates.

While three years were spent in preparing the work for a Second Vatican Council, Pope John found time to devote to the problem of feeding a hungry and ever more populated world. He was born a countryman. All his brothers were tillers of the soil; and when he went to see the prisoners in the gaol which Rome dedicates to the Queen of Heaven, he told them that he once visited two cousins who were in prison for poaching. The remark so shocked some people in the Vatican that the *Osservatore Romano* omitted it from the report of his prison address.

Countrymen poach because they are poor; and to mark the seventieth anniversary of Pope Leo XIII's *Rerum novarum*, Pope John issued, in 1961, his long Encyclical Letter *Mater et Magistra*. He wished to show the injustice of giving the worker on the land a standard of living distinctly lower than that of the worker in the town. The Encyclical Letter appeared just when many hundreds of southern Italians were leaving their homes to find work in the factories of Turin or Milan. Hitherto farmers had encouraged a son or two to go abroad to prevent an excessive fragmentation of the family land; but now whole farmsteads were left unoccupied and unsold. Through almost unavoidable neglect, the amount of cultivated land in Italy was rapidly shrinking.

At this time, FAO was led by B. R. Sen, an imaginative Indian who had been the Famine Commissioner during a major war-time famine in Bengal. He was convinced that foresight and adequate preparation could have prevented its enormous toll of human life. Foresight and preparation alone can avert disastrous consequences when, at the end of this century, the world's population is more than doubled. In its origin, FAO is an association of Governments. In far too many Governments, however, the Ministry of Agriculture is regarded only as a Cinderella post. The war against hunger cannot be left to office-seeking Ministers; it must be waged by the people. With Pope John's full blessing, B. R. Sen launched a Freedom from Hunger Campaign.

Food and population are inseparable problems. *Mater et Magistra* assumed that the increase in population would present no insoluble problem in this century. Yet, sooner or later, Rome would be bound to give a verdict on birth control—an issue which Thomas Malthus, an English clergyman, had the courage to face more than three half-centuries ago. From which side of the Tiber would the verdict come? From the offices of FAO, close to the Baths of Caracalla? Or from the Vatican? Pope John wanted to bring the Church right into the centre of contemporary life. No problems should be shirked, and now, as the opening of the Second Vatican Council drew nearer, everything depended on the Bishops' response.

Some of them believed that the Second Vatican Council would be, like the first, a buttress of orthodoxy. Cardinal Ottaviani, Secretary of the Holy Office, felt certain that the right to put erroneous books on the Index would not be challenged. 'The red light which stops the reading of certain books,' he declared, 'is like a traffic signal. Nobody complains about traffic signals that he is an intelligent and practical person who can judge for himself.'

Cardinal Bea, on the other hand, tried hard to create a firm bridge between Catholics and non-Catholics. As a Biblical scholar, he saw that the Scriptures provided the best basis for all ecumenical discussions. He also insisted that baptism made people members of the mystical body of Christ, though not always in the fullest sense understood by Catholics. This meant that the observer delegates whom the non-Roman Churches sent to the Vatican Council played their part by right of baptism. No observer delegates had attended the First Vatican Council, but the invitations which Pope John sent to the non-Roman Churches were nearly all taken seriously. As head of the Anglican delegation of observer delegates, Michael Ramsey—Geoffrey Fisher's successor as Archbishop of Canterbury—chose John Moorman, Bishop of Ripon, to lead the Anglican delegation. This choice was appreciated in Rome all the more because the Bishop of Ripon had written scholarly books on Francis of Assisi.

Almost seven hundred Bishops attended the opening session of the First Vatican Council on December 8th, 1869. Nearly all came from Europe, and most were Italian. At the opening of the Second Vatican Council on October 11th, 1962, about two thousand five hundred Bishops walked in the procession from the Vatican to St. Peter's. A thousand Bishops, of whom almost four hundred were Italian, came from Europe. About one hundred Fathers represented the religious orders. The other Bishops were from the two Americas, Asia and Oceania. The Church had become truly international and cosmopolitan. No one, however, pretended that the great majority of Bishops were prophets or philosophers, or even well-trained theologians. Very much depended on the few who were as visionary as the Pope. More than ever, the Church needed 'a touch of holy madness'.

In his opening address to the Council, Pope John showed full confidence in the future. He dissociated himself entirely from the pessimists. 'In the existing state of society,' he declared, 'they see nothing but ruin and calamity; they are in the habit of saying that our age is much worse than past centuries; they behave as though history, which teaches us about life, had nothing to teach them, and as though, at the time of past Councils, everything was perfect in the matter of Christian doctrine, public behaviour, and the proper freedom of the Church. It seems to us necessary to express our complete disagreement with these prophets of woe, who give news only of catastrophe, as though the world were nearing its end.'

Yet a pessimist had only to glance at the schemes drawn up by the Council's ten preparatory Commissions to realize that the future looked dim. At the head of each Commission was the head of the corresponding department of the Curia, and each scheme was expressed in ultra-conservative language. The Curia did not want things to be changed. It reckoned, however, without the Bishops from Northern Europe. In particular, the French Bishops who had known and loved Angelo Roncalli went to the Council well briefed.

At the very first meeting of the Council Fathers in general congregation there was a show-down. The Curia presented them with lists of candidates for membership of the various Commissions. Thereupon Cardinal Lienart, Bishop of Lille, rose to read a statement. The Council Fathers, he said, should not vote immediately. They should first meet together in their regional and national groups and consider among themselves the qualifications of the various candidates. The Bishops agreed, and within half an hour the first general congregation came abruptly to an end.

From that moment the Curia lost its full control of the Council. As session followed session, the outer world watched with ever-growing sympathy the efforts of progressive Bishops to win the Council Fathers to their way of thinking. Cardinal Leo Suenens, Archbishop of Malines-Brussels, asked for a complete re-organization of the seminaries, so as to bring them into real contact with the modern world; Cardinal Paul Léger—later to leave his archdiocese of Montreal to work in the leper colonies of Africa—argued that it was wrong for the Church to sponsor only one school of philosophy or to impose a Western system of thought on non-Western seminaries; and the Patriarch Maximos IV Saigh declared that the Curia 'should not take the place of the college of the Apostles which lives in the Bishops, who are their successors'.

To those familiar with the history of the Inquisition, nothing gave more surprise than the success of the American Bishops in their demand for a declaration of religious freedom. 'Such freedom,' the declaration stated, 'requires that man must be free from coercion, either by individuals or by social groups or by any human power, in such wise that in religious matters no one should be forced to act, or be prevented from acting, according to his conscience, in private or in public, always within due limits . . . '

Pope John did not live long enough to witness all these triumphs. During his last summer stay at Castelgandolfo, he suddenly exclaimed: 'I know what my own contribution to the Council will be—suffering.' When he was carried in the gestatorial chair through St. Peter's Square on the opening day of the Council, people who stood nearest to him in the crowd noticed that he was in pain. Little more than a fortnight later—on October 28th, the fourth anniversary of his election—the doctors' diagnoses showed that he had cancer.

Thoughts of his own suffering he put aside when a crisis in Cuba seemed to bring the world to the brink of another World War. He appealed directly to two men: Nikita Khrushchev, an avowed atheist; and John Kennedy, the first Catholic to become President of the United States. The nearness of catastrophe made him impatient to complete his Encyclical Letter *Pacem in terris*; it was the first Encyclical Letter ever to be addressed to 'all men of good will'. In it he drew a firm distinction between Communism and the Communist; between the 'error' of Communism and 'the man who errs'. There were fields in which the Communist and the non-Communist could work together. To the end of his life Pope John held that the things which united men are more important than those which divide them, and he did not refuse to receive Nikita Khrushchev's daughter and son-in-law when they arrived in Rome. 'He has the strong hands of a worker, like my father.' So said the daughter.

In April 1963, a general election increased the Communist strength by more than a million additional votes. One Italian out of every four, in fact, had voted for the Communists. Right-wing critics blamed the dying Pope. Someone known in the Vatican said that it would take 'fifty years to get things right again'. When death came, the bronze door of the Vatican was shut. The black aristocracy, in turn, closed the outer doors of their palaces. Yet one dame insisted that the outer door of her husband's palace should be flung wide open. She had no wish 'to show deference to a Communist Pope'.

'He who enters the Conclave a Pope comes out a Cardinal.' This time, however, thousands were convinced that Cardinal Montini would be the new Pontiff, and—on the morning of June 21st, 1963— he stood on the outer balcony of St. Peter's to give the people his first blessing as Pope Paul VI.

Though Pope Paul agreed to recall the Council, his ideas were not always those of Pope John. In the presence of the observer delegates, John had taken care never to stress his primacy, but Paul more than once pointedly reminded the Council Fathers that he represented Peter. No one called him, as they had called John, a stranger to the Vatican. Even the patient way in which he gave each visitor his undivided attention betokened the days when he listened to Cardinals and Bishops whom it grieved not to be speaking directly with the Pontiff.

He saw two sides to every question, and John once jokingly named him Hamlet. If he recognized the justice of the complaints which the Bishops from Northern Europe levelled against the Curia, he knew that the system, though needing a drastic reform, was not without merit. The Curia had been manned almost exclusively by Italians. Yet they understood each other. They preferred the timelessness of their own inherited methods to any hustling by Bishops who were north-erners or Americans. On the other side of the Tiber is FAO's inter-national staff recruited from more than one hundred countries and on a basis of geographical representation. No one imagines that it has won freedom from friction.

If elected in 1958, and not in 1963, the new Pope would have been unlikely to call a Council of the Church. Yet he almost certainly would have taken the name of Paul. The Apostle Paul travelled from Jerusalem to Rome, and Pope Paul went from Rome to Jerusalem. It was the first papal journey outside Italy since Napoleon's day. Few were more appreciative than Patriarch Athanagoras, who went himself to Jeru-salem and prayed with the Bishop of Rome on the Mount of Olives. There followed a papal journey to Bombay, the Indian city in which Gandhi's influence had been stronger. Pope Paul, it seemed, was making amends for Pius XI's disinclination to receive the Hindu teacher of *satyagraha*. He moved into the world, but it was a world in which Christians are greatly outnumbered by non-Christians, as on the day when the Apostle Paul set out for Rome in bondage.

The Second Vatican Council was John's idea; the long journeys were Paul's. The actual decisions of the Council may not have been too revolutionary. For the Bishops, the dominant change has been the creation of a Synod, which now meets periodically to advise the Pope. Many more non-Italians have been brought into the Curia, in which no one may hold office for more than five years. For all Cardinals, Archbishops and Bishops a normal retiring age of seventy-five has been introduced. On one occasion, Pope Paul praised Pope Celestine V for abdicating when he realized that his physical and mental powers were not equal to the burden of his office. Was it a hint that Pope Paul might himself abdicate when—in September, 1972—he reaches the age of seventy-five?

For priests and laymen, the changes have been mainly liturgical. Rosmini's plea that 'the people should be actors in the liturgy as well as hearers' was at last heeded. Latin has lost its monopoly, and the language of the Church is once more the language of the people. There are many other changes: some are more verbal than real. The Holy Office has changed its name, but not its character. Lay folk are now called 'the people of God', but they still play no part in the rule of the Church.

It is not in isolation, however, that the Second Vatican Council can be judged. Only one Council Father out of every ten had a chance to speak in St. Peter's. The set speeches were often but a pale reflection of what the Fathers thought or said among themselves. John opened the floodgates. No one has yet succeeded in closing them.

Dutch theologians in Nijmegen have composed a widely read 'New Catechism'. Don Enzo Mazzi—once parish priest in Florence's working-class district of Isolotto—told his former parishioners that the Church began, and should have continued, at their own level; it was not meant to become hierarchic, as did the Jewish theocracy. In October 1969, when the Synod of Bishops met in the Vatican, Cardinal Suenens expounded his ideas on how a Pope ought to be elected. While he spoke, progressive priests from various countries were meeting in the nearby hall of the Waldensian church, since no Catholic hall was made available for their use. Most were dressed like laymen. The Church, they claimed, belongs to the people, not the people to the Church.

The Synod of Bishops may yet prove to be the most permanent legacy of the Second Vatican Council. It offers the arena for the discussion of several major problems which, for one reason or another, the Council Fathers had left alone. Pope John, for instance, had decided to refer the problem of birth control to a special Commission, When this Commission failed to reach agreement, many thought that Pope Paul should seek the advice of the Synod of Bishops. Instead, he issued an Encyclical Letter *Humanae vitae*, in which he upheld the traditional Catholic attitude to birth control. Most of the weightiest protests against this Encyclical Letter were made by Catholics.

In February 1970, eighty-four theological teachers in the universities

eminaries of Bonn, Fribourg, Ratisbon, Tubingen, Vienna, Salzburg
Munich published an open letter in which they asked the Bishops
heir own countries to plead urgently in Rome for a dialogue on
ical celibacy. Holland, they stated, was not the only country in
ich celibacy raised grave issues. It 'could provoke a schism in the
Catholic Church'.

On the same day the Vatican published an instruction from Cardinal
an Wright, President of the Congregation for the Clergy. It asked
t, on each successive Holy Thursday, priests should gather round
eir Bishop and answer a question which he puts to them: 'Do you
sh to be more intimately united and close to the Lord Jesus by
nouncing yourselves in the joy of your consecration by means of
libacy and by means of obedience to your Bishop?' Instead of a
dialogue comes a renewal of vows. It must hurt many honest minds
as much as did the anti-Modernist oath once imposed on teachers in the
seminaries. Yet unfettered dialogue might convince hundreds of theological students in Holland and elsewhere that the Roman discipline of
celibacy is just and that its hardships and loneliness are well worthwhile.

Pope Paul has spoken of 'a practically schismatic ferment' among
dissident priests. For that matter, there is ferment in the Gregorian
University, stronghold of Jesuit influence in Rome and nursery of
several Popes. Among its present students are men who will be the
Church's leaders when the phantasmagoric twenty-first century is
reached. They have youth's right to look ahead. If authority oppresses
them or a dialogue is denied, they can forgo ordination. They will
not thereby cease to be religious. In a world with a rapidly increasing
population, the number of ordinands is shrinking. In February 1970,
the Vatican published figures to show that, within the previous three
years, the number of students in the western countries who were
training to become priests had fallen by almost twenty thousand.
Numbers, however, are not all-important. The crisis of authority at
least shows that the Church is alive.

The 'schismatic ferment' is really a second Reformation. Martin
Luther, Thomas Cranmer, Hugh Latimer, Nicholas Ridley and John
Knox were all Catholic priests before they became Protestants. Not a
little of their thinking was more Catholic than contemporaries admitted. The Second Reformation will be the work of men and women
assured by the second Vatican Council that all truly baptized believers
in Christ are in real communion with the Catholic Church. It will be
a more charitable Reformation than the first if words like heresy and
schism are used with the utmost prudence, and if no one cries
'anathema!'

Dante's universal Emperor was almost a figment of the imagination. Pope and Emperor came nearer to each other when Paul went to New York to address the General Assembly of the United Nations. For all their imperfections, the United Nations Organization and its specialized agencies like FAO in Rome and the International Labour Organization in Geneva mark definite steps towards world government, while workers for European unity are striving to ensure that supranational government shall be based on the people's consent. The universal Emperor will be Demos. If Demos reigns, must the Pope still exclude the 'people of God' from any share in the rule of the Church?

A partial answer may be that Demos is still far from becoming the universal Emperor, just as the progressive Cardinals, Bishops, priests and seminarists are still far from winning their battle. Demos can be as reactionary as any former Pope. Many are the humble lay people who resent the liturgical changes, and some have protested inside a Roman church. Rome's secular air can be deceptive. Its population has increased more than tenfold since the city became Italy's capital city and will soon exceed three millions. Yet the Roman himself is little changed. At heart he is a Catholic, and when Italy enjoyed a spell of prosperity, he had to call it the 'economic miracle'.

When Palmiro Togliatti died, a million people watched, or walked in, the long procession from the Piazza Venezia to the forecourt of St. John's Lateran. Each municipal council, or commune, which had elected a Communist mayor sent a delegation to carry its banner in the procession. Nearly every banner bore an image of the commune's patron saint. While the hearse was driven slowly past them, some onlookers raised the clenched fist. Others made the sign of the cross. A few made the sign of the cross immediately after they had raised their closed fist. With the façade of St. John's Lateran as a backcloth, and flanked on either side with Communist mayors holding their colourful and religious banners, Luigi Longo addressed the vast crowd and publicly expressed his thanks to Pope Paul for having asked the people to pray for Togliatti when he was about to die. The scene cannot have been so very different when, in the Holy Year of 1300, Dante saw Boniface VIII carried in state towards the Lateran Church.

In Naples, the people's attachment to the Church is even more stubborn. Among changes sponsored by the Council Fathers was a reform of the liturgical calendar. Accordingly, in 1969, a few saints were reduced in status, and their veneration was made regional rather than universal. The demoted saints included Januarius, the miracle-working patron of Naples. When the news reached the Neapolitans, they were furious. Many went to the Cathedral and waited to see their

saint liquefying his blood, just as their forebears had done on the day—
September 19th, 1870—when Pius IX climbed the Holy Stairs on his
knees and drove for the last time through the streets of Rome. Again
they were impatient. *'Faccia gialla: fang' o' miracolo!'* 'Yellow face, get on
with the miracle!'

The saint did as he was told. What is a century in the life of Rome
or Naples?

House of Savoy: founded by Duke Humbert I, who died about 1047

Last Kings in the Senior Line

Victor Amadeus III, King of Sardinia (1726–1796), succeeded his father, Charles Emmanuel III, in 1773.

Charles Emmanuel IV (1751–1819), succeeded 1796, abdicated 1802.

Victor Emmanuel I (1759–1824) succeeded 1802, abdicated 1821.

Charles Felix (1765–1831) succeeded 1821.

Maria Cristina (1812–1836) married Ferdinand II, King of the Two Sicilies (King 'Bomba'), declared 'Venerable' by Pope Pius IX.

Francis II, last King of the Two Sicilies (1836–1894) married Maria Sofia of Bavaria (1841–1925), succeeded 1859, went into exile in 1861.

Kings in the Cadet Line

Victor Emmanuel I and Charles Felix died without male issue. In 1814 the Congress of Vienna recognized Charles Albert, Prince of Carignano and a descendant of Charles Emmanuel I ('Charles Emmanuel the Great' who died in 1630) as the eventual heir to the throne of Sardinia.

Charles Albert (1798–1849), married Maria Teresa of Tuscany

Ferdinand, Duke of Genoa (1822–1855) married Elizabeth of Saxony

Victor Emmanuel II (1820–1878), succeeded as last King of Sardinia in 1849, declared first King of Italy in 1861, married Maria Adelaide of Austria

Humbert I (1844–1900), succeeded father in 1878, married his first cousin, Margaret

Margaret, first Queen of Italy

Victor Emmanuel III (1869–1948), married Helen of Montenegro, succeeded father in 1900, abdicated in 1946

Humbert II (1904–) succeeded on May 9th, 1946, and went into exile after a referendum held on June 6th, 1946; married Marie José, daughter of Albert, King of the Belgians.

ACKNOWLEDGMENTS

The Bodley Head: From Letters from *Hilaire Belloc* and *The Life of Hilaire Belloc* by Robert Speiaght.

Constable & Company Limited: From *Letters of George Gissing to His Family*.

Harcourt Brace Jovanovich, Inc., and Rupert Hart-Davis Limited: From *The Letters of Oscar Wilde*, edited by Rupert Hart-Davis.

Methuen & Co Ltd.: From *Two Englishwomen in Rome* by Matilda Lucas.

John Murray (Publishers) Ltd.: From *The Letters of Queen Victoria*.

W. W. Norton & Company Inc. and Sidgwick & Jackson Ltd: Reprinted from *Letters to a Young Poet* by Rainer Maria Rilke. Translation by M.D. Herter Norton. Copyright 1934 by W. W. Norton & Company, Inc. Copyright renewed © 1962 by M.D. Herter Norton. Revised edition Copyright 1954 by W.W. Norton & Company, Inc. Reprinted by permission.

Oxford University Press: From *Massimo d'Azeglio* by Ronald Marshall. From *Vernon Lee* by Peter Gunn.

Charles Scribner's Sons: From *The Letters of George Santayana*, edited by Daniel M. Cory.

The Viking Press, Inc.: From *William James: A Biography* by Gay Wilson Allen. Copyright © 1967 by Gay Wilson Allen. From *James Joyce* by Herbert Gorman. Copyright 1924 by B. W. Huebsch, Inc.

BIBLIOGRAPHY

ALLEN, Gay Wilson: William James (*Hart-Davis*) 1967

ANDREOTTI, Giulio: La Sciarada di Papa Mastai (*Rizzoli*) 1967

BAKER, Paul R.: The Fortunate Pilgrims. Americans in Italy, 1800–1860 (*Harvard University Press*) 1964

BARRETT, William E.: Paolo VI (*Edizioni Librarie Italiane*) 1964

BEDESCHI, Lorenzo: La Curia Romana durante la Crisi Modernista (*Guarda*) 1968

BELLOC, Hilaire: The Path to Rome (*Nelson*) 1902

BERENSON, Bernard: Rumour and Reflection (*Constable*) 1952

BERKELEY, G. F.-H. and J.: Italy in the Making, Volume III (*Cambridge University Press*)

BINCHY, D. A.: Church and State in Fascist Italy (*Oxford University Press*) 1940

BULL, George: Vatican Politics and the Second Vatican Council, 1962–1965 (*Oxford University Press*)

CAPONIGRI, A. Robert: History and Liberty. The Historical Writings of Benedetto Croce (*Routledge*) 1955

CORY, Daniel (ed.): The Letters of George Santayana (*Constable*) 1935

CROCE, Benedetto: Storia del Regno di Napoli (*Laterza*) 1966 (first published 1925)

— —: Storia d'Europa (*Laterza*) 1965 (first published 1932)

— —: Storia d'Italia dal 1871 al 1915 (*Laterza*) 1965 (first published 1928)

DE GASPERI, Maria Romana Catti: La Nostra Patria Europa (*Mondadori*) 1969

D'IDEVILLE, Henri: Il Re, il Conte e la Rosina (*Longanesi*) 1967

DOWNIE, R. Angus: James George Frazer (*Watts*) 1940

FINER, Herman: Mussolini's Italy (*Cass*) 1964

FOTHERGILL, Brian: Nicholas Wiseman (*Faber and Faber*) 1963

GILSON, Etienne: Dante the Philosopher (*Sheed and Ward*)

GISSING, George: Letters of George Gissing to his Family (*Constable*) 1927

GORMAN, Herbert: James Joyce (*Bodley Head*) 1941

GREGOROVIUS, Ferdinand: Diari Romani, 1852–1874 (*Spinozi*) 1965

— —: Passeggiate Romane (*Spinozi*) 1965

GROSSKURTH, Phyllis: John Addington Symonds (*Longmans*)

GUNN, Peter: Vernon Lee (*Oxford University Press*) 1964

HALES, E. E. Y.: Pio Nono (*Eyre and Spottiswoode*) 1954

— —: Pope John and His Revolution (*Eyre and Spottiswoode*) 1965

HARE, Augustus: The Story of My Life (*Allen*)

— —: The Years with Mother (*Allen and Unwin*) 1952

HART-DAVIS, Rupert (ed.): The Letters of Oscar Wilde (*Hart-Davis*) *1962*

HASLIP, Joan: The Lonely Empress. A Biography of Elizabeth of Austria (*Weidenfeld and Nicolson*)

HATCH, Alden: Crown of Glory. The Life of Pope Pius XII (*Heinemann*)

HIBBERT, Christopher and WALSHE, Seamus: Garibaldi and His Enemies (*Longmans*) *1965*

HURN, David Abner: Archbishop Thomas Roberts, S.J. (*Darton, Longman and Todd*)

HYDE, H. Montgomery: Oscar Wilde. The Aftermath (*Methuen*) *1963*

JAMES, Henry: Italian Hours (*Grove Press*)

KING, Bolton: A History of Italian Unity (*Nisbet*) *1899*

—— and OKEY, Thomas: Italy Today (*Nisbet*) *1901*

——: Life of Mazzini (*Dent*)

KLIBANSKY, Raymond (ed): Benito Mussolini, Memoirs, 1942–1943 (*Weidenfeld and Nicolson*) *1949*

LAWRENCE, D. H.: Etruscan Places (*Secker*)

——: Twilight in Italy (*Heinemann*)

LEEMING, Bernard: The Vatican Council and Christian Unity (*Darton, Longman and Todd*)

LEETHAM, Claude: Rosmini. Priest, Philosopher and Patriot (*Longmans*)

LUCAS, Matilda: Two Englishwomen in Rome, 1871–1900 (*Methuen*)

MACARTNEY, M. H. H.: The Rebuilding of Italy (*Cambridge University Press*) *1966*

MACGREGOR-HASTIE, Roy: Pope Paul VI (*Muller*)

MACK SMITH, Denis: Italy, a Modern History (*University of Michigan Press*) *1959*

MACMILLAN, Harold: The Blast of War (*Macmillan*) *1967*

——: Garibaldi (*Hutchinson*) *1957*

MAGNUS, Philip: Gladstone (*Murray*)

——: Life of King Edward VII (*Murray*)

MARSHALL, Ronald: Massimo d'Azeglio (*Oxford University Press*) *1966*

MASSINGHAM, Hugh and Pauline: The Englishman Abroad (*Phoenix House*) *1962*

MILLER, Edward: Prince of Librarians. The Life and Times of Antonio Panizzi (*Deutsch*) *1967*

MONTI, Antonio: Vittorio Emanuele (*Garzante*) *1941*

MUGGERIDGE, Malcolm (ed): Ciano's Diary, 1939–1943 (*Heinemann*) *1947*

MUNTHE, Axel: The Story of San Michele (*Murray*) *1929*

MUSSOLINI, Benito: Memoirs, 1942–1943 (*Weidenfeld and Nicolson*) *1949*

NARDELLI, Frederick and LIVINGSTON, Arthur: D'Annunzio (*Cape*) *1931*

NEILL, Stephen (ed.): Twentieth Century Christianity (*Collins*) *1961*

NICHOLS, Peter: Piedmont and the English (*Evelyn*) *1966*

ORIGO, Iris: War in Val D'Orcia (*Cape*) *1947*

PACKE, Michael St. John: The Bombs of Orsini (*Secker and Warburg*) *1957*

PADELLARO, Nazareno: Portrait of Pius XII (*Dent*) *1956*

PARRIS, John: The Lion of Caprera (Barker) 1962

PILLON, Giorgio: I Savoia nella Bufera (Tempo) 1969

POPE-HENNESSY, James: Queen Mary (Allen and Unwin) 1959

PRAZ, Mario: The House of Life (Methuen) 1964

RHODES, Anthony: The Poet as Superman. A Life of Gabriele D'Annunzio (Weidenfeld and Nicolson) 1959

RILKE, Rainer Maria: Letters to a Young Poet, translated by M. D. Herder Morton (Norton, New York) 1962

ROGERS, Neville: Keats, Shelley and Rome (Johnson)

ROLFE, Fr.: Hadrian the Seventh (Chatto and Windus) 1904

SALVEMINI, Gaetano: Mazzini (Cape) 1956

—— and LA PIANCI, George: What To Do with Italy (Duell, Sloan and Pearce) 1943

SAPORITI, Piero: Empty Balcony (Gollancz) 1947

SENCOURT, Robert: The Life of Newman (Dacre Press) 1948

SERMONETA, Duchess of: Sparkle Distant Worlds (Hutchinson)

——: Things Past (Hutchinson) 1930

SPEAIGHT, Robert: Letters from Hilaire Belloc (Hollis and Carter)

—— (ed.): The Life of Hilaire Belloc (Hollis and Carter) 1957

SPRIGGE, Cecil: The Development of Modern Italy (Yale) 1944

TREVELYAN, George Macaulay: Garibaldi and the Thousand (Longmans) 1948

——: Garibaldi's Defense of the Roman Republic (Longmans) 1907

TREVOR, Muriel: Newman. Light in Winter (Macmillan)

——: Pope John (Macmillan) 1967

VASILI, Paul: Roma Umbertina (Edizioni del Borghese) 1968

VIDLER: Prophecy and Papacy (S.C.M. Press)

VILLARI, L.: The Awakening of Italy (Methuen) 1924

——: Italian Life in Town and Country (Newnes) 1902

——: Italy (Hollis and Carter) 1961

WATERFIELD, Lina: Castle in Italy (Murray) 1961

WEBSTER, Richard A.: Christian Democracy in Italy (Hollis and Carter) 1961

WYNNE, George: Early Americans in Rome (Dapa Book)

BIOGRAPHICAL NOTES

Popes of the Nineteenth and Twentieth Centuries

Pius VII (1800–1823)

Barnaba Luigi Gregorio Chiaramonti, born 1742. Elected at a Conclave held in Venice. Crowned Napoleon as Emperor in Notre-Dame, 1804. Restored the Jesuits. Pleaded for a better treatment of Napoleon exiled in St. Helena.

Leo XII (1823–1829)

Nicola Annibale Sermattei della Genga, born 1760. Held in 1825 the first jubilee since the French Revolution of 1789. Compelled the Jews of Rome periodically to hear a Christian sermon.

Pius VIII (1829–1830)

Francesco Saverio Castiglioni, born 1761. Recognized Louis-Philippe as King of the French. Reigned only for 20 months.

Gregory XVI (1830–1846)

Mauro Cappellari, born 1765. A political reactionary remembered chiefly for his condemnation of Lamennais' advocacy of Christian Democracy.

Pius IX (1846–1878)

Count Giovanni-Maria Mastai Ferretti, born 1792. Longest reigning of all the Popes. At first hailed as a liberal, he fled from Rome in 1848 and did not return until 1850. Promulgated in 1854 the dogma of the Immaculate Conception of the Virgin Mary. Convened the First Vatican Council (1869–1870), at which he promulgated the dogma of papal infallibility. On the entry of Italian troops into Rome in September 1870, the last Pope-King became the first 'prisoner of the Vatican'.

Leo XIII (1878–1903)

Count Gioacchino Pecci, born 1810. Worked unsuccessfully for the restoration of the Temporal Power. Issued a record number of Encyclical Letters, of which the most famous was *Rerum novarum* (1891). Named John Henry Newman as his first Cardinal.

Pius X (1903–1914)

Giuseppe Sarto, born of a humble family in 1835. Condemned Modernism. On the outbreak of the First World War, less than three weeks before his death, he refused the Ambassador's request that he should bless Austrian troops. First Pope to be canonized since Pius V (1566–1572).

Benedict XV (1914–1922)

Marquis Giacomo Della Chiesa, born 1854. On the third anniversary of the First World War appealed to all the belligerents to end their 'useless carnage'. In Italy's first post-war election of November 1919, allowed Catholics full freedom to vote and to stand for Parliament.

Pius XI (1922–1939)

Achille Ratti, born 1857. Concentrated on work in the mission field and consecrated six Chinese Bishops. As his Secretary of State, Cardinal Gasparri signed with Benito Mussolini the Lateran Pacts of 1929, thus settling the 'Roman Question' which had made each Pope since 1870 the 'prisoner of the Vatican'. To mark disapproval of Nazi creed and methods, retired to Castelgandolfo when Hitler paid a state visit to Rome.

Pius XII (1939–1958)

Eugenio Pacelli, born 1876 and the first Roman to become Pope since Innocent XIII (1721–1724). Attempted both to avoid the outbreak of a new World War and to persuade Italy to remain neutral. Worked unceasingly to protect refugees from political and racial persecution. Promulgated in 1950 the dogma of the Assumption of the Virgin.

John XXIII (1958–1963)

Angelo Roncalli, born of a humble family in 1881. First future Pope to serve in the Italian Army. Convened the Second Vatican Council (1962–1964). Issued in 1963 *Pacem in terris*, the first Encyclical Letter ever to be addressed to 'all men of good will'.

Paul VI (1963–   )

Giovanni Battista Montini, born 1897. First reigning Pope to travel by air and to make journeys outside Europe. Presided over first Synod of Bishops. In Encyclical Letter *Humanae vitae* upheld traditional Catholic attitude to birth control. Required priests each Holy Thursday to renew vows of celibacy and obedience to their Bishops.

Provisionary Head of the Italian State

Enrico De Nicola (1946–1948)

Neapolitan, born 1877 and died 1959. President of the Chamber of Deputies, 1920–1923. President of the Senate, 1951–1952.

Presidents of the Italian Republic

Luigi Einaudi (1948–1955)

Born in 1874. Liberal and Piedmontese. Returned to public life after the fall of Fascism. Made Governor of the Bank of Italy in 1945 and Minister of the Balance in 1947.

Giovanni Gronchi (1955–1962)

Born in 1887. Tuscan and Christian Democrat. Elected President of the Chamber of Deputies in 1948.

Antonio Segni (1962–1964)

Born in 1891. Sardinian and Christian Democrat. Former university professor, Prime Minister and Foreign Minister. Champion of the Treaty of Rome which, in 1957, brought the European Economic Community to birth. Resigned because of ill health.

Giuseppe Saragat (1964–   )

Born in 1898. Piedmontese and Social Democrat. Lived in exile during the Fascist regime. President of the Constituent Assembly in 1946. Elected President of the Republic when Foreign Minister.

INDEX